MW01194084

SINCERELY
HELD

CLASS | NEW
200 | STUDIES
| IN
| RELIGION

EDITED BY Kathryn Lofton AND John Lardas Modern

SINCERELY HELD

American Secularism and Its Believers

CHARLES MCCRARY

The University of Chicago Press

Chicago and London

The University of Chicago Press, Chicago 60637
The University of Chicago Press, Ltd., London
© 2022 by The University of Chicago
All rights reserved. No part of this book may be used or reproduced in any
manner whatsoever without written permission, except in the case of brief
quotations in critical articles and reviews. For more information, contact the
University of Chicago Press, 1427 E. 60th St., Chicago, IL 60637.
Published 2022
Printed in the United States of America

31 30 29 28 27 26 25 24 23 22   1 2 3 4 5

ISBN-13: 978-0-226-81793-4 (cloth)
ISBN-13: 978-0-226-81795-8 (paper)
ISBN-13: 978-0-226-81794-1 (e-book)
DOI: https://doi.org/10.7208/chicago/9780226817941.001.0001

Library of Congress Cataloging-in-Publication Data

Names: McCrary, Charles A. (Charles Alistair), 1990– author.
Title: Sincerely held : American secularism and its believers / Charles McCrary.
Other titles: Class 200, new studies in religion.
Description: Chicago : University of Chicago Press, 2022. | Series: Class 200: new
    studies in religion | Includes bibliographical references and index.
Identifiers: LCCN 2021038204 | ISBN 9780226817934 (cloth) | ISBN 9780226817958
    (paperback) | ISBN 9780226817941 (e-book)
Subjects: LCSH: Freedom of religion—United States. | Religion and state—United
    States. | Secularism—Government policy—United States.
Classification: LCC KF4783.M33 2022 | DDC 342.7308/52—dc23
LC record available at https://lccn.loc.gov/2021038204

♾ This paper meets the requirements of ANSI/NISO Z39.48-1992
(Permanence of Paper).

For my friends

_____

CONTENTS

INTRODUCTION

The Character of American Secularism

GUY BALLARD FIRST MET WITH Saint Germain in 1930 on Mount Shasta in Northern California. The spectral saint was one of the "Ascended Masters," supernatural once-humans now living in the cosmic realm.[1] These Masters, some of whom were also recognized by Theosophists as Masters of Ancient Wisdom, met with Guy, his wife Edna, and occasionally their son Donald throughout the next decade. The Ballards received the Masters' teachings and wisdom, which they then circulated through public talks, pamphlets, and books. Their movement, the "I AM" Activity, grew rapidly throughout the 1930s. They drew large crowds to their miraculous healing ceremonies, and they blended Theosophist and eclectic esoteric traditions with a variety of magical, political, and Christian motifs. At its peak, the movement reached over one million followers and even more sympathizers, attendees, and readers.[2]

---

1. According to the Saint Germain Foundation, which was founded by the Ballards and still exists, the Ascended Masters are "those Beings who are wholly Divine, for They have made the Ascension as Beloved Jesus did. They are the elder brothers, the teachers of mankind on this Earth. Having lived through human experience, They have by Their own self-effort and Love of God become wholly Perfect and wield Power without limit." https://www.saintgermainfoundation.org/saint-germain.

2. There is a small body of literature on the "I AM" Activity, though numerous texts mention them in passing. For a historical overview, see Charles S. Braden, *These Also Believe: A Study of Modern American Cults and Minority Religious Movements* (Macmillan, 1949); and Robert Ellwood, "Making New Religions: The Mighty 'I AM,'" *History Today* 38, no. 6 (June, 1988): 6–12. On "I AM" material culture and art, see Erika Doss, "The Chart of

The Masters met with Guy Ballard for the last time in 1939, when his unexpected death cut their correspondence short. Guy's death caused problems for the movement, but for more than just the obvious reasons. The Ballards had claimed that Guy was immortal. With one of their central claims revealed to have been false, perhaps the whole thing had been a sham. But, despite Guy's death, Edna and Donald continued to promote their teachings, holding meetings and sending out books and pamphlets. Within a few months they were indicted for sending fraudulent materials through the mail. They had solicited money ("love offerings" or donations, they argued, not payments) while propagating apparently untrue beliefs, including purported miraculous healings, accounts of shaking hands with manifested spiritual figures like Jesus, and of course Guy's immortality.

The criminal indictment alleged that Edna and Donald "well knew" these beliefs to be untrue. The Ballards contended that they had not committed a crime but, rather, practiced their religion. The Supreme Court of the United States heard the case in 1944, and their decision came down to one question: "Did these defendants honestly and in good faith believe those things?" I will return to this case in more detail later in this introduction, because the court's opinion and two dissents outlined the sides and stakes of conversations that persist today, both in the courts and beyond, about "sincerely held religious belief." By focusing on the claimants' sincerity, the *Ballard* case initiated the "sincerity test." Secular courts, when evaluating an individual's petition for religious freedom, putatively set aside the question of veracity—is this religious belief really true?—and consider instead whether the believer holds that belief sincerely.[3]

---

the Magic Presence," Object Narrative, *Conversations: An Online Journal of the Center for the Study of Material and Visual Cultures of Religion* (2014). Catherine Albanese places the Ballards and the "I AM" Activity in the context of California New Thought and Theosophy in *A Republic of Mind and Spirit*, 467–470. On "I AM" and the law, see Gray-Hildenbrand, "Negotiating Authority."

For Guy Ballard's account of his meeting with Saint Germain, see Godfré Ray King, *Unveiled Mysteries* (Saint Germain Press, 1934), 1–32. See also Saint Germain Foundation, *The History of the "I AM" Activity and Saint Germain Foundation: In the Ascended Masters' Words and the Recollections of Those Who Were There* (Saint Germain Press, 2003).

3. United States v. Ballard, 322 U.S. 78 (1944); and Ballard v. United States, 138 F.2d 540 (9th Cir. 1944). The case was retried because women had been excluded from the grand jury. See Ballard v. United States, 329 U.S. 187 (1946).

PLOTS

The *Ballard* case is an inflection point in a story—or a few stories, braided together—about sincerity and the secular in the United States. First, it can be situated at the beginning of a linear story about U.S. religious freedom over the past eight decades. In the 1940s courts were expanding the concept of religious freedom, and sincere belief turned out to be a useful standard for sorting the religious from the not-religious. In the twenty-first century, the sincerity test itself is somewhat weak and often easy to pass. But, rather than focus too narrowly on the test itself, I argue that the logic of the sincerity test and the character of the sincere believer continue to exert substantial influence on U.S. politics, culture, and religious freedom jurisprudence and legislation. A variety of interested actors have taken this idea—that if a belief really is religious, then its veracity is off the table and the interrogator's gaze shifts to the believer's sincerity—and run with it in the 2010s and 2020s. The phrase "sincerely held religious belief" has appeared with increasing frequency in state- and local-level legislation protecting religious freedom, proposed and supported by white Christians on the political right. Sincere believers garner accommodations and exemptions. In other words, sincere beliefs let people break laws, specifically antidiscrimination laws.

In 2020 legislators in Iowa introduced a bill that would define "bona fide religious purpose," a phrase from the state's 1965 civil rights act. The proposed bill would add a subsection explaining, "'*Bona fide religious purpose*' means any lawful purpose that furthers a sincerely held religious belief, whether or not compelled by, or central to, a system of religious belief, and without regard to the correctness, validity, or plausibility of the religious belief."[4] The sincere believer is an identity, a protected class whose rights are to be secured and defended. It is implicitly (and sometimes explicitly) defined against the faker. This bill was held up because opponents found it "too broad," but it is instructive nonetheless.[5] What does it mean to have a

---

4. Iowa H.F. 2130. Introduced Feb. 17, 2020. https://legiscan.com/IA/text/HF2130/id /2111026.

5. Shane Vander Hart, "Religious Liberty Bill in Iowa House Considered 'Too Broad,'" *Caffeinated Thoughts*, Feb. 19, 2020. https://caffeinatedthoughts.com/2020/02/religious -liberty-bill-in-iowa-house-considered-too-broad/.

"sincerely held religious belief" that could be "furthered" by your actions? Who is this bill's made-up class of persons, the sincere believer?[6]

A second way to situate *Ballard* is within an American tale of frauds, charlatans, and the long rise of a "post-truth" era. This second story tracks most closely with the chronology of this book. It begins in the nineteenth-century United States, when the specter of fraud haunted the economy and society at large. Through investigations of con men, humbugs, fakers, and fortune-tellers, Americans set the terms that led not only to the Ballards' conviction for mail fraud but also to the possibility of religious belief as an argument against accusations of fraudulence. The truly religious was necessarily not fraudulent. In this imaginary, the Ballards, debunked knaves preying on foolish followers, played foils to the character of the sincere believer.[7] "Sincerely held religious belief" became a cultural, political, and legal figure in a nation replete with scams.

Third, *Ballard* has a place in a wide-lens secularization narrative. At its broadest, this story begins with the Protestant Reformation, modernity, the Enlightenment, and colonialism. Many secularization narratives written by philosophers, sociologists, and historians in the twentieth century sketched

6. By "made-up," I mean to refer to Ian Hacking, "Making Up People," *London Review of Books* 28, nos. 16–17 (August 2006): 23–26. While Hacking is particularly concerned here with the type of subjects produced by "the human sciences," his terminology is apt to this study, because I am interested in how legal discourse, situated within the broader culture, produces "kinds of people that in a certain sense did not exist before." The twenty-first-century U.S. sincere believer, in some sense, is a made-up person. Crucially, for Hacking, the human sciences make up people because of a will to systematize and classify. While not all imaginings of the sincere believer are biologized or medicalized (although, as I will argue, they are not really pathologized, since the sincere believer is distinguished from the fanatical or superstitious believer by their rationality), this type of religious belief is increasingly understood as a fundamental aspect of the human. See Sullivan, *A Ministry of Presence.*

7. As I will discuss elsewhere in this book, the sincere believer's foil is not only the fraudulent huckster. Because sincerity is also an affective style, believers who are not solemn and whose religious performance is parodic or ironic have sometimes been labeled, by scholars and others, as unserious or insincere. David Chidester's *Authentic Fakes* productively explores these boundaries. On parodic religions, see Cusack, *Invented Religions.* On how the Satanic Temple rides a line and achieves a sort of ironic sincerity, see Laycock, *Speak of the Devil,* especially chap. 5, "Religion or Trolls?" Other scholars have shown how parodic and campy performances do serious religious work and are "real" religious practices. See, e.g., Wilcox, *Queer Nuns,* and Petro, "Ray Navarro's Jesus Camp." On the complications of performing sincere presentations of the religious self to others while cultivating personal authenticity and knowledge of self, see Khabeer, *Muslim Cool,* and Jackson, *Real Black.*

a similar arc, from the ritualistic, enchanted, and institutional religion of medieval and early modern European Catholicism to the belief-centric, disenchanted, and individual religion of Euro-American Protestantism.[8] This arc ended—or will end or should end, eventually—in either the dissolution of religion altogether or in the fulfillment of good religion, a sort of disenchanted liberal Protestantism. In some ways, traditional secularization narratives perpetuate stories European Protestants told about themselves. In both their rivalries with Catholics and their imperial endeavors, "the conceptual mechanism that allowed [the secular state] to sift the religious (as the realm of toleration and freedom) from the secular (as the realm of state interference) always involved an implicit notion of false religion."[9] These models of secularization were also structured by a deep, anti-Semitic, Christian supersessionism and, in the United States, a combination of settler colonialist and anti-immigrant nationalism.[10] By the late nineteenth century, such "progress" narratives had been grafted onto social-scientific, colonialist studies that charted humans' evolutionary progress through a potted history of religion: from primitive, tribal superstitions to more formalized systems and institutions to the most transcendently abstract.[11]

8. This body of scholarship is vast, and customarily this would be the place for a footnote containing a long list of books. Those citations are coming, in what I hope is a more helpful format than a list. For now, though, I will mention, on the history of the study of religion as a colonialist endeavor, see Masuzawa, *The Invention of World Religions*, and Chidester, *Empire of Religion*. For an example of a grand narrative of Western secularity that centers the advent of the liberal individual believer, see Taylor, *A Secular Age*. See also, generally, Asad, *Genealogies of Religion*.

9. De Roover, "Secular Law and the Realm of False Religion," 52.

10. See Carter, *Race*; Anidjar, *Blood*; and Yelle, *The Language of Disenchantment*.

11. These stories are full of tense ironies. Within many, something called "religion" (or a religious impulse or religiosity) is taken to be universal, a constitutive part of the human, and yet the final stage of civilizational progress would see humans transcend religion altogether. And yet, in similar if not identical narratives, it is *secularity* that is taken to be universal. Religion is the particular, historically embedded, and unreasonable, and the eventual enlightenment of the world will usher in a secular age. The problem with that story, though, as scholars since Max Weber have understood, is that what passes for secular is in fact quite Christian, specifically Protestant, in its genealogical foundations (see Janet R. Jakobsen and Ann Pellegrini, "Introduction: Times Like These," in Jakobsen and Pellegrini, *Secularisms*; and Weber, *The Protestant Ethic and the "Spirit" of Capitalism*). Individuality, rationality, and modernity are all revealed to be fictions of a self-aggrandizing white, European, imperialist, patriarchal teleological storytelling. Modernization and secularization, themselves Christian projects, then lead to the eventual end of Christianity. As Peter Berger memorably put it, Christianity is "its own gravedigger" (*The Sacred Canopy*, 129).

SECULARISM AND THE SECULAR

This book is a study of the character of the sincere believer. Its narrative arc, loosely tethered to a particular history of American religious freedom, shows how secular authorities have imagined religion as individual belief. In this process, religion has become unmoored from its formal institutional contexts and further internalized. In some cases, sincerely held ethical or philosophical or spiritual beliefs are in effect equal to traditionally religious ones. These developments have carried significant implications for religious freedom in the United States and elsewhere. Individuals can appeal directly to the state on their own behalf, free from strictures of a religious body but also without institutional support. When judges, for example, attempt to isolate a person's religious belief, they inevitably read that belief through the person's markers of identity and difference. In this way, the individual must perform in such a way as to be legible as religious and as sincere. The judge, or whoever is evaluating the religiosity of someone's belief and the sincerity with which they hold it, creates the sincere believer by reading them as such. This process of translation exposes the contours of American secularism and secularization as a disciplinary regime, even as religious freedom guarantees a widening range of rights and protections. "Sincerely held religious belief," now central to the modern regime of American religious freedom, was produced by and within a liberal order that ensures freedoms by policing boundaries and disciplining subjects.[12]

12. Many critiques of American religious freedom follow Sullivan, *The Impossibility of Religious Freedom*, which argues, in part, that the elevation of "sincerity" in free exercise cases (especially under the Religious Freedom Restoration Act and its state-level versions) led to confusion between orthodoxy and personal belief. Sullivan further argues that the liberal order constrained religion such that "the precondition for political participation by religion increasingly became cooperation with liberal theories and forms of governance" (10). Despite voluminous literature critiquing the institution of freedom itself, interrogating its genealogies and paradoxes, "freedom" tends to escape the critical gaze of religion scholars, who focus more on the first word in "religious freedom." Exceptions include Wenger, *Religious Freedom*; Curtis, *The Production of American Religious Freedom*; and Thomas, *Faking Liberties*. Critiques of freedom that have been most influential for my thinking include Patterson, *Freedom in the Making of Western Culture*; Rana, *The Two Faces of American Freedom*; and Reddy, *Freedom with Violence*.

Some scholars critique religious freedom from the other direction, arguing that it's a good thing but often bad because it is unequally applied. David Sehat, for instance, argues that "the frequent invocation of religious freedom has obscured that in actual practice

My approach to these topics is enabled by the past two decades of scholarship in secularism studies. Secularism is a complex, usefully polysemous concept that does a lot of work.[13] In a variety of fields, such as religious studies, philosophy, sociology, anthropology, and literary studies, scholars have defined and theorized and critiqued secularism and the secular. The result, now, is a cacophonous and daunting field or constellation of subfields. There are many ways one might map these conversations and missed conversations. Here, my mapping is designed to plot this book within it, explaining how I approach these questions and situate my contributions.

Sincerely Held takes up Talal Asad's question "What is the connection between 'the secular' as an epistemic category and 'secularism' as a political doctrine?"[14] It seeks to answer that question, in the U.S. context, through attention to sincerity and the sincere believer. By "the secular" I mean a commonsense "social imaginary," the framework for thinking and determining what is reasonable under the racializing conditions of enlightened modernity. By "secularism" I mean political projects of governance that produce, regulate, and enforce secularity, especially the boundaries between

---

Christian moral and religious ideas pervaded American law and society and formed critical boundaries circumscribing that freedom" (*The Myth of American Religious Freedom*, 283). This makes sense only if one believes that religious freedom is not itself a mechanism to draw boundaries and circumscribe freedoms. Similarly, Kathryn Gin Lum and Paul Harvey, even as they recognize the constructedness of religion and race, argue that the project of pluralism is regrettably "incomplete" because "when challenged, the power of the state does not recognize all 'religion' equally" ("Introduction," in *The Oxford Handbook of Religion and Race in American History*, ed. Gin Lum and Harvey, 14). I think that is a description of how religious freedom has worked and is supposed to work, not of its deficiencies.

I agree that religious freedom is not applied equally to all people. That is clearly true. I am less inclined to argue that some people who are not receiving religious freedom *should* receive it. I am more inclined to argue that religious freedom will never be equitable, because it necessarily depends on a colonialist liberal model of the subject. In the short term, religious freedom might be a good way to ensure your rights, if you can get it, but more thoroughgoing and lasting justice and liberation will not happen through "religion."

13. Taylor, "The Polysemy of the Secular"; and Blankholm, "The Political Advantages of a Polysemous Secular." Joan Wallach Scott defines secularism as "a discursive operation of power whose generative effects need to be examined critically in their historical contexts" (*Sex and Secularism*, 4). Scott's project, in that book, is to analyze secularism as a category her subjects use, not to employ it as an analytic framework herself. While I follow Scott's approach in some ways, such as her interest in a Foucauldian "history of the present," secularism is not a relevant category for many of my subjects, and unlike Scott I do use "secularism" as my own analytic term.

14. Asad, *Formations of the Secular*, 1.

religion and not-religion, or between good religion and bad.[15] Much of the scholarly literature on secularism in the United States has focused more on the secular or secularity than on "projects of secular*ism*."[16] The analysis

15. Saba Mahmood made a similar distinction between "secularity" and "political secularism." For Mahmood, secularity is "a historical product with specific epistemological, political, and moral entailments," and political secularism is "the modern state's sovereign power to reorganize substantive features of religious life, stipulating what religion is or ought to be, assigning its proper content, and disseminating concomitant subjectivities, ethical frameworks, and quotidian practices" (*Religious Difference in a Secular Age*, 3).

For José Casanova, the secular is "a central modern epistemic category—theologico-philosophical, legal-political, and cultural-anthropological—to construct, codify, grasp, and experience a realm or reality differentiated from 'the religious'" ("The Secular and Secularisms," 1049). Secularism refers to "a whole range of modern secular worldviews and ideologies that may be consciously held and explicitly elaborated into philosophies of history and normative-ideological state projects, into projects of modernity and cultural programs. Or, alternatively, it may be viewed as an epistemic knowledge regime that may be unreflexively held and phenomenologically assumed as the taken-for-granted normal structure of modern reality, as a modern *doxa* or as an 'unthought'" (1051). See also José Casanova, "The Secular, Secularizations, Secularisms," in Calhoun, Juergensmeyer, and VanAntwerpen, *Rethinking Secularism*, 54–74.

In this book, I would categorize Casanova's second definition of secularism (following "alternatively") as the secular. The secular is an "epistemic knowledge regime," a way of knowing or sensing what is real. This is similar to what Peter Berger described as secularism's "plausibility structure" (*The Sacred Canopy*). Likewise, John Modern regards secularism as "a conceptual environment—emergent since at least the Protestant Reformation and early Enlightenment—that has made 'religion' a recognizable and vital thing in the world" (*Secularism in Antebellum America*, 7). Again, I would call this the secular or, following Mahmood, secularity, albeit an especially ghostly iteration of it, much more an "unthought" or *doxa* than a "normative-ideological state project."

16. Of Modern's *Secularism in Antebellum America*, Michael Warner offered the following critique: "Those versions of secularism that are localizable as projects of governance, ethics, or struggle are so flattened as to be barely distinguishable from their background conditioning." It is one thing to interrogate the "conditions of possibility" (Taylor, *A Secular Age*) and the frames of the thinkable, but perhaps another to study the lived effects of this line-drawing—or the sometimes violent, always disciplinary, acts by which the lines, such as those between religion and not-religion, are drawn. Thus, Warner suggests, these scholars examine literary archives for secular aesthetics and ideas, more so than on-the-ground acts of governance and regulation, so we might say they are more about "the secular" than "secularism." For this reason, "a distinction between *secularity* and *secularism* is analytically necessary here." He notes that this also brings challenges, such as the question, "What is the relation between secularity (as background) and those projects of secular*ism* that can appear as specific positions against that background?" (Warner, "Was Antebellum America Secular?").

in this book is geared toward secularism and secular governance, particularly regarding religious freedom, with attention to specific sites where it is administered and the agents on all sides of the encounter. These include judges, of course, but also a wide range of actors, including police officers, private investigators, bureaucrats, and board members, in addition to the claimants and their advocates and, increasingly, adversely affected third parties.[17] In order to understand these projects of secularism, though—why some people have religious freedom and some do not, why some believers and not others are counted as sincere—we cannot consider them apart from their "background."[18]

The study of secularism and the secular in the United States has been most illuminating and innovative among scholars of literature. They examine literary archives for secular aesthetics and ideas, more than on-the-ground acts of governance and regulation. The most incisive scholarship in this area, however, attends to power relations and material realities, even if their main objects of scrutiny are literary texts. Scholars of nineteenth-century American literature, such as Tracy Fessenden, John Lardas Modern, Emily Ogden, Peter Coviello, and Lindsay Reckson, have shown how the secular is produced through the racial and gendered contracts of liberalism.[19] Hussein Ali Agrama argued that many scholars, including Asad, have implicitly considered the secular primary to secularism and thus argued that secular governance emerges from a secular epistemics or worldview. But, he contends, secularism and the secular have a "mutually constitutive character," which is "part of the paradoxical quality of secularism's power."[20] Agrama draws our

---

17. American religious freedom, like any other sort of freedom, can be traced genealogically, but any genealogy is inadequate that cites power or capital in abstract senses but fails to account for their lived histories. Attention to specific actors also helps scholars be more specific about power itself. This is a generally applicable point, but I am drawing it here from Wendy Brown, who writes, "Insofar as 'the state' is not an entity or a unity, it does not harbor and deploy only one kind of political power; to start the story a bit earlier, political power does not come in only one variety. Any attempt to reduce or define power as such . . . obscures that, for example, social workers, the Pentagon, and the police are not simply difference faces of the state in an indigent woman's life but different *kinds* of power" (*States of Injury: Power and Freedom in Late Modernity* [Princeton University Press, 1995], 175).

18. "Background" here refers to the Warner quotation in n. 16 above.

19. Fessenden, *Culture and Redemption*; Modern, *Secularism in Antebellum America*; Ogden, *Credulity*; Coviello, *Make Yourselves Gods*; and Reckson, *Realist Ecstasy*. See also Pateman, *The Sexual Contract*, and Mills, *The Racial Contract*.

20. Agrama, *Questioning Secularism*, 2.

attention beyond the often-observed relationship between the secular and the religious, as they constantly define and redefine each other, and instead toward the similar dynamics between the secular and secularism. In much the same way that racialization produces racial imaginaries and racial difference, secularism produces secular epistemics and religious difference.[21]

Secularism and the secular, in the United States, have been Protestant in their content and orientation, leading some scholars to identify a "Protestant secular" or "Protestant secularism."[22] The U.S. Protestant secular valorizes free choice, individual belief, and an implicitly white and male liberal subject—and then universalizes, or overrepresents, that formation.[23] This particularly Euro-American construction is then exported through human rights discourse and the promotion of "religious freedom" as a worldwide value and policy agenda. This story is historically accurate in many cases, and careful studies have shown how Protestant conceptions of religion, backed by U.S. political and military power, shaped and continue to shape domestic and international politics.[24] However, too much emphasis on Protestantism can cause the term to lose specificity and thus analytic utility, asserting a more stable and coherent "Protestant" than is historically accurate and, at the same time, often failing to explain what exactly is "Protes-

21. Saba Mahmood has shown how the secularist principle of religious equality helps construct religious difference. "Secularism," she suggests, "entails a form of national-political structuration organized around the problem of religious difference, a problem whose resolution takes strikingly similar forms across geographic contexts" (*Religious Difference in a Secular Age*, 10).

22. For an overview of this concept and the relevant scholarship, see McCrary and Wheatley, "The Protestant Secular," and Greenberg, "Is Religious Freedom Protestant?" Greenberg argues—provocatively and, to me, persuasively—that "this story has a very distinct past, and one with considerable baggage. For the conflation of religious freedom, secularism, and Protestantism is not new, nor has it always served egalitarian goals; it was originally developed two centuries ago by arch-conservative Catholics, who used it in their attacks against the French Revolution and its ideals of legal equality and democracy" (75).

23. In this sense, the sincere believer is an instance of what Sylvia Wynter called the "overrepresentation of Man" ("Unsettling the Coloniality").

24. Among the many works in this area, see esp. Thomas, *Faking Liberties*, on how U.S. policy makers helped to shape conceptions and practices of religious freedom in occupied Japan. See also Su, *Exporting Freedom*, on U.S. policy makers' uses of religious freedom in the long twentieth century, culminating in a chapter on the Iraq War and the inclusion of religious freedom in the U.S.-written Iraqi constitution. See Hurd, *Beyond Religious Freedom*, for a critique of more recent uses of "religious freedom" as a criterion for offering or not offering international aid and humanitarian support.

tant" about a given cultural artifact or political ideology. Imprecise uses of the term "Protestant secular" also can obscure the role of members of other religions, especially Jews, in shaping the contours of the U.S. secular.[25] Further, scholars should not assume that the secular is always coterminous with Protestantism, Westernness, and whiteness. Secularism studies arose in the context of postcolonial scholarship, specifically as a way to theorize and critique South Asian politics in the 1990s. Now, though, as Agrama has argued, many studies are "general inquiries into secularism and 'local' inquiries into how it takes shape primarily in the countries of the global South, as if they were merely derivative forms of the secular."[26] For this reason, I aim to analyze the secularism operative with the U.S. regime of free exercise law as an iteration of secularism that should be provincialized, not taken as a sort of baseline or ideal form, even—or especially—as it presents itself as such.[27]

This book traces a genealogy of secularism as a project of governance, through a primary archive of free exercise jurisprudence and legislation (but not limited to this scope), with sustained attention to the idea of the secular and how conceptions of (true) religion became common sense. I am showing how, to quote Jakob De Roover again, "judges and other secular authorities are bound to smuggle in one particular theological conception of religion. That is, a specific religious language becomes the metalanguage to discuss

25. Some of the litigants who advanced American religious freedom in the twentieth century, for example, were Jews and/or represented by Jewish lawyers. This does not necessarily mean that they were playing by something other than Protestant secular rules, but it does mean that those rules, which are flexible, were not made only by Protestants. See, e.g., Gaston, *Imagining Judeo-Christian America*, and Stahl, "A Jewish America and a Protestant Civil Religion."

A distinction between form and content might be helpful here. Most scholars of the Protestant secular, I think, are sketching the form of the U.S. secular more so than its content. So, in this way, non-Protestants might contribute to the content of the secular, even as its form, its general shape and foundation, remains Protestant. See esp. Modern, *Secularism in Antebellum America*, and Fessenden, *Culture and Redemption*.

26. Agrama, "Notes on the Idea of Theorizing Secularism."

27. My use of provincializing here is borrowed from Chakrabarty, *Provincializing Europe*. On secularisms and their variegations, see Jakobsen and Pellegrini, eds., *Secularisms*; and Warner, VanAntwerpen, and Calhoun, eds., *Varieties of Secularism in a Secular Age*, especially Saba Mahmood's chapter, "Can Secularism Be Other-wise?" As Agrama ("Notes on the Idea of Theorizing Secularism") has argued, some collections like this still take Western/Christian secularism as axiomatic and then, from there, move on to other "global" versions.

and decide on matters of religion in courts of law and serves as the standard to reject certain practices as not 'truly' religious."[28] What I am suggesting is that sincerely held religious belief exists within a form, specifically a white U.S. Protestant one, that operates as a secular metalanguage. This metalanguage is most recognizably expressed in particular styles of performance, in accordance with what Elizabeth Markovits called the "meta-discursive claim to 'truth-telling.'"[29] In short, *Sincerely Held* studies how the sincere believer makes sense (the secular) and how this subjectivity has been imagined and regulated, mainly but not exclusively by agents of the state (secularism). By way of further introduction, I offer some orienting arguments around each of the words in the vexing phrase "sincerely held religious belief."'

SINCERELY

To be sincere, a person must represent themselves publicly as they truly are privately; they express the internal.[30] A sincere believer, then, must be a stable subject, someone with agency, not one who is superstitious, spirit-possessed, or unduly influenced.[31] The buffered self, to borrow Charles Taylor's term, is buffered not just from spirits, but from the state. This individualized public/private binary, a model of liberal society inscribed onto subjects, is tenuous. It requires maintenance and vigilance, and modern subjects need to remind themselves of their own modernity.[32] In this context, the sincere believer is a secular subject: this believer is not *impressed* upon but, rather, *expresses* their beliefs.[33] They might have been impressed upon

28. De Roover, "Secular Law and the Realm of False Religion," 42. On "smuggling," see also Smith, *The Disenchantment of Secular Discourse*, 34–39.

29. Markovits, *The Politics of Sincerity*, 30.

30. For an accessible and engaging history of the concept of sincerity, see R. Jay Magill Jr., *Sincerity: How a Moral Idea Born Five Hundred Years Ago Inspired Religious Wars, Modern Art, Hipster Chic, and the Curious Notion That We All Have Something to Say (No Matter How Dull)* (W. W. Norton, 2012).

31. On undue influence, see Bradley Kime's forthcoming dissertation (Ph.D. diss., University of Virginia).

32. See Ogden, *Credulity*.

33. Kyla Schuller has analyzed "impressibility" in the nineteenth-century United States. Though Schuller does not engage with literature on the secular, her arguments relate closely

at some point—by spirits, gods, texts; "compelled" to belief—but, after being taken hold of, they reassert their agency and hold the belief.[34] A sincere belief is private, held somewhere inside, but expressed in public. For this reason, sincerity must be discursive, using language faithfully to represent an interior state. Sincerity publicizes the private. "In being sincere," Webb Keane explains, "I am not only producing words that reveal my interior state but am producing them *for you*; I am making myself (as an inner self) available for you in the form of external, publicly available expressions."[35] In many religious freedom cases, this publicness takes on an additional meaning. In order to be proved a legitimate claimant, one must demonstrate the sincerity of one's religious belief—and do so not only in public, but *to* public, state institutions. Sincerity is therefore about recognition: state agents more readily recognize people who look, act, and talk like them, who speak the language and metalanguage of sincere belief.[36] In the phrase "sincerely held

---

to conversations in secularism studies. She demonstrates how "sentimentalism was elaborated in the nineteenth century as a central biopolitical technology to regulate the vulnerability of the civilized body" (*The Biopolitics of Feeling*, 10). Thus, she offers a needed corrective to rigid distinctions between the porous and buffered selves, showing the gendered and racialized nature of an impressible (porous) self that is nonetheless "civilized" by virtue of its impressibility.

34. Lincoln Mullen has studied nineteenth-century U.S. religious converts and found that "religious choice was in no simple sense a new kind of freedom; it is better understood as an obligation." He continues, "Rarely did converts write about their conversion in terms of taking advantage of a religious freedom, though that is often the mode in which scholars write about religious choice. Almost all converts described themselves as compelled to convert" (*The Chance of Salvation*, 16). Attempts to work out this tension between the believer-as-secular-agent and believer-as-compelled, I argue, produce modern secularity.

35. Keane, *Christian Moderns*, 211. See also Keane, "Sincerity, 'Modernity,' and the Protestants."

36. Spencer Dew makes this point vividly when showing how Aliites, like many other religious minorities, "turn to the legal system in order to find recognition and accommodation as well as to speak to their own higher law" (*The Aliites*, 108). In some cases, the content of one's belief or structure of the religious group—as in a "cult"—makes the believer unrecognizable as religious. As Dew notes, whiteness and membership in "mainstream" religions both authenticate one's religiosity and make for easier translations in the language of secular law. Other believers are labeled insincere not because of minoritization, per se, but because their religions are parodic or "fiction-based," as in the Church of the Flying Spaghetti Monster. See Markus Altena Davidsen, "Fiction-Based Religion: Conceptualising a New Category against History-Based Religion and Fandom," *Culture and Religion* 14 (2013): 378–395. Thanks to Jolyon Thomas for the latter reference and suggestion.

religious belief," sincerity appears in the adverbial form. This calls our attention to sincerity's style—in this case, a way of holding belief. Jason Bivins has argued that "sincerity—as an affective quality of the secular—governs the relation between authentic and inauthentic religion."[37] Generic qualities, aesthetics, and forms make performances legible. Publics evaluate individuals' sincerity by look and feel. Sincerity, fundamentally discursive, is also performed and performative.[38]

Some political theorists who advocate for deliberative democracy have found sincerity troubling because the content of words and proposals can be overshadowed by theater and personality. Elizabeth Markovits has called the widespread standard of politicians' performed authenticity the "sincerity norm." "There is a meta-discursive claim to 'truth-telling' at work in the sincerity norm," she explains.[39] Publics evaluate whether the speaker is truthful, more than or even as a substitute for whether a claim is true. Similarly, Ann Pellegrini, noting the affective nature of sincere performances, argues that "religious sincerity" directs our attention "to larger questions concerning the politics of public feelings." She cautions that "we cannot just say all feelings are equal."[40] Truth and truthfulness are related, but they are different. Someone can be sincere even while speaking a falsehood. And, conversely, someone can be untruthful—pandering, bullshitting, outright misrepresenting themselves—although the content of what they are saying might correspond closely with empirical reality.

In his 1828 dictionary, Noah Webster defined the adjective "sincere" as "being in reality what it appears to be; not feigned; not simulated; not assumed or said for the sake of appearance; real; not hypocritical or pretended."[41] This

37. Jason Bivins, "The Secular," in *Religion, Law, USA*, ed. Dubler and Weiner, 220. Ann Pellegrini also argues that sincerity talk leads to affect. But, it's always about performance, perhaps even performing belief *to* oneself ("Religion, Secularism, and a Democratic Politics of 'As If'").

38. By performative I mean performative speech, that is, utterances that make something happen. Sincere beliefs become "real" by being performed. See Butler, *Bodies that Matter*; and J. L. Austin, *How to Do Things With Words*, 2nd ed., ed. J. O. Urmson and Marina Sbisà (Harvard University Press, 1975 [1955]).

39. Markovits, *The Politics of Sincerity*, 30.

40. Pellegrini, "Religion, Secularism, and a Democratic Politics of 'As If,'" 1348.

41. Noah Webster, *American Dictionary of the English Language* (1828), online ed. This is the second definition. The first, "pure; unmixed," was already largely out of use. Based on this meaning, Webster purported that the word derived from the Latin *sine* (without) and *cera* (wax), referring to pure or unmixed honey (other etymologists thought it could refer to furniture without wax plugging holes and painted over). Modern linguists find this etymol-

definition is largely negative. The sincere is *not* feigned, *not* simulated. The real is understood against the fake, just as the disenchanted subject defines their modernity by debunking others' enchantments. Webster then offered a somewhat more positive definition: "being in reality what it appears to be." The word "sincere" referred to things before it referred to people, but by the 1820s sincerity was often about people and their intentions, such that Webster's definition for the noun "sincerity" began with "honesty of mind or intention" and included "freedom from hypocrisy, disguise or false pretense." Sincerity was never far from suspicions and accusations of insincerity.

Being in reality what it appears to be. Webster's anxious definition admits to the inevitability of masquerade in public life. For this reason, the twentieth-century literary critic Lionel Trilling argued that sincerity arose as an ethic—"a salient, perhaps a definitive, characteristic of Western culture"— with the rise of the individual and decline of feudalism.[42] No longer strictly divided by social classes and defined by predetermined roles in village life, certain Europeans developed an ethic of sincerity. Trilling quotes Polonius's famous lines in *Hamlet*: "This above all: to thine own self be true / And it doth follow, as the night the day / Thou canst not then be false to any man." It is a public ethic, for settings where people know what you appear to be but not necessarily who you are. In public societies, we play roles and we wear masks. To be sincere does not mean to be maskless, if that is even possible,

---

ogy spurious. The Latin *sincērus* means "clean, pure, sound," and Romance languages all have similar words, but how exactly *sincērus* originated is unclear. It appears, though, that both senses of the English word—unmixed and unfeigned—first arose at about the same time. The *Oxford English Dictionary* records uses meaning, first, "not falsified or corrupted in any way" (e.g., re: doctrine), and, second, "pure, unmixed; free from any foreign element or ingredient," both "of immaterial things" and "of colours or substances." The first known uses of each of these senses date to the same ten-year period (1536–1546). The *OED*'s earliest citation is from 1533, with a slightly different meaning: "characterized by the absence of all dissimulation or pretence; honest, straightforward," citing the English Protestant martyr John Frith's reference to "Master Wycleve" as "noted . . . to be a man . . . of a very syncere lyfe." *Oxford English Dictionary Online*, s.v. "Sincere."

42. Trilling, *Sincerity and Authenticity*, 6. Larry Siedentop offers a similar narrative, although, while both are secularization narratives, Siedentop's affords more explanatory power to "Christian egalitarianism," which allowed people to imagine selves behind or beneath social roles. "Social positions could no longer be regarded as 'fated' or inescapable," he writes. "This was the secular translation of the Christian idea of the 'soul'" (*Inventing the Individual*, 348).

but to craft a persona that matches one's private self. *Wearing a mask that looks just like what's under it.*

HELD

The point of sincere belief is not really to hold it, but to express it, to press it out. "Held" might seem the least significant piece of this formulation. And yet, it adds something to our sketch of the character of the sincere believer. This believer is a holder. How does one hold a belief sincerely? Like a parent holds a child, like a prison holds an incarcerated person, like a candelabrum holds a candle, like a wrestler holds an opponent? Often, in the twenty-first century, courts treat religious beliefs almost like categories of identity, similar to race or gender, imagined as more or less stable markers of who you are. As I will explain in detail in chapter 5, in the 1965 case *United States v. Seeger* the Supreme Court described "sincere and meaningful belief" as that which "occupies [a place] in the life of its possessor."[43] We should linger on the word "possessor."

The modern secular subject, Talal Asad writes, is "a sovereign, self-owning agent."[44] Thus, if the sincere believer is a secular subject, to possess a belief one must also be self-possessed. In this way, the "possessor" is a quite revealing iteration of secular subjectivity. The good believer possesses belief, and the bad believer merely acts, ritualistically, unable to hold a belief—or, worse, is not a possessor but the possessed.[45] And indeed, a persistent marker of bad religion or superstition is insufficient agency and flimsy subjectivity. As Lindsay Reckson demonstrates in her study of secularism and ecstatic performance, ecstasy entails *being beside*, which "signals a crucial displacement of the self."[46] These performances, like the "frenzy" of a Black church or camp meeting or the Ghost Dance, become racialized in part through their unrecognizability as (good) religion. Ecstasy, while in

43. United States v. Seeger, 380 U.S. 163, 176 (1965).

44. Asad, *Formations of the Secular*, 135.

45. On possession, spirits, and politics, and how spirit possession relates to political sovereignty and property rights, see J. Brent Crosson, ed., "What Possessed You? Spirits, Property, and Political Sovereignty at the Limits of 'Possession,'" special issue, *Ethnos* 84, no. 4 (2019).

46. Reckson, *Realist Ecstasy*, 17.

some primal sense religious, is not sincere because it is neither discursively expressed to others nor held by a holder.[47] Defining such performances as outside the bounds of (good) religion is the racializing, disciplinary work of secularism, in an affective and stylistic key.

Another way to make the point, with reference to the secular, is to say that the belief holder is disenchanted. If one is enchanted, they are the one being held, by a ghost, spirit, demon—or their deluded belief therein, enchanted by belief itself. Moderns found enchantment nameable only once something called disenchantment was imagined. Thus, Emily Ogden argues, "enchantment can *only* be modern!"[48] But the point of being a secular modern, as Ogden shows, is not to eliminate all bad belief, but to use the credulity of others—in other words, to possess someone else by managing their belief. As in the case of Charles Poyen, who tried to use mesmeric techniques to enchant his enslaved laborers, this possession, this *holding*, can be starkly literal.[49] Far from being an inconsequential part of the formation, "held"

47. A striking example of this distinction can be found in intra-Pentecostal discussions of glossolalia (ecstatic speech) and xenoglossy (speaking real languages unknown to the speaker). Glossolalia is ecstatic, an experience in which the Holy Spirit moves animates an individual who has surrendered their agency. Xenoglossy, on the other hand, while also the work of superhuman agencies, is a tool for one's missionary intentions. As some Pentecostals, particularly white members of the Assemblies of God, attempted to become more mainstream evangelicals, they argued that all "speaking in tongues" was meaningful and discursive: if not xenoglossy per se, then it contained specific meanings understood by God (and, perhaps, other spirits, like angels or demons) and interpretable by others. They also distinguished between "private prayer languages" spoken only to God and public displays of tongues for which an interpreter ought to be present. On the possibilities of glossolalia and the coloniality of xenoglossy (or xenolalia), see Crawley, *Blackpentecostal Breath*, 211–236. See also Nicholas Harkness, *Glossolalia and the Problem of Language* (University of Chicago Press, 2020).

48. Ogden, *Credulity*, 9.

49. Ogden, *Credulity*, 68–101. Ogden also goes on to expose a latent assumption held by some scholars that agency entails the manipulation of others. For instance, Miles Coverdale, the protagonist of Nathaniel Hawthorne's *The Blithedale Romance* (1852), has been castigated by critics for, as Ogden puts it, "not being much of an agent," because he undertakes "an experiment in a kind of selfhood that neither veils nor enslaves others" (184, 183).

It is worth mentioning here that Coverdale is also the novel's narrator, and, like Melville's narrator in *The Confidence-Man* (discussed in chap. 1 of this book), he breaks in for a chapter-long, fourth-wall-breaking examination and defense of his own actions—although, very much unlike Melville's narrator, Coverdale appears to be sincere, even painfully so. He is self-critical, admitting, "I have made but a poor and dim figure in my own narrative,

exposes much about sincerely held religious belief, namely the agentive force required for a self-owning individual to exercise religion freely. Belief is property.[50]

RELIGIOUS

The category "religion," while still undertheorized by scholars in many disciplines, has been critiqued thoroughly within religious studies. Some scholars debate whether there is indeed some transhistorical essential thing that might be called "religion." I am not concerned with whether religion exists or who is truly religious, but instead with how that label is applied or not applied. Religious freedom is an arena in which this question obviously matters. Religion carries many different meanings, complicated by the fact that it is a term used both by scholars and by the people we study. I do not think there are proper or improper applications of the label "religious" (although some might make more or less sense within a given culture, such as that of constitutional law or a particular theological tradition).[51] I focus less on these normative questions and more on the (also normative) questions of whether people apply "religious" to work that has good, just, and equitable effects. There are good and bad uses of religion and religious freedom, but none of them is, on my view, faithful to any essential meaning of the terms. For now, the important point is to ask what work "religious" does in the figuration "sincerely held religious belief." Simply, it modifies "belief," specifying that only certain beliefs, religious ones, count. Which beliefs—and which believers—count as religious is always an open question, subject to contestation. Rather than argue about who and what should be counted among the

---

establishing no separate interest, and suffering my colorless life to take its hue from other lives." But in the novel's final line (spoiler alert), he confesses his deeply held, deeply secret love for another character. Nathaniel Hawthorne, *The Blithedale Romance* (Penguin Classics, 1986 [1852]), 245–247.

50. Harris, "Whiteness as Property." I would not argue that the sincere believer or secular subject is white per se, but I would note, quoting Harris, that "becoming white increased the possibility of controlling critical aspects of one's life rather than being the object of others' domination" (1713).

51. On the culture of constitutional law, see Berger, *Law's Religion*.

religious, the more pertinent questions ask why "religious" sincere beliefs wield such political power and how that power is used.

BELIEF

———————

In the landmark Supreme Court case *Reynolds v. United States* (1879), the Court found that the U.S. Constitution's First Amendment's protection of the free exercise of religion applied only to belief, not necessarily to action.[52] People are free to believe what they will, but that is as far as their exercise is guaranteed. Other words might follow "religious," such as "ritual," "community," "law," or "violence." But when the law—in the realm of free exercise, at least—sees religion, it sees belief. Many scholars also emphasize beliefs and belief systems, sometimes imagining the other stuff of religion, like ritual, as the expression or manifestation or symbol of interior belief, such that religious enactments exist on the sincerity–ritual spectrum.[53] But many other scholars, if even they recognize the value in studying beliefs, have argued that the supposed tension between ritual and sincerity is in fact a Protestant preoccupation improperly universalized.[54] Many religious people, it turns out, are not so hung up on belief. Nevertheless, belief remains a central category in legal evaluations of religion, and often in scholarly ones as well.[55]

The sincerity test—considering the sincerity with which someone holds a belief but not the truth of the belief itself—calls attention to how religious belief is assumed to be unlike other types of belief. A religious belief is quali-

———

52. Reynolds v. United States, 98 U.S. 145 (1879).

53. Seligman, Weller, Puett, and Simon, *Ritual and Its Consequences*; and Adam B. Seligman, "Ritual, the Self, and Sincerity," *Social Research* 76, no. 4 (Winter, 2009): 1073–1096.

54. See, e.g., Orsi, *History and Presence*.

55. Lopez, "Belief"; and Bell, "Belief." My thinking about belief and religious studies was also influenced by conversations with Bradley Kime, as well as by reading a draft of a chapter from his dissertation.

For a defense of belief as a category for religious studies, see Jason N. Blum, "Belief: Problems and Pseudo-Problems," *Journal of the American Academy of Religion* 86, no. 3 (Sept., 2018): 642–664. He argues that to stop studying individual belief "would mean evacuating the discipline of any minimally reasonable conception of what it is to be a human subject, and eliminate many of the basic theoretical means by which religion needs to be interpreted and can be explained" (644).

tatively different from an argument, conclusion, or reason. Analyzing Britain's Religion or Belief Regulations of 2003 and 2010's Equality Act, Yvonne Sherwood has written, "If belief is the leftover space to describe that which is not of truth, reason, or philosophy, then it is potentially ubiquitous—and deliriously free."[56] In the United States, the Equal Employment Opportunity Commission (EEOC), founded under Title VII of the Civil Rights Act of 1964, determined in 1970 that a claimant who was religiously unaffiliated nevertheless held her beliefs "with the strength of traditional religious convictions."[57] Unmoored from institution and specific content, belief floats free, anchored only by the strength with which the holder holds it. In the Pew Research Center's 2015 report on "America's Changing Religious Landscape," one group of believers stands out: 6.9 percent of respondents claimed that their religious identity was "nothing in particular" *and* claimed that religion was "somewhat or very important" to their lives. What Pew labeled the "Nothing in particulars (religion important)" are thinkable, legible, only in a secular age organized around sincerity.

THE SINCERITY TEST

The Ballards' alleged crime was sending fraudulent material through the mail, raising money through claims they allegedly knew were false. Propagating these beliefs, then, was not religion but fraud. As Jenna Gray-Hildenbrand argued, "State prosecutors hoped the jury would see the line between 'religion' and crime as clearly as they did. Thus . . . the prosecution built its entire case on the assumption that 'religion' was a belief system, or, at the very least, belief was the most important feature from which all other 'religious' qualities derive."[58] Religion was believed in good faith, and

---

56. Yvonne Sherwood, "On the Freedom of the Concepts of Religion and Belief," in *Politics of Religious Freedom*, ed. Sullivan, Hurd, Mahmood, and Danchin, 32. She continues, "In a giddy and bizarre demonstration of the freedom of the concept of belief, the legal odd couple 'religion or belief' now means, effectively, 'secular, not religious, but as intense as religious belief'" (33).

57. EEOC Dec. No. 71–779, *summarized* at 3 F.E.P. Cas. 172 (Dec. 21, 1970). See Weiner, "The Corporately Produced Conscience."

58. Gray-Hildenbrand, "Negotiating Authority," 145.

so demonstrable bad faith rendered a practice necessarily irreligious.[59] In their criminal trial, the Ballards initially did not describe their "activity" as a religion.[60] The state's suspicion of them stemmed in part from their politics, including their associations with right-wing movements like William Dudley Pelley's Silver Shirt Legion. They saw themselves as patriotic Americans, but others understood them as dangerous fascists with an enchanted group of hoodwinked followers. The Ballards changed course and made a free exercise defense, now self-identifying as religious. In advocating for their religious freedom, the Ballards did not attempt to upend the distinction between religion and fraud. Instead, they seized on it to argue that their beliefs and practices were religious and, ergo, not fraudulent.

The state's case against the Ballards depended on demonstrating their fraudulence, bad faith, and trickery—and thus their irreligiosity. They contrasted the "I AM" Activity with recognized religion and likened it to a scam. The state's attorney Ralph Lazarus emphasized the Ballards' "commercialism," alleging that they sought only to make money. Such a motive, he implied, was inherently irreligious and directly contradicted the teachings of Jesus, who was "opposed to commercialism, was opposed to any of that nature whatsoever." (This distinction would not last; the most prominent religious freedom case of the 2010s found a large for-profit corporation to be a sincere believer.[61]) And yet, the Ballards used stories about shaking Jesus's hand to gain attention and sell books. They did not just sully religion with commercialism, Lazarus alleged. Even worse: they were selling a false bill of goods, duping followers with fantastical promises of healing and fake stories about Ascended Masters, celestial visions, and Christly handshakes.

When the case made it to the Supreme Court, the decision hinged on the nature of the Ballards' beliefs, namely, whether they were sincere and religious. Despite all the deliberation at the lower levels about the nature

---

59. See Barry Nobel, "Religious Healing and American Courts in the Twentieth Century: The Liberties and Liabilities of Healers, Patients, and Parents" (Ph.D. diss., University of California–Santa Barbara, 1991), 55–59. See also American School of Magnetic Healing v. McAnnulty, 187 U.S. 94 (1902).

60. U.S. v. Edna Ballard et al., District Court of the US for the Central District of California; Central Division; Criminal Docket 14471; Record Group 21; National Archives and Records Administration—Pacific Region (Riverside). See Gray-Hildenbrand, "Negotiating Authority," 141n27.

61. Burwell v. Hobby Lobby Stores, Inc., 573 U.S. 682 (2014). See also Schwartzman, Flanders, and Robinson, eds., The Rise of Corporate Religious Liberty.

of religion, the Supreme Court generally agreed that the Ballards' beliefs were religious. But the Court's real question was whether they were sincere. Their beliefs certainly seemed false, perhaps even unbelievable, but it was possible that they truly did believe them. The district court had instructed the jury, "Whether that is true or not is not the concern of this Court and is not the concern of this jury. . . . The issue is: did these defendants honestly and in good faith believe those things? If they did, they should be acquitted. I cannot make it any clearer than that."[62] Supreme Court Justice William O. Douglas quoted this sentence approvingly, making sincerity and fraud the linchpins of the case. In the majority opinion, he penned the oft-quoted line, "Heresy trials are foreign to our Constitution." "Men may believe what they cannot prove," he wrote; "religious experiences which are as real as life to some may be incomprehensible to others."[63] Legal scholars and judges have interpreted this statement as a defining moment for secular neutrality, erecting a wall of separation between facts that might be disproven and beliefs that cannot, in a secularist context, be evaluated. Douglas's key intervention, then, was to separate veracity from sincerity, at least in matters of religious belief.

Other justices disagreed with the conclusion that sincerity and veracity could be separated. There were two dissents. Chief Justice Harlan Stone (joined by Owen Roberts and Felix Frankfurter) believed that sincerity and veracity were inseparable issues, and thus courts should continue to evaluate both. In the other dissent, Justice Robert H. Jackson agreed that veracity and sincerity were inextricably bound together, but from there reached the opposite conclusion: that neither should be up for legal debate. Jackson summarized, "The trial judge, obviously troubled, ruled that the court could not try whether the statements were untrue, but could inquire whether the defendants knew them to be untrue; and, if so, they could be convicted." He admitted, "I find it difficult to reconcile this conclusion with our traditional religious freedoms. . . . How can the Government prove these persons knew something to be false which it cannot prove to be false?" When one is being insincere, he or she knows the belief isn't true. But, doesn't then the law, at least implicitly, also assume it isn't true?

62. *Ballard*, U.S. 322 at 81.

63. *Ballard*, U.S. 322 at 86. He further quoted a 1872 decision holding that secular courts could not adjudicate decisions made by religious courts: "The law knows no heresy, and is committed to the support of no dogma, the establishment of no sect." Watson v. Jones, 80 U.S. 679, 728 (1872).

The three opinions presented three conceptual models. If sincerity and veracity cannot be considered separately, either (1) both can be evaluated by the courts or (2) neither can be evaluated. Or, there was another option, the one on which Douglas's majority opinion rested: (3) we can somehow divorce sincerity from veracity. This allows courts to test sincerity without getting into the messy business of adjudicating theological truth—at least not explicitly or officially. But how? When Justice Jackson asked, "How can the Government prove these persons knew something to be false which it cannot prove to be false?" he identified a nagging problem of secularization. In a disestablished secular state, courts shouldn't be "talking theology all day."[64] But, Jackson argued, the theological assumption of certain religious claims' veracity and others' falsehood had always been implicit within religious freedom law. And he was right. Even if courts set aside veracity, judges and other state agents have their own ideas about what it true, which inevitably colors their evaluations of what is believable and, thus, believed. It is much easier to conclude that someone sincerely believes if their belief seems reasonable. Veracity and sincerely remain linked, even as they are officially separated. Similarly, when the secular state classifies and regulates religion, as it must do to protect and promote religious freedom, they will always find certain beliefs more obviously "religious" than others. These evaluations, Jackson recognized, are always in some sense normative.

Since 1944 the sincerity test's secularist principle—separating veracity and sincerity—has taken root in religion law in the United States and beyond. Courts still cite this principle often, and the phrase "sincerely held religious belief" has been written into laws. The eighty-year rise of sincerity abetted the expansion of religious freedom, but it also contributed to what Winnifred Sullivan called the "impossibility" of religious freedom. In a series of cases throughout the second half of the twentieth century, courts treated free exercise as a matter of individual sincere belief, loosely if at all connected to orthodoxy. In some cases, courts had used a "centrality" test to determine religiosity, requiring that a belief be both religious and nontrivial, something central to one's religion and not an idiosyncratic personal belief. That standard was overturned in the 1981 case *Thomas v. Review Board*, in which the U.S. Supreme Court held that the Indiana Supreme Court had improperly "dissected" a claimant's religious belief, in part by comparing it to the beliefs of other members of his church and finding his belief to be more a "personal philosophical choice" than a sincerely held religious

64. Sullivan, *The Impossibility of Religious Freedom*, 4.

belief.[65] And yet, at the same time, many judges depended on models of religion they knew and understood, which often meant Protestantism. Often, unsuccessful claimants have been religious and/or racial minorities who were unable to convince state authorities that their beliefs were legitimately religious. Native Americans have had a particularly difficult time, as their cultural and political practices and knowledges do not translate easily to the language and metalanguage of "sincerely held religious belief."[66]

Legal scholars have debated the role of sincerity and the sincerity test. Many of them, following Justice Jackson in *Ballard*, are concerned that sincerity tests inevitably favor more orthodox believers, whose beliefs seem most believable. There is "a thin line between sincerity and verity," to quote Anna Su.[67] Heresy trials may be foreign to the Constitution, but "legal constructions of religion establish a normative framework for regulating social and legal relations among those who might have different ideas and attitudes about religion and what exercises of it are entitled to legal protection."[68] Furthermore, because judges and juries—as well as other actors along the way, such as prison officials—evaluate an individual's sincerity, other biases can easily shape whether a claimant is "read" as sincere or not. While churches and corporations are increasingly important players in religious freedom law, investigations into sincerity remain inquisitions into a person's belief, often pitting some individuals' rights against others'. The sincerity test is supposed to put everyone on equal footing under the law, but it also makes them stand alone.[69]

Despite these problems, some legal scholars maintain that a sincerity test is necessary and effective. And the potential benefits are clear: it relieves courts of the messy business of theology, and it allows claimants to speak

65. Thomas v. Review Board of the Indiana Employment Division, 450 U.S. 707 (1981).

66. This has been particularly acute with regard to land-use claims, such as in Lyng v. Northwest Indian Cemetery Protective Association, 485 U.S. 439 (1988). On this case, see Lloyd, *Arguing for This Land*. Lloyd argues, based on close readings of the evidence submitted to the court, that the case was never really about religion but about sovereignty and dignity. On land-use claims and secular translations, see McNally, *Defend the Sacred*, and Howe, *Landscapes of the Secular*, 79–116.

67. Su, "Judging Religious Sincerity," 41.

68. Su, "Judging Religious Sincerity," 29.

69. This has been the case in matters of religious freedom and antidiscrimination law in recent years. William Eskridge Jr. accurately predicted in 2011 that what he called "equality-liberty clashes," between civil rights and religious freedom, would increasingly "involve religious *individuals*, rather than religious *organizations* or *associations*" ("Noah's Curse," 710).

for themselves without having to pass a test of orthodoxy. Beyond the concerns described above, though, practical questions remain. How are courts actually supposed to test sincerity? And can they? Courts frequently evaluate truth claims, and in fact they have extensive experience in "ferreting out insincerity."[70] Determining whether or not people are lying is, indeed, a major part of the judicial process. On the other hand, though, questioning religious sincerity might be a different kind of fact-finding, a qualitatively different sort of investigation. There might be something special about *religious* sincerity. If the central conceit of the *Ballard* decision holds, then courts must take care not to slide into theological judgments or tests of religious orthodoxy.[71] Justice Jackson's argument, with which many scholars agree, is that this is just not possible.

PLOTS

In closing, I will briefly lay out the plan for the book.[72] At the outset of this introduction, I situated the *Ballard* case in three entwined thematic narratives. The first narrates the legal history of sincerity, especially the sincerity test, as an aspect of religious freedom jurisprudence in the United States. The second centers on frauds and hucksters, because sincerity is performed against the backdrop of insincerity, or at least the threat or specter thereof. The third is a broad story about secularization and the deinstitutionalization

70. Adams and Barmore, "Questioning Sincerity," 60.

71. Nathan Chapman calls this the "no-orthodoxy" principle. Evaluating the truth of a religious claim is not exactly the same as judging its orthodoxy, within a tradition. But, Chapman argues, they are hard to separate and, at any rate, the courts should not do either. Chapman, "Adjudicating Religious Sincerity."

72. Thanks to the many people who responded to my tweets about chapter outlines in book introductions. Taken together, they helped me understand what work an outline needs to do and how readers might use it. And, more basically, they convinced me to write one. So, here you go. But while we're here in this sincere footnote, I will admit that I still do this with hesitation. For me, much of the fun of reading an academic monograph—and, even more, discussing it with friends—is detecting the resonances among the chapters, digging up submerged arguments, pulling out themes, and figuring out how to use it. The following chapter outline is my attempt to explain my choices—why I chose the topics and archives I did—and in so doing to provide a guide to the logic of the book. It's all quite post hoc and incomplete, though, and I think that if you read the book you can do a more interesting and useful-to-you job of it.

of religion. Each of the eight chapters picks up these threads, with different archives, although the book is not a collection of case studies. Nor is it a straightforward linear history; however, it is mostly chronological, as I offer a genealogical treatment of sincerely held religious belief. There are many stories one could tell about the rise of sincerely held religious belief in the United States. In this chapter outline, I will try to explain why I am telling this one.

I begin with a chapter on antebellum schemes and scams, with brief reference to the same in the twenty-first century. Through a reading of Herman Melville's novel *The Confidence-Man*, I develop some of the key questions and frameworks for the rest of the book. I show how the character of the sincere believer was formed through its others, such as the con man, the knave, and the fool. This first chapter argues, finally, that the ideal of sincerely held religious belief relies on the fiction of the bounded liberal individual, which disintegrates in Melville's destabilizing text. The second chapter turns more directly to secular governance, later in the nineteenth century. Taking inspiration from Melville's invocation of the Inquisition, I consider the ways that internal states are investigated and calculated by state authorities. If secularism is disenchanting, then calculation is one of its primary modes. The main historical actors in this chapter are Anthony Comstock and his agents of the New York Society for the Suppression of Vice. Comstock's obsession with fraudulence and true value, I argue, was foundational to his project of investigating and regulating people's private and public lives. Continuing with many of the first two chapters' themes— fraud, masquerade, urban anonymity and vice, policing and investigation— the third chapter turns finally to religious freedom. In the early twentieth century, hundreds of people, mostly white Spiritualist women, were arrested for "pretending to tell fortunes." A few of them claimed that their practices were not fraudulent and were, in fact, religious. The deliberations in court, as well as discussion law journals, turned up tricky questions: Is all fortune-telling fake? Does it matter if someone really believes she is telling fortunes? Although these claimants were unsuccessful, they pressed at some of the very issues that the sincerity test in *Ballard* intended to solve.

After *Ballard*, perhaps the most prominent sincerity case of the mid-twentieth century was *United States v. Seeger* (1965). In that case, a conscientious objector who did not affirm a belief in a Supreme Being was found to have a sincere religious belief. *Seeger* cited *Ballard*'s sincerity test, and many courts after have cited *Seeger* as a key case that broadened the meaning of "religious belief." However, *Seeger* was not technically a First Amendment case and was not precisely about the free exercise of religion, even though later courts have generally treated it that way. It was actually about interpreting the phrase "religious training and belief" in the draft act. This point matters, I argue, because a deeper study of the draft act and the procedures of the Selective Service show how highly theoretical judicial and scholarly questions about definitions are produced through tangled bureaucracies, paperwork, and idiosyncratic individual lives. To that end, chapter 4 tells the story of the draft act of 1940, which exempted from combat those who objected to war "by reason of religious training and belief," a vague phrase contested in federal courts and clarified in the 1948 draft act. This chapter explains the arduous bureaucratic processes by which the state evaluated petitioners' religiosity and sincerity, which included multiple hearings for and an FBI investigation into each conscientious objector. Chapter 5 continues this story through a detailed narration of the *Seeger* case, based on close readings of the court cases as well as archival research in Seeger's personal papers.[73]

With this historical background established, chapter 6 situates *Seeger* in the context of secularization narratives written in the late 1960s and early 1970s. One of the central ways of defining religious belief, in the context of the draft, was to define it against the political and the "merely personal." For this reason, believers who could be read as more political than religious—such as Black objectors who had also participated in the civil rights movement—more often lost their cases. I argue that *Seeger* redefined religious belief according to its style more than its content, so that religious belief was less about believing in a certain set of content called "religion" and more about believing religiously. This redefinition is how sincerely held religious belief, individualized and deinstitutionalized, became such a flexible and capacious standard in the 1970s and beyond.

Wide as the gyres of the "religious" grew, not everyone won their religious freedom cases. Believing religiously was always more accessible to those whose performance of religion and sincerity was most legible to secular authorities—which is to say, white people, especially Christians or liberal

---

73. I take methodological inspiration, if not an exact model, from Gordon, *The Spirit of the Law*. Through a series of meticulously researched case studies, Gordon shows how the "new constitutional world" of the mid-twentieth century was built by "hard labor" that "fell primarily on believers and religious practitioners" (5). In this way, Gordon's work goes far beyond the discourse-analysis approach that many religious studies scholars have taken to Supreme Court cases.

post-Protestants, who generally had a much easier time being recognized. Even so, by the late 1970s a number of judges and legal scholars wanted to rein in the excesses, as they saw it, of the sincerity test. The "religious" was too broad. Chapter 7 follows these debates as they culminated in the 1981 Third Circuit Court case *Africa v. Pennsylvania*. The case dealt with Frank Africa, a minister in MOVE, a radical religious group in Philadelphia. Africa requested dietary accommodations while incarcerated, but the court, using guidelines established two years earlier, found that his beliefs were not really religious. The chapter concludes with an analysis of Blackness, anti-Blackness, and secularity. The eighth and final chapter carries the story forward to the 2010s, surveying the new politics of sincerely held religious belief in that decade. In particular, I focus on the Christian legal movement and its use of sincerely held religious belief to exempt its claimants from anti-discrimination laws. The twenty-first-century politics of religious freedom is not *all* about sex and gender, but I focus on these issues because they are most prominent and pertinent, both legally and culturally. Taken together, the eight chapters offer a cultural history of "sincerely held religious belief." That politically useful formation has come to make sense in the twenty-first century. There are many ways that one might chart its rise, but my wager is that we can trace it through instances of secular governance in which the character of the sincere believer was crafted, shaped, and reshaped.

01

KNAVES, FOOLS, AND SINCERE BELIEVERS

PROMOTING HIS THEN-FORTHCOMING TELEVISION SHOW in the fall of 2017, Mike Huckabee assessed the character of his first guest: President Donald Trump. Huckabee's new show was "religious programming," broadcast on the evangelical Trinity Broadcasting Network, but it would also include "political" content. He had experience in both arenas, as a former Fox News television host, Baptist pastor, and governor of Arkansas. Huckabee was aware that his first guest was not often considered a model of Christian piety. "Nobody pretends that he would be an ideal Sunday-school teacher, to be fair," Huckabee conceded. "I don't think he is a person who is deeply acquainted with the Bible and he's not known to set attendance records at church."[1] So why Trump? Trump respected "the Christian community," Huckabee said, and he had styled himself as a champion for religious liberty, which in the 2010s had become a rallying point for conservative Christians who felt that pluralism was just a cloak for anti-Christian oppression.

Emma Green, the journalist interviewing Huckabee, didn't buy it. Donald Trump, she thought, was nothing like a sincere believer. She quoted Huckabee's own words, from his book *Character Makes a Difference*: "Character is that which causes you to make the same decision in public as you would make in private."[2] Green cited Trump's many private actions "that don't necessarily show strong character." But she slightly missed the point

---

1. Emma Green, "Mike Huckabee and the Rise of Christian Media under Trump," *Atlantic*, Sept. 17, 2017.

2. Mike Huckabee, *Character Makes a Difference: Where I'm From, Where I've Been, What I Believe* (B&H Publishing, 2007).

of Huckabee's definition. He clarified, "To me, character is if you're the same in public as you are in private, and I think that in many ways, that's what's appealing about [Trump]. . . . Even his tweets, for example, are very transparent about what he's thinking, what he's feeling." Character is when the inner and outer, the private and public, the heart and the mouth, are in sync. Mask off. Or, a mask that looks just like what's under it. For Huckabee, Trump's public and private vulgarity show character because they are *both* vulgar. He's consistent; or, sincere. Sincerity, then, like character, becomes a moral good in and of itself, regardless of content. And Trump "has not pretended that he's sitting on the front row of church or that he's memorized any Bible verses. And I think ['the Christian community' is] frankly refreshed by the honesty. But more importantly," Huckabee pivoted, "they want a president who simply respects them—who recognizes that underneath all the Bill of Rights is religious liberty."[3] These two pieces—the valorization of sincere belief apart from the truth of the belief itself and strategic religiopolitical alliances formed in the name of religious liberty—characterize the twenty-first-century politics of sincerely held religious belief.

The discourse of sincerity is never far from the specter of the fraud, and in this way it is fitting that the 2010s saw the rise of both "sincerely held religious belief" and fears that a new "post-truth" era was upon us. Finding sincerity, in practice, entails investigating fakes. The politics of sincerity is a debunking game. But when a debunker investigates another's sincerity and accuses them of duplicity, they are not (necessarily) saying the belief is false; they are saying, "You do not really believe what you claim to believe." To debunk a sincerity claim is to prove that the interior, that hidden place where we hold beliefs, has not been faithfully represented by the external mask. The key, though, as Huckabee explained, is that the game is not really about the content. It's not about the truth or goodness or accuracy of what someone says. Likewise, the cleavage of sincerity from veracity is fundamental to the regime of religious freedom, stemming from the sincerity test and *U.S. v. Ballard* (1944), itself a case involving accused charlatans and fraud charges.

The early twenty-first century, a time when the figure of "sincerely held religious belief" inflected cultural politics and religious freedom law, is also an age of scams. Jia Tolentino has told the story of the millennial generation in seven scams, culminating in the "definitive scam": "the election of an open

3. Green, "Mike Huckabee and the Rise of Christian Media under Trump."

con artist to the presidency in 2016."[4] What does it mean to call Trump an "open con artist"? And how does that accusation correspond to Huckabee's defense of his character? Tolentino was far from the only observer to call Trump a confidence man. The language of cons—especially "grifters" and "grifting"—was invoked frequently in analyses of Trump and his milieu. This chapter takes up the suggestion that Herman Melville's 1857 novel *The Confidence-Man* might help index twenty-first-century schemes and scams. More generally, through Melville this chapter offers a character sketch of the sincere believer as a secular subject, realized against the duplicitous fraud. Melville's confidence man calls liberal subjectivity itself, and thus the possibility of the sincere believer, into question. The idea of sincere belief depends on stable categories and consistent characters. Melville reminds us, though, that we are never really on firm ground.

The term "confidence man" first appeared in print in 1849, applied to a swindler named Samuel Thompson.[5] A series of pieces in the *New York Herald*, probably written by the editor, James Houston, captured the public's attention (likely including Melville's, as he was in New York at the time). Unlike the elaborate confidence games described in works like David Maurer's classic *The Big Con* (1940) and dramatized in twentieth-century popular culture, Thompson's method was not complicated. The *Herald* reported that he directly asked his victims for their "confidence," as in, "Have you confidence in me to trust me with your watch until to-morrow?"[6] It was an old trick, noteworthy in this case only for Thompson's bluntness, his willingness to say the quiet part aloud. Jean Braucher and Barak Orbach have argued convincingly that Houston "wrote the story of Thompson as a sketch to illustrate" a typology he already "had in mind."[7] Thus, the confidence man entered the world of print and public discourse as already an

---

4. Tolentino, *Trick Mirror*, 190. The academic job market is not one of the seven scams Tolentino mentions, though it is implicated in some of the others, including the market crash and the student debt disaster. And her observation that "the pipe dream is becoming the dominant structure of aspiration" (194) feels increasingly relevant to the academic humanities.

5. Numerous scholars have made this claim as they have traced the term's history. See Braucher and Orbach, "Scamming," 251n16.

6. "Arrest of the Confidence Man," *New York Herald*, July 8, 1849. This account was brought to scholars' attention by Bergmann, "The Original Confidence Man."

7. Braucher and Orbach, "Scamming," 287.

abstraction, a collection of others' desires rather than a single or singular historical actor.

Debunking even the most obvious and open cons requires a significant set of beliefs. These are the same beliefs required for "sincerely held religious belief" to make intuitive sense. In both cases, you have to believe, at least, in the belief holder—that they exist, that they can hold a belief, that they are wearing a mask, that the mask is hiding something real, that the mask can be removed, and that you're the one who can pull it off. There is a pleasure in debunking—in sniffing out bullshit, unmasking smooth operators, shining spotlights.[8] As Tolentino writes, "Stories about blatant con artists allow us to have the scam both ways: we get the pleasure of seeing the scammer exposed and humiliated, but also the retrospective, vicarious thrill of watching the scammer take people for a ride."[9] This debunker's delight is what many people took from the American novelist Philip Roth's suggestion that *The Confidence-Man* might help people understand Trump. By reading this "darkly pessimistic" book, Roth advised, we might learn how to spot a fake.[10] But to approach the con in this way gives the game away, since we know who the fake is—who has the bad belief and who is truly rational—from the outset.[11] It reassures us that we're not the ones getting conned. From a comfortably enlightened position, we can sift through the rhetoric and see what's really going on out there. I begin this first chapter with Melville's book because it does *not* afford us such a foothold. Real and fake, sincere and insincere, religious and secular—there are no bright lines between them, and there is no vantage point from which to revel in the cheap thrill of the debunker. It is not a book for self-confident, self-owning agents.[12]

8. On debunking and secularism, see Ogden, *Credulity*, and Caleb Smith's review, "The Art of Debunking," *Immanent Frame*, Feb. 22, 2019. Smith writes, "Secularism would authorize itself, indeed it would summon itself into being, by disenchanting all this bunk."

9. Tolentino, *Trick Mirror*, 182.

10. Judith Thurman, "Philip Roth E-mails on Trump," *New Yorker*, Jan. 30, 2017. As Bergmann noted, some contemporary reviewers read it this way as well. According to the *Newark Daily Advertiser*, "a certain class of persons, those who read police reports, will relish this record of trickery and deceit" (May 23, 1857; quoted in Bergmann, "The Original Confidence Man," 575).

11. Sarah Hammerschlag makes a similar point in "Believing in the USA."

12. Asad, *Formations of the Secular*, 135.

"WHEN ALL IS BOUND UP TOGETHER, IT'S SOMETIMES CONFUSING"

Melville's novel inhabits and interrogates a world of humbug, suspicion, and fakery.[13] Set on April 1 and published on the same date, *The Confidence-Man* dramatizes cycles of distrust and confusion in an "environment of strangerhood"—in its form as well as content.[14] The narrative, such as it is, begins and ends aboard the Mississippi River steamboat *Fidèle*. We never leave the ship, but the ship never stays put. The cast of characters, like the setting, remains in constant flux: "Though always full of strangers, she continually, in some degree, adds to, or replaces them with strangers still more strange; like Rio Janeiro fountain, fed from the Corcovado mountains, which is ever overflowing with strange waters, but never with the same strange particles in every part."[15] A series of vignettes follows a confidence man (or perhaps multiple confidence men), who appears in a succession of guises (or perhaps altogether shape-shifting), swindling his fellow passengers out of large and small sums of money by appealing to their "confidence."[16]

13. I am engaging Melville here as a conversation partner more than a primary source. However, I do think that *The Confidence-Man*, weird and difficult as it is, represents anxieties of the antebellum period more than it critiques them from an outsider's perspective. As Lara Langer Cohen has noted, many critics have explained the icy reception of the book through the prism of their "investment in the figure of Melville as an alienated visionary, whose gimlet eye sees through a world of pretense and sham that blinds his more gullible contemporaries" (*The Fabrication of American Literature*, 173). I am guilty of sharing this investment sometimes. But in the case of *The Confidence-Man*, at least, I am persuaded, like Cohen, that aspects of the novel are "more symptomatic than idiosyncratic" (174). Melville understood things more sharply than others, perhaps, and he certainly explained the world in a singular voice, but the ideas in *The Confidence-Man* are not original (and, as the narrator admits, neither are the characters).

14. The phrase "environment of strangerhood" is borrowed from Halttunen, *Confidence Men and Painted Women*. See esp. chap. 2, "Hypocrisy and Sincerity in the World of Strangers," 33–55.

15. Melville, *The Confidence-Man*, 15. Subsequent references will be made parenthetically in the text.

16. According to most critics' interpretations, in keeping with the singular of the title, there is one confidence man. However, the text never explicitly says so, and even if it did, we might be wrong to trust it. The text also suggests that the confidence man is a devilish figure, an allegory for the devil or even the devil himself. Parker and Niemeyer highlight

As the novel wears on and the *Fidèle* heads south, the pace slows, and the confidence man changes character less rapidly. But this does not offer greater clarity. In the early chapters, characters flit in and out of scenes, usually never to return, but it remains relatively clear who the confidence man is. He's the one who goes around asking nameless stock characters for money, preying on their weaknesses. In later chapters, beginning with the introduction of Charlie Noble, a run-of-the-mill riverboat charlatan, it becomes difficult to keep track of who the real confidence man is. As Lara Langer Cohen has put it, "The second half of the novel foregoes a clear demarcation between confidence men and dupes entirely to stage a series of encounters between competing tricksters."[17] Lost in a world of strange particles, the reader, like most of the characters and perhaps even the narrator, scrambles futilely for sure footing.

Like a confidence man, the narrator presents himself as honest and forthcoming, even reassuring. In three separate chapters, including the penultimate one, the narrator offers self-referential apologies for his own writing.[18] In the first of these, titled "Worth the Consideration of Those to Whom It May Prove Worth Considering," he admits that the characters so far have not been very consistent. The previous chapter had ended with a country merchant's leaving a table "with the air of one, mortified at having been tempted by his own honest goodness, accidentally stimulated into making mad disclosures—to himself as to another—of the queer, unaccountable caprices of his natural heart" (74). Earlier, when approached by a man he did not recognize but who knew his name, the country merchant had replied, "'Why,' a bit chafed perhaps, 'I hope I know myself'" (27). As it turns out, he did not. After multiple scenes in which certain characters are called upon to vouch for others, whose stories cannot be taken at face value, the country merchant cannot account for himself to himself. He is an inconsistent character, the narrator admits. However, he contends, this is what makes him true. "That fiction, where every character can, by reason

---

these themes in their Norton critical edition. Melville's text contains numerous biblical allusions to the devil as well as references to Milton's *Paradise Lost*. See Thomas L. McHaney, "*The Confidence-Man* and Satan's Disguises in *Paradise Lost*," in Melville, *The Confidence-Man*, 447–452.

17. Cohen, *The Fabrication of American Literature*, 164.

18. Some of the language in these chapters repeats phrasing the confidence man uses. This fact and others have led some critics to suggest that the narrator himself is the confidence man. See Cohen, *The Fabrication of American Literature*, 166.

of its consistency, be comprehended at a glance, either exhibits but sections of character, making them appear for wholes, or else is very untrue to reality" (75). The narrator might be unreliable, but he tells it like it is, which might change.[19]

Like the country merchant, many characters find themselves struggling to maintain internal consistency. They try to keep their views of themselves, what they understand their character to be, in line with their feelings and actions. And it's disorienting; selves disintegrate.[20] Sianne Ngai suggests that *The Confidence-Man* "might be described as an exploration of the new emotional economy produced by the general migration of 'trust' from personal relationships to abstract systems."[21] In other words, it is a novel about the secularization of trust, abstracted and set in a context rife with and even structured by confusion, masquerade, and counterfeiting.

In the closing scene, an old man pores over a Bible by lamplight. The cosmopolitan Frank Goodman, the last of the confidence man's personas, strikes up a conversation about apocrypha. "Fact is," the cosmopolitan says, "when all is bound up together, it's sometimes confusing. The uncanonical part should be bound distinct."[22] A "juvenile peddler" interrupts the discussion to hawk some goods. He sells the old man a "traveler's patent lock" and pickpocket-proof "money-belt." Then, as lagniappe, he includes a Counterfeit Detector. The old man is initially grateful, but when he attempts to use the gift, he is troubled. Checking two bills against the Detector, he studies them but cannot reach a verdict on their authenticity: "I don't know, I don't know . . . there's so many marks of all sorts to go by, it makes it a kind of

19. On the narrator, see Kemper, "*The Confidence-Man.*" Kemper writes, "Like the confidence man, the narrator counts on and preys on man's insistent craving to move from doubt to certainty. Melville is suggesting that fiction, by its nature and at its very inception, is a deception" (26).

20. I am referring here to Lionel Trilling's reading of Hegel's reading in *Phenomenology of Mind* of Diderot's *Rameau's Nephew*. For Hegel, "base" life, which is antagonistic to external power, is counterpoised to "noble" life, whose relation to external power is premised on rational commitment to it. When the base self rejects noble life, realizing that the moral of "right" conduct is in fact just "approved" conduct, the self loses "its wholeness; its selfhood is 'disintegrated'; the self is 'alienated' from itself" (Trilling, *Sincerity and Authenticity*, 37–38).

21. Ngai, *Ugly Feelings*, 40.

22. For further discussion of this scene and the gold standard, see Taylor, "Discrediting God."

uncertain" (247). But as with apocrypha and the true word, fakes and real bills were not bound distinct.

"THERE'S SO MANY MARKS OF ALL SORTS TO GO BY"

Searching for truth, antebellum Americans investigated fakes. The fake is an imitation, a falsified version of something that does in fact exist. Legal tender sets the conditions of possibility for a counterfeit. As Paul Johnson has noted, "Every forgery points to an original."[23] In Melville's disorienting text, however, signs point to signs that point to other signs. The existence of an original, not to mention its knowability, is an open question. Other people's sincerity, and even our own, can never be known with certainty. But people tried. Melville's narrator reminds us that, while "some mathematicians are yet in hopes of hitting upon an exact method of determining the longitude, the more earnest psychologists may, in the face of previous failures, still cherish expectations with regard to some mode of fallibility discovering the heart of man" (77). In the meantime, many took to debunking, directing their energies toward the unmasking of fakes.

The antebellum obsession with fakes was the flip side of an obsession with empirical truth. Theologians, scientists, and other seekers believed that the world was knowable, that truth could be ascertained through common sense and direct observation. The problem was that what appeared to be real might in fact be fake. The specter of the fake was not new in the nineteenth century. Indeed, Johnson argues, "Potential fakery is part of the furniture of every religious enactment."[24] Fakecraft, Johnson's term for the ritual processes by which religious actors construct fakes and investigate them—is the believer sincere? is the conversion genuine? is that ghost really possessing him? does that potion work?—bespeaks what is important to a religion. Any culture has its ideas about what's real and what's fake, as well as its procedures for making these distinctions. These particular sets of concerns enable groups to police authenticity within the group and "also constitute and maintain boundaries between religions."[25] Fakecraft is thus central to

---

23. Johnson, "Fakecraft," 106.
24. Johnson, "Fakecraft," 111.
25. Johnson, "Fakecraft," 119.

the secular business of making religion.[26] Fakecraft is not only a task for self-consciously religious actors, though; it is also one way that secular states identify religions and even produce religious difference.[27]

Nineteenth-century U.S. thought was dominated by commonsense empiricism, a secular metaphysics that set the terms by which the fake and the real would be construed. Drawn from Scottish common sense realism, this style of reasoning permeated U.S. Protestant theology as well as scientific, social, and political thought. Many thinkers approached and engaged the world as empiricists, even to opposite purposes and conclusions.[28] Common-sense theorists found within and imposed on the world a systematicity, with evidentiary feedback loops, that was amenable to republicanism.[29] If truth were readily ascertainable for everyone, then "common people" had access not only to theological truth but, potentially, to the authority that could come with it.[30] Common sense was secular because it subjected everything to theoretically nonsectarian calculations. As Max Weber wrote, "The increasing intellectualization and rationalization . . . means that principally there are no mysterious incalculable forces that come into play, but rather that one can, in principle, master all things by calcula-

26. Dressler and Mandair, eds., *Secularism and Religion-Making*.

27. On the production of religious difference as a technique of political secularism, see Mahmood, *Religious Difference in a Secular Age*.

28. See, e.g., Rusert, *Fugitive Science*, on how African American thinkers engaged with, modified, and repudiated white empiricist science, including race science, and crafted their own literatures.

29. Historians of American religion have long recognized the centrality of common sense to American theology, as well as its "democratizing" applications. What has been less common is the immanent critique of scholars' own frameworks' indebtedness to this tradition, especially in the way this nexus has determined what is taken to be "religion" in the first place. See Sydney E. Ahlstrom, "The Scottish Philosophy and American Theology," *Church History* 24, no. 3 (Sept., 1955): 257–272; Mark A. Noll, "Common Sense Traditions and American Evangelical Thought," *American Quarterly* 37, no. 2 (Summer, 1985): 216–238; Mark A. Noll, *America's God: From Jonathan Edwards to Abraham Lincoln* (Oxford University Press, 2002); and E. Brooks Holifield, *Theology in America: Christian Thought from the Age of the Puritans to the Civil War* (Yale University Press, 2003). On the transatlantic political history of common sense, see Sophia Rosenfeld, *Common Sense: A Political History* (Princeton University Press, 2011). On feedback loops and commonsense Protestant thought, see Modern, *Secularism in Antebellum America*, 25.

30. Nathan O. Hatch, *The Democratization of American Christianity* (Yale University Press, 1989) offers less explicit discussion of Scottish thought but does find a pervasive democratizing trend wherein theological truth and authority was available to "common people."

tion. This means that the world is disenchanted."[31] Thus, a factish fetishization of that which is calculable led to the rationalization of everything, in more or less desperate attempts to account for ghosts.[32]

Debunking—sorting the real from the fake, the sincere believer from the con man—was a crucial task in the work of disenchantment.[33] As Emily Ogden has demonstrated, nineteenth-century Americans became modern and secular by aiming others "*away* from modernity." They managed and leveraged the credulity of others in order to reassure themselves of their own modern rationality, lest it slip from their grasp.[34] Most antebellum white Protestant Americans, like most Christian moderns, believed that good religion was defined by interior states and individual beliefs, particularly with regard to questions of authentic conversion. Sincerity's centrality to American religion is owed, at least in part, to the rituals of investigation that would find and debunk shams. And the nineteenth-century United States was full of shams.

Mundane daily encounters, including commercial transactions, occurred between increasingly urban and mobile parties who were unlikely to know each other personally. Without close knowledge of business partners or fellow travelers, Americans developed systems to gauge the trustworthiness

31. Weber, "Science as a Vocation," 139.

32. The terminology of "factish" is from Bruno Latour, *On the Modern Cult of the Factish Gods* (Duke University Press, 2010). Ogden, *Credulity* applies this aspect of Latour's thought to secularism studies. In a response to Ogden's book, Donovan Schaefer connects the factish and fetish, with reference to "Science as a Vocation" ("*Credulity*, or Science as an Intoxication," *Immanent Frame*, Feb. 22, 2019). See also Asad, *Secular Translations*, 15–16.

33. On disenchantment classifying and containing religion, rather than eradicating it, see Josephson-Storm, *The Myth of Disenchantment*. John Modern argues for a Protestant secular genealogy of disenchantment, which "already signified a process of securing the boundary between (Protestant) facts and (Catholic) fancies, certainty and uncertainty, legitimacy and illegitimacy" (*Secularism in Antebellum America*, 126). He elaborates: "To be clear, mysterious incalculable forces still came into play. Yet they were encountered with expectations of transparency, assumptions of calculability, and ambitions of certainty. Their existence was at best momentary. What this state of disenchantment portended, with its submission to future calculability and infinite progress, is in part an evacuation of moral reflection, *a refusal to acknowledge the self as a relational entity*" (126n17; emphasis added).

34. Ogden, *Credulity*, 17. Ogden is building on the argument of Talal Asad, who writes: "Assumptions about the integrated character of 'modernity' are themselves part of practical and political reality. They direct the way in which people committed to it act in critical situations. These people *aim* at 'modernity,' and expect others (especially in the 'non-West') to do so too" (*Formations of the Secular*, 13).

of others. These systems fit neatly with the Protestant-secular calculative reason that catalogued characters and bodies, from discourses on "hereditary heathenism" to phrenological examinations and race science.[35] To these, middle-class Americans added the accoutrements of what Karen Halttunen called "the sentimental ideal of sincerity": styles of dress, grooming, speech, and so on that were meant to display inner character through outward performance.[36] Sentimentalists celebrated literature, especially poetry, that seemed to be unfiltered expressions of the heart. Likewise, sentimental fashion strove for an ideal of transparency. As a piece in *Godey's Lady's Book* put it, "In a woman of true beauty, 'the body charms because the soul is seen.'"[37] To write, speak, pray, or emote in ways that reflected or represented the inner world was to be sincere.[38] Sincerity was a bodily performance, a matter of style.[39] There was a problem, though. Once a style was widely recognized as enacting or evincing sincerity, it could just as easily be faked.

35. "Hereditary heathenism" is borrowed from Rebecca Anne Goetz, *The Baptism of Early Virginia: How Christianity Created Race* (Johns Hopkins University Press, 2012). In the 1850s, rigid racial hierarchies and polygenetic theories were ascending in popularity in race science, as propagated by white ethnologists.

36. Halttunen, *Confidence Men and Painted Women*. On secularism, race, and performance, see Reckson, *Realist Ecstasy*.

37. Cited in Halttunen, *Confidence Men and Painted Women*, 71.

38. While sincerity in some sense is likely a transcultural, even universal concept (I would venture that few to no societies lack concepts of lying and truth-telling), its particular *aesthetic* shapes in the United States are a specific historical product. Specifically, stylistic representations of "inner worlds" are products of nineteenth-century U.S. culture. I am thinking especially with Sarah Blackwood, who has argued that in the nineteenth century, "proliferating representational images of human body, the soma, began to characterize the inner life as 'deep'" (*The Portrait's Subject*, 2). Her careful study of portraiture in its various forms produced ideas about interiority, rather than merely expressing them. Developments in photography, painting, sculpture, portrait fiction, and other forms were part of an "aesthetic progression" from understanding portraiture as "*expressive* of something else (a sitter's inner life, an artist's genius, et cetera) and toward an understanding of portraiture *as* the thing itself, as inner life/psychology/consciousness/genius itself" (124). Blackwood shows how consciousness was not revealed or ascertained, as if it were a timeless and stable object that humans have always sought, but rather developed as a "historically situated aesthetic object" (136).

39. And in this way, the politics of sincerity and aesthetics of sentimentalism were technologies of a biopolitical Protestant secular that rendered some subjects as trustworthy, authentically religious believers. See Schuller, *The Biopolitics of Feeling*. For further discussion of biopower and secularism, see Coviello, *Make Yourselves Gods*.

A dizzying cycle of sign and signification kept people unsure of whom to trust and, at the same time, dependent on their looping rationalities and rituals of fakecraft.

Money was no more trustworthy than people. In both cases, fakes circulated among the genuine. Many Americans assumed that gold possessed natural value. But gold was scarce and, besides, far too valuable for everyday transactions. They had to use representations of value, such as paper money and bank notes, rather than something imbued with the "real presence" of value.[40] This belief, that materials such as gold held inherent value that was evident from their appearance and constitution, mapped onto racist ideologies that found phenotypical evidences of immutable interior states.[41] Gold and money also reveal connections between the two meanings of "sincere"—the modern use referring to persons' self-representation and the archaic sense applying to things' purity. One might not know by simply looking at a bar of gold whether its core had been pumped with tin. But most Americans did know that real sincere gold, gold through and through, was inherently good. On the gold standard, paper money was like an honest person's clothes; it represented true value. A sign of sincerity, but only a sign.

After the destruction of the Second National Bank, orchestrated by President Andrew Jackson and his administration, paper money was no longer produced or backed by the federal government. Instead, bills were issued by thousands of local banks and even retailers. Banks frequently failed, leaving deposited money unreturned. A retailer might print bills, issuing them in exchange for specie, but if that retailer went out of business or skipped town, what good was that piece of paper? It was hard to tell which bills were "real" and which were counterfeit in the first place, especially if one lacked a trained eye or reference materials. Even with the aid of such materials it could be very difficult, as the old man could attest after his experience with the young peddler's Counterfeit Detector. Authentic bills usually had no apparently different qualities from fake ones. Unlike lustrous and beautiful gold, nothing about a bill or bank note seemed obviously valuable.[42] Making matters worse, a large proportion of antebellum bills in circulation

40. By using the phrase "real presence," I mean to gesture to Orsi, *History and Presence*, and suggest that paper-money-as-symbol is analogous to Protestant understanding of the Eucharist, counterpoised to Catholic beliefs in "real presence."

41. On racism, gold, and paper money, see Michael O'Malley, *Face Value: The Entwined Histories of Money and Race in America* (University of Chicago Press, 2012).

42. Murphy, *Other People's Money*.

were indeed counterfeit—in some times and places, as many as half. As the historian Stephen Mihm has described, anyone in this period doing business "had to rely on the 'look' of the person presenting [a note or bill]—that is, clues to their class status derived from the way they moved, talked, and handled the money. But all these emblems could be counterfeited, and were no more fixed and certain than was the amount of gold and silver backing the bills."[43] Confidence men, in turn, mimicked these behaviors, just as counterfeiters did with genuine bills, and thus markers of sincerity quickly became associated with fraud. So middle-class Americans forged new markers of sincerity, which were then appropriated again by "passers," and on the cycle went.

Fakecraft, which included accusations of fakery and the investigations thereof, situated in social and economic context, made and reinforced religious difference. Anti-Mormon debunkers, for example, often employed economic tropes in their accusations. One polemicist wrote, in an 1841 work titled *The Mormons; Or, Knavery Exposed*, "May the Mormons be ashamed of their counterfeit bible, which by their own testimony is shown to be as gross a trick as their counterfeit bank notes."[44] It worked the other way, too. Some apologists used the same tropes to defend their own, true religions. In 1844 a writer in the *New York Evangelist* performed a bit a fakecraft in a piece entitled "True Coin and its Counterfeit."[45] They pointed out that some people reason "that because there are counterfeits in religion, therefore there can be no true coin—no true piety towards God. But the argument is absurd. It disproves itself." There must be a true coin; if not, there's nothing to fake.

43. Mihm, *A Nation of Counterfeiters*, 211.

44. Lee, *The Mormons, Or, Knavery Exposed*, 3. Quoted in J. Spencer Fluhman, *"A Peculiar People": Anti-Mormonism and the Making of Religion in Nineteenth-Century America* (University of North Carolina Press, 2011), 46.

Joseph Smith was frequently accused of being a charlatan, his "swindle" often cast in economic terms, both literally and metaphorically. See Laurie F. Maffly-Kipp, "Tracking the Sincere Believer: 'Authentic' Religion and the Enduring Legacy of Joseph Smith Jr.," in *Joseph Smith Jr.: Reappraisals after Two Centuries*, ed. Reid L. Neilson and Terryl L. Givens (Oxford University Press, 2009). Maffly-Kipp notes an early twentieth-century anti-Mormon polemicist's likening of Smith's founding story, and indeed Mormonism as a religion, to a theatrical production. She explains that because that author judged "that Smith's intentions were not honest, the religion itself is rendered a sham. Religious *truth* is thus linked to Smith's personal *sincerity*—defined as genuine, honest, and free of duplicity" (176). Defenses of the truth of Mormonism, Maffly-Kipp shows, have depended on constructing Smith as a sincere believer.

45. "True Coin and Its Counterfeit," *New York Evangelist*, June 20, 1844, 98.

The writer continued, "True religion, then—genuine piety, which is pure and holy love to God, and which becomes at once the solace and salvation of the soul, remains the same, notwithstanding all counterfeits," just as real currency is not delegitimated simply because its fraudulent doubles still circulate.[46]

Fakes caused intradenominational problems too. While Protestants spun tales of Catholic deception and Mormon coercion, they also feared imposter preachers among their own ranks. Thus, they devised rituals—fakecraft—to identify them. Methodist itinerants, for example, rode the nation and beyond, preaching, teaching, and counseling. How was one to know if the ragged young man approaching on horseback, seeking hospitality and an audience, was indeed a real preacher who had really been called to preach and had been authenticated by his denomination?[47] For their part, circuit riders themselves worried about these questions too and devised complex narrative structures for convincing others—and themselves—of their authenticity.[48] Unlike Methodists, Baptists lacked a centralized denominational authority that endorsed and directed their ministers. One side effect of congregational independence was a lack of networks of authentication. When preachers or parishioners moved from one congregation to another, communities lacked formal procedures to ensure a smooth transition or even to know who these newcomers really were. To solve this problem, many churches developed a paperwork ritual. They began to issue "letters of dismission" to outgoing members in good standing. These letters would vouch for the individual Baptist moving from one church to another, assuring the receiving church that their new congregant had not left their previous church amid disgrace or scandal.[49] "Strange particles"

46. On "cash value," see also William James, *Pragmatism* (Charles Scribner's Sons, 1907).

47. Circuit preachers depended upon hospitality on their travels, often from women, sometimes dubbed "sisters and mothers in Israel." See Gregory A. Schneider, *The Way of the Cross Leads Home: The Domestication of American Methodism* (Indiana University Press, 1993).

48. See Charles McCrary, "The Myth of the Circuit Rider: American Methodist Autobiography and the Croaks of Nostalgia," *Soundings* 100, no. 1 (Jan., 2017): 54–87. For a catalog of tropes used in Methodist writings, see Donald E. Byrne, Jr., *No Foot of Land: Folklore of Methodist Itinerants* (Scarecrow Press and the American Theological Library Association, 1975).

49. Thanks to Jacob Hicks for discussing these letters with me, and for showing me some examples from his archival research at the Library of Virginia. See Monica Najar, *Evangelizing the South: A Social History of Church and State in Early America* (Oxford Uni-

flowed throughout antebellum America, and sincere believers developed ritual forms of fakecraft to make them less strange, to manage the haunting distrust.

"DISTRUST IS A STAGE TO CONFIDENCE"

One could argue that questions of authenticity and fakery miss the point of much religious ritual. To make such an argument, one might first point out that sincere belief is not a universal concern but a particularly Protestant one. Thus, when scholars universalize a Protestant preoccupation, they not only misunderstand the social worlds of many of their subjects, but they further the colonialist project of ranking the "religions" according to how closely they hew to a white, Protestant model. Rather than abandoning the category of religion altogether, though, one might posit a different provisional theory of religion, perhaps finding religious authenticity in unexpected places. David Chidester, for example, argues that pieces of popular culture do "real religious work" and notes how "the production, circulation, and consumption of popular culture can operate like religion." Chidester defends the analytical utility of "religion" to understand humanity—"forming a human community, focusing human desire, and entering into human relations of exchange"—even as he also interrogates categories of authenticity and what constitutes a "real" religion.[50] Also attending to popular culture and consumption, Kathryn Lofton argues that "*religion* is a word that has captured our sociality. . . . Religion is a name for social organization."[51] David Walker suggests a ritual theory drawn from P. T. Barnum's investigations into humbugs. For Barnum, Walker writes, "in order to be considered a humbug (rather than a fraud, a cheat, or someone insufficiently interesting to have any moniker at all), one needed to provide a service. There had to be 'something there.'"[52] Even if trickery were afoot, there could be "something in it."

---

versity Press, 2008), 98–106. Najar argues that these letters were designed to keep churches in "good order," and that they "provided a kind of introduction and a guarantor of past good conduct" (98). See also John G. Crawley, *Primitive Baptists of the Wiregrass South: 1815 to the Present* (University Press of Florida, 2013 [1998]), 41–43.

50. Chidester, *Authentic Fakes*, 2.

51. Lofton, *Consuming Religion*, xi.

52. Walker, "The Humbug in American Religion," 40.

The humbug is a fake, but, courting its own investigation, it is a fake that points to the real. In these ways (and many more), the category of religion has been produced by investigations into the "really real." Whether or not the term has analytical utility for scholars, our inquiries, from debunking to reenchantment, often portend investigatory rituals.

From spirit possessions to genuine conversation to the presence of Christ in the Eucharist, the Protestant-secular history of religion has investigated the unseen real by inspecting fakes. In the mid-nineteenth century, the subject of religious investigation du jour was Spiritualism.[53] Not all or even most Spiritualist mediums staged theatrical performances or attempted to draw large audiences, and most carried on their business apart from professional debunkers and sensationalist coverage. However, from the earliest days of the Spiritualist movement, investigators from both within and without looked into potential fakes. The very "efficacy" of mediums and their practices, Erika Dyson has argued, "is not necessarily the result of genuine powers but results from both deferral and theatricality, from a mediation between the 'real' and the 'really made up.'"[54] One might press further on what makes "genuine powers" genuine, but the larger point is that questions of sincerity and efficacy, while different, are related. Investigating the sincerity of a Spiritualist medium—or whether the audience or other participant really believes in it—is not the same as asking whether the medium is really channeling a spirit. But these issues run together. Rather than argue that debunking investigations did real religious work—although they might have, depending on one's theory of religion—I suggest that debunking did real secular work. By this I mean that mediating between the real and the really made-up was a secular project that demarcated true religion from false.

In practice, the drawing of the lines took more dimensions than two— more than just real versus really made-up—as the category of the humbug illustrates. A humbug is not fraudulent per se. It is a sort of trick that from the outset acknowledges that it might be a trick. Barnum and his fellow peddlers of humbuggery invited critical inquiry. They presented an object

53. As Emily Ogden has shown, Spiritualists, targets of many debunking efforts, attempted to establish and perform their own modernity by debunking others, namely mesmerists. Ogden, *Credulity*, 216–226.

54. Dyson, "Spiritualism and Crime," 293. Similarly, Ann Braude wrote of the Fox sisters and early Spiritualism, "The interpretations of investigators, rather than the manifestations themselves, provided the content of the new religion" (*Radical Spirits*, 19).

of fascination and invited the viewer, the consumer, to believe it or not. As David Walker has explained, "The important thing, [Barnum] thought, was to provide a space wherein people could play with the boundary between marvel and analysis and between credulity and skepticism; and where they could think through the conditions of modern life."[55] What bothered Barnum were outright frauds, which did not invite inquiry but instead tried to dupe the unsuspecting. There's nothing playful about baldly exploiting a rube, and there is no entertainment value in it either. This is why Barnum attempted to expose Spiritualist mediums as frauds. His staged investigations, as well as actual criminal trials of exposed mediums such as William Mumler, captivated audiences and served, as Barnum would have it, as occasions for the public to engage in debunking rituals.[56] "Artful deception in the Age of Barnum," James Cook has observed, "routinely involved a calculated intermixing of the genuine and the fake, enchantment and disenchantment, energetic public exposé and momentary suspension of disbelief."[57] These admixtures could be playful, but they were complex social rituals with high stakes and heavy consequences. And in an environment of strangerhood, counterfeiting, and a crisis of trust, the pertinent questions were often about whom, more than what, to believe.

Who and what were not easily separated. People had to place confidence in people in order to place confidence in things. Melville's confidence man repeatedly leverages this social fact to his own advantage. He argues that confidence, in and of itself, is a virtue—a democratic, Christian virtue. Then he exploits it. In the guise of the man in the traveling cap, the confidence man fetches a glass of water for an elderly miser with a nasty cough, asking

55. Walker, "The Humbug in American Religion," 40. Elsewhere, Walker wrote, "If we take religion to entail the recasting of historically contingent social conditions as intellectual heuristics and community blueprints, then people do 'genuine' religious work whenever they help others situate themselves as humans relative to super- and sub-humans in place and time" ("James Strang's Letter of Appointment," *Frequencies: A Collaborative Genealogy of Spirituality*, Nov. 21, 2011). While it is not my purpose here to adjudicate the authenticity of religious experience, it is worth highlighting the staying power of these questions of what constitutes real religious work, and how a certain type of functionalist definition of religion produced in particular nineteenth-century contexts still offers something useful to religious studies scholars and American jurists.

56. Louis Kaplan, *The Strange Case of William Mumler, Spirit Photographer* (University of Minnesota Press, 2008); Peter Manseau, *The Apparitionists: A Tale of Phantoms, Fraud, Photography, and the Man Who Captured Lincoln's Ghost* (Houghton Mifflin Harcourt, 2017); and Lindsey, *A Communion of Shadows*, 113–157.

57. Cook, *The Arts of Deception*, 17.

only for confidence in return. The sick man freely offers confidence, and so his helper suggests he put that confidence to good use and asks for a hundred dollars, which he will invest on his behalf. The sick man, finding his helper's countenance to be "honest," even though the light is dim and the face hard to see, eventually hands over the money. His confidence in the man with the traveling cap leaves him down a hundred dollars and lacking a receipt. He was tricked once, and he still has a cough. But he retained his critical faculties, his ability to debunk.

In the next scene, an herb-doctor (who, the reader intuits, is the confidence man's next persona) attempts to sell the sick man a remedy. At first he is hesitant to trust another stranger. But after some philosophical wrangling about nature and goodness, the herb-doctor persuades the sick man to purchase some natural medicine. After the money and goods are exchanged, the herb-doctor invites investigation. He tells his client how to inspect the vials: if genuine, they will have the word "confidence" printed as a watermark on the label. Confused and upset, the sick man objects. Throughout their entire conversation, the herb-doctor has been preaching confidence, but now he seems to encourage distrust. The herb-doctor clarifies, then, that he had encouraged, specifically, "confidence in the genuine medicine, and the genuine *me*." This does not add up, for the sick man. How can he have confidence and distrust at the same time? He protests, "But to doubt, to suspect, to prove—to have all this wearing work to be doing continually—how opposed to confidence. It is evil!" The herb-doctor replies, "From evil comes good. Distrust is a stage to confidence" (89). This is fakecraft: looking for a fake, the sick man finds the real (or doesn't). The medicine, in this way, is a sort of humbug. There might be "something in it," but the sick man needs to investigate, literally to hold it up to the light, to be sure.[58] And yet, the proof he will find (or not), the marker of authenticity, is still confidence.

"HE PONDERS THE MYSTERY OF HUMAN SUBJECTIVITY IN GENERAL"

Several chapters later the herb-doctor has been debunked, at least according to his debunkers. He attempts to sell a "Samaritan Pain Dissuader," an

---

58. The novel does not include a scene in which the sick man inspects the labels, so the reader never finds out whether they have the watermark.

elixir of "pure vegetable extract," for fifty cents. And he guarantees a five-hundred-dollar payout if it does not "remove the acutest pain within less than ten minutes" (90). After an initially tepid response, a few people begin buying the nostrum. But then a gigantic man steals the scene, denouncing the herb-doctor as a phony and arguing loudly about opiates and pain. He finally yells, "Profane fiddler on the heart-strings! Snake!" At this, the herb-doctor decries the "wrathful blow" and "coward assault" and makes a quick departure (94–95), upon which a few travelers analyze what just happened. "But do you think it the fair thing to unmask an operator that way?" one asks. Another responds, "Fair? It is right."

Their debate hinges on the politics of sincerity. They agree that the herb-doctor's cures are fake. But it is not the cures that have been unmasked; it's the "operator." The question then becomes whether the herb-doctor knew his fakes were fakes. If he did know and was intentionally deceiving others for personal profit, he should be condemned as a "knave." Perhaps, however, he believed in his own quackery, in which case he would be not a knave but a "fool" (95).[59] The politics of knaves and fools is subsequent to investigations of humbugs. No longer does the audience play with the ambiguity of fact and falsehood. Knave/fool is a disenchanted dichotomy, rooted firmly in the secular discourse of sincerity. The knave is not authentically religious, because he is duplicitous and insincere. The fool is not authentically secular, for his insufficiently buffered self is irrational and credulous.[60]

The knave/fool distinction is simple enough. When we try putting it into practice, however, difficulties arise stemming from the unknowability of motive but also the shiftiness of character. The herb-doctor was unmasked

59. Later in the conversation, a third character suggests that the herb-doctor was a secret Jesuit, for "the better to accomplish their secret designs, they assume, at times I am told, the most singular masques; sometimes, in appearance, the absurdest" (98). This third option leaves the knave-fool debate unresolved. The charge that there was something Catholic about the herb-doctor was not baseless. On the label of each bottle of the Samaritan Pain Dissuader was an "engraving of a countenance full of soft pity as that of the Romish-painted Madonna," and the herb-doctor said the medicine was a "thrice-blessed discovery of that disinterested friend of humanity whose portrait you see" (90). What might be understood as a sectarian (i.e., "Romish") image is instead cast as nonsectarian and humanistic. It is a secular medicine, natural and universal, yet given authority (and garnering suspicion?) by its quasi-religious imprimatur.

60. Recall the anti-Mormon propaganda cited in note 45 above (Lee, *The Mormons, Or, Knavery Exposed*). Lee's sense of the word "knavery" rests on exactly the dichotomy I am describing here. For Lee, Joseph Smith and other Mormon leaders were knaves exploiting foolish followers.

because his cures were determined to be fake, but the "inquest into [his] true character" was inconclusive.[61] He's selling a fake—but is *he* a fake? At this point in the novel, characters have changed their minds, been surprised by their own reactions, and questioned their own internal consistency. The herb-doctor had told the sick man to have confidence in "the genuine *me*," but it is unclear whether there really is a genuine person under the series of masquerades. And if that genuine person is supposed to be consistent (a belief holder, capable of self-possession), then the possibility of anyone's being genuine has already been called into question by a number of characters and quite explicitly by the narrator.

Into this chaos steps the backwoods Missouri bachelor Pitch. He is thoroughly distrustful, with a dour view of human nature and a heap of skepticism toward the natural world. The herb-doctor reenters the scene and introduces himself as "one who has confidence in nature, and confidence in man, with some little modest confidence in himself." Pitch ridicules this "Confession of Faith" and asks him if more men are knaves or fools. With confidence in nothing, having investigated humbugs and found nothing in them, Pitch concludes that all must be either knaves or fools. There are two types of people in this world. And, in his estimation, the fools far outnumber the knaves "for the same reason that I think oats are numerically more than horses. Don't knaves munch up fools just as horses do oats?" (112).

Pitch is a secular subject. He constructs his own rationality over and against the irrational gullibility of others. His world is disenchanted. He pulls off every mask—but, tragically, he ends up with nothing to hold on to. After the herb-doctor departs again, seemingly bested, Pitch encounters a man from the Philosophical Intelligence Office. (Again, the reader intuits that this new character, too, is a guise of the confidence man. This is not, however, immediately clear to Pitch.) The P.I.O. officer offers to sell Pitch the services of an indentured servant boy.[62] This turns into a protracted philosophical discussion about human nature, in which Pitch argues that all boys are "rascals" and thus men are too. As the conversation wears on, Pitch grows frustrated with his interlocutor's arguments, charging, "You pun with ideas as another man may with words" (128). By the end of the exchange, he

61. "Inquest into the True Character of the Herb-Doctor" is the title of chap. 18, in which the knave-fool discussion occurs.

62. In the previous chapter, Pitch had told the herb-doctor he was "now started to get me made some kind of machine to do the sort of work which boys are supposed to be fitted for" (113).

gives in and decides to purchase a boy's services after all having been assured that this particular boy is honest "as the day is long. . . . Such, at least, were the marginal observations on the phrenological chart of his head, submitted to me by the mother." The appeal to reasonable calculation, to science, seems to work. Pitch maintains that he has not really changed his mind, but he concedes to try the boy "for the sake purely of a scientific experiment." But the P.I.O. officer demands not tentative experimentation but full confidence, which Pitch finally gives (132–133). Shortly afterward Pitch gazes over the swampy, mosquito-infested scene at twilight and begins to suspect that "he, the philosopher, had unwittingly been betrayed into being an unphilosophical dupe." He is not, after all, the stable subject capable of sincere and unchanging belief. He is, in fact, credulous. "He ponders the mystery of human subjectivity in general" (134).

Pitch was a mark, the target of a confidence game. "Big-time confidence games," David Maurer explained in his classic *The Big Con*, "are in reality only carefully rehearsed plays in which every member of the cast *except the mark* knows his part perfectly."[63] In Melville's text, it is not clear how big the con really is and exactly who is in on it, but it *is* clear that Pitch is the mark: "He is living in a fantastic, grotesque world which resembles the real one so closely that he cannot distinguish the difference."[64] Maurer is a sort of debunker, offering readers a peek behind the curtain, whereas Melville's narrator seems to live in a fantastic, grotesque world too—and so do the readers. At any rate, we know that Pitch is a mark. After the mark realizes he has been conned, he needs to be "cooled out." A confidence man's accomplice consoles the mark to keep him calm and deliver "instruction in the philosophy of taking a loss," as Erving Goffman phrased it.[65] The mark is not who he thought he was. He has lost his role in society, or what he thought it was, "involuntarily deprived of his position or involvement and made in return something that is considered a lesser thing to be."[66] Pitch, the philosopher, is not so rational after all. He is dissociated from his role, his subjectivity disintegrated. He is in desperate need of cooling out. Just in time, a man with a voice "sweet as a seraph's" addresses Pitch with a "cordial

---

63. Maurer, *The Big Con*, 101.

64. Maurer, *The Big Con*, 101–102.

65. Goffman, "On Cooling the Mark Out," 452.

66. Goffman, "On Cooling the Mark Out," 453. See also Alexander S. Dent, "The Devil in the Deal: Notes toward an Anthropology of Confidence," *Anthropological Quarterly* 90, no. 4 (Fall, 2017): 1007–1024.

slap on the shoulder" and a listening ear. This character, it turns out, is the confidence man's final guise, the cosmopolitan. He offers some instruction in loss-taking. "Life is a pic-nic *en costume*," he advises, and "one must take a part, assume a character, stand ready in a sensible way to play the fool" (139).

The Confidence-Man calls into question the very possibility of a sincere believer. Some critics have suggested that the book imagines an alternative sort of personhood, one grounded in the social rather than the indissoluble individual.[67] Pitch is an enlightened secular subject, but his selfhood falls apart. Struggling to keep it together, he twice asserts, flailing, "My name is Pitch; I stick to what I say" (122, 130). These two sentences are the only occasions in which the novel includes Pitch's name. In every other case, he is the "Missouri bachelor" or the "backwoodsman." When he feels his own subjectivity crumbling, he blurts out his name as if it might hold him together, like the hot tar sealing the boards of a leaking ship (that substance commonly known, in the nineteenth century, as pitch).[68] "I stick to what I say." It's not much to stick to. The Missouri bachelor does not realize, to quote Jennifer Greiman, that "multitudes are present within the appearance of the singular, and names . . . are merely the words that gather them together."[69] Instead, he rather pitiably sticks to his own words; they're all he has.

The confidence man, by contrast, has everyone else's words and desires. Perhaps he does not have a self, nothing under the mask. Or, perhaps, he's not him but everyone else.[70] He is not a "mirror" for society or a blank slate onto which others write their desires. Instead, like the *Fidèle*, he is a container for strange particles, an amalgamation of society. It is not that he lacks a self, then, but that his self is not an atomic individual. Rachel Cole

---

67. This type of scholarship, which I think includes much work on the postsecular, responds to the limits of debunking as an epistemic mode of scholarship, as laid out by Bruno Latour: "Can we devise another powerful descriptive tool that deals this time with matters of concern and whose import then will no longer be to debunk but to protect and to care, as Donna Haraway would put it? Is it really possible to transform the critical urge in the ethos of someone who adds reality to matters of fact and not subtract reality? To put it another way, what's the difference between deconstruction and constructivism?" (Latour, "Has Critique Run Out of Steam?," 32).

68. Given this fact, Mark Noble has aptly described Pitch's name as a joke. He argues, "In light of the stickiness of saying anything at all, the joke implies that thinking subjects never quite stick to what they say but remain stuck nevertheless to the contingencies and indeterminacies concealed within identic claims" ("Reading Melville Reading Character," 244).

69. Greiman, *Democracy's Spectacle*, 193.

70. See Gordon, *Ghostly Matters* on "complex personhood."

has argued that he "represents an irreducibly social form of personhood, in which the person is created in both the eyes and image of someone else."[71] This type of personhood is even more public than that of the sincere believer. The sincere believer has an honest public persona, which relies on an individualized public/private distinction. Melville's confidence man is neither sincere nor insincere. He might seem like a monster, someone without personhood or character. But, following Mark Noble, we might ask if "what looks like the collapse of character is rather the ground for social relationship as Melville understands it."[72]

"STRANGE PARTICLES"

Sincere believers traffic in words. Sincerity must be discursive, Webb Keane has argued, such that "nondiscursive actions are sincere only insofar as they can be translated into discourse or be treated as some sort of signification."[73] If publics (and counterpublics) are networks, discursively but also affectively created and maintained, then sincerity does not necessarily require atomization and rigid boundaries between subjects. In this way, masks can be media through which to make connections rather than to obscure intentions. And in many cases, to speak in the voice of "another" might be sincere, not duplicitous.

In the confusing run of chapters in the middle of *The Confidence-Man*, the cosmopolitan engages with a Transcendentalist type named Mark Winsome. The two quickly tire of each other, at which point Winsome calls over his disciple, Egbert. Egbert is a repository for and repeater of Winsome's philosophy. He understands it, believes it, lives it. "Indeed, it is by you that I myself best understand myself," Winsome tells him. "For to every philosophy are certain rear parts, very important parts, and these, like the rear of one's head, are best seen by reflection" (199). Winsome passes Egbert on to the cosmopolitan and exits the conversation (physically). And then the cosmopolitan makes a strange suggestion. Instead of Egbert explaining Winsome's philosophy from "first principles," he will explain it through a staged dialogue in character. The cosmopolitan, whose name is Frank Goodman,

71. Cole, "At the Limits of Identity," 396.
72. Noble, "Reading Melville Reading Character," 240.
73. Keane, *Christian Moderns*, 209n8.

will play a character named Frank. Egbert will play a character named Charlie. They then reenact a conversation had with Charlie Noble, the riverboat con man, a few chapters earlier. The sequence is thickly layered. Characters play characters playing characters. The centerpiece is a full short story, told by "Charlie" (played by Egbert) in order to explain Winsome's philosophy to "Frank" (played by Frank). The story is told neither in the voice of Charlie nor in that of Egbert, but in that of whoever told it to him, because "unhappily the original storyteller here has so tyrannized over me, that it is quite impossible for me to repeat his incidents without sliding into his style" (208).

This weird, playful sequence models an alternative form of sincerity. Here, sincere discourse flows *through* others, not just *to* them. It is not a network of buffered selves. Further, the passage seems to suggest that masquerade can be a more sincere means of ascertaining truth than speaking in one's "own" distinct voice. When Charlie refuses Frank's fervent pleas for money, Frank accuses, "Oh, this, all along, is not you, Charlie, but some ventriloquist who usurps your larynx. It is Mark Winsome that speaks, not Charlie."[74] Charlie replies, "If so, thank heaven, the voice of Mark Winsome is not alien but congenial to my larynx" (207). Can a person be sincere if someone else's voice is congenial to their larynx? The question almost fails to make sense. The person of Egbert-*cum*-Charlie, channeling Mark Winsome, is of course not straightforwardly sincere, a single individual expressing his private beliefs earnestly through public discourse. But he is not insincere either. His masquerade aims to reveal. After a while, Frank angrily terminates the conversation over his objections to Egbert's/Charlie's/Winsome's "inhuman philosophy" and lack of confidence in humanity. Egbert, now alone, is left "at a loss to determine where exactly the fictitious character had been dropped, and the real one, if any, resumed. If any, because, with pointed meaning, there occurred to him, as he gazed after the cosmopolitan, these familiar lines: 'All the world's a stage / And all the men and women merely players, / Who have their exits and their entrances, / And one man in his time plays many parts'" (224).[75] Fakecraft, as discussed above, refers to the rituals by which social actors investigate fakes and artifice in order to discover the real to which it points. *The Confidence-Man* suggests that the

---

74. It is not clear why "Charlie" would know who Mark Winsome is. The masks are hard to keep in place.

75. William Shakespeare, *As You Like It*, act 2, scene 7, lines 139–142. Erving Goffman, in slight disagreement, writes, "All the world is not, of course, a stage, but the crucial ways in which it isn't are not easy to specify" (*The Presentation of Self in Everyday Life*, 72).

real is society, a world of "strange particles" in which the real is not within each particle but in their movements, each mask simultaneously a cover over and window into "infinite socialities."[76]

To contain infinite socialities is to diverge from a secular model of sincere religious belief. But, by some definitions, such personhood might be religious. Émile Durkheim, for example, argued that religion is "eminently social."[77] The gods or the sacred represent society itself. Scholars who work in a broad Durkheimian lineage, which includes many in religious studies, study discourse, ritual, and texts about gods in order to study people. However, as a secular pursuit, the academic study of religion also can perpetuate models of personhood that are foreign to the people under study. The study of religion has often centered individual belief as a primary object of inquiry.[78] And so have other secular institutions, such as the law. Sincerely held religious belief is not eminently social. It has social elements and social expressions, but its core is atomistic, indissoluble.

The liberal regime of religious freedom protects individual sincere religion. Thinking with *The Confidence-Man* might allow us to think otherwise about our selves and religion. Melville was not debunking the logic of his day so much as uncovering it, turning it over, and inspecting it. The novel is not simply a rebuke of secular subjectivity or the possibility of sincerity. Rather, it dramatizes what many people still feel and know: that we imagine ourselves as rational and autonomous individuals, but we feel influences from unknown places and are given to the "caprices of [our] natural heart" (74). Secular modernity aims to rein something in, gods or spirits or "subtle agencies" or infinite socialities.[79] U.S. secularism is a containment strategy. But, like the strange particles in the "Rio Janeiro fountain," beliefs and

---

76. Shortly after the publication of *Moby-Dick*, and six years before that of *The Confidence-Man*, Melville wrote, "Infinite socialities are within me." John Modern interprets this quip as Melville "refusing to answer the question of ultimate reference, the question of what exactly [*Moby-Dick*] was about" (*Secularism in Antebellum America*, xxii). See also John Lardas Modern, "Confused Parchments, Infinite Socialities," *Immanent Frame*, Mar. 4, 2013.

77. Durkheim, *The Elementary Forms*.

78. Lopez, "Belief."

79. Melville, *Moby-Dick*, 110. As Parker and Hayford (editors of the Norton critical edition cited) mention in a footnote, the title of this chapter, "Enter Ahab; To Him, Stubb," is the first use of stage directions. These stage directions, like much else in the book, seem to indicate some "subtle agencies" and thus call into question the singular, rational, choosing subject who is aware of their own motivations and in control of their fate.

believers spill and flow. It is hard to pin down, to track, to surveil, a single strange particle. It is also difficult to count strange particles up. Yet, the "power of the modern state," as Talal Asad writes, "depends on using a distinctive language: the language of numbers."[80] The next chapter turns to state-sponsored projects of calculation and technologies of secularism.

80. Asad, *Secular Translations*, 99.

SECULAR GOVERNANCE IN COLUMNS AND ROWS

IF *THE CONFIDENCE-MAN*'S STEAMER is a "world of unregulated miscellany," then Anthony Comstock's world was one of miscellany quite regulated.[1] Beginning in the 1870s and continuing until his death in 1915, Comstock regulated mail and morals, trying to keep people in line. Taking Comstock and his New York Society for the Suppression of Vice (NYSSV) as its point of departure, this chapter analyzes the processes of documentation, surveillance, and calculation that are central to modern secular governance. In this way, perhaps unexpectedly, Comstock's morality policing belongs to a history of religious freedom and secularism as it imagined and enforced the character of the sincere believer. While he catalogued threats to moral order and documented his many arrests, Comstock created the sincere believer by detailing its others. It was that type of believer, then, who would become the truly religious and thus whose religious freedom would be protected. As Jolyon Thomas has written, there is an "inherently coercive nature of religious freedom."[2] It sets the grammars and vocabularies into which, by "certain tyrannies of translation," believers must give an account of their beliefs.[3] Many agents of the secular state dictate the terms by which belief might or might not guarantee free exercise. But the regulation of religion takes place outside the courts as well. Sometimes secularism is a police operation. And

---

1. The quotation is from Cole, "At the Limits of Identity," 396.

2. Thomas, *Faking Liberties*, 5.

3. Fred Moten, "B 3," Feb. 6, 2010, https://www.poetryfoundation.org/harriet/2010/02/b-3.

it often takes an inquisitional approach. This is especially the case when sincerity is at issue, as agents probe subjects' inner consciences—extracting the belief, translating it, rendering it legible, holding it up to the light.

Comstock had a reputation—and still does, including among historians of religion—for his fixation on sex. That reputation is well earned. But, at least during the late 1870s and 1880s, he was just as fixated on fraud and what might be categorized generally as financial crimes. In that era, as in Melville's antebellum period, trust was at a premium. The U.S. economy was regulated only loosely, and investors found it difficult to discern the differences between "legitimate" and "illegitimate" forms of market activity. Futures markets, stock trading, railroad bonds, bucket shops, and lotteries thrived in these decades. Bubbles swelled and burst, and the nation plunged into the Long Depression of 1873–1879. This was the setting for the early years of the NYSSV. The Society was founded in 1872, and the Comstock laws, which banned the circulation of "obscene" materials, were passed in 1873. In 1880 Comstock published a book titled *Frauds Exposed; Or, How the People Are Deceived and Robbed, and Youth Corrupted*. The text cast light onto a shadowy society of trickery and deceit, warning readers of urban life's vicious traps and pitfalls.

This chapter opens with a discussion of *Frauds Exposed*, where Comstock articulates a familiar framework of knaves and fools. Next, it riffs on Comstock's remark, "I was called the 'great Inquisitor of the Nineteenth Century'—the courts 'Inquisitions.'"[4] Thinking about an Inquisition and fears thereof can provide insight into the politics of sincere belief and the persistent problem of investigating interiority. The chapter then considers the roles of documentation and calculation in secular governance generally before finally returning to the NYSSV and their police work.

KNAVES, FOOLS, AND SINCERE BELIEVERS

Frauds Exposed presented a compendium of hucksterism and deception. In the course of its five-hundred-plus pages the book detailed a litany of duplicitous schemes. Chapter after chapter exposed various frauds—lotteries, divining rods, confidence schemes, quackery—and their threats to the public. Comstock peppered the text with anecdotes and vignettes, telling

4. Comstock, *Frauds Exposed*, 411.

of the various scoundrels he and the Society had arrested. He explained how schemes work, giving detailed descriptions of lottery frauds, bogus stocks, and sundry switcheroos and "sawdust swindles" (in which the mark is left with what he believes to be a bag of counterfeit cash but is, in fact, a sack of wood shavings).[5] *Frauds Exposed* also reproduced dozens of advertisements and circulars, showing readers exactly what and whom to watch out for. It was not unlike Melville's juvenile peddler's Counterfeit Detector, pages of fakes implying the existence of something real. With this detector, Comstock aimed "to warn honest and simple-minded persons" about the many damnable schemes of "the sharper."[6]

Comstock detailed a world of knaves and fools. Whereas the Missouri bachelor Pitch likened knaves and fools to horses and oats, Comstock chose a more carnivorous metaphor: "[The fools'] race will never perish from the face of the earth, so long as there are knaves to prey upon them," he wrote. "Like certain species of fishes, they fill their place in nature as sustenance for the sharks."[7] But unlike Pitch, who thought all people either knaves or fools, Comstock imagined a class of sincere believers in the middle. The knaves and fools on either side were beyond saving. "This book is not written for the fools; I do not hope to teach them wisdom," he wrote. No, his public was the "many respectable persons" who "sometimes fall a prey to swindlers."[8] This public was made up of sincere believers, neither insincere knaves nor credulous fools.[9]

Anything could be faked, Comstock warned, and just about everything had been. "Every thing of value has its counterfeit," he wrote, in anticipation of his audience's doubt that a whole section on counterfeit sewing machines was warranted.[10] Frauds represented value where there was in fact none,

---

5. On such schemes and nineteenth-century gambling more generally, both fraudulent and nonfraudulent, see Fabian, *Card Sharps and Bucket Shops*. George Pickering Burnham offered a concise and helpful explanation of sawdust swindles (or "the sawdust game") in *American Counterfeits, How Detected, and How Avoided* (Boston: A. W. Lovering, 1879), 400–407. This game, he wrote, "is played by only two parties; to wit, sharp knaves and dull fools" (400).

6. Comstock, *Frauds Exposed*, 5.

7. Comstock, *Frauds Exposed*, 13.

8. Comstock, *Frauds Exposed*, 13. I am using the term "publics" to mean the intended audience, imagined through rhetoric, not necessarily the audience Comstock's discourse actually reached. See Warner, "Publics and Counterpublics," in *Publics and Counterpublics*.

9. Comstock even used the word "credulous" to describe "fools" (*Frauds Exposed*, 13).

10. Comstock, *Frauds Exposed*, 262.

a thin veneer over cheap materials. In *Frauds Exposed* Comstock further developed this theory of value, arguing that usefulness, healthfulness, artfulness, and moral rectitude imbued a thing with worth. If it was well made and could be put to good use, it was good. And, thus, it could and would be faked. Here, he anticipated Paul Johnson's point about fakes: "Every forgery points to an original, like a visible fold of rope that implies many coils beneath the surface, of unknown reach."[11] New York's social and economic worlds were riddled with counterfeits, and Comstock's role was to expose them, to rip off the masks and show nothing of true value underneath.

There might seem to be little connection between Comstock's antifraud mission and his regulation of sex and "obscenity." However, reading his 1883 follow-up *Traps for the Young* and 1887's *Morals versus Art* through the frameworks established in *Frauds Exposed*, we can see how Comstock's theory of value structured his concerns with obscenity. Obscenity led people astray because it tricked them into believing that there was something of value where there was not. This point comes through clearly in Comstock's writings on art. He stridently opposed reproductions and was skeptical of photography in general because, among other reasons, fraudsters could manipulate images and use them to make fakes. Comstock was not alone in this concern. Molly McGarry has shown how critics of William Mumler (the famous spirit photographer and subject of many exposés and a fraud case) expressed "fear that a dangerous technological double could compete for the status of the original and displace the real thing."[12] Such worrying about real things and fakes, McGarry suggests, might account for Comstock's "otherwise puzzling concern with the mischief caused not only by pornographic photographs but also by artistic reproductions of all kinds."[13] These reproductions were, for Comstock, counterfeits.

Comstock had a sort of labor theory of value, fetishizing the work of artists, manufacturers, and craftsmen that imbued a product with inherent value. He advanced what McGarry has called a "bizarre argument": that a painting imparts beauty but a photograph, even a photograph of the same beautiful painting, was offensive. Likewise, a reproduction of a painting of a woman was immoral, whereas the original painting was not.[14] In *Traps for the Young*, he explained that in reproduction "the labor of the artist is

11. Johnson, "Fakecraft," 106.

12. McGarry, *Ghosts of Futures Past*, 111.

13. McGarry, *Ghosts of Futures Past*, 111.

14. McGarry, *Ghosts of Futures Past*, 113.

robbed of its *true value* when his picture is caricatured by such a process."[15]
J. Lorand Matory argues that the discourse of the "fetish," as it developed as a
discourse between Europeans and Africans in the sixteenth and seventeenth
centuries, was a "bilateral *disagreement* over the proper value and agency of
people and things."[16] I would argue that Comstock and his enemy "liberals"
disagreed about things' value. But, on Comstock's account, this was not a
disagreement so much as a contest between light and darkness—in a very
real sense, between God and Satan.[17] He presented his work as a form of
debunking fakecraft, unmasking the fakes to preserve and protect the real.
Sincere believers, unlike fools, were able to see the truth—if only the knaves
and their frauds were exposed.

Toward the end of *Frauds Exposed*, Comstock turned his attention away
from the professional swindlers and to the "infidels and liberals who defend
these moral cancer-planters."[18] People such as the famed freethinker Robert Ingersoll accused him of opposing free speech and the free press. Their
"liberal fraud," Comstock warned, was *the greatest curse to the youth of
this country.*"[19] Ingersoll led a petition against the Comstock law, with sev-
enty thousand signers, but they all "dealt in falsehood and misrepresentation," Comstock alleged. "Facts were suppressed."[20] It was not just a matter
of lying, but also a disagreement about value. The liberals claimed to value
liberty, but they misapprehended what true liberty was. Just like the "free
lovers"—who take the word "love" and "distort and prostitute its meaning";
"it should be spelled l-u-s-t, to be rightly understood"—liberals did not
understand the real meaning of the words they used for themselves.[21] To
them, liberty "means that they may, without let or hindrance, blaspheme
and deride the holiest things, while any one opposed to their views is to
be held to strict accountability."[22] In their disagreement about the meaning

---

15. Comstock, *Traps for the Young*, 172.

16. Matory, *The Fetish Revisited*, 14. On the fetish and the development of religious
categories and their racializing work, see Johnson, *African American Religions*, 56–106.

17. Comstock mentioned Satan repeatedly throughout *Traps for the Young*, blaming
him directly for the traps and snares endangering young urban men. Also, recall Melville's
frequent insinuations that the confidence man is, if not Satan, a devilish figure.

18. Comstock, *Frauds Exposed*, 5.

19. Comstock, *Frauds Exposed*, 388.

20. Comstock, *Frauds Exposed*, 421. In these pages, he also responded to the attacks in
De Robigne Mortimer Bennett, *Anthony Comstock: His Career of Cruelty and Crime* (1878).

21. Comstock, *Traps for the Young*, 158.

22. Comstock, *Frauds Exposed*, 394.

of liberty, Comstock imagined his position as true and the liberals' as not only false but fake.

How people debunk fakes reveals what is important to their conceptualizations of the real. Johnson explains that as a religious tradition "applies discourses of the fake and the real, they apply that hinge to different sets of concerns—to different doors and windows, so to say."[23] Comstock applied the hinge of fake/real, or counterfeit/valuable or vicious/moral, to lots of doors and windows, as we've seen. But the doors and windows he cared most about, ultimately, were those separating the bourgeois domestic home from the world of public commerce and free-flowing exchange. Protecting the purity of white children and women meant, for Comstock, damming up the poisoned channels of words and images flooding the streets in order to keep them out of homes.[24] In this way, through surveillance and policing, Comstock regulated the public and private spheres to protect "pure" womanhood. Imagining white women as vulnerable and impressionable (two qualities by which their whiteness and femininity were constructed), Comstock tried to maintain their purity, which is to say, their value.[25] Critics from the nineteenth century through today have mocked Comstock for being terrified of sex. But what really terrified him, I would suggest, was queerness, sexuality as "unregulated miscellany," the messy flows of flesh and image. So he tried to contain the excesses of sexual, economic, and religious life by accounting for them, naming deviance and deviants to produce their other, the good and sincere citizen.

AUTO-DA-FÉ

On a personal copy of *The Confidence-Man*, Herman Melville wrote, "Dedicated to the victims of Auto da Fe," referring to the public rituals in Iberian Inquisition trials in which imprisoned heretics were sentenced and punished, most famously through burning at the stake.[26] Some critics have

23. Johnson, "Fakecraft," 119.

24. See McGarry, *Ghosts of Futures Past*, 118–119; and, generally, Werbel, *Lust on Trial*.

25. On impressibility and on womanhood as a racial concept, see Schuller, *The Biopolitics of Feeling*. I am also indebted here, in thinking about the racial dimensions to Comstock's antiqueerness manifest in policing regimes, to Snorton, *Black on Both Sides*.

26. The burning is likely what Melville had in mind. *Auto-da-fé* is mentioned one time in the text of *The Confidence-Man*: in the final scene, in which the young child interrogates

argued that this dedication indicates Melville's own identification with said victims, after the low-church evangelical press pilloried his works and made him a victim of their inquisition, as it were.[27] Others have suggested that victims of *auto-da-fé*—literally, "act of faith"—are those victimized by their own confidence, faith itself being "the ultimate confidence game."[28] In other works, most famously "The Town-Ho's Story" in *Moby-Dick*, Melville had invoked the Inquisition as an example of unjust tyranny, anachronistically antidemocratic.[29] He was far from the only author to do so.

In the nineteenth century, American Protestant authors made the Inquisition a common theme, in many cases as a part of anti-Catholic invective.[30] In these broadsides, the Inquisition was properly understood as a *Catholic project*, and thus it demonstrated the differences between (good) Protestant settler empires and (bad) Catholic settler empires. References to the Inquisition often served to link Catholicism with slavery or other states of unfreedom.[31] Joseph F. Berg, pastor of the First German Reformed Church of Philadelphia, averred that enslaved people in the South were free "when compared with the man who breathes the atmosphere of liberty, and yet

----

the old man and gives him the Counterfeit Detector. "All pointed and fluttering, the rags of the little fellow's red-flannel shirt, mixed with those of his yellow coat, flamed about him like the painted flames in the robes of a victim in *auto-da-fé*" (243).

27. Hershel Parker, "The Confidence-Man's Masquerade," in Melville, *The Confidence-Man*, 293–303, at 301; see also 243n2.

28. Taylor, "Discrediting God," 615.

29. John Cyril Barton, "'An Unquestionable Source?' Melville's 'The Town-Ho's Story,' the Inquisition, and W. B. Stevenson's Twenty Years' Residence in South America," *Nineteenth-Century Literature* 68, no. 2 (Sept., 2013): 145–179.

30. See, e.g., B. F. Ellis, *A History of the Romish Inquisition Compiled from Various Authors* (Hanover, IN, 1835); J. F. Berg, *Mysteries of the Inquisition* (Philadelphia, 1846); D. Achilli, *Dealings with the Inquisition; Or, Papal Rome, Her Priests and Her Jesuits* (New York, 1851); Theodore Dwight, *The Roman Republic of 1849; with Accounts of the Inquisition and the Siege of Rome* (New York, 1851); and Joseph S. Wilson, *The Inquisition* (Milwaukee, 1853).

31. For an overview, see Maura Jane Farrelley, *Anti-Catholicism in America, 1620–1860* (Cambridge University Press, 2017). Ray Allen Billington, *The Protestant Crusade, 1800–1860: A Study of the Origins of American Nativism* (Macmillan, 1938), remains a useful resource, and Billington gives more attention to mentions of the Inquisition than many later studies. The Italian Revolutions of 1848 brought another wave of anti-Catholic literature and Protestant anxieties about freedom in the United States. See Peter R. D'Agostino, *Rome in America: Transnational Catholic Ideology from the Risorgimento to Fascism* (University of North Carolina Press, 2004), especially chap. 1, "The Roman Question and the Battle for Civilization, 1815–1878."

voluntarily fetters his soul, and surrenders himself, bound hand and foot, to the sovereign will and pleasure of a popish priest."[32] When liberals likened Comstockery to the Inquisition, it was part of their argument that he limited their freedoms of speech and press (which Comstock argued were not truly free or freeing, when speech and press were used in service of propagating vicious traps). It was an argument about freedom. Anti-Catholicism was central to Protestant secular articulations of true religion and freedom. In the "Bible wars" of Philadelphia and Cincinnati, the sermons of Lyman Beecher, Samuel F. B. Morse's conspiracy theories, and the 1834 burning of the convent in Charlestown, Massachusetts, Protestant rhetoric and action instituted a United States defined by individual freedom and official disestablishmentarianism.[33] Even earlier, in James Madison's writings on religious freedom, Elizabeth Fenton notes, "the Inquisition metonymically represents all forms of religious oppression."[34]

Much of the anti-Catholic discourse alleged not just that Catholics were unfree but that the priests and other church officials were deceptive, tricky, and insincere. In 1835 some printers in New York republished the English Puritan Richard Baxter's 1659 treatise *Jesuit Juggling: Forty Popish Frauds Detected and Disclosed*. In form, Baxter's text was not so different from such nineteenth-century compendia as David Reese's 1838 *Humbugs of New-York* or P. T. Barnum's 1865 *The Humbugs of the World* (or Comstock's *Frauds Exposed*)—guidebooks on frauds and how to spot them.[35] It was a remarkable example of the Puritan ideal of sincerity as true religion. He wrote,

32. Joseph F. Berg, *The Confessional; or, an Exposition of the Doctrine of Auricular Confession as Taught in the Standards of the Roman Church* (Philadelphia: Isaac Ashmead, 1841), 75. See also Berg, *Lectures on Romanism* (Philadelphia: D. Weidner and I. Ashmead, 1840).

33. Franchot, *Roads to Rome*; Fessenden, *Culture and Redemption*; and Fenton, *Religious Liberties*. Anti-Catholicism also shaped nascent U.S. foreign policy, for Catholics were imagined as both a vast global network of imperial power (including states one might go to war with, fighting over colonized land) and inherently foreign and unfree traitors. See Corrigan, *Religious Intolerance, America, and the World*, esp. 56–101. On how anti-Catholicism helped lead to the Mexican-American War and shaped U.S. soldiers' perceptions of their mission, see Pinheiro, *Missionaries of Republicanism*.

34. Fenton, *Religious Liberties*, 29.

35. Maurer's *The Big Con*, discussed in the previous chapter, might be read as part of this same genre, albeit with a somewhat different goal. Geoffrey O'Brien calls *The Big Con* "a systematic breakdown, something like a poetics of the scam" and "essentially a taxonomy of crimes, a work of abstraction, offering a Platonic ideal or skeletal outline of perfect scams" ("A Nation of Grifters, Fixers, and Marks" 729, 730).

"But as plain dealing in religion is better than juggling, so, we had rather that open Papists were tolerated, than those juggling deceivers," the Jesuits and Friars.[36] Bad as "Papists" were, to Baxter, they were tolerable if they were sincere. The publishers who reissued Baxter's guide assured their antebellum readers that "the coflagrations [sic] of the Auto da Fe, and the indiscriminate massacre of Protestants by the blood-hounds of the Mother of Harlots, who furnished the blood of the Saints with which she became drunken, have passed away not to be reiterated." But, they warned, "the Romish priestly assassins will not surrender their stilettos, their poison, their frauds, and their long enjoyed supremacy without a struggle."[37] In these ways, the Protestant secular was realized through fears of Catholic governance. Protestant secularism, a form of governance itself, was the enactment and enforcement of this ideology.

Protestants imagined freedom in general and religious freedom in particular as essentially incompatible with Catholicism.[38] As Fenton put it, nineteenth-century U.S. secularism appears "not as the condition of being without religion but, rather, as the condition of being without Catholicism."[39] Although the historiography of anti-Catholicism largely focuses on white Protestants (with some good reason, because anti-Catholicism was linked closely with nativism and anti-immigrant politics aimed at Irish and Italians), some Black Protestants envisioned their own freedoms in anti-Catholic terms as well. For instance, David Walker, the antislavery activist, celebrated the Haitian Revolution but lamented that Haiti, the "glory of the blacks and terror of tyrants," was a beacon of freedom in every way but one: it was "plagued with that scourge of nations, the Catholic religion."[40] Other sorts of nationalists agreed that a truly free nation could not be a Catholic nation. The problem, or one of the problems, was again that Catholics were

36. Richard Baxter, *Jesuit Juggling: Forty Popish Frauds Detected and Disclosed*, 1st American ed. with an introductory address (New York: Craighead and Allen, 1835 [1659]), 31.

37. Baxter, *Jesuit Juggling*, xx. The introduction was an address "to the ministers, officers, and members of all the Protestant churches in the United States."

38. On Catholic visions of freedom in the United States in a variety of contexts, including but not limited to responses to Protestant competition and accusation, see McGreevy, *Catholicism and American Freedom*.

39. Fenton, *Religious Liberties*, 7.

40. David Walker, *Appeal to the Coloured Citizens of the World*, ed. Peter P. Hinks (Penn State University Press, 2000), 23.

sneaky. In the American Protestant imagination, Catholics lurked among the Protestants (this is one reason cartoonists like Thomas Nast depicted Irish people as identifiable racial others), cloaking their "foreign allegiances" and theocratic tendencies.[41]

Fears of Catholic secrecy were animated by an anxious politics of sincerity, the same confusion about masks and cloaks and "strange particles" Melville dramatized in *The Confidence-Man*. Stories about Jesuit jugglers and the like reinforced in American Protestants a "view of their religious opponents as potential traitors, as practitioners of dark arts scheming to overthrow the social and political order."[42] Secrecy was enticing; it made for good stories. "Escaped nun" tales like Maria Monk's *The Awful Disclosures of the Hotel Dieu Nunnery of Montreal* and Rebecca Reed's *Six Months in a Convent* "titillated readers with spectacles of gender inversion and sexual transgression," of "young women losing their femininity and sometimes their very humanity within convent walls."[43] Such narratives underscored the gendered nature of publicness and privacy, as well as the grasping desire to regulate and solidify what seemed wild and fluid. Although the Spanish Inquisition formally ended in 1834, the same year Protestants set the Ursuline convent in Charlestown aflame, the Inquisition had by then become a popular source of entertainment as well as political polemic. As they reveled in inquisitional maleficence, American Protestants reinforced their own secular ideologies of public/private separation and liberal subjectivity. Edgar Allan Poe's "The Pit and the Pendulum" was probably the most famous Inquisition fiction of the period and the work of "the ultimate stylist of Protestant captivity," in Jenny Franchot's memorable turn of phrase. In that story, Poe "uncovers the self-preoccupation at the heart of a tradition of practiced tremblings before the specter of the Inquisition."[44] The Inquisition was a dramatist's setting for the anxious experience of forming a secular subject.

41. See Fessenden, *Culture and Redemption*, 76–83.

42. Corrigan, *Religious Intolerance, America, and the World*, 60.

43. Kara M. French, "Prejudice for Profit: Escaped Nun Stories and American Catholic Print Culture," *Journal of the Early Republic* 39, no. 3 (Fall, 2019): 503–535, at 516. See also Yacovazzi, *Escaped Nuns*. Yacovazzi shows how escaped-nun stories were motifs through which to think and argue about freedom and nation across overlapping themes and topics including gender, immigration, and slavery.

44. Franchot, *Roads to Rome*, 167.

BLOOD AND FAKERY

Beyond the nineteenth-century anti-Catholic rhetoric, historical studies of the Inquisition are useful for thinking about secularism as a political project driven by investigative, calculative practices. There is perhaps something inquisitional about the sincerity test itself. Protestant conceptions of freedom and good order—extensions of that Puritan self-interrogation and, as Richard Baxter showcased, association of true religion with sincerity—demonized Catholics, and yet, those same polemicists employed tactics that might be called inquisitional. Without siding with Comstock's detractors, I want to suggest that there was indeed something inquisitional about Comstock, that perhaps he was the "great Inquisitor of the Nineteenth Century." Comstock's tactics of racial, gendered, and moral governance was backed by governmental power. And, as I will discuss later in the chapter, one of Comstock's methods of policing fraudulence and immorality was to categorize, catalogue, and document.

On the Iberian Peninsula as well as in the Americas, Inquisition officials exposed frauds. Their trial records contain a "profusion of terms such as *fignir* (to feign or dissimulate), *embuste* (a trick or fraud), *impostura* (imposture), and *embaucar* (to fool or deceive)."[45] Exposing frauds was not an essentially Protestant project. Here I return to Johnson's argument about fakecraft: that all religions have systems for sorting the real from the fake. For U.S. Protestants, and eventually for courts in religious freedom cases, fake religion is either duplicitous (knavish) or superstitious and credulous (foolish). Crucially, then, the sincere believer is a liberal individual subject, *choosing* to believe rationally and independently from coercion by an institution, whether governmental or ecclesial or both. Inquisitional politics were different, since the sincere believers they imagined were sincere in a different sense, "unmixed" and "pure," not individual believers but true members of the Church. Still, there are important and instructive similarities.[46] Andrew Keitt explains that women "were more likely to be charged with feigning raptures and revelations because of ingrained cultural assumptions about female duplicity. Moreover, women were thought to be

---

45. Keitt, *Inventing the Sacred*, 1.

46. In the Americas, generally inquisitors were more concerned with "superstitious" and blasphemous practices than with revealing the "true" identities of *conversos*, as they were in Spain and Portugal. Tortorici, *Sins Against Nature*, 12.

especially prone to demonic deception for psychological reasons."[47] Considering how women figured as both crafty knaves and impressionable fools, we might hear echoes of Inquisition in Comstock's efforts to quash women's rights, particularly the sexual freedom and spiritual authority claimed by such women as Ida Craddock and Victoria Woodhull, and, at the same time, to protect white women from corrupting influences.

Scholars of American religions have shown how inquisitional ideas and practices led to the creation of race in the Americas. Part of this history slots into larger Afro-Atlantic discourses about the fetish, materiality, and agency discussed above, as Europeans took different worldviews to be deficient or even diabolical, racializing the populations who held them.[48] There were live debates among inquisitors and their opponents about how to categorize and define certain Afro-Atlantic practices as magic, fetish, error, or fake.[49] The general point, for scholars sketching a larger argument about religion and race, has been that religious differences eventually became understood as all-but-immutable characteristics and ranked accordingly. What I want to emphasize here, more as a tool for theorizing secular governance than as a genealogical argument about race, is that inquisitors wrote their worldviews into policy. Racialization is a project of colonial states, specifically by European (and Euro-American) empires who rule by excluding some people from the government of their own state on the basis of allegedly natural differences.[50] Historians have argued that one such ideological pol-

47. Keitt, *Inventing the Sacred*, 5–6. Keitt also mentions numerous "cross-dressing" and gender-nonconforming people as targets of inquisitional tactics. On women's experience of the Inquisition in New Spain, see Delgado, *Laywomen*. See also Tortorici, *Sins against Nature*, on the processes of cataloguing and archiving "unnatural" sexuality in New Spain. Tortorici also offers clear and detailed explanations of the investigative procedures and courtroom proceedings.

48. Matory, *The Fetish Revisited*. On the contests between African and European worldviews in the context of the Inquisition, see James H. Sweet, *Domingos Álavares, African Healing, and the Intellectual History of the Atlantic World* (University of North Carolina Press, 2011).

49. See, e.g., Fromont, "Paper, Ink, Vodun, and the Inquisition." Fromont explains how *feiticeiros* ("magicians") has a few meanings, according to early dictionaries, one of them being from "the adjective *feitiço* meaning something not natural, but artfully created, or fake, pretend, factitious" (466). Focusing on the *bolsas de mandinga*, a type of amulet, Fromont shows how such objects and practices forced European colonizers "to think anew about immaterial forces and their material manifestations" (498).

50. Hesse, "Racialized Modernity." Hesse describes three types of racialization: cultural, epistemological, and governmental. Governmental racialization, particularly germane

icy, *limpieza de sangre* (purity of blood), was foundational to the entwined histories of religion-making and race-making. After the Reconquista, Spanish and Portuguese leaders differentiated "Old Christians," those whose families had been Christians for generations, from "New Christians," recent converts (*conversos*) often accused of still secretly practicing their original religions (Judaism and Islam). As María Elena Martínez has shown, the *limpieza* idea racialized subjects, marking them as essentially different and thus disempowered—subjects to be governed, not governors.[51]

Limpieza de sangre was not only an idea; it was a bureaucratic system. Spanish subjects who would immigrate to the Americas were required to obtain proof, called a *probanza*, of their blood purity, usually from local judges. The *probanza* was, basically, paperwork. In Spain and New Spain, a *probanza* was often required to hold official positions, both secular and ecclesial. Though there were inconsistencies, local variations, and uncertainties in the historical record, the Spanish crown developed bureaucratic procedures for issuing this documentation. Martínez explains, "Done well before the Inquisition had regularized purity investigations, the probanza included the main questions (regarding legitimacy, limpieza, place of birth, moral conduct, and reputation) later contained in Holy Office questionnaires."[52] In the colonial Americas, the *sistema de castas* (caste system) was less fixed. People's *calidad* (quality), including "spiritual status," was sorted and ranked by physical and nonphysical characteristics, but these were not (only) "racial" or biological. However, over time *limpieza de sangre* provided the ideological and theological backing for phenotypical markers to be viewed as "the exteriorization of moral impurity."[53] In this way,

---

here, is "characterized by the social routinization and institutionalization of regulatory, administrative power (e.g. laws, rules, policies, discipline, precepts) exercised by Europeanized ('white') assemblages over non-Europeanized ('non-white') assemblages as if this was a normal, inviolable or natural social arrangement of races" (656).

51. Martínez, *Genealogical Fictions*.

52. Martínez, *Genealogical Fictions*, 130.

53. Jessica Delgado and Kelsey Moss, "Religion and Race in the Early Modern Iberian Atlantic," in *The Oxford Handbook of Religion and Race in American History*, ed. Gin Lum and Harvey, 46. This essay is a helpful historical and historiographical overview, especially with regard to how religious categories are racialized, and if offers productive suggestions for complementary work in Iberian colonial history and critical race studies. "In the case of the early modern Iberian Atlantic, we must continue to analyze the particular historical operations—*limpieza de sangre*, the Inquisition, notions of *calidad* and spiritual status, colonial governance, dress, and physical appearance—that all functioned as critical elements in a larger system whose ultimate effect was the racialization of Jewish, Muslim,

through state practices of identifying and sorting and policing, religious identity became racialized and even the source of race itself.[54]

Melville's reference to *auto-da-fé*, whatever he meant when he scrawled that dedication, might be read productively against the context of nineteenth-century anti-Catholicism and its central role in scholarship on the Protestant secular, as well as recent scholarship on the Inquisition and racialization. Nineteenth-century Protestants feared and opposed Catholic ideology because it troubled their normative view of freedom and subjectship, but inquisitional containment strategies proved useful to the most ardent proponents of Protestant secular governance. Talal Asad has described how inquisitional methods produced truth, inflicting physical pain to squeeze out words: "Verbal discourse was the indispensable medium of the truth. Secret thoughts had to be made available in the form of utterances—words as inner signs brought out as meaningful sounds."[55] This was, in so many words, a sincerity test—a test of faith, an extractive procedure to reveal what was *really* inside, under the mask.

Nineteenth-century exposés and unmaskings constructed the secular subject by fingering everyone else.[56] In moralistic keys, they catalogued impurities to assure themselves of their own cleanliness. Scholars of race and religion in the United States have shown how both Protestantism and whiteness can operate as "unmarked" categories. The secular also represents a putatively universal yet in fact particular form. In this interplay between the unmarked and unmasked, we can see how the white Protestant secular

---

African, and native bodies and souls" (57). Though I am not at all a historian of the Iberian Atlantic, in these pages I am trying to take up, in my own way, their offer of a "framework for studying the diverse history of racisms" rather than a "linear trajectory of the history of race" (57). As scholars think race and religion together, as in the construction of the "religio-racial," I think it is important to attune ourselves to histories of racial governance *as* secular governance. This focus could also return secularism studies to its postcolonial roots.

54. "For White Europeans," Sylvester Johnson has argued, "Christianity was an essentialist constitution that was 'in the blood' in both a literal and a figurative sense. In this context, the principle of *limpieza de sangre* (purity of blood) was among the most formidable and pervasive of juridical and theological principles in Europe and throughout Europe's colonies in the Americas" (*African American Religions*, 88).

55. Asad, *Genealogies of Religion*, 93. He continues, "The words were not identical with the truth, in the way that the bodily marks of someone who had submitted to the ordeal were identical with it. For so long as the rules of the ordeal were properly followed, the marks it produced could not lie" (93).

56. Thanks to Tracy Fessenden, who suggested this point and the evocative language.

subject instantiates their own power by surveilling and policing, specifically through unmasking or exposing, their others. Investigative procedures are often underrecognized components of religious freedom, but they often constitute the form of secularism by which the sincere believer is construed and protected. And in many cases, religious believers' interactions with the secular state are not cast in terms of freedom or rights; they do not take place in federal court, and attorneys are not present. Believers' rights hinge on various state agents' evaluations of their interior states, based on interpretations of external signs. Sincere speech can be free and freeing. But that depends on a variety of factors, including who's asking the questions.[57]

PEOPLE WITH PAPERS

The legal regime of religious freedom proposes a certain theory of religion and the person. Benjamin Berger identified three elements of law's conception of religion: "(1) religion as essentially individual, (2) religion as centrally addressed to autonomy and choice, and (3) religion as private."[58] This type of religion has become defined by and all but equated with sincerely held belief. There is a problem, though. Religious belief, to be legible as both religious and sincere, must accord with Berger's three elements, but it cannot be too individual, too private, or totally idiosyncratic. Religious beliefs are personal but not "merely personal."[59] Josef Treboho Ansorge has aptly explained the dynamic: "Radical individual identity is always established through recourse to a layering of various group identities. . . . An individual can only be known to the sovereign through supra-individual categories."[60] Recalling the previous chapter's discussion of masquerade and authentic selfhood, we might understand these supraindividual categories as masks that permit sincere expressions of private selves. These masks are not necessarily covering something else up so much as they are the public version of the imagined interiority. Or they *create* the imagined interiority. An apparent tension persists between the Protestant secular imagination of

57. See Agrama, *Questioning Secularism*.

58. Berger, *Law's Religion*, 66.

59. This is the language from the Military Selective Service Act of 1948, discussed at length in chaps. 4 and 5.

60. Ansorge, *Identify and Sort*, 11.

the individual believer and the project of governing subjects according to their characteristics. This tension can be explained, if not really resolved, by examining the centrality of calculative reason to secular governance.

To protect religious believers, state authorities must identify the religious and differentiate it from the secular. The sincere presentation of self requires intelligibility through classification. Abstract language and calculation thus enable what Talal Asad calls an "alarming development that goes beyond the nation-state: life rendered as signs—that is, as computable and translatable information."[61] We are data.[62] On Asad's view, a transparently sincere self, whose inner secrets are on full view to the sovereign, is the fulfillment of the secularizing project: "Secularization's greatest achievement lies in the future, in eliminating decisively the distance between the mask and its wearer."[63] Whereas a radically sincere self might be liberating in the sense that it is social and fosters community, it might also totally undermine privacy and essentially make whole persons visible to the state, which in turn can surveil and sort them. The sorting process is inherently reliant on abstraction and calculation.[64]

A crucial aspect of the calculative nature of secularism is documentation.[65] Just as the Spanish Inquisitors required a *probanza*, modern secular subjects use paperwork to verify people's identities and evaluate their sincerity. Melville dramatized this too. Early in *The Confidence-Man*, a crowd of passengers gathers around the confidence man's second guise, a "Negro

61. Asad, *Secular Translations*, 100.

62. Cheney-Lippold, *We Are Data*.

63. Asad, *Secular Translations*, 126.

64. "The liberal democratic state is secular because and to the extent that it depends crucially on the language of numbers: it is a calculation that finally determines to whom the state belongs" (Asad, *Secular Translations*, 134). See also Viswanathan, *Outside the Fold*.

65. Some citizens participate in this sorting via documentation, even making it fundamental to their own identification as citizens and religious subjects. For example, an Alabaman named Sheila described to a *Washington Post* reporter in 2018 her belief that President Obama had "awakened a sleeping *Christian* nation." Elaborating on this, she described how she felt threatened by religious minorities, particularly Muslims, as well as immigrants. She explained the problem with immigrants through calculative reason and recourse to documentation: "'Unpapered people,' Sheila said, adding that she had seen them in the county emergency room and they got treated before her. 'And then the Americans are not served.'" Stephanie McCrummen, "Judgment Days," *Washington Post*, July 21, 2018. Sheila is a white Christian nationalist whose legitimacy—as an American and a Christian—even her personhood, is marked by bureaucracy and state regulation. She is a "papered" person.

cripple" referred to as "Guinea," who plays tambourine and catches coins in his mouth. A man with a wooden leg, a "fellow-limper," accuses him of being a sham, a white person painted black and faking a disability (19–20). At this accusation, the crowd turns to the pleasures of debunking, for they, "finding themselves left sole judges in the case, could not resist the opportunity of acting the part" (20). In their judicial role, their first request for evidence is, "among other things, asking him, had he any documentary proof, any plain paper about him, attesting that his case was not a spurious one" (21). He does not have papers. But he has the word of other people—specifically, the word of white men who will vouch for him. He describes a number of fellow passengers, most of whom, the reader learns, are future guises of the confidence man.

A few chapters later, one such character discusses Guinea with a young clergyman whose initial suspicions had led him not to give money. Now, talking with a white man who claims to know Guinea and calls him "honest" and "grateful," the clergyman laments his own "spirit of distrust" and gives some money: "Hand it to Guinea when you see him; say it comes from one who has full belief in his honesty, and is sincerely sorry for having indulged, however transiently, in a contrary thought" (42). Without missing a beat, the white man accepts the money and immediately asks for more, on behalf of a (fake) charity. The clergyman hesitates but then gives more. However, he asks, "Of course you have papers?" The man receiving the money assures him, "Let me take down name and amount. We publish these names" (43). In many other cases, documentation and statistics—recall, for instance, Pitch's confidence in a boy's goodness based in part of a report on his phrenological chart (133)—serve as means of verification.[66] In a world of strangers and signs and masks, documentation offers certainty. As Melville's text shows, documentation is still a representation of the social. But it's hard to put "infinite socialities" into rows and columns.

What was so disconcerting about Guinea, for the other passengers aboard the *Fidèle*, was not that he was unclassifiable; it was that easy classifications so ready to hand might be fake. His Blackness, houselessness, and disability were data according to which the other passengers could classify him as one

---

66. Francis Galton, who coined the term "eugenics," later would praise "statistics" as "the only tools by which an opening can be cut through the formidable thicket of difficulties that bars the path of those who pursue the Science of man" (*Natural Inheritance* [1889], 63). On the connections between statistics and eugenics, see Aubrey Clayton, "How Eugenics Shaped Statistics," *Nautilus* 92 (Oct., 2020).

dependent on charity—and classify themselves as charitable, Christian, and white. Fake pauperism and fake Blackness destabilized beneficent whiteness. Thus, as Susan Ryan has shown, nineteenth-century Americans developed a style of "investigative philanthropy," complete with manuals written by "arbiters of need." The Guinea scene thus "exposes the intimate relationship in antebellum America between knowing race and knowing benevolence, even as it establishes, quite literally and materially, the questions of identity and trust that dominate the rest of the novel."[67] For many Americans, race has been one of the surest sorting mechanisms. It was also a way that exterior signs were naturalized as evidence of interior states.[68] Surveillance is a form of "social sorting," as David Lyon has argued. In the late twentieth and early twenty-first centuries, Lyon contended, the point of surveillance became "to plan, predict, and prevent by classifying and assessing those profiles as risks."[69] In earlier periods, though, we also see calculative reason as a predictive technology of surveillance. Indeed, the racialized caste system of the Iberian Americas, manufacturing religio-racial classifications through *limpieza de sangre*, was in part a predictive system that assessed individuals' potential for public service, church work, and criminality.

SURVEILLANCE AND SINCERITY

Surveillance shifts the object of policing from crimes to criminals. For example, as I discuss in the next chapter, vagrancy laws criminalized people's statuses, not their actions. It was illegal to be a certain type of person. Vagrants, then, had difficulty being recognized as religious, since religiosity and criminality were seen as an incongruous, if not mutually exclusive, pair. In turn, such vagrants were not intended to receive the protections of religious freedom, since they were not truly religious. It remained, for some, a mark on their person. In the twenty-first century these legacies persist,

---

67. Ryan, "Misgivings," 690, 693, 697.

68. See Simone Browne, *Dark Matters: On the Surveillance of Blackness* (Duke University Press, 2015). See also "Race, Communities, and Informers," ed. Simone Browne, Katherine McKittrick, and Ronak K. Kapadia, special issue, *Surveillance and Society* 15, no. 1 (2017).

69. David Lyon, "Surveillance as Social Sorting: Computer Codes and Mobile Bodies," in *Surveillance as Social Sorting*, ed. Lyon, 13. See also Sarah Brayne, *Predict and Surveil: Data, Discretion, and the Future of Policing* (Oxford University Press, 2020).

and religion remains a category of governance and surveillance.[70] This is especially notable in federal agencies' surveillance of Black and/or Muslim groups. For example, FBI agents infiltrated the Moorish Science Temple of America and the Nation of Islam, and they closely surveil Muslim organizations, African American religious leaders, and others.[71]

Americans developed complicated systems of implicitly and explicitly acknowledged social codes, ways of looking sincere. How-to guides for young urban businessmen, novels about "character," detective stories, "investigative philanthropy" tracts, and other texts and subgenres, including police manuals, were bound up with the surveillance work of the state. Comstock's *Frauds Exposed* and *Traps for the Young*, written while he was conducting surveillance and police work, belong in that genre. Desperate to maintain the tenuous politics of subjectivity—and policeable selves—many Americans doubled down on supposedly immutable characteristics such as sex and phenotype. "Sciences" like phrenology systematized character. Along with later developments in "characterology," these arts and sciences tried to get inside the person by dismantling the stark distinctions between interior and exterior. In his study of character in the nineteenth century, James Salazar has noted the staying power of the intellectual scaffolding supporting surveillance, including governmentalized self-surveillance. Phrenology itself waned in popularity, but, Salazar writes, "the underlying physiognomic premise out of which it grew—that character could be read in the physical form and details of the body and could also literally be re-formed through the performances and representations of the body"—did not.[72] Legal and scholarly discourses of "religion" have followed a similar intellectual trajectory. The cognitive study of religion, for example, which coincides with what Winnifred Sullivan has called the "New Establishment," imagines religion as a distinct and integral aspect of human experience.[73]

---

70. See "Race/Religion/War," ed. Keith P. Feldman and Leerom Medovoi, special issue, *Social Text* 34, no. 4 (Dec., 2016).

71. Johnson, *African American Religions*; Johnson and Weitzman, eds., *The FBI and Religion*; and Rana, *Terrifying Muslims*.

72. Salazar, *Bodies of Reform*, 26. See also Blackwood, *The Portrait's Subject*.

73. American psychology, especially in its early stages, was particularly concerned with religious experience. Psychological studies of religion formed the basis for much of the early history of the study of religion, particularly in the United States. In this way, my project on sincerity and belief provides some insights for a history of the intellectual context within which religious studies as a "discipline" arose. See, e.g., Taves, *Fits, Trances, and Visions*; Christopher G. White, *Unsettled Minds: Psychology and the American Search for Spiritual*

Isolating it, as courts have to do when protecting religious belief (but not political or philosophical belief), continues to be a tricky task.

From the nineteenth century on, writers, scholars, and a wide assortment of actors engaged in policing projects devised ways to solve the inquisitional problem of sincerity through the observation and surveillance of bodies. For example, Mary Ann O'Farrell has explained how blushing could be understood "as an instrument by which the body is enlisted in the production of legibility in order to serve at surveillance's creation of domesticable bodies."[74] The unknowability of inner thoughts and beliefs necessitated this domestication via publicization, or, in other words, surveillance. This technique worked in the same way that supposedly involuntary responses to conviction and conversion—weeping, "the jerks," glossolalia—presented evidence of spiritual change. Ideas about blushing, sweating, twitching, and other actions included in the category "body language" were appropriated by law enforcement professionals who developed strategies for interrogation and learned to "read" people, as they tried to detect guilty parties as well as discover "natural-born" criminals.

The science of body language often reinforced extant assumptions about trustworthiness and sincerity. An 1872 piece in the *Phrenological Journal of Science and Health* pointed out that the blush was an inadequate technique when applied to certain people. For instance, "It is often the case that the most innocent and virtuous are so bashful that it is next to impossible for them to look even an inferior squarely and steadily in the eye." Furthermore, the "African, the Asiatic, and the North American Indian may *feel* a blush, though—owing to the color of his skin—he may not *show* it."[75] Likewise, according to some racist theories, Jews were incapable of blushing, and these theories were used to explain why they supposedly could cheat and swindle so deftly. In a society where social and financial interactions required people to deal face-to-face with strangers, Americans made every effort to establish-

Assurance, 1830–1940 (University of California Press, 2008); and Jodie Boyer, "Religion, 'Moral Insanity,' and Psychology in Nineteenth-Century America," *Religion and American Culture* 24, no. 1 (Winter, 2014): 70–99.

74. Mary Ann O'Farrell, *Telling Complexions: The Nineteenth-Century English Novel and the Blush* (Duke University Press, 1997), 6. See also Annamarie Jagose, *Orgasmology* (Duke University Press, 2012), on subjective experience, performance, and faking it. And on the "project of legibility," see James C. Scott, *Seeing Like a State: How Certain Schemes to Improve the Human Condition Have Failed* (Yale University Press, 1998).

75. "Blushing," *Phrenological Journal and Science of Health* 54, no. 3 (Mar., 1872): 195.

ment with certainty who was trustworthy. These efforts continued through the invention of the polygraph, or lie detector test, in the 1920s.[76]

Scientistic imaginations of sincerity, from phrenology to body language studies to early psychological experiments to the polygraph, often went hand in hand with surveillance technologies. As Asad writes, "Surveillance takes place by infiltration, and its purpose is to look for signs of actual or potential betrayal—signs of possibility that need to be translated into *certainty* so that appropriate action can be taken."[77] A total infiltration might look something like scientific lie detection. Like the Iberian Inquisitors, polygraph operators found truth in blood.[78] Sincerely held religious beliefs can be expressed by translating private feelings into public discourse. In many cases, though, inquests into sincerity, always reliant on signs, seek to push past the signs, to infiltrate and surveil, to get inside. Anthony Comstock did not just write books and deliver speeches. He surveilled, documented, calculated, and literally policed. In the final section of this chapter, I turn to Comstock's NYSSV.

SUPPRESSING VICE

It feels odd to argue that Anthony Comstock was a sort of secularist. He was a religious zealot who called his opponents "infidels." He was, by most

76. Geoffrey C. Bunn, *The Truth Machine: A Social History of the Lie Detector* (Johns Hopkins University Press, 2012); Ken Alder, *The Lie Detectors: The History of An American Obsession* (Free Press, 2007); and David T. Lykken, *A Tremor in the Blood: Uses and Abuses of the Lie Detector* (Basic Books, 1998 [1980]).

77. Asad, *Secular Translations*, 117.

78. This literature is substantial. John Augustus Larson and Leonarde Keeler, who are credited with inventing the polygraph, were police officers in Berkeley, California. Larson held a Ph.D. in psychology. Many of his studies and methods focused on blood pressure. See, e.g., J. A. Larson, "Present Police and Legal Methods for the Determination of the Innocence or Guilt of the Suspect," *Journal of the American Institute of Criminal Law and Criminology* 16, no. 2 (Aug., 1925): 219–271; and George Walker Hanley, John Augustus Larson, and Leonarde Keeler, *Lying and Its Detection: A Study of Deception and Deception Tests* (University of Chicago Press, 1932). See also Fred E. Inbau, "Scientific Evidence in Criminal Cases. II. Methods of Detecting Deception," *Journal of Criminal Law and Criminology* 24, no. 6 (Mar.–Apr., 1934): 1140–1158; and Paul V. Trovillo, "Deception Test Criteria: How One Can Determine Truth and Falsehood from Polygraphic Records," *Journal of Criminal Law and Criminology* 33, no. 4 (Nov.–Dec., 1942): 338–358.

accounts, *not* secular. But I am arguing that the NYSSV enacted a doctrine of political secularism. By this, I mean that the Society enforced a particular conception of religious or moral subjectship, documenting and policing persons by classifying them, presenting these regulatory projects as universal goods rather than sectarian projects, and used public and state means to do so. Perhaps it stretches the scholarly uses of "secular" too far; if Comstock is secular, who isn't? The important point, though, is that secularism defines and regulates "religion," and in so doing constructs a model of the sincere believer as a form, a "measurable type," that is protected by various means, including policing its others.[79] The NYSSV was not a governmental agency, nor was it affiliated with a church. It had wealthy financial backers and had begun as a subgroup of the Young Men's Christian Association (YMCA). Comstock worked as a United States Postal Inspector, and the U.S. Congress, not an ecclesiastical or missionary organization, passed the Comstock laws. The NYSSV was not exactly a governmental agency, but it did work on behalf of the "public" and was granted, by the state, the power to arrest people. That work—which was, in short, regulatory police work—was a form of secular governance.

In 1872 a New York City police officer allegedly allowed an erotica dealer to escape arrest. Incensed, Comstock filed a complaint against the officer. Then he decided to take matters into his own hands.[80] He sought funding from the YMCA, whose Committee for the Suppression of Vice was already surveilling the erotic book trade and protecting young men from the traps of urban life. Soon, after securing more funding sources, Comstock founded the NYSSV as its own organization, with a founding membership of all eight YMCA Committee members along with nine more.[81] The city had granted

79. On this dynamic see, e.g., Adcock, *The Limits of Tolerance*. The term "measurable type" is borrowed from Cheney-Lippold, *We Are Data*. I also have in mind here Wernimont, *Numbered Lives*, which is an excellent companion to Asad's work on secularism and calculative reason. Wernimont studies a wide variety of methods of quantification, of counting up life and death. "What a deep history allows, and what we urgently need," she argues, "is to see the ways in which the forms of quantum human-technological media encounters are and have long been cocreative with the production of racializing and gendering notions of 'truth,' the state, and Anglo-American subjectivity" (6). While this book does not contain much analysis of technology per se, I hope it contributes to conversations on how secularism surveils and documents human life in order to account for, rather than eradicate, ghosts.

80. This origin story is relayed in Dennis, *Licentious Gotham*, 238.

81. Dennis, *Licentious Gotham*, 253.

the power to arrest to the YMCA's Committee. It then extended that power to the NYSSV. In the following decades in New York and other cities, local governments would deputize dozens of such committees, often for narrow purposes, such as enforcing specific laws like the Raines law, an 1896 New York state law that forbade establishments (except hotels) to serve alcohol on Sundays.[82] In this period cities also forged partnerships with private surveillance and security agencies like the Pinkertons.[83] From the 1870s until his death, Comstock and his agents arrested hundreds of people for a variety of crimes, leading to oppressive fines and prison sentences.

The NYSSV's and Comstock's work depended on common but often overlooked processes, such as postal inspection, by which secular authorities police religions. Many different state and parastate agents intervene in individuals' self-categorizations and identities and redefine them for the state's own regulatory purposes. In these ways, oftentimes as a component of the promotion and protection of religious freedom, liberal states police the boundaries of the religious by affording that label to some people but denying it to others.[84] Scholars of secularism should focus not only on how state agents (and not-quite-state agents, like the NYSSV) define religion and regulate religious communities, but also on how their "religious" and "secular" categories and ethical frameworks inform and frame their policing. Agents of secular states—judges, police officers, IRS agents, even postal inspectors—maintain their own ideas about what the religious is, as well as their own ideas that scholars might call religious or ethical, which shape their regulatory interactions with dissident subjects.

Comstock developed a shared framework for financial panic and moral panic, both of which threatened the middle-class domestic sphere and bourgeois society. There was a link between moral rectitude and social capital, and many worked to maintain the former in order to shore up the latter. Upper-class New Yorkers, including J. Pierpont Morgan and numerous prominent old-money families, supported the NYSSV at its founding. Sven Beckert has surmised, "Social capital, it seemed to them, was an integral part of what it meant to be bourgeois, and the consumption of pornography was

82. The Committee of Fourteen, one such group, published reports that are easily available online. See, e.g., Committee of Fourteen, *The Social Evil in New York City: A Study of Law Enforcement* (New York: Andrew H. Kellogg, 1910).

83. Fronc, *New York Undercover*.

84. Wenger, *Religious Freedom*.

a direct threat to this goal."[85] According to Nicola Beisel, 83.5 percent of New Yorkers who contributed to the NYSSV between 1872 and 1892 were from the upper classes.[86] This financing of vice-suppression programs stemmed in part from concern for the moral health of the middle class but also from fear of the poor (not that these are two entirely different reasons) and a desire to regulate their activities at a time when churches exercised little cross-class influence.[87] At the heart of Comstock's regulatory secularism was an attempt to firm up the indistinct edges of the public and private spheres. Because the mail could transmit information and objects throughout the nation, Comstock saw the postal service as a potential vehicle for spreading learning and morality and, at the same time, a system through which all manner of contagion could seep into public and private space.[88]

Comstock understood the public as an affectively bonded community, defined by love for their children and fear of their monstrous others. In her analysis of the cultural politics of fear, Sara Ahmed has argued that "the economy of fear works to contain the bodies of others, *a containment whose 'success' relies on its failure, as it must keep open the very grounds of fear.*"[89] The project of containment is never complete, and thus fears are never fully quelled. Comstock *wanted* the public to be afraid. As Ahmed explains, fear of the other gives meaning to performances of love for one's own community. This love entails security, and thus security "includes the transforma-

85. Sven Beckert, *The Monied Metropolis: New York City and the Consolidation of the American Bourgeoisie, 1850–1896* (Cambridge University Press, 2001), 263.

86. Beisel, *Imperiled Innocents*, 50. She also shows that 92.3 percent of Bostonians contributing to the New England Society for the Suppression of Vice from 1885 to 1892 were upper-class.

87. Paul Boyer, *Urban Masses and Moral Order in America, 1820–1920* (Harvard University Press, 1978), makes a version of this argument. Boyer wrote, "In earlier days, Protestant churchmen confronting the city had been sustained by the sense that between themselves and all levels of the city population—from the wealthiest to the poorest—existed a bond of shared religious loyalties and institutional ties rooted in the preurban era. . . . The evaporation of this confidence in the late nineteenth century underlay the uncertain and sometimes almost panicky efforts of American Protestantism to develop new urban strategies in these years" (142). Kyle B. Roberts, *Evangelical Gotham: Religion and the Making of New York City, 1783–1860* (University of Chicago Press, 2016) offers a similar secularization narrative.

88. McGarry, *Ghosts of Futures Past*, 117.

89. Ahmed, *The Cultural Politics of Emotion*, 67.

tion of democratic citizenship into policing."[90] Comstock's good citizenship, his civil service, required him to alert the public to danger. Throughout *Frauds Exposed*, he used fearmongering language, particularly corporeal metaphors of public health and contagion: poison in public fountains, cancers, bloodsucking leeches. Modern society produced the conditions for such treachery, and regular citizens, caught in the maelstrom of modernity, fell prey to it. In these ways, Comstock's morality was both secular and religious, in conventional senses, and his particular moralizing was shaped by economic contexts and his ideas of publicness and sincerity.

Many critics argued that Comstock's idea of the public good was not, in fact, good. And, more practically, critics and defenders debated the merits of the NYSSV's tactics. Some of Comstock's bitterest enemies, such as Robert Ingersoll and Victoria Woodhull, argued that the whole project was based on flawed ideology, regulating practices that needed no regulation. Other critics focused specifically on the tactics, noting that, for all the talk of fraud and con men, Comstock used fake letters, aliases, and undercover accomplices to trick pornographers into mailing him materials. Entrapment was one of the Society's most common methods.[91] In an 1882 exchange in the *North American Review*, Comstock defended the Society, explaining that his agents were appointed as "peace officers" by the sheriff, "under the provisions of the Code of Criminal Procedure."[92] Some people had called for the Society to disband, but, Comstock suggested, that energy would be better directed toward the many pornographic publications and sleazy dime novels, tawdry crime reporting, "blasphemies of infidel publications," and "all schemes for corrupting the rising generation."[93] Octavius Brooks Frothingham, a Unitarian minister and critic of the NYSSV, admitted that Comstock and his agents had done some good, but their whole approach was wrong: "The position assumed by these champions is that of belligerency. The rules they adopt are rules of war." They claimed to protect the public good, but in fact they antagonized the public.

Frothingham alleged that the NYSSV was not secular, for their operations were "uniformly sectarian in their character." He wondered how such

---

90. Ahmed, *The Cultural Politics of Emotion*, 75, 78. On religion, surveillance, and security as love, see Kevin Lewis O'Neill, *Secure the Soul: Christian Piety and Gang Prevention in Guatemala* (University of California Press, 2015).

91. Werbel, *Lust on Trial*, 270.

92. Comstock, Frothingham, and Buckley, "The Suppression of Vice," 485.

93. Comstock, Frothingham, and Buckley, "The Suppression of Vice," 488.

sectarianism might be mistaken for something universal: "Mr. Comstock makes frequent use of the words 'obscene,' 'indecent,' and so forth. Are we prepared to accept his definition of such words of the definition of his society?" Not only was Comstock a sectarian enemy of free inquiry, but the Society itself, through its policing and regulation, materially limited the free exchange of ideas.[94] In the forum's final piece, J. M. Buckley, a polemicist and Comstock affiliate who wrote the foreword to *Traps for the Young*, demonstrated Frothingham's points. "The passions are normally and gradually developed in man as in the lower animals," he wrote, "but the brutes are under no restraint." Policing by the Society, which certainly saw its fellow citizens as enemies, was necessary, because these fellow citizens were not fully human. They were "brutes" and "monsters, whose only type in nature is the octopus."[95] With scientistic pretensions to universality, Comstock and his allies defended their projects on the basis of secularity.

COLUMNS AND ROWS

This chapter concludes with a brief meditation on a material object: the NYSSV's big ledger book. The Society kept detailed records of each arrest it made from 1872 through the 1940s. It recorded, by hand, the name and address of the arrestee, their age, any known aliases, nationality, religion, education, marital status, number of children, and occupation, as well as information about the arrest—who issued the warrant, the offense charged, the arresting officer, information on jail and bail, inventory of stock seized, the judge, and the sentence—and, last, "remarks."[96] In the earliest years of the Society, most of the crimes were the sort Comstock is most famous for

94. Comstock, Frothingham, and Buckley, "The Suppression of Vice," 491–492.

95. Comstock, Frothingham, and Buckley, "The Suppression of Vice," 495, 497. Buckley's metaphorical octopus was not original; cephalopods were a common metaphor for creeping evils. See Jacques Schnier, "Morphology of a Symbol: The Octopus," *American Imago* 13, no. 1 (Spring, 1956): 3–31; and Melody Jue, "Vampire Squid Media," *Grey Room* 57 (Fall, 2014): 82–105. Many thanks to Jeff Wheatley for these references and for his own as-yet-unpublished work on cephalopods.

96. New York Society for the Suppression of Vice Records, Manuscript Division, Library of Congress. Hereafter cited as NYSSV Records. Thanks to the archivists at the LOC for sending the microfilm reels to me in Tallahassee. And thanks to Nicholas Meier for laboriously and tediously scanning them into hundreds of PDFs.

opposing: sending pornographic pictures through the mail, providing abortion services, selling "immoral rubber goods." But soon there was a noticeable shift. From the late 1870s to the 1890s, well over half of the Society's arrests were for what could be classified broadly as financial crimes. The ledger is full of gambling, green-goods games, lottery scams, and the types of schemes and swindles detailed in *Frauds Exposed*.

The records exemplify the calculative reason of secular governance. They expose fraudulent criminals and sort their categories of identification and actions into little boxes. These records hold hundreds of stories and scant details of stories—glimpses into untold backstories. Some arrestees were apparently professional criminals. One man's occupation was listed as "sawdust swindler and member of a gang." Others, usually those committing crimes related to abortion and/or contraception, were college-educated doctors. Often, they were recorded as "quack" or "quack + abortionist," or, for one Edward Harvey, "magic, quack, abortionist." (Harvey was arrested for "mailing abortion articles.") In general, U.S. Protestants received the label "doctor" or "physician," though sometimes in conjunction with "quack," whereas others were simply "quacks." The listed nationalities throughout the book included many Irish, German, English, and American, as well as "Southerner," "born in Ohio," and, as late as 1929, "Negro." Religions included many Jews, Catholics, and Protestants (sometimes with specific denominations listed, though often just "Protestant")—but also "none to speak of," "Spiritualist and free-lover," "free lover," and a few entries, for those of Chinese nationality, for "heathen."

The record book offers a fascinating window into the lives of late nineteenth- and early twentieth-century New Yorkers—the incredible diversity and the vibrancy of urban life, contrasted with the Society's ever-futile attempts to regulate. Fifty-year-old German Jews were arrested alongside their fourteen-year-old Irish Catholic employees for advertising "devices to prevent conception." For most of the people listed, the Society's book is likely the most significant extant historical record they have, a keyhole view into a full, dynamic life. And that is one tragic aspect of all this—the lives damaged, even ruined, by these indictments. Some of the fines were massive and certainly led to financial and personal collapse. Some of the sentences were exceptionally harsh. One man, upon his third arrest for mailing obscene pictures, was sentenced to ten years at hard labor.[97]

Bureaucratic systems of governance rely on classification and categoriza-

97. NYSSV Records, reel 1.

tion, which must be imposed on subjects and often does not fit neatly. The world is unruly, full of miscellany, and it is hard to catalogue it, to discipline it with the straight lines and boxes of a record book. That unruliness peeks through in entries like "free-lover" in the "religion" column. Why did Comstock find that to be the most apt descriptor of someone's religion? Comstock's fellow exposer John B. Ellis had written that while not all Spiritualists were free lovers, "it may be said that all Free Lovers, with rare exceptions, are spiritualists."[98] So perhaps "free-lover" was basically interchangeable with "Spiritualist." But why, then, would he choose the former? Was there something in the logic of Comstock's moral regulation and secular governance that found "free-lover" a better name for a deviant religion?

When Comstock identified hucksters and swindlers, quacks and abortionists, he exposed them to the public. Identification and exposure were part of the same process of "social sorting," of which surveillance and the modern police state is a key part. And by identifying them as "public foes," Comstock rendered them as (potential) objects of surveillance. Comstock's more rhetorical projects were thus intimately connected with his police work, just as the secular and secularism work in tandem. The NYSSV ledger sits at the intersection of these two fields, an artifact of what we could call "paperwork secularism," the mundane processes by which people are classified, their religions, nationalities, races, and legal status recorded and thus imposed. And certainly there were material consequences. Thousands of people were arrested, thousands of books and pictures were burned, and tens of thousands of pieces of mail were confiscated and processed and catalogued. Just as secularism is about both intellectual genealogies and political actions, regulation involves classification, social sorting, surveillance, and physical violence.

Anthony Comstock continued his work with the NYSSV for the rest of his life, but in 1883, the same year *Traps for the Young* was published, he moved out of the city. A few years later Alice Ashley moved into Comstock's neighborhood, Brooklyn's Clinton Hill, about a thousand feet away from Comstock's former home on Grand Avenue. She was just the sort of person Comstock would have wanted to keep out. From her home, Ashley conducted Spiritualist séances, flower readings, and, allegedly, told fortunes.

---

98. John B. Ellis, *Free Love and Its Votaries; Or American Spiritualism Unmasked . . .* (United States Publishing Co., 1870), 473; quoted in McGarry, *Ghosts of Futures Past*, 97.

3

TELLING FORTUNES

ON A MARCH DAY IN 1917, just down the block from Anthony Comstock's former home in Brooklyn, someone paid Alice Ashley a visit. As they sat across the table from each other, the visitor asked Ashley questions about her life and her future, and Ashley responded with insight and predictions. What happened next was disputed. The visitor claimed that Ashley requested a dollar as a fee; Ashley claimed that the visitor slid an unsolicited dollar across the table. This visit, as it turned out, was a police sting. And the visitor, Margaret Goodwin Seller, was a police informant who regularly worked to suppress vice and expose "fortune-tellers." Shortly after their encounter, Ashley was arrested as a "disorderly person," a category that, in the New York Code of Criminal Procedure, included "persons pretending to tell fortunes."[1]

Appealing her conviction, Ashley argued that the state had violated her right to free exercise of religion, for her so-called fortune-telling (a label she rejected) was in fact part of her religious practice as a Spiritualist. Since 1879, when the U.S. Supreme Court ruled in *Reynolds v. United States* that the free exercise of religion applies to beliefs, not necessarily actions, states had faced difficult questions in interpreting their own free exercise laws.[2] There

---

1. People v. Ashley, 184 App. Div. 520 (N.Y. 1918); N.Y. Code of Criminal Procedure, § 899.

2. Because *Reynolds* held that the First Amendment's religion clauses applied only to federal law, not to state law, the early twentieth-century fortune-telling cases analyzed here were not, strictly speaking, First Amendment cases. However, all states had protections for religious freedom in their constitutions, and many judges used *Reynolds* to interpret these constitutional meanings. The religion clauses were not incorporated against the states until the 1940s. The free exercise clause was incorporated via Cantwell v. Connecticut, 310 U.S. 296 (1940), and the establishment clause through Everson v. Board of Education, 330 U.S. 1 (1947).

was the perennial question about what counted as "religious," but, beyond that, merely attaining the label "religious" did not guarantee protection. And plenty of hazy categories—superstition, fanaticism, magic—hovered between secular knowledge and (good) religion.[3] Ashley's case, along with dozens of similar cases in the same period, illustrated the politics of secular governance at a moment just before, and perhaps anticipating, the modern regime of religious freedom and the sincerity test.

The bans on fortune-telling were based on centuries-old English vagrancy laws. In many U.S. states and other British colonies and former colonies, the bans had been passed earlier in the nineteenth century, but state and para-state actors set about enforcing them more stringently in the late nineteenth and early twentieth centuries. The resultant arrests and prosecutions—only a few of which led to court cases, and in those cases only a few defendants waged religious freedom defenses—make for a rich and strange data set. Some scholars have studied these cases in recent years, situating them in the context of (post-)colonial governance, histories of Spiritualism, and the development of religious freedom.[4] Taking place in the years leading up to *Ballard* and the sincerity test (and afterward, though less frequently), these cases were occasions to consider the theological capacities of state actors, whether and how they might make pronouncements on the truth or falsity of religious beliefs and practices. To do this, claimants and judges and others first had to wade into debates about religion and its limits.

By the early twentieth century, for many secular authorities, the linkage of sincere belief with true religion was common sense. Fraudulence and duplicity, then, were clear signs of irreligion. One trial judge made this distinction quite explicit, writing of one claimant's faith healing practices and communications with an angel, "I do not think this is religion; you cannot make this religion with me; it is too fakey."[5] This implicit theory of religion's limits—not too fakey—was an obstacle to Spiritualists' and others' religious

3. On superstition as a third category in a "trinary," rather than the religious-secular binary, see Josephson-Storm, "The Superstition, Secularism, and Religion Trinary."

4. The most comprehensive of these is Patrick, *Faith or Fraud*. He studies the regulation of fortune-telling and the "crafty sciences" in England, Canada, Australia, and the United States. Patrick concludes with a discussion of these cases' relevance for contemporary religious freedom law, particularly as it relates to "spiritual counselling" and the "spiritual but not religious." Other legal scholars have found contemporary resonances in the cases too. See, e.g., Corcos, "Seeing It Coming"; and Jones, "Did Fortune Tellers See This Coming?"

5. Jageriskey v. Detroit United Railway, 163 Mich. 631, 128 N.W. 726 (1910), 727. On good faith, bad faith, and religious freedom, see also Barry Nobel, "Religious Healing

freedom. Erika White Dyson has shown how Spiritualists intentionally represented themselves as "respectable and sincere religionists."[6] The assumption that their practices and beliefs were inherently fraudulent, that it was fake, was widespread and, more important, seemed to be woven into the statutes that banned the practices. Ashley was arrested for being a person who *pretended* to tell fortunes, so her conviction implied a judgment on her sincerity and thus the authenticity, legitimacy, and truth of her religious belief.[7] When accused fortune-tellers like Ashley—most of whom were white female Spiritualists—described their practices as religious or based in religious belief, they did not necessarily try to upend presumptions that religiosity precluded fakery or that religious beliefs should be sincere. They argued that their practices were, in fact, *not* too fakey.

"THOSE WHO PRETEND"

For six years during the 1890s, Eliza Dean met regularly with Hannah Ross, who channeled Dean's deceased husband. Dean paid the medium for her services in the form of bonds. Eventually, though, she began to doubt Ross's mediumship. The final straw came during a séance in which Dean com-

---

and American Courts in the Twentieth Century: The Liberties and Liabilities of Healers, Patients, and Parents" (Ph.D. diss., University of California–Santa Barbara, 1991), 55–59.

6. Dyson, "Spiritualism and Crime," 94. Dyson is primarily interested in how Spiritualism became an established organized religion and the internal debates about whether and how to organize. One argument for organization, she shows, was that becoming an established church would afford Spiritualists better opportunities to receive religious freedom protections and avoid fraud and vagrancy charges.

Johnson, "Spirits on the Stage," claims to provide "a new way of interpreting Spiritualism that acknowledges the reality of fraud in mediumistic practice without portraying spiritualist believers—those who really believed they saw spirits in public séances—as unintelligent or dim-witted" (24). What interests me about Johnson's claim is that he uses the concept of sincerity to talk about true religiosity and as justification for his own scholarly imperative to "take religion seriously." For Johnson, public mediumship practices were religious and are worth studying because people "really believed" them, even though he acknowledges that in many cases the performances were "fake." Sincere belief made them, in some sense, "real." On the politics of the scholarly injunction to take religion seriously, see Pritchard, "Seriously, What Does 'Taking Religion Seriously' Mean?"

7. In addition to Dyson, "Spiritualism and Crime," see Pietruska, *Looking Forward*, 241–243.

plained to her husband about how much money she had paid the medium. Through Ross, the husband replied, "Well, if I had as much again I would give it to the medium." Dean concluded, "That is never my husband talking, nor is it a spirit. That is Mrs. Ross herself." She successfully sued Ross to recoup her considerable lost assets, alleging that they had been obtained fraudulently. Ross appealed to the Massachusetts Supreme Judicial Court, which upheld the award.[8] Ross tried multiple arguments, none of which persuaded the judge, who repeatedly dismissed the notion that her mediumship could have been anything but duplicitous. Ross argued that her practices were legitimate because they were not fake, and thus she had not obtained the money from Dean fraudulently—she had obtained it by actually channeling the deceased Mr. Dean. And, more to the point, Ross contended, no one could say otherwise. She plainly asserted, "[N]o one can say that spirits do not speak through mediums."[9] The court did not consider this argument, since Ross did not raise it at trial and thus could not introduce it on appeal. She lost again, and Dean collected her payment. Although her point was brushed aside, it was not the first or last time an accused fortune-teller would raise this issue.[10]

In 1915 a New York astrologer and palmist named Maude Malcolm also objected to her charge as a person "pretending to tell fortunes." She was not pretending; she was *really* telling fortunes. She argued that the wording of the statute necessitates that "an element of deceit or fraud must be shown in order to justify a conviction."[11] And since she had neither deceived nor defrauded, she was not guilty. The trial judge saw it differently. On his interpretation, *really* telling fortunes was not possible. Thus, anyone who told fortunes must be pretending, whether or not they acknowledged or recognized it. The practice itself was inherently fraudulent. And, he reasoned, the legislature agreed, which is why they used the word "pretending" in the statute—to indicate their "disbelief in human power to prophesy future events."[12] If this were the case, then intent to deceive was not a relevant question. All pretending—or claiming, alleging, asserting, or professing—to tell fortunes was necessarily duplicitous.

8. Dean v. Ross, 178 Mass. 397 (1901).

9. *Dean*, 178 Mass. at 402.

10. A number of claimants protested the label "fortune-telling" in part because it was linked with "pretending." See Pietruska, *Looking Forward*, 220–227.

11. People v. Malcolm, 90 Misc. 517, 520 (N.Y. Misc. 1915).

12. *Malcolm*, 90 N.Y. Misc. at 520. In his decision in *Ashley*, Judge William Kelly approvingly quoted this portion of Nott's opinion.

Even (or especially) when judges tried to avoid the issue, fortune-telling cases showed the narrowness of what Anna Su has called the "thin line between sincerity and verity."[13] Although the sincerity test was designed to avoid judgments about theological truth, assumptions about practices' and beliefs' legitimacy and believability nevertheless inflect evaluations of claimants' sincerity. In his dissent in *United States v. Ballard* (1944), the fraud case in which the sincerity test was proposed, Justice Jackson had raised this very issue. He asked, "How can the Government prove these persons knew something to be false which it cannot prove to be false?"[14] The assumption of certain claims' veracity and others' falsehood had always been implicit within religious freedom law, Jackson argued. In the case of fortune-telling, the statutes themselves seemed to imply a disbelief in the veracity of the practice.

At a moment before the sincerity test, and before the fuller development of religious freedom jurisprudence and the incorporation of the First Amendment's religion clauses against the states, cases like Malcolm's and Ross's illustrate another aspect of sincerity politics. They did not argue that they sincerely believed in their practices. Rather, they argued that their practices were real. There is a difference between saying "I believe this is true" and "this is true." As we will see, eventually some mediums (and at least one law professor) began to argue that so-called fortune-telling was a religious activity and ought to be protected as such. But for most, on both sides, the debate about fortune-telling's legitimacy and legality was inextricable from questions about its efficacy. Some thought this should be a settled question, that of course these practices were both unreal and, in some sense, unbelievable. In such a specifically disenchanted world, purported believers in the "crafty sciences"—predicting the future, channeling the dead, learning from palm lines or tea leaves or flowers—had to fall on one side or the other of a familiar dichotomy.

"There are only two kinds of [Spiritualist] mediums," said Harry Houdini, the famous illusionist and debunker. "Those who are mental degenerates and who ought to be under observation, and those who are deliberate cheats and frauds."[15] Testifying before a subcommittee of the House of Representatives in favor of a ban on fortune-telling in the District of Columbia,

---

13. Su, "Questioning Sincerity," 41.

14. *Ballard*, 322 U.S. at 93.

15. *Hearings before the Subcommittee on Judiciary of the Committee on the District of Columbia*, House of Representatives, 69th Congress, First Session on HR 8989 (Feb. 2,

Houdini allowed that some might truly believe but thought it possible only if they were fools or, even beyond foolish, mentally unwell. The rest were knowing cheats, fakers, knaves. While Houdini took aim at the mediums, others focused on those who might consult them. In 1895 the chemist and historian of science Henry Carrington Bolton wrote in the pages of the *Journal of American Folklore* about the sort of people who might believe in such things, "the superstitious who ignorantly believe that mankind has power over the supernatural. In this class fall numbers of 'silly women, ever learning, never able to come to the truth.'" He added speculatively, "Probably a large proportion of this credulous class are of foreign birth."[16] This class needed the law's protection. Indeed, according to one New York court, "The plain object of the [anti-fortune-telling] statute here is to protect the fool and credulously weak from the knavery" of those who would dupe them.[17] This judgment on the veracity of a belief foreclosed the possibility of the believer's sincerity. If these practices were always fake, then belief in them had to be either duplicitous or credulous. Fortune-tellers, then, were either knaves or fools, but not sincere believers.

ROGUES AND VAGABONDS

"Fortune-telling"—like superstition or obeah or, sometimes, religion—is generally not a term people use to describe their own practices. It is, rather, a term of governance. The term was listed alongside other "crafty sciences" in vagrancy laws throughout the United States, as well as England, South Africa, the Caribbean, Australia, and elsewhere. These laws were applied differently in different times and places. They were not enforced in such a way that tightly defined fortune-telling or palmistry or crafty sciences. Practices that might have been policed under the statutes were widespread. The legal scholar Jeremy Patrick has argued that "fortune-telling is a practice that has historical manifestations in many, if not all, world cultures."[18]

May 18, 20, 21, 1926). On this testimony, see Alicia Puglionesi, "In 1926, Houdini Spent 4 Days Shaming Congress for Being in Thrall to Fortune-Tellers," *Atlas Obscura*, Oct. 11, 2016.

16. Henry Carrington Bolton, "Fortune-Telling in America To-Day: A Study in Advertisements," *Journal of American Folklore* 8, no. 31 (Oct.–Dec., 1895): 299–307, 306. Bolton was quoting 2 Timothy 3:6.

17. People ex rel Priess v. Adams, 33 NY Crim Rep 326, 344 (Magis. Ct. 1914).

18. Patrick, *Faith or Fraud*, 13.

It is true that means of predicting the future have been and continue to be practiced all over the world. What makes some methods "spiritual" or "religious" and others, like meteorology, "scientific" or "secular" is a different question.[19] The point of this chapter is not to study historical examples of actual fortune-telling but to show how the label signified a certain type of subject, the fortune-teller, and how she was policed.

Most fortune-telling bans drew their language from English law, specifically the Vagrancy Act of 1824. Vagrancy is a crime of status, not action. One does not really commit vagrancy; rather, one *is* a vagrant. As the legal historian Risa Goluboff has put it, "Vagrancy laws made it a crime to be a certain type of person."[20] Thus, they were notoriously flexible. U.S. police in many cities used vagrancy laws against queer communities. British officials used them, both in the metropole and in the colonies, to police the economic lives of racialized subjects, especially practitioners of Afro-Atlantic religions, casting them as charlatans and frauds.[21] And local police and politicians leveraged vagrancy statutes against labor leaders throughout the United States in the early twentieth century.[22] In the United States vagrancy laws were struck down finally in the 1970s, when the Supreme Court recognized their clearly discriminatory uses.[23]

The 1824 law was far from the first English vagrancy statute; in fact, it was meant to consolidate many other laws "relating to idle and disorderly Persons, Rogues and Vagabonds, incorrigible Rogues and other Vagrants in England."[24] These three categories had been developed over the course

19. In *Looking Forward*, Jamie Pietruska studied many of these same fortune-telling cases, plotting them in a history of nineteenth- and early twentieth-century prediction.

20. Goluboff, *Vagrant Nation*, 2. See also A. L. Beier and Paul Ocobock, eds., *Cast Out: Vagrancy and Homelessness in Global and Historical Perspective* (Ohio State University Press, 2009). Euan Cameron has argued that the church in England, whether Catholic or Protestant, supported vagrancy statutes because they helped control the poor and stamped out "folk" practices that undermined church hierarchy and uniformity (*Enchanted Europe*, 175).

21. Boaz, "Fraud, Vagrancy, and the 'Pretended' Exercise."

22. Ahmed A. White, "A Different Kind of Labor Law: Vagrancy Law and the Regulation of Harvest Labor, 1913–1924," *University of Colorado Law Review* 75, no. 3 (2004): 667–743.

23. Papachristou v. Jacksonville, 405 U.S. 156 (1972). On the fuller twentieth-century history, see Goluboff, *Vagrant Nation*.

24. Vagrancy Act, 1824, 3 Geo. IV., c. 4. "Rogues and vagabonds" included "those who pretend to tell fortunes, or use any subtle craft, means, or device, by palmistry or otherwise, to deceive and impose on any one; those who publicly expose any obscene print, picture, or other indecent exhibition; those who publicly expose their persons obscenely; those who

of centuries, with shifting definitions and varying correspondent punishments. On the first page of his compendious 1887 history of vagrants and vagrancy, Charles James Ribton-Turner admitted that his task was difficult because it required one to "trace out, in fact, the vicissitudes of the servile classes from the time they are servile by inheritance or by destiny, until they become free members of society, and leave only a remnant who are servile or abject from choice, and whose history becomes a record of hypocrisy, humbug, and habitual idleness."[25] In practice, neither English nor U.S. law enforcement was so careful in determining the socioeconomic causes of a person's vagrancy. Who exactly counted as a vagrant—and what type of vagrant—was never clearly explicated and oftentimes depended solely upon the judgment of the arresting authority.[26]

Because vagrancy is a crime of status, English law could not point to a specific action and label it vagrancy. Instead, the law identified vagrants by long lists of activities that might be used to indicate vagrancy. Fortune-telling was one such practice. Thus, U.S. state laws generally included fortune-telling in such a list, drawn from the 1824 act. North Carolina's statute (repealed in 2004), for instance, declared, "It shall be unlawful for any person to practice the arts of phrenology, palmistry, clairvoyance, fortune-telling and other crafts of a similar kind."[27] Other states went into greater detail. Pennsylvania singled out anyone who "pretends for gain or lucre, to tell fortunes or predict future events, by cards, tokens, the inspection of the head or hands of any person, or by the age of anyone, or by consulting

---

endeavor by the exposure of wounds or deformities to gather alms; those who endeavor to collect charitable contributions under any false or fraudulent pretence . . . those who publicly play or bet at any game or pretended game of chance. . . ." Cited in Ribton-Turner, *A History of Vagrants and Vagrancy*, 236.

For an overview of secondary sources on vagrancy laws, see Goluboff, *Vagrant Nation*, 351n7. On vagrancy in the nineteenth-century United States, see Novak, *The People's Welfare*, 167–171.

The Vagrancy Act consolidated other laws, including the Witchcraft Act of 1735, which itself repealed the ban on "witchcraft" (dating, in various iterations, to 1542), but criminalized claims to use "magical powers." These were replaced by the Fraudulent Mediums Act of 1951, which was repealed in 2008. See "Witchcraft," http://www.parliament.uk/about/living -heritage/transformingsociety/private-lives/religion/overview/witchcraft/.

25. Ribton-Turner, *A History of Vagrants and Vagrancy*, vii.

26. On the history of English vagrancy laws, see James Fitzjames Stephen, *A History of Criminal Law in England*, vol. 3 (Macmillan, 1883), 266–275. See also Slack, *Poverty and Policy*.

27. NC Gen Stat § 14–401.5.

the movements of the heavenly bodies, or in any other manner" and goes on to mention hexes, health guarantees, locating lost items, "necromancy," putting "bad luck on a person or animal," and advising clients to take "what are commonly called love powders or potions," among other offenses.[28] U.S. vagrancy laws were "derivative, sprawling, and overlapping," and they allowed police considerable interpretive leeway.[29] While legal authorities could use the laws' capaciousness to their advantage, defendants could at least attempt to seize on their vagueness. Accused vagrants could protest their convictions by denying the state's labels—fortune-teller, palmister, juggler, whatever the charge—and reclaiming their own practices. Indeed, as this chapter will detail more fully below, Alice Ashley's defense parsed the differences between "fortune-telling," "foretelling," "prophecy," and other labels.

From the English statutes emerge two defining characteristics of "rogues and vagabonds," the category of vagrants including fortune-tellers: their shifty placelessness and their insincerity. Regarding the first, wanderers normally were sent back to their home village, literally put in their place.[30] This was perhaps the most enduring and pervasive feature of these laws.[31] Even centuries later, vagrancy laws were, Goluboff writes, "linked to a conception of postwar American society—as they had been linked to a conception of sixteenth-century English society—in which everyone had a proper place," and they could be used to police "anyone who threatened . . . to move 'out of place' socially, culturally, politically, racially, sexually, economically, or spatially."[32] Furthermore, in an early instance of policing for profit, individual constables were rewarded, starting in 1744, for vagrancy arrests: two shillings per vagrant, and five or ten for repeat offenders and "incorrigible rogues."[33] Around the turn of the twentieth century Spiritualist mediums

---

28. PA Code ch. 71 § 7104.

29. Goluboff, *Vagrant Nation*, 9.

30. See Slack, *Poverty and Policy*, 96–97. See also Beier, *Masterless Men*, 222.

31. On legal restrictions of movement in urban spaces, see Ron Levi, "Loitering in the City That Works: On Circulation, Activity, and Police in Governing Urban Spaces," in *Police and the Liberal State*, ed. Markus D. Dubber (Stanford University Press, 2008), 178–199.

32. Goluboff, *Vagrant Nation*, 3.

33. Ribton-Turner, *A History of Vagrants and Vagrancy*, 200. These rogues often turned to entertainment, such as legerdemain and fortune-telling, as a way to subsist. It is important to note that simply being an entertainer was not illegal in most cases. The 1740 statute banned not all entertainers but those "without authority, by virtue of letters patent." The historian A. L. Beier explains, "Not all showpeople were vagabonds by law, because those

were arrested on a range of charges, many of which can be traced to vagrancy statutes and other English poor laws.[34] As police power and antivice crusades expanded in tandem, agencies from the local to the federal level sought to put the poor in their place as well as root out fraudulence.[35] Antifortune-telling statutes, and vagrancy laws more generally, afforded opportunities to do both. Police stings like the one during which Alice Ashley was arrested were part of a growing trend in policing, stemming in part from their partnership with antivice groups and support from the popular press.[36]

VAGRANCY AND THE HISTORY OF RELIGIONS

While religious people generally make money, accusations of illegitimacy and hucksterism tend to arise when either "too much" money is made or the profit motive seems central. This is one reason the dollar on Ashley's table—and who initiated its transaction—mattered. Most of the statutes included a phrase like "for gain or lucre" or "for profit." As Alana Piper has shown,

---

patronized by noblemen and corporations were protected. Royal licenses and the establishment of permanent companies were additional ways to escape prosecution" (*Masterless Men*, 97). Patronage and licensure legitimated entertainers' livelihoods. Vagrants were by nature out of place in the traditional or legitimate economy. A fortune-teller, dancer, or juggler who obtained some form of authorization was, by definition, not a vagrant. Nevertheless, there were certain forms of entertainment—those based on "pretending"—that remained particularly suspect.

34. Erika Dyson identified four kinds of criminal charges with which Spiritualists were most commonly charged: (1) "obtaining money under false pretenses," (2) mail fraud, (3) practicing medicine without a license, and (4) being "fortune-tellers, which was a species of vagrancy in some states, and a disorderly persons charge in others" ("Spiritualism and Crime," 189–190).

35. William McAdoo, as New York City police commissioner and later as chief magistrate, unsuccessfully advocated the expansion of vagrancy statutes' purview; see McAdoo, *Guarding a Great City* (Harper and Bros., 1906), 320, cited in Dyson, "Spiritualism and Crime," 367n134. Tammy Stone-Gordon, "'Fifty-Cent Sybils,'" also mentions police crackdowns on fortune-tellers in New York after 1910. Four women in particular did a significant amount of the undercover sting work. For a firsthand account, see "How I Had 54 Persons Arrested and What I Found Out about Palm-Reading," *Ladies' Home Journal* 28 (Aug., 1911).

36. See Fronc, *New York Undercover*, and Dubber, *The Police Power*. On the press and advertising bans, see Stone-Gordon, chap. 6, "'Wholesale Raids on Fortunetellers': Urban Myths and the End of Seer-Centered Advertising," in "'Fifty-Cent Sybils.'"

in early twentieth-century Australia "the increased policing of fortune-telling . . . resulted partially from its growing professionalization."[37] The scene between Ashley and Seller illustrates how the policing of fortune-telling, as it cracked down on certain forms of women's work, also created new jobs for women, such as undercover police informant. The cases, along with contemporary academic and legal scholarship on them, offer examples not only of the racialized and gendered nature of secular governance, but also of how ideas, including scholarly ideas, about religion and its histories are entwined with governance.

Blewett Lee—a Mississippi-born lawyer, son of the Confederate lieutenant general Stephen D. Lee, and faculty member at the University of Chicago Law School—wrote a series of articles about fortune-telling and similar cases in the 1920s in which he recognized potential religious freedom issues and attempted to locate the crafty sciences in a history of religions.[38] Though many jurists and legislators dismissed the possibility of fortune-telling and spirit communication, Lee was not so epistemically hubristic. He cautioned, "Enough people believe that spirits are concerned to give their views a kind of religious standing and protection under the wise legal policy of refusing to condemn religious beliefs so long as no serious public mischief results from the believers. . . . Under all the circumstances, therefore, the law cannot very well take the dogmatic position that every phenomenon of the class called spiritualistic is a delusion."[39] To assume that all fortune-tellers were knaves or hucksters was dogmatic and, further, led to unjust discrimination. "Let us be as incredulous of messages from the dead as we can," Lee wrote, "but let us not persecute people for believing in such messages on evidence which satisfies them, if not us. After all, it is at least possible that we may be mistaken in some of our own religious views."[40] Neither Lee's brand of liberal

---

37. Piper, "Women's Work," 38.

38. Stephen D. Lee's papers are available at the University of North Carolina–Chapel Hill, to which they were donated by Blewett Lee in 1941. The Lee home in Columbus, Mississippi, where Blewett was reared, is now a museum and is on the National Register of Historic Places. See United States Department of the Interior National Park Service, *S. D. Lee House National Register of Historic Places Nomination Form*, 1969, 71.5.28.0001. Blewett Lee is mentioned as an original Chicago Law School faculty member in Bernard D. Meltzer, "The University of Chicago Law School: Ruminations and Reminiscences," *University of Chicago Law Review* 70 (2003): 236.

39. Lee, "Spiritualism and Crime," 440.

40. Lee, "The Fortune-Teller," 262. Lee declined to comment in his writings whether he believed in these practices, but he apparently was not involved with any Spiritualist

tolerance nor his sympathies to Spiritualism were uncommon among his set of academics. However, he did take a wider view than most as to what ought to count as "religion," particularly for religious freedom purposes.[41] And he did so, in part, by disentangling veracity and sincerity, the same secularist move the Supreme Court would make a few decades later.

Lee understood religion and spirituality as universal human phenomena. The way he plotted that universality, though, mostly tracked with common evolutionary secularization stories, positing a progression from the primitive to the enlightened. In one 1922 essay, for example, he cited the anthropologists Andrew Lang and E. B. Tylor as authorities on the evolution of religion.[42] In some ways Lee reiterated the common assumption that fortune-telling was a premodern, superstitious practice, "modernity's foil."[43] "The calling of foretelling the future by occult powers is most ancient, and seems to have existed everywhere," he wrote. "The human mind has developed similar superstitions throughout the world."[44] Unlike other legal thinkers, Lee did not draw from this framework the lesson that religion was modern and thus premodern superstitions should not be protected as religions. Instead, he understood fortune-telling, automatic writing, trance mediumship, and other practices as essentially the same as modern religion, since they fulfilled the same basic roles in individual and communal life. Lee thus reflected an undercurrent of social scientific interest in magic that cut against the supposed secularization of modernity and the popularity of debunking.[45] For Lee, all people had access to the religious, to the spiritual realm, although some people accessed it in more modern ways than others.

---

or similar society. In a 1921 essay, he disclaimed "any desire to take a position one way or another upon the occurrence or the real nature of what are called psychic phenomena," admitting that he knew "nothing more about them than may properly be expected of one who is moderately acquainted with the literature of the subject and has always been fond of ghosts." A helpful footnote to that sentence advised, "The safest place to search for ghosts (always excepting the Bible) is in the ENCYCLOPEDIA BRITANNICA" (Lee, "Psychic Phenomena and the Law," 625n1).

41. On scholarly affinities with and participation in Spiritualism and various "occult" activities, beliefs, and societies, see Josephson-Storm, *The Myth of Disenchantment*.

42. Lee, "Spiritualism and Crime."

43. This phrase is from Styers, *Making Magic*, 26.

44. Lee, "The Fortune-Teller," 251.

45. See Josephson-Storm, *The Myth of Disenchantment*. These were the sorts of people, including Sir Arthur Conan Doyle, at whom Harry Houdini took aim when he remarked, "The ancients' childish belief in demonology and witchcraft; the superstitions of the civilized and uncivilized, and those marvellous mysteries of past ages are all laughed at by the

White women, most of them Spiritualists, accounted for the majority of fortune-telling arrests and almost all of the resultant court cases, but they were of course not the only people in the United States performing what LaShawn Harris has called "supernatural labor." For example, at the same time white women such as Alice Ashley and Maude Malcolm were arrested for telling fortunes, Black women in New York were "creat[ing] new occupational identities and entrepreneurial opportunities for themselves, selling magical paraphernalia, distributing policy numbers to gamblers, and establishing home- and church-based religious centers and magic and healing businesses."[46] As Harris has shown, these supernatural laborers blended traditions and practices, sometimes incorporating orientalist imagery and language, and in many cases would consider themselves religious. They also faced accusations of knavery and preying on fools. One observer wrote, "There are an estimated 200 spiritualists in Harlem, most of them hiding behind the guise of religion."[47] Black people and Black religion are largely absent from the archive of fortune-telling arrests and religious freedom cases. They are not absent, however, from the history of vagrancy laws and enforcement. In fact, as Danielle Boaz has demonstrated, vagrancy laws provided the model for obeah laws, which created a category ("obeah") in order to regulate African diasporic ritual practices.[48]

The popular press often discussed fortune-telling in racialized terms, with reference to "Negro superstitions" and "gypsies," and Black people and

---

full grown sense of the present generation; yet we are asked, in all seriousness, by a few scientists and scholars, to accept as absolute truth such testimony as is built up by their pet mediums" (Harry Houdini, *A Magician Among the Spirits* [Harper and Brothers, 1924], xx). At the time of his death, Houdini was collaborating with the horror writer H. P. Lovecraft on a work entitled "The Cancer of Superstition." The extant thirty-one-page manuscript was discovered in 2016. Alison Flood, "Lost HP Lovecraft Work Commissioned by Houdini Escapes Shackles of History," *Guardian*, Mar. 16, 2016.

46. Harris, *Sex Workers, Psychics, and Number Runners*, 97. On similar practices and cultures in an earlier period, see Shane White, "The Gold Diggers of 1833: African American Dreams, Fortune-Telling, Treasure-Seeking, and Policy in Antebellum New York City," *Journal of Social History* 47, no. 3 (Spring, 2014): 673–695.

47. Marvel Cooke, "Million Dollar Take," *New York Amsterdam News*, May 25, 1940, 11. Quoted in Harris, *Sex Workers, Psychics, and Number Runners*, 115.

48. Boaz, "Fraud, Vagrancy, and the 'Pretended' Exercise"; and Boaz, "Obeah, Vagrancy, and Boundaries of Religious Freedom." See also Diana Paton, *The Cultural Politics of Obeah: Religion, Colonialism and Modernity in the Caribbean World* (Cambridge University Press, 2015), esp. chap. 5, "Obeah in the Courts, 1890–1939."

Roma were occasionally arrested for fortune-telling.[49] For the most part, though, the enforcement of fortune-telling bans in the late nineteenth and early twentieth centuries were aimed at white Spiritualist women who, for a fee, channeled dead spirits to give advice or predict the future.[50] Unlike those groups who were racialized as premodern and superstitious, these Spiritualists were supposed to be modern subjects, and their superstitious dabbling troubled courts and lawmakers. Exposing the incompleteness of modernization and secularization, the "myth of disenchantment," Spiritualists posed problems for those with an interest in defending the "modern" as well as "religion." In addition to these ghostly concerns, Spiritualist politics often contested and undermined patriarchal power.[51]

49. Carol Silverman, "Everyday Drama: Impression Management of Urban Gypsies," *Urban Anthropology* 11, nos. 3–4 (Fall–Winter, 1982): 377–398. Some of the English statutes specifically outlawed *pretending* to be "gypsies." The British historian Frank Aydelotte noted this in his early twentieth-century treatment of vagrancy: "There are several statutes against English vagabonds disguising themselves as gipsies or wandering in company with them, which indicates that there were some relations between the two races. English vagabonds soon began to practise the fortune-telling which made the gipsies so welcome to the country people everywhere" (*Elizabethan Rogues and Vagabonds* [Clarendon Press, 1913], 18). Some municipalities in the United States picked up on this idea. Front Royal, Virginia, for instance, outlawed "fortunetelling or practicing magic art" with this language: "It shall be unlawful for any company of gypsies or other strolling company or person to receive compensation or reward for pretending to tell fortunes or to practice any so-called 'magic art'" (Municipal Code 110–17). The statute was repealed in 2014.

50. There were a few local exceptions, as when bans responded directly to specific incidents. For example, in 1915 the police chief of Anaconda, Montana issued an order "stopping all spiritualists, mediums, trance mediums, clairvoyants and similar practitioners from continuing their readings and prophecies. This order was issued as the result of the investigations made at the time Tina Haakla, a kitchen maid at the Silver Bow club, was duped out of $565 by Katherine Boboska, a gypsy who claimed Indian blood and the power of healing disease" ("Mediums Are Under Police Chief's Ban; An Indian Practitioner Starts the Trouble," *Anaconda Standard*, July 30, 1915, 7).

Tammy Stone-Gordon, in her study of seers and the press, notes that in New York's arrest reports from 1909 to 1917 (during the heaviest crackdown on mediumistic practices), only eight "mentioned the seer's ethnic or religious affiliation: African-American (2), Muslim, Japanese, German Spiritualist, Hindu, Gypsy and Syrian" ("'Fifty-Cent Sybils,'" 241).

51. See McGarry, *Ghosts of Futures Past*, and Braude, *Radical Spirits*. Class was a relevant factor as well. Even "purely" as a form of entertainment, by the late nineteenth century fortune-telling and spiritual mediumship were considered less "respectable" as the "entertainment industry was swiftly moving toward professionalization and regulation" (Johnson, "Spirits on the Stage," 14).

There is at least one exception, *Cooper v. Livingston*, in which a Black woman was arrested for telling fortunes. That case, along with Blewett Lee's commentary on it, illustrates how the evolutionary history of religions and the imagination of "religion" itself has been structured by racialization. For Lee, all religion shared some common essence, but he thought historically and genealogically about specific practices and practitioners. The *Cooper* case took place in Florida in 1883. A Black woman named E. G. Magruder had collected a $250 note for using "conjure" and "incantations" to attempt to cure a sick man.[52] When the man died, his family brought suit to recoup the assets. The court found in the family's favor, concluding that "'conjuring' over a sick man 'to make him well' is not a valid consideration for a promissory note; and that no man with a healthy mind would voluntarily give a note for $250, with interest at two per cent, a month, for the services of a conjurer."[53] The dying man must either have agreed to pay because he was of unsound mind or, as his widow claimed, not actually have agreed to the payment or even desired Magruder's services. The court cited previous decisions in which "such persons" were treated as "rogues and vagabonds" (terminology from the Vagrancy Act and its predecessors dating to the sixteenth century) and referred to Magruder as a "fortune teller."

Lee chided the Florida court for failing to understand the history of religion and the history of "rogues and vagabonds," and for their inability to differentiate among seemingly similar practices. Invoking his Mississippi roots, he wrote, "A Southerner cannot help feeling that the court went to the wrong place for information about conjuring" when they cited Webster's dictionary and English common law. Magruder's healing practices, in Lee's estimation, "would probably hark back to African magic rather than to medieval superstition in England. Probably this fortune teller was guilty of nothing more than magical ceremonies of a kind which are found everywhere among primitive peoples."[54] The phrase "hark back" reveals what

52. Cooper v. Livingston, 19 Fla. 684 (1883). The case does not mention Magruder's race explicitly anywhere, but in several places it is implied that she was Black, and Lee makes this assumption as well. Magruder lived in LaVilla, a historically Black town, incorporated into the city of Jacksonville in 1887.

53. *Cooper*, 19 Fla at 694.

54. Lee, "The Conjurer," 371. On Afro-Atlantic religions and charges of fraudulence by British officials, see Boaz, "Fraud, Vagrancy, and the 'Pretended' Exercise." For more instances of encounters between African and Afro-Atlantic conjure practices and U.S. law, see Chireau, *Black Magic*, 206nn4, 5.

Homi Bhabha called the "ambivalent temporality of modernity."[55] Modernity is figured both spatially and temporally, and "hark back" evokes both registers. Modernity is, as Sylvester Johnson has written, "*not really* an era so much as it is *an effect of the subjectivity* of Western conquerors."[56] The fortune-teller or conjurer is not a fully Western subject, because they hark back temporally to medieval superstitions or spatially to Africa (notice that "African magic" has no temporal signifier whereas "medieval English superstition" does)—or both spatially and temporally to what's "found everywhere among primitive peoples." The subjectivity of Western conquerors, on the other hand, is constructed through putatively race-neutral appeals to "sanity." The court in *Cooper* held that "no man with a healthy mind" would believe in conjuration. Sincerely held religious belief in conjuration, then, was an impossibility.

Drawing from ongoing legal considerations of responsibility and consciousness, and seeking to restore the original antifraud intent of the statutes, Lee advocated a legal standard of religious sincerity. He thoughtfully considered how one might evaluate religious sincerity, anticipating twenty-first-century debates about the sincerity test. Fakecraft was hard work, and investigations into individual motivation and intention—especially when involving spiritual claims or altered states such as trances—were tricky. Lee recognized this, and he expressed frustration over judges who never even considered it. Discussing *People v. Hill*, a New York case wherein a medium was arrested at a "public religious service of a Spiritualist Society" in which "there was prayer, singing and public speaking," he lamented that "the thing which nobody paid any attention to was that Hill testified firmly and with apparent sincerity that he really saw and heard spirits, and his performance at the meetings which he conducted was a usual feature of spiritualistic public religious services."[57] Hill was a "default legal person," a rational actor,

55. Homi K. Bhabha, "Race, Time and the Revision of Modernity," in *The Post-Colonial Studies Reader*, ed. B. Ashcroft, G. Griffiths, and H. Tiffin (Routledge, 2006), 219–223. See also Michel Foucault, "What Is Enlightenment," in *The Foucault Reader*, ed. Paul Rabinow (Pantheon, 1984). He writes, "I know that modernity is often spoken of as an epoch, or at least as a set of features characteristic of an epoch; situated on a calendar, it would be preceded by a more or less naive or archaic premodernity, and followed by an enigmatic and troubling 'postmodernity'" (37).

56. Johnson, *African American Religions*, 153.

57. Lee, "The Fortune-Teller," 265.

a sincere believer.[58] And yet the court had treated him as though he was not truly religious. What's more, they attempted to regulate his religious practice itself. Lee sarcastically added, "It is quite a compliment to our legal profession that it must be consulted before a man can safely undertake to communicate with angels even at church."[59] Laws designed to prosecute the deceitful had instead been misused, Lee thought, to burden the free exercise of sincere believers. And they had done it, as Anthony Comstock had, through policing and regulation.

"THE SPIRIT OF REGULATION"

"Verily, the spirit of regulation is abroad in the land," an Oklahoma judge lamented in 1922, balking at the criminal conviction of a trance medium. States regulated "the mediums of communication between human beings such as the telephone and telegraph. Now this state proposes to regulate the mediums of communication with the spirit world."[60] Regulation takes many shapes, but it often involves licensure and paperwork. Secularism runs on a spirit of regulation, categorizing the religious and nonreligious in columns and rows. These procedures do not just catalogue or record religion but produce religious difference.[61] Rather than controverting the foundations of American religious freedom, these are the mechanisms by which it is (provisionally and unequally) ensured. By regulating fortune-telling and policing fortune-tellers, states protected certain freedoms by restricting others, and in so doing determined not only which beliefs were religious, but which believers.

Rogues and vagabonds, in the English statutes and those based on them, were defined by their "false pretenses" and lack of proper licensure.

58. Susanna Blumenthal has analyzed what she calls the nineteenth-century "default legal person," "who possessed a set of intellectual, moral, and volitional faculties that enabled him to follow the precepts of reason and natural justice, as well as those of the positive law" (*Law and the Modern Mind*, 9). She explains how certain religious beliefs, including Spiritualist beliefs in mediumship or ghosts, were sometimes treated as evidence of the believer's insanity or, at least, insufficient faculties of reason.

59. Lee, "The Fortune-Teller," 266.

60. McMasters v. State, 21 Okl. Cr. 318, 327 (1922).

61. Mahmood, *Religious Difference in a Secular Age*.

In 1865 Charles Colchester was arrested in upstate New York for performing magic without a license and was required to become licensed as a juggler. Colchester was a Spiritualist, and he claimed that "he is not a juggler; that spiritualism is not jugglery, and that the United States Government . . . has no right to force him to acknowledge his religion all humbug and deception by obliging him to accept and pay for a license as a juggler."[62] David Walker has analyzed this fascinating trial, in which a variety of characters, including the judge, newspaper writers, and expert witnesses, deliberated over Colchester's profession—and, with it, the nature of religion, ritual, and belief. Some witnesses, themselves practitioners of legerdemain, attempted to demonstrate that Colchester knew the "tricks of the trade" and thus was not really a medium. Other witnesses tried to debunk Colchester's claims with common methods of demonstration, pointing out his failure to answer sealed questions. There are many interesting points to be drawn from this case, several of which Walker raises. Relevant to our purposes here is the fact that sincerity and veracity were at issue. Walker writes, "It was evidently an open question whether belief was a prerequisite or effect of ritual participation, just as whether veracity—the presumed grounds of belief—was necessary for religious character, aesthetics, or utility."[63] The trial produced a variety of questions. If Colchester was using skillful sleight-of-hand tricks, were his actions categorically not religious? Did it matter, and in what ways, that Colchester's beliefs appeared not to be true?

Colchester was charged with *unlicensed* jugglery. This licensure process was reminiscent of the 1824 Vagrancy Act's allowance for deceptive entertainment only when performers were sponsored and accounted for by patrons. For Colchester, to register as a juggler—a label that implied duplicity—would be to admit the falsehood of his religion and, further, to mark his practices as nonreligious or even irreligious. Some states' anti-fortune-telling legislation specifically banned only unlicensed practice. In Ohio, for example, "whoever, not having been licensed so to do, represents himself to be an astrologer, fortune-teller, clairvoyant or palmister, shall be fined not less than twenty-five dollars nor more than one hundred dollars or imprisoned in jail not less than thirty days nor more than three months, or both."[64] (The effectiveness of this statute was compromised by the fact that,

62. Walker, "The Humbug in American Religion," 46. The quotation is from the *New York Herald*.

63. Walker, "The Humbug in American Religion," 50.

64. OH Code § 13145.

as one appellate court noted in 1928, neither the state of Ohio nor the city of Cleveland actually issued any such licenses.[65]) Laws across the country included provisions allowing for certain harmless forms of entertainment— rendered harmless by their context, not their content.[66] Sometimes fortune- telling was just for fun, not *really* faking anyone out or *pretending* to be real. These stipulations, allowing for fortune-telling as entertainment and/or not for profit, indicated that whether persons or activities were real societal dangers depended on the setting, namely, whether they took place outside official or legitimate venues.

"ATTENDED WITH SUPERSTITIOUS CREDULITY AND . . . TINGED WITH HYPOCRISY"

Arrested fortune-tellers often had little legal recourse, but a small number of Spiritualists contested their convictions with appeals to religious freedom. As discussed above, they had at least two factors working against them. First, state officials often seemed to consider their practices inherently fraudu- lent and cast doubt on their sincerity. Such aspersions were written into the language and history of vagrancy statutes. Second, these defendants often lacked security and power. The status of being religious, if attained, might offer the protections of religious freedom. In the early twentieth century, though, individual "religious belief," regardless of how sincerely it was held, was not usually sufficient to establish religiosity; instead, membership in an official, recognized religious organization was required. However, Spiritual- ists disagreed about how official to be. From the start of the movement, many held antiorganizational principles and harbored doubts about hierarchical organized religion. In the late nineteenth century, though, with the founding of the National Spiritualist Association (NSA) in 1893, they moved toward organization.[67] The NSA president Harrison D. Barrett borrowed terminol-

---

65. Davis v. State, 118 Ohio St. 25 (1928).

66. For example, North Carolina's law specified that the listed practices were legal when not done for profit, although only when "in connection with school or church socials, pro- vided such socials are held in school or church buildings." NC Gen Stat § 14–401.5.

67. See Dyson, chap. 2, "They Speak in Thunder Tones, 'ORGANIZATION!' The Founding of the National Spiritualist Association," in "Spiritualism and Crime," 33–118.

For the most part, members of the NSA and other Spiritualist societies did not receive any sort of ministerial exemption until the mid-twentieth century. Christine Corcos has

ogy straight from vagrancy statutes when in 1896 he declared that he would bar any "fortune-teller, card reader, charm seller, love powder giver, or other imposter" from membership.[68] Thus, when accused fortune-tellers called on the NSA for help, they were asking for support from an organization founded in part to separate Spiritualism from the very crimes of which the defendants were accused.[69]

A number of defendants, from New York to Georgia to Washington, went to court to defend their free exercise. In some cases practitioners were associated with Spiritualist churches and national organizations; in others, their operations were more freelance. One defendant, L. D. McMasters, had been charged in Oklahoma with violating the state's statute, passed in 1915, that criminalized accepting any fee, gift, or donation in exchange for "pretending or professing to tell fortunes by the use of any subtle craft, means or device whatsoever, either by palmistry, clairvoyancy or otherwise."[70] She appealed her conviction, arguing that the law infringed on her free exercise of religion. As evidence of her religious bona fides, McMasters cited her membership in the National Spiritualist Association. Her attorney explained that she was not only a member but "regularly licensed to give spiritual advice to others; that many of the tenets, beliefs and practices of this cult are religious in their nature, including the practice of communicating with departed spirits."[71] McMasters allegedly accepted a one-dollar fee from a young woman named Bessie Jones and in return channeled, via trance, the spirit of Minnehaha.[72] According to Jones's testimony, McMasters went into a trance and delivered to her a message from Minnehaha correctly stating that Jones currently was unemployed but predicting that she soon would

---

noted that, in a few cases, such exemptions were written into vagrancy statutes earlier in the twentieth century, in Illinois (1911), New York (1929), and Nebraska (1940), though she does note that the New York amendment was not interpreted in such a way until 1943 ("Seeing It Coming," 53–63). See also Corcos, "The Scrying Game," 3n10.

68. Harrison D. Barrett, "Protection for Mediums," *Washington Post*, Dec. 14, 1896.

69. On Spiritualists' attempts to fashion themselves as modern and religious, over and against the credulity of mesmerists (and others, as Barrett's remarks illustrate), see Ogden, *Credulity*, chap. 5, "The Spirit of Benjamin Franklin." Ogden shows how Spiritualists "shaped a narrative in which mesmerism was the primitive practice that they had rationalized" (224).

70. Section 1, chap. 59, Oklahoma Session Laws of 1915. As cited in *McMasters*, 21 Okl. Cr. at 320.

71. *McMasters*, 21 Okl. Cr. at 320.

72. On mediums channeling Native Americans, see McGarry, *Ghosts of Futures Past*, chap. 2, "Indian Guides: Haunted Subjects and the Politics of Vanishing."

receive an offer and accept it. She also forecast a love triangle and fore-told that, after that had been resolved, Jones would marry a wealthy man. McMasters took a dollar, then gave Jones six calling cards and asked her to help advertise by distributing them among her friends. She had no doubt violated the letter of the law, but she sought exemption from it, since to apply it to her was to violate of her free exercise of religion.

Although sincere religious beliefs are individual, once again the case hinged primarily on the nature of the claimant's church. The court consid-ered the nature of the NSA at some length. The judges mulled over the asso-ciation's stated reasons for forming and the benefits of assembling, in their constitution's words, "the various spiritual societies of the United States into one general association for promoting mutual aid and co-operation" in their various "enterprises germane to the phenomena, science, philosophy, and religion of Spiritualism." Here Spiritualism was described as a religion, but not *only* as a religion. Upon consideration of the NSA's stated tenets, Judge E. S. Bessey situated these beliefs within a sketched history of religion: "Ever since the dawn of history there have been those who have believed in the influence of good and evil spirits. The devil himself was a fallen angel, cast out of heaven." Even the "writings of Dante, of Shakespeare and of Milton, as well as the modern poets," he added, "abound with examples of the belief in spirits."[73] Bessey, for his part, did not discount the possibility of commu-nication with the dead.[74] He thought McMasters's claim was dubious, since Minnehaha was a fictional character and thus lacked a spirit to channel. However, he allowed for the possibility that McMasters was not a knave but actually a fool, duped by "some unknown, playful spirit" falsely claiming to

---

73. *McMasters*, 21 Okl. Cr. at 322.

74. Perhaps it is not surprising that those legal thinkers who believed—or at least found it possible to believe—in the "reality" of the practices in question tended to write in defendants' favor. It is easier to "take seriously" others' beliefs when one is sympathetic to or in agreement with them. And vice versa. In *The Impossibility of Religious Freedom*, Winnifred Sullivan makes a similar point, noting the difficulties Judge Kenneth Ryskamp had in understanding claimants' religious practices and his tendency to attempt analogies or connections to his own religious beliefs and practices. This point again underscores the fact that individual background and experience matter, even when objectivity and fairness—blind justice—are stated principles. While scholars should not pin too much on individual judges' religious backgrounds, as if religious belief were a sure cipher for a person's deepest motivations (though this is how "religion" is often added to certain his-torical conversations), it can be analytically fruitful to focus on specific agents rather than a monolithic secular state.

be Minnehaha. The court could ponder these matters but not rule on them. Bessey made the point with a Prohibition-era joke, noting that the court had "no jurisdiction over any spirits except those banned by the prohibitory law, such as 'Bourbon,' 'Mountain Dew,' 'Forked Lightning,' and like distillates."[75] The regulation of religious activities was none of the court's business.

While the spirits themselves fell outside the court's regulatory powers, Spiritualists did not. The court's consideration of its capacity to regulate McMasters and her activities came down to the question of whether she was really religious. For this reason, the nature of the NSA was a sticking point. Among the Association's stated principles was the Golden Rule, which was biblical and thus religious, but yet somehow insufficiently religious, since plenty of nonreligious organizations—"the Masonic Order, the Elks, the Rotary Club, or the Boy Scouts"—believed in it too. Beyond the institutional context, the substance of McMasters's/Minnehaha's message, Bessey wrote, "sounds very secular to this court. It seems very like a Gypsy fortune teller, or the reading of the palm by some wrinkled old hag, or the interpretations of a crystal gazer in a freak side show." Whether it was religious or not, it was "attended with superstitious credulity and in the instant case tinged with hypocrisy."[76] Too fakey. Ultimately, the court ruled that it did not matter either way, since religious people still had to follow the law, and McMasters clearly had broken it.

"A COVER FOR SOME OLD-TIME WRONGDOING"

Alice Ashley, with whom this chapter opened, was not successful in her attempts to convince the judge that whatever happened during that police sting was sincere religion. But her defense hinted toward eventually successful strategies for demonstrating sincere belief, and it raised key issues that would come up repeatedly in religious freedom law. There was the matter of whether she was "pretending" to tell fortunes, and what that might mean. But she also raised another, perhaps even more fundamental issue. Ashley disputed the descriptor "fortune-telling" itself. She had only given

75. *McMasters*, 21 Okl. Cr. at 326.
76. *McMasters*, 21 Okl. Cr. at 323.

"advice" to Margaret Seller, she claimed.[77] She could predict the future, but that would not rightly be called fortune-telling. The correct term would be "prophesying" or "foretelling," religious practices that were not equivalent to fortune-telling and not mentioned in the vagrancy statute.

Like some other accused fortune-tellers—and, we will see, like many religious freedom claimants—Ashley used her institutional membership to demonstrate her religiosity. As Winnifred Sullivan has shown, even in the twenty-first century, "the church" persists as a conceptual and even phenomenological touchpoint for "religion" in law.[78] Before the sincerity test, in the early twentieth century, defining belief as "religious" remained largely a matter of membership and official doctrine. Some, like McMasters, were able to point out that their churches were incorporated, which provided a modicum of legitimacy.[79] Others, like Spokane's F. F. Neitzel, proved their membership in organizations such as the National Astrological Society.[80] The state often rejected the authority of these alternative licensures in a period of growing bureaucracy and the consolidation and protection of official secular knowledge. By these rejections, the secular state maintained the exclusive right to determine which beliefs were religious and who was authorized to hold them.

Ashley testified that she was a minister in the Brooklyn Spiritualist Society.[81] She was licensed by the New York Association of Spiritualists and the NSA, and she had been involved with NSA-related organizations

77. According to Sellers's testimony, Ashley (whom she apparently knew as "Jessie Ashley") closed her eyes and told her, "You are extremely sensitive owing to the fact that you have been dominated by somebody." Seller asked, "Will I get a position and will I get married?," to which Ashley responded, "The spirit of your Mother appears and advises you to use your own judgment. You will get the position for which you are looking very soon, and you will also marry and have two or three in the family." *Ashley*, 184 N.Y. App. Div. brief for defendant appellant.

78. Sullivan, *Church State Corporation*.

79. See also *Davis*, cited above at n. 65. Gertrude Davis was a pastor at the Asti-Universal Church in Cleveland. As in the McMasters case, the judge determined, citing State v. Neitzel, 69 Wash. 597, 125 Pac. 939 (1912), and *Reynolds*, that it was not legally relevant whether she was a pastor or not, nor whether the church was religious or not, since Davis "would have no greater right as a spiritualist or as a message bearer to tell fortunes contrary to the statute than the members of any other religious or secular group or system of religion or denominational religion."

80. *Neitzel*, 69 Wash. 597, 125 Pac. 939.

81. *Ashley*, 184 N.Y. App. Div. at 521.

since the 1890s.[82] The size and nature of the Brooklyn Spiritualist Society is unclear. The case brief mentioned that she "claimed" to be a minister but said nothing about the organization. Ashley had advertised her services in the *Brooklyn Daily Eagle* as early as 1898.[83] The paper announced daily "consultations" by appointment, as well as "seances Tuesdays, 2:30 P.M.; Wednesdays and Sundays, 8 P.M.; class Mondays, 8 P.M.," and "short talks, followed by flower readings," all led by "Mrs. Ashley."[84] The Sunday meetings usually took place in a public hall, but Ashley hosted the other services in her home. How many people attended, who those people were, whether the society had official ties to a national association—the answers to these questions are unknown. However, Ashley herself did have at least one national institutional connection. Dr. George B. Warne, of Chicago, the president of the NSA and founder of the periodical *National Spiritualist*, testified at trial as a witness for the defendant and vouched for her credentials.

As an authority in his church, and as a man, Warne answered the court's questions about his and Ashley's religion. Asked to explain why what Ashley did was not fortune-telling, Warne offered two answers. First, he explained that "foretelling," as practiced by mediums like Ashley, was "done directly under the inspiration of a spirit outside of the individual medium" and "was not in any way controlled by society." This communication did not require a special certification or training or acculturation, nor was it "confined to any creed or nationality." When spirits want to speak, they speak. On the other hand, the practice the law intended to prevent was done intentionally "for the sake of compensation or gain." The judge agreed that the purpose of fortune-telling bans, dating to early English vagrancy laws, "was the more effectually to prevent such practices whereby ignorant persons were frequently deluded and defrauded."[85] No one disputed that Ashley

82. Dyson, "Spiritualism and Crime," 305–306. Dyson found Ashley's applications for licensure in the Archives of the National Spiritualist Association of Churches, Lily Dale, NY.

83. Dyson, "Spiritualism and Crime," 306n7. Dyson reports that this is the earliest date she had found Ashley offering services in her home, but the notice she cites advertised a Sunday afternoon meeting at Tax Hall ("Religious Notices," *Brooklyn Eagle*, Apr. 16, 1898). The earliest advertisement I have found that lists Ashley's home address is from the following January. It announces "a spiritual meeting, especially devoted to tests" at her home on Tuesdays and Wednesdays in addition to the Sunday Tax Hall meeting ("Religious Notices," *Brooklyn Eagle*, Jan. 21, 1899).

84. "List of Sermons," *Brooklyn Daily Eagle*, May 11, 1907.

85. *Ashley*, 184 N.Y. App. Div. at 523.

had received a dollar. Thus, the legality of her actions hinged on whether she had told a fortune in order to be paid or, instead, she had foretold or given advice under a spirit's inspiration as part of her practice as a member of a religious community and then received a dollar as an unsolicited donation.[86]

Trying a second tactic to distinguish foretelling from fortune-telling, Warne turned to a well-known and reputable source: the Bible. "The foretelling," Warne exposited, "if practiced by mediums, comes under the same classification as a prophesy [sic] of the Old Testament. . . . You will find it recorded in substance by Paul." Judge William J. Kelly, a trustee at the (Roman Catholic) Church of St. Joseph, debated the biblical merits of Warne's distinction.[87] He doubted that whatever Ashley did was similar to the work of the Hebrew prophets. He did agree, though, that the prophets were not fortune-tellers, since the Deuteronomy advises the Lord's people not to "consult . . . soothsayers, or observe . . . dreams and omens. Neither let there be any wizard,—Nor charmer, nor any one that consulteth pythonic spirits, or fortune-tellers, or that seeketh truth from the dead. For the Lord abhorreth these things."[88] Looking next to the New Testament, Kelly noted that the apostle Paul "not only condemned witchcraft and fortune telling by the method of summoning departed spirits, which was the method followed by the defendant here, but, as we know, he had very decided views against women acting as prophets or ministers."[89] (Kelly and Warne brought

---

86. For a similar argument but in a much earlier case, with a different outcome, see State of Ohio v. Abigail Church. Gallia Common Pleas Court, May Term, 1823. Printed in *Reprint of Ohio Cases Published in the Weekly Law Gazette, Law and Bank Bulletin, American Law Register, Ohio Law Journal*, vol. 3 (Norwalk, OH: Lansing Printing, 1897), 85–91.

The issue of monetary payment, which came up in many fortune-telling cases and was included in many of the statutes, has come up repeatedly in the history of religion and law. Charging fees for certain religious services is legal, of course, but courts also have found that fixed pricing indicates a quid pro quo exchange and is thus taxable. Hernandez v. Commissioner, 490 U.S. 680 (1989).

87. The biographical information on Kelly is from "William J. Kelly," Historical Society of the New York Courts.

88. Kelly was quoting Deuteronomy 18:10–12 from the Douay-Rheims Bible. Translations of this passage vary significantly. As mentioned above, the same passage was cited in *Mitchell*, 222 Ala. at 389. It is worth noting that at the time of this translation (the early seventeenth century), English law classed "wizards" alongside fortune-tellers as vagabonds, distinguished from witches. See Beier, *Masterless Men*, 103–105.

89. *Ashley*, 184 N.Y. App. Div. at 522.

up other questions, such as how the Hebrew prophets made money—was "prophet" a *job*?—to which the biblical text offered no clear answers.) In general, a biblically based argument was a good way to prove the "religious" authenticity of a particular practice, but in this case Kelly remained unconvinced by Warne's exegetical efforts.

In the end, neither of Ashley's arguments—that she didn't tell a fortune or charge a fee, and that what she did do was a religious, even biblical practice— convinced Judge Kelly. Citing the Supreme Court's ruling in *Reynolds*, Kelly opined, "The State may not interfere with the religious beliefs and opinions of a citizen, but it may prohibit acts and practices which are deemed to be detrimental to the community."[90] That sentence was quoted in the 1920 annotations of New York's Bill of Rights, in the article guaranteeing "freedom of worship; religious liberty" (article 1, section 3).[91] Kelly concluded by noting that religious freedom is important, but religious claims always "should be carefully examined to see that they are not a cover for some old-time wrongdoing or indecency sought to be brought to life again. This seems to be such a case." Among the assumptions implicit in this statement is one that religious beliefs and practices necessarily cannot be "wrongdoing." These practices might be a cover for wrongdoing—sin masquerading as religion.[92] Like many agents of secular governance before him and after, Kelly defined true religion against its fakes.

INDIVIDUAL BELIEF

Just as individual sincere belief, apart from questions of the belief's veracity, was becoming a legal standard for free exercise claims, Spiritualists were making gains by appealing not to individual belief but to church member-

90. In addition to *Reynolds*, he cited The Late Corporation of the Church of Jesus Christ of Latter-Day Saints v. United States, 136 U.S. 1 (1890), and People v. Pierson, 176 N.Y. 201 (1903).

91. Robert C. Cumming and Frank B. Gilbert, eds., *Annotated Consolidated Laws of the State of New York*, 2nd ed., vol. 1 (Banks, 1920), 2.

92. See also Dill v. Hamilton, 137 Neb. 723, 291 N.W. 62 (1940), wherein the Supreme Court of Nebraska held that "the police power to prohibit public exhibitions for money-making purposes or 'for gain' extends to harmful, immoral, or indecent performances, though conducted in the name of religion. These are evils against which the statute is directed."

ship. In 1923 the Supreme Court of New Jersey protected an "act of prediction" because it was "made as a part of the public service of a Spiritualist
Church."[93] A few years later New York changed its statute, adding a sort
of ministerial exemption to the fortune-telling ban: "but this subdivision
shall not be construed to interfere with the belief, practices or usages of an
incorporated ecclesiastical governing body or the duly licensed teachers or
ministers thereof acting in good faith and without personal fee."[94] Blewett
Lee, for one, thought the law was "certainly a step in the right direction."[95]
In 1943 a court solidified this step by finding that because the Spiritualist Church had been incorporated in New York, its ministers should be
exempt from the statute.[96] Although these changes granted more freedom
to a certain set of (mostly white) Spiritualists, by requiring incorporation
and licensure, these changed further imbricated the state in the regulation
of religion and religious authority. From the middle of the twentieth century
on, religious freedom protections expanded considerably, especially after
the First Amendment was incorporated against the states. One important
change was the deinstitutionalization of religious belief, so that believers
no longer needed to prove membership in an organization to receive religious freedom protections. And yet, it was the legitimation of Spiritualism
as a religion, through their own organizational efforts and incorporation
through the state, that afforded New York Spiritualists their freedoms.

As this chapter has shown, early twentieth-century legal scholars and
jurists, as well as defendants, struggled with (or against) the implications of a
secular state evaluating religious truth or falsehood of religious claims. They
thus anticipated the sincerity test. That eventual solution—to try claimants
on the basis of their sincerity, leaving questions of religious truth aside—
was neither obvious nor inevitable. Blewett Lee proposed something like
this resolution, but it was not immediately or easily accepted, particularly
because the religious practices in question, specifically Spiritualist practices, were often understood to be fraudulent, insincere, or insufficiently
religious. Indeed, the eventual legal triumph of some Spiritualists was due in

93. State v. Delaney, 122 Atl. 890 (NJ 1923). See also Chester J. Antieau, "The Limitation of Religious Liberty," *Fordham Law Review* 18, no. 2 (1949): 221–241, which discusses
fortune-telling, noting the exceptionality of *Delaney* in 237n108.

94. N.Y. Laws 1929, c. 344.

95. Lee, "The Fortune-Teller Again," 56.

96. People on Complaint of Mirsberger, 46 N.Y.S. 2d 206 (1943). Corcos has argued that
this case "prefigured" the Supreme Court's decision in *Ballard* ("The Scrying Game," 101).

part to their self-conscious efforts to look like a "real" church or religion.[97] Just as Spiritualists and others were turning to incorporation and group membership to defend their religious freedom, in a different legal arena—conscientious objection to war—the law formally disregarded group affiliation and isolated individual believers' beliefs.

97. Dyson, "Spiritualism and Crime."

04

"RELIGIOUS TRAINING AND BELIEF"

FROM 1940 UNTIL THE EARLY 1970S, thousands upon thousands of men in the United States explained their religious beliefs, carefully and precisely and sometimes at great length, on paper. And thousands of other men read those explanations, conferred with each other, interviewed the believers, and decided their fate. That fate could be military service, a work camp, prison, or perhaps a return to regular life. The men filling out the paperwork were conscientious objectors, who opposed war because of their religious beliefs. And their stories—and the vast bureaucracy through which they were interpreted and processed—shaped the administration of religious freedom and the rise of sincerely held religious belief.

With the advent of the sincerity test in *United States v. Ballard* in 1944, religious freedom depended more and more on investigation. If an individual's belief were to be protected, agents of the state would need to find that belief deep inside and determine that it was both religious and sincere. The sincerity test came to shape free exercise law and, eventually, popular understandings of what religion is into the twenty-first century. This occurred in a number of arenas, the most prominent of which was the courts. In the 1930s and 1940s, a slow-building sea change in First Amendment jurisprudence was under way, led prominently by Jehovah's Witnesses.[1] In cases in 1940 and 1947, the Supreme Court incorporated the free exercise and establishment clauses, respectively, against the states, meaning that the clauses applied not only to actions by the federal government but to those of states

---

1. See Peters, *Judging Jehovah's Witnesses*, and M. James Penton, "Jehovah's Witnesses and the Secular State: A Historical Analysis of Doctrine," *Journal of Church and State* 21, no. 1 (Winter, 1979): 55–72.

as well.[2] This change dramatically expanded the number of potential and actual cases. Because of ordinary religious actors and skilled lawyers, courts protected the free exercise of a growing number of believers, and religious freedom was beginning to be conceptualized as a civil right, even a human right, that might take precedence over other liberal goods, such as national unity or public order. This era of expansion led to *United States v. Seeger*, the 1965 conscientious objection case that included religiously unaffiliated nontheists within the purview of the authentically and sincerely religious. It is a story of religious freedom, individual sincere belief, and the rights of conscience. But it is also a story of paperwork, bureaucracy, and investigation.

Although the conscientious objection court cases dealt with the definition of religion and have since been cited by courts and scholars as useful for free exercise cases, they were not First Amendment cases. Conscientious objection is not a constitutional right; it is statutory, granted by Congress. To understand *Seeger*, then, and its place in the history of sincerely held religious belief, we must wade into a bureaucratic morass. Despite its pretensions to orderliness and fairness, the Selective Service system, including its procedures for handling conscientious objection claims, did not run smoothly and uniformly. It was a mess, and nearly all conscientious objection cases ended mired somewhere in it, with objectors' paperwork accepted or rejected, a panel accepting or rejecting their appeal, and the ensuing consequences. A select few objectors' cases made it to federal courts, where judges carefully considered the language of the draft acts and the meaning of "religious training and belief." Administrative and judicial logics are different, and the circumstances of their thinking are different. But both of them are essential to secular governance and, in this case, the rise of sincerely held religious belief and the remaking of U.S. religious freedom.

Close readings of the cases and laws illuminate complex discursive work—here, nearly endless parsing of the phrase "religious training and belief"—that ensures or denies freedom. But such readings are incomplete without analysis of what goes in to the "making of law," the multifaceted processes in which members of Congress, conscientious objectors, draft counselors, activists, lawyers, and federal judges all participated. Although the court decisions are carefully measured statements of secular ideology, delineating the parameters of the religious, they were not detached from or dis-

2. Minersville School District v. Gobitis, 310 U.S. 586 (1940); West Virginia State Board of Education v. Barnette, 319 U.S. 624 (1943). See Gordon, *The Spirit of the Law*, chap. 2, "The Worship of Idols."

interested in the politics that led to them. Scholars of religion have analyzed these Supreme Court cases, especially *Seeger*, which turns on the sort of definitional questions (with actual stakes, winners, and losers) to which certain religion scholars gravitate. Other historians, as Megan Threlkeld has noted, have tended to focus on either the cases on the one hand or conscientious objectors and the peace movement on the other.[3] This chapter attempts to examine both, offering a reading of the cases that is grounded in analysis of the bureaucratic procedures that led to them. Saba Mahmood argued that "the two dimensions of political secularism—its regulatory impulse and its promise of freedom—are thoroughly intertwined, each necessary to the enactment of the other."[4] If the mid-century conscientious objection cases expanded the "promise of [religious] freedom," that promise enacted and was enacted by regulatory procedures. This history begins with the Selective Training and Service Act.

SECTION 5(G)

In 1940 Congress passed a new draft act requiring men between the ages of twenty-one and thirty-six to register for the Selective Service.[5] During World War II, the Selective Service, a complex system of sorting and tracking, not only determined whom would be drafted into the armed forces to fight overseas but also oversaw sweeping manpower mobilization efforts. The 1940 act required "alternative service" for those unable to fight, and administrators used deferments and exemptions to slot men into work sectors of "national importance." Conscientious objectors (COs) made up only a small percentage of the men processed by the system, and their claims would be evaluated and investigated. The resultant court cases had an outsized influence on the history of religious freedom and sincerely held religious belief, as they handled fundamental liberal issues such as the nature of individual freedom, the limits of state power, the definition of "religious," and the character of the sincere believer. But, in the narrowest sense, they

3. Threlkeld, "'The War Power Is Not a Blank Check.'"
4. Mahmood, *Religious Difference in a Secular Age*, 21.
5. Selective Service Training and Service Act of 1940, Pub.L. 76–783, 54 Stat. 85 (1940). On the history of this act, including President Franklin Roosevelt's support for the idea and the lobbying efforts that led to the bill, see Flynn, *The Draft*, 9–52.

were about interpreting a single vexing passage: section 5(g) of the Selective Training and Service Act.

The 1940 act identified the conscientious objector as "any person ... who, by reason of religious training and belief, is conscientiously opposed to participation in war in any form."[6] This language marked a significant change from the previous draft act of 1917, which required objectors to be members of a historic peace church, such as the Mennonites or the Society of Friends (Quakers). The 1940 act eliminated the membership requirement, so now it was up to the individual believer to prove his conscientious opposition. While this change greatly raised the number of potentially successful objectors, it was actually a partial failure for pacifists. During the drafting of the bill, a coalition of representatives from peace churches, the Fellowship of Reconciliation, and the War Resisters League testified before Congress to argue for the protection of nonreligious objectors too. Some members of Congress seemed amenable to the idea that humanistic or philosophical objections to war might be worth protecting alongside religious ones, yet questions about sincerity lingered. They wanted, as one historian phrased it, "a satisfactory standard of sincere conscientious objection, and it was on this point that the pacifist argument on behalf of secular conscientious objection failed."[7] At least for the time being, "secular" objectors would not be covered by section 5(g). Refiguring the terminology, though, I would argue that "secular" objectors were the *only* kinds of objectors covered. The conscientious objector became an iteration of the sincere believer: a secular subject, often coded as white and masculine, whose beliefs are rational, deeply held, and individualistic rather than ritualistic or communal.[8]

6. 54 Stat. 885 at 889.

7. Glen, "Secular Conscientious Objection," 61.

8. Although the 1940 act made significant changes, the imagination of the CO as a sincere believer rather than simply a church member was not new. In 1919, before he became Chief Justice of the Supreme Court, Harlan Stone argued that "both morals and sound policy require that the state should not violate the conscience of the individual. All our history gives confirmation to the view that liberty of conscience has a moral and social value which makes it worthy of preservation at the hands of the state. So deep in its significance and vital, indeed, is it to the integrity of man's moral and spiritual nature that nothing short of the self-preservation of the state should warrant its violation" ("The Conscientious Objector," *Columbia University Quarterly* 21, no. 4 [Oct., 1919]: 253–272, at 269). By locating conscience at the very core of the person, Stone naturalized religious belief as part of "man." This passage was quoted by Justice Tom Clark in support of the Court's opinion in *Seeger*, 380 U.S. at 170.

What counted as "religious training and belief?" That was a question for the courts. But federal courts turned out conflicting interpretations, and so Congress tried to clarify by amending the section in the draft act of 1948. Between 1940 and 1948 there were numerous cases and much debate in law journals about how best to interpret the statute. The first question, though, was not about what "religious training and belief" meant or why consciences should be protected; it was about *how* to protect consciences. Procedural problems produced theoretical questions, and vice versa. Hard cases led to statutory changes, which led to more hard cases, which eventually led to *Seeger*, which led to another statutory change. But what happened in courts and Congress was only a slice of the story of conscientious objection in this period.

The court cases were culminations—or, sometimes, not-quite-endings—of processes that began years earlier. The question of what to do with conscientious objectors led to mundane logistical problems to be worked out at numerous stages by various agents of the secular state. Judges drew from philosophy, literature, and history to write carefully considered opinions. But the secular always intersected with and even stemmed from governing techniques of political secularism. Before judges ever heard their cases, conscientious objectors had already interacted with local draft boards, federal investigators, generals, and sometimes police officers and prison guards. And they did not face the state alone. Lawyers, advocacy groups, and some religious denominations and parachurch organizations provided advice, counsel, and financial support. These parties, with varied and often conflicted interests, made law together.[9]

A BUREAUCRATIC PROCESS

Before the courts tried to define "religious training and belief," other state actors had to assess a petitioner's sincerity and religiosity. Dozens of conscientious objection cases wound their way through the federal courts in the 1940s, and more followed until the draft was suspended in 1973. Each case revolved around the assessment of an individual believer's sincerity and religiosity as he subjected them to scrutiny and attempted to translate

9. The "making of law" is relational, produced by networks and interactions. See Latour, *The Making of Law*.

them into the language of the state. Conscientious objector organizations paid attention to these shifting standards and helped objectors choose their words with shrewd precision. Dozens of cases made it to federal courts, but thousands began and ended at the local level, before the hundreds of local draft boards across the country. All of these cases exposed individuals' idiosyncratic lives and beliefs to the formal, calculative reason of state bureaucracy. They filled out forms. The forms, by asking questions and providing the blanks on which to write, disciplined believers into certain expressions of belief. In this way, the character of the conscientious objector as sincere believer was formalized.

The sincerity question, then, was whether they filled out their forms accurately. To become legible as a sincere believer—as someone whose "religious training and belief" is *the* source of his objection to all wars—a petitioner had to translate his beliefs into the appropriate language and, when it came to in-person hearings, to comport himself properly. He presented his case to numerous state actors across multiple formats. As much as the forms disciplined and formalized, and although judges and legislators attempted to develop workable tests, sincerity remained an intensely personal matter. There is no general standard, no definition to check it against. It is always about *this* believer, not the abstracted belief. There is no sincere belief as such—only sincere believers and beliefs sincerely held. These beliefs, imagined to reside inside the individual, had to be extracted, examined, and investigated.

The bureaucratic steps of the labyrinthine draft process, much more than the federal judiciary, is where most cases were decided. First, the objector requested a Form 47. Ideally, this would happen when he first registered for the Selective Service, but often it happened later, because of age or changed beliefs or, commonly, because he had received a student deferment or other exemption at first and thus had not felt a need to register as a conscientious objector. (Draft counselors always advised against this last strategy, since a declaration of conscientious objection when one didn't "need" it would be helpful evidence of consistency and sincerity later on.) Form 47 reproduced the language of section 5(g) of the draft act, below which petitioners would sign their names to indicate their objection. The form then instructed the petitioner to "describe the nature of your belief which is the basis of your claim" and "explain how, when, and from whom or from what source you received the training and acquired the belief." It asked for evidence—"describe the actions and behavior in your life which in your opinion most conspicuously demonstrate the consistency and depth of your religious conviction"—and about past public expressions, such as speeches or writings. Many petitioners' reasons for objection did not precisely fit the available wording, and so they attached longer written explanations of their beliefs.

Petitioners then appeared before a local draft board, staffed by at least three and usually five community volunteers, all men, mostly veterans. There were about six thousand local boards throughout the country.[10] These boards dealt not only with conscientious objectors but with all inductees and those seeking deferments as students, fathers, ministers, agricultural workers, and other exempt categories. The Selective Service developed policies and procedures for separating the legitimate claims from the fraudulent. Marriages and childbirths, for instance, were sometimes suspiciously conveniently timed. Amy Rutenberg has described the investigatory operations undertaken by local boards, including the Selective Service's "detailed policy on determining the date of a baby's conception that included discussion of a woman's menstrual cycle and methods of counting forward from the first day of her last period or the baby's quickening and backward from its delivery date."[11] In the first years of U.S. involvement in World War II, deferments and exemptions were relatively easy to get, so the Selective Service added stricter guidelines and tried to crack down on fraudulent claims.[12]

When an applicant issued a conscientious objection claim, the local board would evaluate his file and potentially ask follow-up or clarifying questions, after which it could approve or reject the application for exemption. If, upon reviewing these written materials, the local board rejected the claim, the registrant then could appeal either in writing or in person. Because the local draft board was not really trained to judge matters of sincerity and religiosity, the Department of Justice supplied boards with legal guides and sets of questions they might ask of an objector. Despite attempts to develop regulatory standards, and despite courts' rulings on the statute's meaning, board members might have their own ideas about who should and should not be afforded the status of conscientious objector.[13] Idiosyncrasies,

10. *Selective Service in Victory: The Fourth Report of the Director of Selective Service, 1944–1945; With a Special Supplement for 1946–1947* (Washington, DC: GPO, 1948), 422.

11. Rutenberg, *Rough Draft*, 25.

12. In an effort to raise the standard, in 1943 the Selective Service created a new class of deferments for men whose families would face "extreme hardship and privation" if they were drafted. See Rutenberg, *Rough Draft*, 45–47.

13. Even into the 1960s, some local board members were either unaware of legal standards or flagrantly disregarded them. One objector's claim was denied, for instance, because

political ideologies, religious prejudice, and racism could shape local boards' decisions. If, for whatever reason, the board rejected the claim again, or if the members were unable to reach a definitive conclusion, the case moved to an appeal board. At this stage the registrant became subject to an FBI investigation.

The petitioner would also interview with a hearing officer, who was appointed by the Department of Justice. Based on that interview and his reading of the FBI's report on their investigation, the hearing officer wrote another report. This was an especially crucial stage, since the Hearing Officer's Report was given to the appeal board and was the main criterion on which they based their decision; it also could be cited in later court cases. In the Circuit Court case of Frederick Reel, for example, the court quoted the hearing officer's summation that Reel was "a sincere philosophic humanitarian, which may be regarded as a sociological concept of the highest order."[14] Which is to say, *sincere* but not *religious*. One supporter, writing on behalf of an objector, recounted his own experiences: "[I] have had to prove my sincerity before a hearing officer and realized, with growing horror, as I sat there that the success or failure of my claim depended on the accordance of our personalities—the hearing officer's and mine. What else could he go on, save personal likes or dislikes?"[15] Hearing officers wielded considerable power. As fact-based and calculative as these investigative, inquisitional procedures were meant to be, a pivotal step involved a powerful man critiquing and evaluating an applicant's affect and self-presentation.

Next, the appeal board reviewed the Hearing Officer's Report along with whatever materials the petitioner submitted. These would include Form 47, sometimes with appended pages for further elaboration. The appeal board did not interview petitioners in person, so their impression of his personality was based solely on these materials. If the appeal board rejected the claim, the file could be passed on to yet another board, the Presidential Appeal Board, staffed primarily by military officers. They issued a simple

---

his local board did not "consider it within its province to grant CO status to any but members of the historic peace churches." Letter from petitioner's mother to Bob Seeley, Feb. 1, 1969. Series V, Box 30 [petitioner name redacted]. Central Committee for Conscientious Objectors Records, Swarthmore College Peace Collection, Swarthmore, PA.

14. United States ex rel. Reel v. Badt, 141 F.2d 845, 847 (1944).

15. Robert G. McGuire to Paul French, Jan. 8, 1943, Series E, 1, Box 19, Center on Conscience and War (CCW) Records, SCPC.

verdict of "accept" or "reject," without additional comment, based on a review of the entire file.[16]

In theory, the 1940 act could open up conscientious objection to a much larger set of applicants. And that is in fact what happened, but bias and inequality nevertheless permeated the system. At its most basic, the process hinged on a panel of mainly white men who were expected to assess the character of an individual they were meeting face to face. Board members had their own political and religious ideas, and most of them were veterans, who were often not very sympathetic toward those who refused to fight for their country. Objectors affiliated with nonsectarian pacifist organizations found their claims routinely denied because they were seen as "political" rather than "religious" actors (and their politics were often strongly opposed by board members). A board refused even to consider the claims of one man who had a German mother and a Japanese father, was the chairman of the Chicago chapter of the War Resisters League, and had been defamed by a district attorney stoking "much newspaper talk of an espionage ring, sedition and sex crimes."[17] He was sentenced to three years at Sandstone Federal Penitentiary in Minnesota, where he served nearly his full time before successfully applying for parole.[18]

Black objectors often faced particularly unsympathetic audiences and, furthermore, lacked institutional support or help from peace organizations.[19] Among the nearly 12,000 conscientious objectors during World

16. In many cases, these materials included a rebuttal to the Hearing Officer's report, written by the petitioner. For more on the procedures outlined here, see Heisler, "The Law versus the Conscientious Objector," which includes citations and descriptions of cases from the author's own files. See also Smith and Bell, "The Conscientious-Objector Program." Smith and Bell both worked for the Conscientious Objector Section of the Selective Service; Bell was the chief of the section. On the Selective Service and administrative procedure more generally, see Wilson, "The Selective Service System."

17. Frank Olmstead to Paul French, Feb. 27, 1942. Details culled from numerous documents in Robert Asahi Chino's file, Series E, 2, Box 5, CCW Records.

18. Ellen Hinton (Secretary to Charles F. Boss Jr.) to Paul Comly French, Sept. 2, 1942; Bob Fangmeier to File Room (NSBRO), office memo, Nov. 27, 1944, Series E, 2, Box 5, CCW Records.

19. This was also true under the 1917 act, when institutional affiliation was required. Members of the Church of God in Christ, for instance, met heavy resistance at local boards and frequently were unable to receive deferments. See Kornweibel, "Investigate Everything," 150–152.

War II, only 122 were Black.[20] Black leaders advocated for more Black people to sit on local draft boards, but General Lewis Hershey, who directed the Selective Service, did nothing of substance to ensure equity. Instead, in his response to a Morgan State College registrar who had spoken out against white supremacy in the draft process, Hershey insisted, "The manner in which the 6,442 local boards throughout the country have exercised their function of selection has served to strengthen the confidence of all citizens, and particularly Negro citizens, in the increasing realization of our democratic aims."[21] Only 250 Black men sat on those boards.[22]

These procedures were not altogether removed from First Amendment issues. In fact, administrative and bureaucratic processes were entwined with the language, logic, and logistics of judicial decisions and constitutional interpretations. For instance, the wording of the questions supplied to local draft boards was designed to slide registrants as cleanly as possible into the categories "sincere" and "religious," as determined by courts' interpretations of federal statutes—which drew their wording from judges' opinions (including dissents, as in the 1948 draft act). While judges and administrators were embroiled in the same system, their logic and ways of thinking were different. Judges had clerks, books, and hours to think about cases. Experts prepared briefs, and specialized attorneys argued on both sides. The judge knew that his opinion should be not only well reasoned and thoroughly considered but also carefully and precisely worded, since it would establish precedent and be quoted and cited again. The local draft board, by contrast, was a panel of volunteers who had dozens of other cases to deal with, and their only sources were a Form 47 and a man appearing before them.[23] Their role was to be cogs in a massive machine, helping it run as smoothly as possible by sorting people appropriately, insofar as they

20. Flynn, *The Draft*, 99.

21. Letter quoted in George Q. Flynn, "Selective Service and American Blacks during World War II," *Journal of Negro History* 69, no. 1 (Winter, 1984): 14–25, at 17.

22. Flynn, *The Draft*, 99.

23. Thanks to Mike McVicar, whose comments on the panel "America's Bureaucracy of Transcendence: Government Legitimation of American Religion" at the 2017 American Academy of Religion Annual Meeting helped me clarify this point about administrative and judicial logics—and the uses of bureaucratic ignorance as well as knowledge. Thanks also to the panelists, Katie Holscher, Mike Graziano, Brad Stoddard, and Sarah Dees, each of whose papers helped me think through this issue.

could discern.[24] This system produced varying results, at times violating due process, as boards mismanaged the procedures out of ignorance, inexperience, prejudice against the petitioner, or occasional outright disagreement with established legal standards.[25]

PAPERWORK, MEDIATION, AND TRANSLATION

Sorting through thousands of conscientious objection claims required massive effort and attention—and reams of paperwork. These enactments of political secularism involved identifying sincere believers and distinguishing "religious training and belief" from other kinds of training and belief. Through conceptual and theoretical these issues could be, their administration was mostly mundane. Secular governance is sometimes violent and dramatic, but sometimes it's paperwork: filling out forms, processing those forms, checking boxes, filing files.[26] The documents themselves were actants in a network that produced the character of the objector as a sincere believer.[27] In his ethnographic study of paperwork and bureaucracy

24. For another example of how judges and administrators think and work differently, and how the latter shape law, see Pascoe, *What Comes Naturally*. Studying miscegenation law in the United States, Pascoe shows how, "in much the same way that a seemingly natural biological 'fact' of race was produced in courtrooms, a seemingly natural documentary 'fact' of race was produced in marriage license bureaus" (133). I am suggesting something similar: that the "fact" of religion was produced by local draft boards and appeal boards just as much as by legislators and judges.

25. Heisler, "The Law versus the Conscientious Objector," offers several examples of due-process problems at the local level (442–466). E. Raymond Wilson, "Evolution of the C.O. Provisions in the 1940 Conscription Bill," *Quaker History* 64, no. 1 (Spring, 1975): 3–15, offers a useful overview.

26. I am grateful to Ronit Stahl for her clarifying conversation about this. I first wrote about this in "Paperwork Secularism and the Governance of American Religions," Nov. 26, 2017, "Religion in American History" blog.

27. A number of scholars have turned recently to paperwork and government bureaucracy as a trove for American religion. I am particularly inspired by Judith Weisenfeld's approach in *New World A-Coming*, which Laura McTighe aptly summarizes: "Weisenfeld attunes us to the manifold roles of state agents, including low-level administrators, in whose hands categorizations of religion and racialization were (and are) made daily. It also illuminates the fissures and fractures in the systems, as those living in the shadows of power

in Pakistan, Matthew Hull argued, "Just as discourse has long been recognized as a dense mediator between subjects and the world, we need to
see graphic artifacts not as neutral purveyors of discourse, but as media-
tors that shape the significance of linguistic signs inscribed on them."[28]
The forms reproduced statutory language, but when objectors signed their
names and added explanations and marked up the language, they altered
that language's meaning. The words that objectors wrote on forms would
be repeated on reports and quoted in court, and they would serve as guides
for future objectors' words. The Form 47s (and their successor, the Form
150s) bore the language of section 5(g), which, when it was amended to section 6(j), borrowed language from the Supreme Court. The Form 47s were
printed, mailed to petitioners, written on with pens or pencils or typed on
with typewriters (sometimes with a draft counselor's help), read by bureaucrats, and filed. The forms themselves—thousands of them, filled out and
marked up—shaped believers' beliefs as well as the meaning of the statute
and, eventually, its words.

The words and the paper mediated a network that included a lot of
people. The stakes of navigating it were high, and objectors needed help
to do so. Many of them, especially those who were not members of historic peace churches, sought representation as they presented their cases
to the Selective Service. In 1940 peace church leaders from the Brethren
Service Committee, the American Friends Service Committee (AFSC), and
the Mennonite Central Committee formed the National Service Board for
Religious Objectors (NSBRO) as an intermediary between objectors and
the government.[29] The Board worked directly with objectors as well as with
General Hershey, the director of the Selective Service, to whom objectors
directed their appeals.[30] The Quaker activist Paul Comly French served

---

contested their governance and built their own subjectivities" (McTighe, "Introduction:
Roundtable: 'Religio-Racial Identity' as Challenge and Critique," *Journal of the American
Academy of Religion* 88, no. 2 [June, 2020]: 299–303, at 302).

28. Hull, *Government of Paper*, 13.

29. The NSBRO later added representatives from the Federal Council of Churches, the
Fellowship of Reconciliation, and other groups. They later merged with the National Inter-
religious Service Board for Conscientious Objectors (NISBCO) and became the Center on
Conscience and War (CCW), which is still in existence. See https://centeronconscience.org.

30. On Hershey, see Nicholas A. Krehbiel, *General Lewis B. Hershey and Conscientious
Objection during World War II* (University of Missouri Press, 2011); and George Q. Flynn,
Lewis B. Hershey, Mr. Selective Service (University of North Carolina Press, 1985).

as the NSBRO's executive secretary.[31] He handled much of the organization's day-to-day correspondence, coaching objectors as they made their way through the system and connecting them with other organizations and resources.

The NSBRO sent out questionnaires to men who wanted to become conscientious objectors. On these one-page documents (NSB-123-A), men recorded their local board number, induction date, the classification from their local board, the classification from the appeal board, the classification they sought, and the outcome of their hearing if they had had one. There were two larger spaces, the first of which was labeled "RELIGION (Religious training and present religious belief which are bases for claim for classification) As much of Form 47 as registrant thinks pertinent." Here, reproducing the section 5(g) phrasing, the NSBRO wanted to know *how* the registrant had explained his religion on his Form 47. This was especially important if he had been unsuccessful in his attempt to become a conscientious objector. There was also space at the bottom of the questionnaire for "pertinent facts," where many objectors wrote about their hearing, sometimes adding pages to correct what they believed to be mistakes and misrepresentations in the Hearing Officer's Report.

If one's claim were at last successful and he were granted conscientious objector status, during this period he avoided military work but still had to do "work of national importance." Beyond raising a military, in this period the draft was for cultivating "manpower," creating essentially a national workforce. As Amy Rutenberg has shown, forms of alternative service often favored middle-class white men. In fact, she argues, the whole national debate about manpower and universal military training was about citizenship and the ideal national subject, who was "implicitly defined as white and male."[32] One could receive a deferment for being a student or married father, or one could receive an alternate assignment if one had expertise in a medi-

31. French had been an influential antiwar activist and a journalist for the *Philadelphia Record*. He also had written two relevant books: *Common Sense Neutrality: Mobilizing for Peace* (Hastings House, 1939) and *We Won't Murder: Being the Story of Men Who Followed Their Conscientious Scruples and Helped Give Life to Democracy* (Hastings House, 1940).

32. Rutenberg, *Rough Draft*, 80. Here she is writing specifically about Universal Military Training, but the point applies more broadly. On citizenship and white heteronormativity in this period, see Margot Canaday, *The Straight State: Sexuality and Citizenship in Twentieth-Century America* (Princeton University Press, 2009).

cal field or the sciences.[33] Agricultural workers received deferments as well, although this standard was not always consistently applied.[34]

Conscientious objectors who did not receive other sorts of deferments were converted to manpower in Civilian Public Service (CPS) camps. The CPS program, designed by peace church leaders in collaboration with the federal government, set up 152 work camps around the country where conscientious objectors labored in manufacturing, forestry, and agriculture. Between 1941 and 1947 some twelve thousand religious objectors were assigned to the CPS camps.[35] The NSBRO also facilitated these assignments, and there was a form for that (NSB 101). Objectors filled out their work history, listed any skills that might be of use, and could indicate what type of work they would like to do or particular camps at which they would prefer to be assigned.[36] Some objectors refused to participate in the alternative service, for a variety of reasons, not least of which was that many of the CPS camps were poorly run, and objectors were subjected to long hours of hard

33. Rutenberg, *Rough Draft*, also shows how ongoing debates about masculinity and the structure of society were central to manpower policy, and how matters of race and class structured the unequal distribution of manpower resources.

34. There were also concerns about "job jumpers," who took a certain job, such as agricultural work, just in time to receive a deferment and then left that line of work. Rutenberg, *Rough Draft*, 46–47.

35. A wonderful digital project on the Civilian Public Service camps collects stories and documents and includes many photographs; see https://civilianpublicservice.org. There is a small body of historical scholarship on the CPS. In addition to archival records, I have consulted Heather T. Frazer and John O'Sullivan, eds., *We Have Just Begun to Not Fight: An Oral History of Conscientious Objectors in Civilian Public Service During World War II* (Twayne, 1996) as well as several local histories. See, e.g., Mitchell L. Robinson, "Men of Peace in a World at War: Civilian Public Service in New York State, 1941–1946," *New York History* 78, no. 2 (Apr., 1997): 173–210; and Charles B. Hirsch, "The Civilian Public Service Camp Program in Indiana," *Indiana Magazine of History* 46, no. 3 (Sept., 1950): 259–281. Some denominational and institutional histories were written in the years immediately following the CPS period. See, e.g., Melvin Gingerich, *Service for Peace: A History of Mennonite Civilian Public Service* (Mennonite Central Committee, 1949); Leslie Eisan, *Pathways of Peace: A History of the Civilian Public Service Program Administered by the Brethren Service Committee* (Brethren Publishing Group, 1948); and Mulford Quickert Sibley and Philip E. Jacob, *Conscription of Conscience: The American State and the Conscientious Objector, 1940–1947* (Cornell University Press, 1952).

36. There was also a space to check which "administrative agency under which you prefer to serve." The options were the American Friends Service Committee, the Brethren Service Committee, the Mennonite Central Committee, and the Association of Catholic Conscientious Objectors.

work without pay. In a few infamous cases, camp administrators conducted experiments on conscientious objectors—starvation, sleep deprivation, or testing the toxicity of seawater or the ability to perform physical labor in extreme weather (e.g., "riding a stationary bike five hours a day every day of the week in the tropical heat").[37] The War Resisters League denounced the CPS because conscription to work (without pay) still stripped objectors of their freedom. During this period more than six thousand men were imprisoned for not reporting to camps, deserting camps, or otherwise failing to cooperate after their conscientious objection claims (and appeals) were denied.

Reading through the NSBRO's files on the imprisoned men shows religious diversity and eclecticism—Swedenborgians, Pentecostals, members of Father Divine's Peace Mission, and at least one minister from the Temple of the Jeweled Cross in Hollywood—that perplexed draft boards and eventually pressed at the edges of statutory interpretation.[38] These files show the impasses, gaps, frustrations, and difficulties as men tried to translate their beliefs into the language of the forms. And sometimes they outright refused to submit to the calculative reason of state bureaucracy. One Jehovah's Witness from Montana sent back the NSBRO questionnaire blank. He could not fill out the "religion" section: "I am a Christian and not a religionist. All religion and all religionists are soon to be destroyed at Armageddon." He should be exempt from service, he argued, but "the draft board have chosen to follow Satan the Devil and will have to answer for their wicked course to God Almighty The Creator of the Universe."[39] His father wrote to General Hershey directly, requesting an agricultural deferment: "Without him I will not be able to operate the farm," he pleaded. "He has spent his whole life farming."[40] Nevertheless, he was assigned to a CPS camp. When he failed to report, staying home to serve as a farmer and a minister of the Gospel,

---

37. Anne M. Yoder, "Human Guinea Pigs in CPS Detached Service, 1943–1946," Nov., 2010, Swarthmore College Peace Collection. https://www.swarthmore.edu/library/peace/conscientiousobjection/CPSResources/MEDICAL%20RESEARCH.pdf. The quoted study was Unit 115.12, directed by Jerome W. Conn and Margaret Johnson at the University of Michigan Hospital. See "CPS Camp Number 115," https://civilianpublicservice.org/camps/115, which has photographs as well as citations of relevant scholarship. See also Taylor, *Acts of Conscience*, esp. 80–88.

38. Series E, 1 and E, 2, CCW Records.

39. Boyd Breazeale to NSBRO, Mar. 20, 1943. Series E, 1, Box 9a, CWW Records.

40. Amos W. Breazeale to Lewis B. Hershey, Apr. 20, 1943. Series E, 1, Box 9a, CCW Records.

he was arrested and served time in federal prison.[41] As the historian Joseph Kip Kosek framed the question, "Had the CPS system been a victory for the Christian nonviolent lobby, or was it rather a timid compromise with a proto-Fascist state?"[42] Some objectors answered with the latter. Many of them submitted willingly to incarceration, their convictions preventing them from working in the CPS camps. Even though the camps were run by peace churches, they were still wrapped up in militarism, in league with an inherently violent state. And it was especially difficult to detach work of "national importance" from the war effort, practically or conceptually, during World War II.

I will offer one extended example to show the winding, difficult path these claims took and the hardships faced by those who maintained their conscientious objection to the whole system. John Andrew Shubin was a dairy farmer in California and a member of the Russian Molokan Christian Holy Jumpers, a small pacifist sect.[43] His grandfather was imprisoned in Russia for refusing to fight, and his father had done the same in California during World War I.[44] John was assigned to a CPS camp and never reported, and he was arrested too. At his criminal hearing, he told Judge Leon Yankwich that he wanted to be exempt "from things relating to war, or anything connected with war." "You are exempt," the judge replied, arguing that work in the camps "is not war activity at all. They make you chop wood. . . . What is there in your religious feeling that prevents you from chopping wood that may be used by the Government to keep people warm?" They went back and forth, with the judge trying to work out a solution that would keep Shubin out of jail. Shubin did not budge. The judge asked him whether he

41. Ralph Beechy (Director, Camp 64, Terry, MT) to NSBRO, July 19, 1943. Series E, 1, Box 9a, CCW Records.

42. Kosek, *Acts of Conscience*, 165.

43. See Pauline V. Young, "The Russian Molokan Community in Los Angeles," *American Journal of Sociology* 35, no. 3 (Nov., 1929): 393–402; and Susan W. Hardwick, "Religion and Migration: The Molokan Experience," *Yearbook of the Association of Pacific Coast Geographers* 55 (1993): 127–141.

44. John Andrew Shubin to NSBRO, Aug. 5, 1945, Series E, 1, Box 74, CCW Records. On Molokans and objection in World War I, see William Haas Moore, "Prisoners in the Promised Land: The Molokans in World War I," *Journal of Arizona History* 14, no. 3 (Winter, 1973): 281–302. Moore mentions a few Shubins, though I cannot find a direct relation between those he mentions and John Andrew Shubin. Shubin is a common last name among Molokans; see the Russian Molokan Cemetery (Commerce, CA) page at https://www.findagrave.com/cemetery/8313/russian-molokan-cemetery. John Andrew Shubin is buried there, along with over two hundred other Shubins.

would reconsider if he could be assured that he would not do "any military work but purely work of national importance," to which Shubin responded, "The Holy Ghost forbids me to accept anything." Finally, Judge Yankwich concluded, "The Holy Ghost won't forbid you to accept a sentence in jail," sentencing him to six months' imprisonment. He concluded, "All right, you fight it out with the Holy Ghost there [in jail]. I say that with all due reverence, gentlemen."[45]

Shubin was sent to Tucson Prison Road Camp, where his religious scruples prevented him from accepting the hard labor required of incarcerated persons. Facing a less sympathetic audience than Judge Yankwich, he was sent to a prison in Texas, where he faced one hundred days of solitary confinement. Upon his release he was malnourished and needed surgery for a double hernia. Less than a year later Shubin was classified as 1-A and required to report to his local board, where he received a deferment for about seven months, at which point he was again classified 1-A. He was called to report to a CPS camp. Again he didn't show, instead going back to work on the dairy farm.[46] The leaders of his church wrote letters on his behalf, explaining their religion and attesting to Shubin's sincerity: "He is a true follower of these teachings for which our fathers were forced to leave Russia because of military conscription. He is very sincere."[47] It didn't work. They wrote again the next month, and the month after that they sent a petition. In an attempt to clear up "this misunderstanding between our sincere young men and the Selective Service Act," the petition outlined the group's history, from their early nineteenth-century forced migration (owing to their refusal to take up arms) to Trans-Caucasia and Siberia to their 1881 migration to the United States. They followed the Holy Spirit to the United States for freedom. They pleaded one more time, "Is there another land on earth that gives the freedom of America[,] and is not the foundation

45. United States v. John Andrew Schubin [sic], District Court of the United States for the Southern District of California Central Division, Criminal Docket no. 15790, Jan. 25, 1943. Box 33, American Civil Liberties Union National Committee on Conscientious Objectors Records. Swarthmore College Peace Collection, Swarthmore, PA. Hereafter cited as NCCO Records.

46. Later that year, he started working on a large potato farm as well. His employer wrote an affidavit seeking an agricultural deferment. Affidavit–Occupational Classification (General) for John Andrew Shubin, Oct. 22, 1945. Series E, 1, Box 74, CCW Records.

47. Leaders of the True Spiritual Christian Jumpers (Molokan) Young Peoples Church to NSBRO, May 14, 1945, Series E, 1, Box 74, CCW Records.

of America—Religious Freedom?"[48] Once again Shubin went to prison in Tucson, this time for eight more months. He was scheduled for conditional release on June 1, 1946.[49] When Shubin had filled out his first paperwork to protest his camp assignment, in August of 1942, he wrote, "We Molokan *true believers* cannot accept the camps or anything else. The Holy Ghost forbids it!" "But," he continued, "we are under your laws (Draft) and we know you are highly educated and intelligent people and we are more or less obscure. But we also know that you cannot truly understand us and our Molokan Christian Holy Jumpers religion and belief."[50] On all counts, he was right.

These are hundreds more stories to be told of objectors whose sincere beliefs were not quite legible as religious. For reasons of class, race, education, national background, immigration status, religious identity, and bad luck, they could not perform the role of the truly religious sincere believer. Each step of the filing and appeals process required that individuals render their beliefs legible, that they express them to secular state agents, who then analyzed whether the registrant's beliefs sufficiently matched the criteria or not. Thus, religious belief—or, more precisely, the expression of religious belief—entered secular, public spaces in order that its holder might be exempted from certain national projects. At the same time, state agents utilized a diverse "repertoire of moves"—hermeneutics, theology, constitutional interpretation, the threat of violence, inquisitional tactics, and affective judgments—to make their determinations.[51]

The registrant's task, seemingly simple though in practice quite complex, was to give an account of himself before the state. He laid out his beliefs plainly yet persuasively, arranged to make an argument but not manipulated or fudged. As one legal scholar summarized, "The burden of persuasion is on the registrant; he must tender sufficient evidence to show that he falls within the statutory standard."[52] In the language games of secular governance, petitioners had to translate their beliefs into the state's language and

48. "Petition of the Religious Sect—True Spiritual Christian Jumpers (Molokan)," sent to NSBRO, Aug. 1, 1945, Series E, 1, Box 74, CCW Records.

49. NSB 133 for John Andrew Shubin, Series E, 1, Box 74, CCW Records.

50. John Andrew Shubin to NSBRO, Aug. 5, 1942, Series E, 1, Box 74, CCW Records.

51. Berger, "Belonging to Law," 49.

52. Reisner, "The Conscientious Objector Exemption," 708. This demonstrates Hussein Ali Agrama's point that secularism also involves "questioning," i.e., inquiring of citizens whether they or their beliefs or actions are religious or secular. In this way, the state's secular governance works in an inquisitorial mode. Agrama, *Questioning Secularism*.

thus become legible.[53] This was hard to do. Some objectors were able to seek help from legal advocacy groups like the American Civil Liberties Union's (ACLU) National Committee on Conscientious Objectors (NCCO).[54] The NCCO offered legal aid, sometimes by writing amicus curiae briefs or providing representation for those petitioners whose claims were denied and who were therefore now classified as ready for combatant service. Even for petitioners whose cases never went to trial, these groups would offer legal counsel, giving specific instructions on how to fill out paperwork or answer hearing officers' questions, even offering line-by-line critiques on copies of individuals' draft forms. Many of these individual correspondences spanned several months, even, in some cases, years. With the help of the NCCO, some claimants made it through to federal courts, and their arguments eventually changed the law.

"CALL IT CONSCIENCE OR GOD": A THEORY OF RELIGION

Which brings us back to section 5(g). That section of the 1940 draft act defined the conscientious objector as "any person . . . who, by reason of religious training and belief, is conscientiously opposed to participation in war in any form."[55] But what did that actually mean? As I have shown, there was a vast infrastructure dealing with conscientious objectors and many levels of bureaucracy through which to process them. The other part of the story is what happened in the courts. The question at hand was always particular—whether this individual petitioner should be exempt from combat. But behind it lurked a more fundamental one: What does "religious training and belief" mean?

53. On secularism as a language game, see Asad, *Secular Translations*.

54. The ACLU was founded in 1920, an outgrowth of the National Civil Liberties Bureau (CLB), which was founded in 1917 to protect conscientious objectors and antiwar activists. After 1920, they expanded their scope to include other civil liberties causes, including free speech, women's rights, and civil rights for African Americans. On the ACLU's early history, see Samuel Walker, *In Defense of American Liberties: A History of the ACLU*, 2nd ed. (Southern Illinois University Press, 1999); and Judy Kutulas, *The American Civil Liberties Union and the Making of Modern Liberalism, 1930–1960* (University of North Carolina Press, 2006).

55. Selective Service Training and Service Act of 1940, Pub.L. 76–783, 54 Stat. 85 (1940).

This question reached the federal courts in 1943, in the landmark case *United States v. Kauten*. Mathias Kauten, originally from St. Louis, worked as a commercial artist in New York. He was arrested for failing to report for induction, which he claimed he did not have to do because he was a conscientious objector. He lost his case because objectors were in fact required to appear for induction and then formally refuse induction at the site. Protocol failures aside, Kauten's case was important because it provided an early opportunity for the federal courts to draw limits around the scope of the draft act's "religious training and belief" clause. The sticking point was that Kauten was not a typical religious believer: he did not affirm a belief in a god. What's more, his beliefs appeared to be particular to the current political situation rather than sincerely held beliefs in a timeless religious creed.

With representation and legal aid from the ACLU, Kauten's case reached the Second Circuit Court of Appeals. Julien Cornell, an up-and-coming civil rights attorney and conscientious objector advocate, argued that supporters of the 1940 draft act "regarded it as providing for conscientious objection derived from deep and sincere conviction, but not for objections based on political or social expediencies. The word 'religious,'" Cornell continued, "refers to these deep-rooted and sincere convictions, not to emanations from the established church."[56] He went on to cite dictionary definitions, philosophers from Auguste Comte to John Dewey, "the scientist's definition of religion" (citing William James and Albert Einstein), Quaker theologians, and Thomas Jefferson and Abraham Lincoln. The common point Cornell extracted from these assorted quotations was that "religion" was not the same as formal theology or established church doctrine. It was sincere and deep conviction, essentially individual.[57]

The argument worked. Judge Augustus Hand, writing for the court, agreed with Cornell and Kauten's definition of "religious." But he did think that courts needed some standards or guidelines by which to recognize the religious and distinguish it from the nonreligious—so he wrote some. First, Hand distinguished between religious beliefs and other beliefs by associating the former with a total objection to war. "Selective" objection (opposing specific wars, not all wars or war in general) was not religious, since

56. United States v. Kauten, 133 F.2d 703 (2d Cir. 1943). Julien Cornell, Brief of Appellant, 6. In Box 20, NCCO Records.

57. Cornell also made these points in his book *The Conscientious Objector and the Law* (John Day, 1943). See also Julien Cornell, "Exemption from the Draft: A Study in Civil Liberties," *Yale Law Journal* 56, no. 2 (Jan., 1947): 258–275.

it stemmed from the temporal and political realities of the day, whereas religion was timeless and not contingent upon earthly circumstance. Total objections to war, Hand wrote, "may justly be regarded as a response of the individual to an inward mentor, call it conscience or God, that is for many persons at the present time the equivalent of what has always been thought a religious impulse."[58] Having drawn a line of demarcation between the religious and the political, Hand explained more carefully what "religion" involved. He did not need a comprehensive, universal definition, since "the content of the term is found in the history of the human race and is incapable of compression into a few words."[59] Instead, it was possible to identify religious impulses, the stuff of religion, its traces.

Without a clear definition, an identifiable, calculable thing to point to and call religion, judges had to search for signs of religious belief. For Hand, sincerity was one of these signs, though not all sincerity was religious. Certainly, people could believe sincerely in philosophical concepts that did not arise from "religious training and belief." Thus, sincerity was a necessary but not sufficient condition for authentic religious belief. Although he did not attempt a formal definition, Hand did explain:

> Religious belief arises from a sense of the inadequacy of reason as a means of relating the individual to his fellow-men and to his universe—a sense common to men in the most primitive and in the most highly civilized societies. It accepts the aid of logic but refuses to be limited by it. It is a belief finding expression in a conscience which categorically requires the believer to disregard elementary self-interest and to accept martyrdom in preference to transgressing its tenets.[60]

He went on to cite Martin Luther, Menander, Socrates, and William Wordsworth on conscience as something like the germ of religion. Like early and mid-twentieth-century scholars of religion, Hand theorized religious belief's basic anthropological social functions. It helped humans relate within groups and across cultural divides, where reason failed. Religious beliefs were held sincerely and conscientiously; they were convictions that went deeper than rational conclusions. Hand argued that religion was prerational, although rational ideas and conscience could be overlaid later onto

58. *Kauten*, 133 F.2d at 708.
59. *Kauten*, 133 F.2d at 708.
60. *Kauten*, 133 F.2d at 708.

religious orientations and affects. In the statute, then, "religious training and belief" had to be the first cause of belief, the affective core from which one might later reason. It was the source of belief, not its content.

In an influential 1978 article, the legal scholar John Sexton marked *Kauten* as a major turning point in constitutional definitions of religion. He contrasted it with *Davis v. Beason* (1890), an early religious freedom case that, like *Reynolds v. United States* (1879), held that free exercise applies strictly to belief and not necessarily action (a number of the fortune-telling cases discussed in the previous chapter also cited *Davis*).[61] "Where *Davis* saw religion as relating man to God," Sexton wrote, "*Kauten* examined the relationship of man to the broad universe and to other men."[62] In this way, religion became a component of the human experience, a way of orienting the individual to the world and others. This change was important, but it did not clarify how courts might know, with any certainty, which beliefs were indeed religious. Was the content of a belief a reliable indicator of one's motivations for believing it? In the *Kauten* decision, the matter was straightforward: *absolute* objections were evidence of religious impulses, but *specific* objections were evidence of something else. The broader standard established in *Kauten* postulated that religious beliefs were essentially different from other classes of belief.

Other petitioners and their lawyers immediately tried to work the *Kauten* standard to their advantage. Results were mixed. Some courts upheld and even furthered this line of interpretation, with the Second Circuit at the cutting edge. A few months after *Kauten*, the court also decided in favor of Randolph Godfrey Phillips, whose beliefs had been found by his local board, the appeal board, and the hearing officer to be political rather than religious. Phillips asserted, "My opposition to war is deep-rooted, based not on political considerations but on a general humanitarian concept which is essentially religious in character."[63] Although his hearing officer recognized that "this case is not without its perplexities," he ultimately concluded that Phillips's beliefs did "more largely result from his political convictions and his dissatisfaction with our present way of life." The court disagreed. Phillips critiqued capitalism and fascism, yes, but his statements were "not

---

61. Davis v. Beason, 133 U.S. 333 (1890). The case upheld an Idaho statute banning "bigamists" and "polygamists"—or one "who teaches, advises, counsels or encourages any person or persona to become bigamists or polygamists . . ."—from voting or holding public office.

62. Sexton, "Note: Toward a Constitutional Definition of Religion," 1061.

63. United States ex rel. Phillips v. Downer, 135 F.2d 521, 523 (1943).

linked to any definite political movement." And, besides, Phillips's political beliefs appeared to be "but a correlative, and not the defining limitation, of the belief against war."[64] In other words, Phillips had reached a political conclusion from a *source* of essentially religious conviction. This subtle distinction—between the source of the belief and its content, with the former being what must be religious—would come up again in conscientious objector cases, including *Seeger*, which reshaped conscientious objection as well as religious freedom.

The Second Circuit kept reconsidering the limits of "religious training and belief" the next year, when they heard the case of Frederick Reel. Reel had long objected to war, and while he argued that his views were in line with the teachings of Christ, Confucius, the Golden Rule, and Reverend John Haynes Holmes, he did not belong to any religious organization and did not believe in a deity.[65] Reel's hearing officer had written, "Among scholars the word 'religion' certainly involved Deity and worship. Polytheism, monotheism, primitive religion, higher religion, ethical religions, universal religions are all terms used by scholars in discussing man's beliefs as to supernatural power and the relationship of humankind to such power. 'Ethical' and 'religious' are not synonymous terms."[66] And in the hearing officer's judgment, Reel's beliefs were merely ethical. In a letter to General Hershey requesting a presidential appeal, Reel cited *Phillips*, noting that the court understood Phillips's "philosophical and humanitarian" beliefs to have "the essence of religious thought."[67] The debate, still, was about religion and not-religion. Reel was sincere, everyone agreed. But the *source* of his belief was in question: was it essentially religious, or was it political or philosophical or some-

64. *Phillips*, 135 F.2d at 525. The particular point of disagreement between Judge Clark and the hearing officer's report was a play Phillips had written, which he submitted as evidence of his long-standing sincere convictions. Clark included a few pages of literary analysis and critique, finding meaning in punctuation choices and noting ambiguities in the final scene. The hearing officer thought it was a political play and thus evidence of political belief, and Clark thought it was a political play that expressed religious beliefs.

65. As evidence of his long-standing belief, Reel attached to his Form 47 a speech he had delivered in 1936 while a student at the University of Wisconsin, titled "The Road to Peace." The Form 47 included the question, "Have you ever given public expression, written or oral, to the views herein expressed as the basis for your claim?" Frederick U. Reel, Form 47, Box 25, NCCO Records.

66. *Reel*, 141 F.2d at 846; quoting the report by Hearing Officer E. Barrett Prettyman. Reel's hearing with Prettyman took place on May 19, 1943.

67. Frederick U. Reel to Lewis B. Hershey, Aug. 27, 1943, Box 25, NCCO Records. He was quoting Reel's hearing officer, as quoted in the case.

thing else? Once again, the justices of the Second Circuit decided in favor of the petitioner, citing their own previous decisions. Reel did not believe in God, per se, but he had a conscience, something "equivalent" to a "religious impulse." That impulse, from something deep inside the individual—"call it conscience or God"—impelled the belief, which then should be protected by the statute.[68]

"WITHOUT THE CONCEPT OF A DEITY": A DIFFERENT THEORY OF RELIGION

According to the *Kauten* standard and its applications in *Phillips* and *Reel*, "religious training and belief" did not mean that a petitioner had to believe in a god or belong to a religious organization. Rather, it referred to the deep source of a belief, something ineffable yet distinct from politics or philosophy. Kauten, Phillips, and Reel—all of whom worked with the NCCO and one of whom (Phillips) went on to work for the ACLU and direct the NCCO in 1944 and 1945—were well connected and had successfully embarked on setting new precedents and shoring up rights for more conscientious objectors.[69] All three were cultured, well-educated white men living in major East Coast cities. In this respect, they had more in common with federal judges than with the volunteers staffing local draft boards.[70] They had progressive,

68. *Reel*, 141 F.2d at 847, quoting *Kauten* 133 F.2d at 708. The court did not order that Reel was exempt from service but said rather that it was "not established just what the holding was" by the Director of Selective Service. *If* the director had denied Reel's exemption even though he acknowledged that Reel's objection was based on "the compelling voice of his conscience," then it should be reversed. But it was not clear if the director had rejected the hearing officer's findings. Thus, the case went back to the district court. There, they found that Reel was not sincere, and the Second Circuit again reversed the ruling. United States v. Badt, 152 F.2d 627 (2d Cir. 1945).

69. Walter H. Waggoner, "Randolph G. Phillips, 71, Dies; Led Many Stockholder Fights," *New York Times*, Oct. 12, 1982.

70. Kauten was from a working-class St. Louis family, and his parents were Hungarian immigrants. He graduated from art school at Washington University in St. Louis before moving to work as an artist in New York (see "Mat Kauten," https://www.pulpartists.com /Kauten.html). Phillips was from Manhattan. He graduated from Columbia University and, by the time of his case, had worked as a financial reporter, a consultant to the U.S. Senate, a speechwriting consultant on Thomas Dewey's gubernatorial campaign, and a corporate consultant (Waggoner, "Randolph G. Phillips"). Frederick Reel, the son of German immi-

antiwar politics and the citations to back them up, and they opened doors wide for future objectors who were like them, people like Dan Seeger, a white, Catholic-raised agnostic from New York.

Not all courts embraced such generous interpretations as the Second Circuit. Things were a little different out in California. Herman Berman, a Jewish socialist living in Los Angeles, filed his Form 47 and cited *Kauten*, *Phillips*, and *Reel*. He argued that "a person's philosophy of life or his political view point, to which his conscience directs him to adhere devotedly, or his devotion to human welfare, without the concept of deity, may be religious in nature."[71] Working with the NCCO, Berman seized on *Kauten's* implication that beliefs were religious not necessarily because of their content but because of the depth of conviction with which they were held. The Ninth Circuit Court held, however, that "no matter how pure and admirable [Berman's] standard may be, and no matter how devotedly he adheres to it, his philosophy and morals and social policy without the concept of a deity cannot be said to be religion in the sense of that term as it is used in the statute."[72] Unlike in *Reel*, in *Berman* belief in a deity was the sine qua non of religion. No god, no religion.

"It would be quite ridiculous," wrote Judge Albert Lee Stephens, "to argue that the use of the word 'religion' could have been understood by the authors of our national charter or by those having to do with its adoption as meaning to be inclusive of morals or of devotion to human welfare or of policy of government."[73] On Stephens's account, secularization and religious change had led to more abstract religious beliefs and more religious diversity, yet the core of religion—"faith"—remained the same. Neither science nor reason nor philosophy would supersede religion. None of these could "fill a life or satisfy the soul hunger to understand the daily joys and sadnesses and disappointments of life or to understand the ultimate purpose of creation. Faith in a supreme power above and beyond the law of all creation mollifies our fears and satisfies our longings."[74] Like other judges (and anthropologists and liberal theologians), Stephens located religion somewhere

---

grants, grew up in Milwaukee and earned a B.A. and J.D. from the University of Wisconsin. At the time of his filing, he was an attorney at the U.S. Department of Labor in Washington, DC (Reel file, Box 25, NCCO Records).

71. Berman v. United States, 156 F.2d 377, 379 (9th Cir.), cert. denied, 329 U.S. 795 (1946).

72. *Berman*, 156 F.2d at 381.

73. *Berman*, 156 F.2d at 379–380.

74. *Berman*, 156 F.2d at 380.

within the human psyche, where it fulfilled an almost therapeutic function. But his definition of religion was narrower: it required "faith in a supreme power."

Religion was timeless and innate, but religions were not. Even in the modern era, Stephens argued, secular philosophies could not replace religious faith. What about nontheistic religions, though? In his dissent, Judge William Denman affirmed the religiosity of Berman's humanism, pointing out that his "religious training" included reading Norman Thomas and Eugene Debs, who were both Christians (and, like Berman, socialists). Berman's beliefs had religious bases and were, for Denman, authentically religious *and* nontheistic. If these were mutually exclusive, "this would exclude all Taoist China and in the Western world all believers in Comte's religion of humanism." Denman added, "This recognition of religion as not requiring a god is excellently stated in Judge Augustus Hand's opinion" in *Kauten*.[75] Stephens, for his part, doubled down on his interpretation, noting that other judges and justices had used similar deity-belief tests when defining "religious." Supreme Court Chief Justice Charles Evans Hughes had written in his dissent in *United States v. Macintosh* (1931) that "the essence of religion is belief in relation to God involving duties superior to those arising from any human relation."[76] Stephens quoted this passage and remarked in a footnote that any implication that Hughes (along with Justices Oliver Wendell

75. *Berman*, 156 F.2d at 384.

76. United States v. Macintosh, 283 U.S. 605, 633–634 (1931). In Hughes's dissent he also invoked sincerity twice, to refer to what people "sincerely believed to be" their "duty of obedience to God" or "allegiance to the will of God" (630, 631). Again, the race and class issues here were pertinent. Macintosh was applying for citizenship, which at that time included an oath to take up arms in defense of the United States. He was a pacifist, an ordained Baptist minister, and a professor at Yale Divinity School. As the legal scholar John Henry Wigmore bluntly argued at the time (a high time for eugenics, restrictive immigration, nationalism, and race science), "He had a good Scottish name and ancestry; therefore presumably a sturdy genuine conscience, and a racial congeniality with the fundamental stock of our nation. His personality thus made it possible to consider squarely the issue of law without any of those lurking prejudices that have often been associated with the type of conscientious objector so prominent in 1917–18" ("United States v. Macintosh—A Symposium," *Illinois Law Review* 26, no. 4 [Dec., 1931], 375). The stunning irony of the phrase "without any of those lurking prejudices" is quite the illustration of how whiteness and the Protestant secular draw power from appearing both neutral and good, unremarkable and yet remarked upon approvingly. Although Macintosh lost his case, it was a contentious 5–4 decision, and Hughes's dissent lived on by lending language to the *Berman* decision and the 1948 draft act.

Holmes, Louis Brandeis, and Harlan F. Stone, who had joined his dissent) had failed to think about Taoism or Comte "would be an unwarranted assertion of their ignorance of the history of religious beliefs."[77] Berman lost his case and was reclassified as ready for induction into the armed forces.

The Second and Ninth Circuits clearly disagreed about how to interpret the statute (although, it should be noted, the decisions were not all unanimous; there were dissents in *Berman* and *Phillips*). Indeed, Berman himself had explicitly based his argument on the Second Circuit rulings, and the Ninth Circuit rejected it. Judge Stephens readily acknowledged, "We take divergent views from these cases [*Kauten, Phillips*, and *Reel*]." He regarded Congress's phrase "religious training and belief" as "plain language . . . written into the statute for the specific purpose of distinguishing between a conscientious social belief, or a sincere devotion to a high moralistic philosophy, and one based upon an individual's belief in his responsibility to an authority higher and beyond any worldly one."[78] Stephens's goal was not different from the Second Circuit judges'. Both were trying to distinguish between the religious and the nonreligious; the disagreement was about where to draw that line. The starkest point of disagreement was whether religious belief required a deity.[79] When Congress drafted a new draft act, they attempted to sort out the confusion.

SECTION 6(J)

In 1948 Congress passed a new draft act that included an amendment to the conscientious objection section, now section 6(j), to clarify the meaning of "religious training and belief." As in 1940, some activists had advocated for the inclusion of "secular" believers. Senator George Malone, a Kansas

77. *Berman*, 156 F.2d at 385n2.

78. *Berman*, 156 F.2d at 380.

79. This debate was not limited to responses to the Second and Ninth Circuit decisions. Even before *Kauten*, people had opined on the meaning of the phrase. For instance, in 1942 Lewis Hershey, director of the Selective Service, wrote that he interpreted the "religious training and belief" clause "in light of its meaning by people who think of religion as a relationship between the individual and something above the plane he lives on, something that lies outside his relationship to man." Lewis Hershey to James Rowe, March 5, 1942; quoted in George Q. Flynn, "Lewis Hershey and the Conscientious Objector: The World War II Experience," *Military Affairs* 47, no. 1 (Feb., 1983), 3.

Republican, introduced a provision that would include those with "humanitarian convictions." Others wanted to make the standard stricter, more in line with the *Berman* decision. Eventually, Congress settled on language that they believed—incorrectly, as it turned out—would limit the reach of the act.[80]

The amendment to section 6(j) expounded, "Religious training and belief in this connection means an individual's belief in relation to a Supreme Being involving duties superior to those arising from any human relation, but does not include essentially political, sociological, or philosophical views or a merely personal moral code."[81] With this addition, they attempted to resolve the tensions between *Kauten* and *Berman*. But they did not seem to perceive fully, or at any rate did not acknowledge, the differences between the two cases. These tensions are evident in Congress's chosen language. For instance, the phrase "in relation to a Supreme Being" seemed to side with the *Berman* conception, since it borrowed language from Chief Justice Hughes's *Macintosh* dissent, which the *Berman* court had also cited. However, the term "Supreme Being" was Congress's, whereas Hughes had written "God." Later courts would try to discern the meaning, if any, in that change. Perhaps because of such ambiguities, Congress believed this language worked to encompass both *Kauten* and *Berman*, which they took to be operating according to essentially the same logic.

Congress's revision—or clarification—defined "religious belief and training" positively, as beliefs "in relation to a Supreme Being," but also negatively, against politics, sociology, philosophy, and personal opinion, the others of religion.[82] Because these positive and negative definitions, each of which was problematic on its own, were supposed to harmonize, many contentious cases resulted from instances in which the two parts seemed to

80. Threlkeld, "'The War Power Is Not a Blank Check,'" 313–314.

81. Military Selective Service Act of 1948, Pub.L. 80–26, 61 Stat. 31. The act is also sometimes called the Elston Act, as it was introduced by Ohio Republican Senators Charles Elston and Robert Taft.

82. The delineation of religion from not-religion is a persistent function of secular governance. For this reason, Jolyon Thomas has advocated using the terms "religion" and "not-religion" rather than "religion" and "the secular" (*Faking Liberties*, 12). Because I argue that "the secular" has content, insofar as it is an intellectual project that grounds subjectivities and conceptions of modernity, I still use the terms. However, I agree with Thomas that, in terms on secular governance, the project of secularism, what regulatory agents identify and sort is more accurately called "not-religion" than "the secular." In these terms, the secular is, rather, the imaginary informing and undergirding this distinction.

cut against each other. It was certainly conceivable that an individual might have a sincerely held belief that he understood to be a matter of conscience, not politics or philosophy, but nevertheless had no relation to a Supreme Being. Herman Berman was one such believer. Or, somewhat differently, a believer might petition for an exemption because his conscience forbade participation in war but his conception of a Supreme Being was unorthodox.

The legislative attempt to bring clarity did not succeed. The statute's ambiguous wording and complicated concepts prompted thorny questions that grew ever sharper with each court case. And there were many more court cases. Even though World War II had ended, the Korean War and the Cold War were just beginning. With the continuation of universal military training and service, the Selective Service by the 1950s had become a system for producing the ideal white American male subject, offering deferments for students and fathers (and the well-connected), slotting people into particular jobs of "national importance," and manipulating the labor force through a vast federal bureaucracy. As Amy Rutenberg has written, it was a "policy of manpower channeling, a form of social engineering designed to coax men into designated fields by offering them deferments from conscription."[83] Throughout the 1950s conscientious objectors continued fighting for their cause, and the courts kept interpreting and reinterpreting the draft act. These years set the stage for the Vietnam era, in which the numbers of objectors and draftees exploded. In the final section of this chapter, I consider one aspect of these cases I so far have mentioned only briefly. By the time a conscientious objector reached a federal courtroom, at the end of the long bureaucratic and legal process, he had compiled a huge stack of paperwork. The federal judiciary had access to this stack, plus another source of information: the results of the FBI investigation.

"F.B.I. REPORTS NO EVIDENCE OF DEEP RELIGIOUS FEELING": FAIR RÉSUMÉS AND THE FACTS OF BELIEF

As jurisprudential debates about interpreting the 1948 act carried on into the 1950s, the investigative aspects of secular governance became even more

---

83. Rutenberg, *Rough Draft*, 112.

central.[84] Every conscientious objector was subject to an investigation of his "background and reputation for sincerity."[85] These investigations were fact-finding missions. Federal courts could not reject local boards' and appeal boards' findings unless there was "no basis in fact for the classification."[86] Thus, the FBI reports were crucial, since their purpose was to discover and present as many facts as possible. Agents probed a registrant's conscience, investigating his "general character, reputation, and religious activities," and they interviewed and recorded written statements from "school officials, employers, fellow employees, neighbors, acquaintances, religious associates, and references listed by the registrant."[87] For instance, one losing defendant was found to be neither religious nor sincere because he claimed to attend church but apparently did so infrequently, if at all. At least, that is what the FBI agents surmised after they interviewed a number of his supposed fellow church members, who said that they did not remember him.[88] Before the

84. The quotation in the section title is from a telegram from Laura Swomley, of the Fellowship of Reconciliation, to an objector, Richard W. Enders, Sept. 25, 1942. (Swomley was also married to John W. Swomley, a Methodist minister and leader in peace movements, civil rights, and church-state separation who had testified before Congress in favor of expansive CO protections in the 1940 draft act.) The telegram notified the objector: "F.B.I. reports 1) no evidence of deep religious feeling 2) no connection between religion and conscientious objection, 3) objection political rather than religious. Even that not firm or thorough. An attitude rather than conviction." The objector wrote a letter the next day to request a presidential appeal, arguing, "My objections to participation in war are fundamentally religious, stemming out of a reverence for human life and human personality (for they are essentially the source of all good) and out of knowledge that war, operating in complete opposition to this belief, is an evil tending to perpetuate and intensify the very evils it is designed to overcome." Richard W. Enders to General Lewis Hershey, Sept. 26, 1942. This sort of language would be more likely to be classified as religious after the 1948 act and certainly after *Seeger* in 1965. In the early 1940s, though, this objector's appeal was denied at every step, despite legal support from a variety of peace groups. He was later imprisoned. Richard W. Enders file, Series E, 1, Box 23, NCCO Records.

85. The quotation is from the syllabus of United States v. Nugent, 346 U.S. 1 (1953).

86. Estep v. United States, 327 U.S. 114 (1946), at 122–123. This "fact-finding" standard was made explicit here.

87. Smith and Bell, "The Conscientious-Objector Program," 701. See also Heisler, "The Law versus the Conscientious Objector."

88. Imboden v. United States, 194 F.2d 508 (6th Cir. 1952). The court in this case also considered that the petitioner originally had registered for an exemption to do farm work and, having been denied that, only then applied for conscientious objector status. If his objection were deeply held and sincere, the court reasoned, he would have attempted to

local draft and appeal boards, it was up to registrants to present themselves as sincere religious believers, and the boards evaluated not only their written statements but their appearance of earnestness. With these facts found and filed, though, any further evidence of the registrant's inner sincerity was to come from further outside of himself.

While the FBI in this period investigated and suppressed queer people, Black communities, religious minorities, and suspected communists, they also applied tactics of domestic surveillance to conscientious objectors.[89] Particularly in their surveillance of racialized religious minorities, the FBI did the secular work of identifying religions and nonreligions, using terms like "cult" for the latter.[90] In the case of the conscientious objectors, the goal of the system was to ensure religious freedom by rooting out the insincere and nonreligious. Many of the issues that arose after 1948 were not only about what "religious training and belief" meant, or whether individuals really believed "in relation to a Supreme Being" (whatever that phrase meant), or the differences between religious and political beliefs. They were also about procedure: how to enforce these distinctions. The FBI and the Department of Justice were significant players in this system of secular governance.

Courts generally found the FBI reports useful, but they puzzled over how exactly to use them. For instance, it was not clear who should have access to the reports. Courts debated whether registrants were entitled to see them. And should judges read the full dossiers, including all the interviews, or just the Department of Justice's summary report? District and appeals courts disagreed on many of these issues, and with so many cases happening around the same time, they sometimes were unable to read one another's opinions before issuing their own. Disagreements among circuit courts sometimes

---

object in the first place. In other cases, petitioners sought other exemptions first or changed their request from 1-A-O to 1-O. Inconsistency was often viewed as a sign of insincerity if not sufficient evidence on its own.

89. On the FBI and religious communities, see Johnson and Weitzman, eds., *The FBI and Religion*.

90. See, e.g., reports on the "Muslim Cult of Islam," the Bureau's term for the Nation of Islam. Much of the Nation of Islam subject file has been made public through Freedom of Information Act requests and is available online. See vault.fbi.gov. See also Karl Evanzz, "The FBI and the Nation of Islam," in *The FBI and Religion*, ed. Johnson and Weitzman, 168–190.

led to further appeals, and several key conscientious objection cases made their way to the U.S. Supreme Court in the 1940s and 1950s.

Registrants had the right to due process, thanks to the 1946 *Estep* case, which guaranteed judicial review of boards' decisions, but there were still questions about just what that due process entailed.[91] For instance, did a registrant have the right to see the FBI reports about him? In *United States v. Nugent* (1953), the Supreme Court answered no. Nugent had asked to see the reports so that he could refute the claims not in his favor. He argued that because he was required to explain his position and defend himself, that it was his right under the statute to know what was said about him and who said it. If the FBI's role was to find facts and the judge's was to consider the Department of Justice's summary of these facts, then petitioners should have had the opportunity to correct the record—and they could not correct a record they could not see. Nugent's case made it to the Supreme Court, where he lost. Justices Felix Frankfurter and Hugo Black each wrote a strong dissent, the latter arguing that "a hearing at which these faceless people are allowed to present their whispered rumors and yet escape the test and torture of cross-examination is not a hearing in the Anglo-American sense."[92] However, Chief Justice Fred Vinson cited "the imperative needs of mobilization and national vigilance" the Selective Service Act was designed to meet, suggesting that too much "litigious interruption" would distract from more important national efforts. He concluded that the Department of Justice met "its duties under § 6(j)" by letting a conscientious objector provide his own paperwork and view a "fair résumé of any adverse evidence in the investigator's report."[93] In other words, the investigative bureaucracy was doing its job, and conscientious objectors did not need to check their work, even when the substance of their work was to search his very self for vestiges of religiosity.

Interested parties continued to debate the line between religion and not-religion throughout the 1950s. When one objector asked what evidence there might be against his claim, his hearing officer cited the results of the FBI investigation: "Some of your references," the officer wrote, "stated that they thought your stand was based on political and sociological grounds. You must show that it is based on religious training and belief, good faith

91. *Estep*, 327 U.S. 114. See also Threlkeld, "'The War Power Is Not a Blank Check,'" 304.
92. *Nugent*, 346 U.S. at 14.
93. *Nugent*, 346 U.S. at 6.

and sincerity."[94] Here we can see the statutory language saturating the hearing officer's and FBI's reports—and, it seems, the references' as well. It was the *Kauten* standard again: essentially religious, *not* political or sociological. One of the claimant's references, according to the Department of Justice's fair résumé, "could not base his claims on teachings of and membership in the Methodist Church of which he was a member." To be clear, the Department of Justice's argument was not that he was insincere or even that he was not religious, but that the content of his pacifistic beliefs did not stem from religion. Rather, the investigation revealed that he "was influenced by the teachings and practices of Ghandi [*sic*] and the Fellowship of Reconciliation."[95] Even though Congress had done away with membership requirements for conscientious objectors, membership in a religious group still could serve as evidence for religious sincerity. But by the same token, beliefs were not inherently religious. The same belief, in terms of content, might be religious for one person and political, sociological, or "merely personal" for another. The confusion about the political-versus-religious designation that courts had fretted over in *Kauten* and *Berman*, and which the 1948 act sought to sharpen, clearly had not dissipated.

State agents, including judges and investigators, searched for sincerity, for the fact of religious belief. But it was hard to find. They set up investigative, administrative, and regulatory procedures to find belief, but believers were fickle and beliefs could change. What did it mean to "hold" a belief? And despite all attempts, none of these cases fully resolved the problem of how to define "religious training and belief." These issues persisted throughout the 1950s as draft counselors and attorneys worked with objectors to navigate the system and courts in turn took up cases and parsed previous decisions again and again. Interpretive definitions of "religious belief" were restrictive and calculative, sorting the religious from the not-religious. The not-religious went to camps, to prison, to war. The religious, often assisted by the NSBRO or NCCO or other organizations that mediated between individual believers and the bureaucratic leviathan, were able to translate their beliefs into the calculable language of the secular state. In so doing, many of them sought to press against the edges of statutory interpretation. By the 1960s, as judicial and popular conceptions of the religious broadened, some objectors contested the Supreme Being requirement. They argued that

94. United States v. Evans, 115 F.Supp. 340, 341 (D.Conn. 1953).
95. *Evans*, 115 F.Supp at 341.

sincerely held beliefs did not require belief in a deity to be authentically religious. And they won, eventually, in the 1965 case *U.S. v. Seeger*. The next chapter analyzes that case, showing how and why the Supreme Court redefined "religious belief" in the draft act and, unintentionally, for hundreds of religious freedom cases in the following decades.

05

SUPREME BEINGS AND THE SUPREME COURT

BY 1965 A QUARTER-CENTURY OF HARD cases and legislative tweaks had, bit by bit, restructured conscientious objection law and procedures. The changes produced a wide variety of outcomes and potential outcomes, many of which seemed to conflict. At the same time, advocacy groups, religious denominations, and draft boards responded to judicial decisions, navigating the shifting legal terrain and, in some cases, intending to reshape it. Courts struggled to craft useful standards by which religious beliefs could be meaningfully and clearly differentiated from an individual's political or social beliefs, and the new amendment in the 1948 draft act, despite the addition of some new questions and revised language, had not made the task much easier. There was more pressure on believers to express themselves persuasively and legibly as religious—and on courts to sort religious beliefs from political or "merely personal" ones. With each court case, the ground shifted a little.

Interpreting and applying the draft act became even more difficult in the 1960s, for two interconnected reasons. First, a few Supreme Court cases had considered nontheists to be authentically religious, which potentially cast doubt on the soundness of the Supreme Being standard. Secondly, the act defined "religious" positively as "in relation to a Supreme Being," but it also defined it negatively, as differentiated from the "essentially political, sociological, or philosophical" and the "merely personal." As legal and popular understandings of the religious expanded, through deinstitutionalization and individualization, it was harder to draw a clear and defensible line between religious and nonreligious beliefs. These issues came to a head in 1965 in *United States v. Seeger*. The case considered the claims of three men—Arno Sascha Jakobson, Forest Britt Peter, and Daniel Andrew

Seeger—whose beliefs the statute strained to cover. Seeger's case presented the most significant difficulty, since he did not believe in a Supreme Being.[1]

In *Seeger*, the Court reconceptualized religious belief as a mode of believing—believing religiously—rather than a belief in a particular set of "religious" content. An individual could be authentically religious, in the eyes of the state, without necessarily adhering to doctrinal standards or belonging to a religious organization. A believer was religious "in his own scheme of things."[2] The Court also developed what has been called the parallel-belief test, stipulating that an objector's belief was religious if it was a "sincere and meaningful belief which occupies in the life of its possessor a place parallel to that filled by the God of those admittedly qualifying for the exemption." It was not about believing in religious content per se but about being religious—and sincerely so. Although "sincere" and "religious" had been considered separately in conscientious objector cases, such that people sometimes passed one prong of the test but not the other, by the 1960s they were starting to collapse back into each other. Religious beliefs were "sincere and meaningful" beliefs. Keeping in mind the previous chapter's exploration of paperwork, bureaucracy, and the vast network of actors who collaborated in the making of law, this chapter turns directly to *Seeger*. Legal scholars and scholars of religion have recognized the case's importance, but few have attended to both the case's religious freedom implications and its context in the complexities of the Selective Service.[3] This chapter offers a narrative explanation of how Peter, Jakobson, and Seeger made their cases, and how nine Supreme Court justices came to agree that they believed religiously.

1. The circuit court cases were United States v. Seeger, 326 F.2d 846 (2d Cir. 1964); United States v. Jakobson 325 F.2d 409 (2d Cir. 1963); and Peter v. United States, 324 F.2d 173 (9th Cir. 1963).

2. *Seeger*, 380 U.S. at 163.

3. Two chapters in Dubler and Weiner, eds., *Religion, Law, USA*, spend time on *Seeger*. Jason Bivins situated the case in the context of the individualization of belief, arguing that *Seeger* "articulated the centrality of sincerity to claims for religious exemption from legal obligation" ("The Secular," 219). Ronit Stahl plots *Seeger* (and *Welsh*, which I discuss in chap. 6) within a story about the rise of conscience, traced through to *Hobby Lobby*. She argues that twenty-first-century applications of *Seeger* and *Welsh* for "complicity-based" exemption claims adopt the rhetoric of conscience while "eschewing the regulatory system that oversaw conscientious objection to war[, which] has created an unbalanced framework in which some religious ideas receive automatic deference while others are ignored" ("Conscience," 54). See also Sullivan, "The Conscience of Contemporary Man." My argument here does not argue against these works so much as build on them, providing a detailed account of *Seeger* and its effects.

"MERELY PERSONAL"

According to the draft act, religious belief was for individuals. But it couldn't be *too* individual, a "merely personal moral code." As the previous chapter explained, section 6(j) of the 1948 act was designed to account for court decisions that had taken seemingly contradictory interpretations of section 5(g) of the 1940 act on "religious training and belief." In *Kauten* (1943), the Second Circuit Court of Appeals took a quite generous stance on what counted, though they used a religious/political test, where each was defined against the other.[4] In *Berman* (1946), the Ninth Circuit Court of Appeals had attempted to create a usable definition of "religious belief," which for them referred to those positions "based upon an individual's belief in his responsibility to an authority higher and beyond any worldly one."[5] Congress tried to make these harmonize, or perhaps strike the same note, by incorporating language from both decisions into the 1948 statute. But this produced new questions. Perhaps the most obvious, and the most pertinent to *Seeger*, was whether a truly religious belief necessarily involved belief in a deity. But there was another thorny issue: how to differentiate between individual religious beliefs and "merely personal moral codes." Religious belief was essentially individual and sincere. It was personal but not "merely" so. So, how did petitioners go beyond the "mere"?

Presenting oneself as a sincere religious believer was a matter of style and legibility. Followers of merely personal codes were inscrutably idiosyncratic. For this reason, even though membership in a religious organization was not required, such affiliation helped. Registrants also cited recognizably religious sources as inspirations for their beliefs. They expressed their beliefs rationally and clearly, though they acknowledged that true faith stretched beyond human understanding. And they understood their beliefs' relevance to the political realities, but they were not too historically located or occasioned, lest they be seen as political beliefs rather than timeless religious scruples. It was a difficult position to stake out, especially for someone who was not a member of a recognizable religious community. And as always, objectors had to stake out this position within the lines on formal paperwork, squeezing their beliefs into the strictures of statutory language, responding sincerely and personally (but not "merely" so) to questionnaires.

4. *Kauten*, 133 F.2d.
5. *Berman*, 156 F.2d. at 380.

Their answers to these questions, their word choices on their paperwork, performed belief.

Britt Peter, Arno Jakobson, and Dan Seeger each objected to war but belonged to no religious group. Their beliefs required some explanation. They each needed space to answer the questions on Form 150 (the successor to Form 47), which asked petitioners to describe the nature of their beliefs and provided enough room for a two- or three-sentence response. Like many other objectors, they wrote longer statements and appended them to the form. These responses were the first and often most the important step toward becoming a conscientious objector. Not only were they read and considered by the local draft boards but if the case went farther, the answers would be the basis for further investigation and consideration. In these three cases, years passed between the initial filing and the court cases, but the answers were still cited and read carefully, even by the Supreme Court.

Successful petitioners often composed detailed and precise responses, and draft counselors and conscientious objector advocates advised doing so. Many petitioners sent drafts of their answers to groups like the Central Committee for Conscientious Objectors (CCCO), where counselors would critique them and offer suggestions and corrections to help petitioners most effectively appear religious and sincere. In addition to their direct assistance, the CCCO published the *Handbook for Conscientious Objectors*, first in 1952 and updated in regular new editions. It contained just over a hundred pages walking objectors through practical questions, describing the paperwork, and offering tips on how to fill it out.[6] Later editions included discussions of specific cases, explaining the court rulings and why certain objectors had been successful. They also produced handbooks for draft counselors that large networks of peace organizations, churches, and other groups could use to help men navigate the system.[7] The handbook crafted a sort of catechesis,

6. An early edition is available freely online through the SCPC. See https://www .swarthmore.edu/library/peace/DG051–099/dg073CentralComm(CCCO)/CCCOHand-book1952.pdf.

7. Other organizations, such as the American Friends Service Committee and War Resisters League, published similar documents. In some cases they shared information and even whole articles, slightly adapted. I saw many of the CCCO pamphlets in the CCCO Records at the SCPC. Some of these materials have been digitized and are available freely online from the SCPC, as well as the Vietnam Center and Sam Johnson Vietnam Archive at Texas Tech University. See https://vva.vietnam.ttu.edu/.

so to speak, such that the recitation of individual sincere beliefs became an increasingly standardized rite.[8]

For those who would become conscientious objectors, the first ritual step was to complete Form 150. The second part of the form, Series II, consisted of questions dealing with "religious training and belief."[9] The first was the most straightforward: "Do you believe in a Supreme Being?" Since the statute defined religious belief as "in relation to a Supreme Being," petitioners had a hard time becoming conscientious objectors if they responded "no." Many men, often at the suggestion of the handbook, tried some version of "It depends on the definition of Supreme Being."[10] At least one petitioner even used a typewriter to type this phrase over the question.[11] The second question in Series II asked petitioners to "describe the nature of your belief which is the basis of your claim [to be a conscientious objector] and state whether or not your belief in a Supreme Being involves duties which to you are superior to those arising from any human relation."[12] It was in response to this question and the following, which asked about the religious training and background, that petitioners affixed their longer answers. Many of these answers are preserved because organizations such as the CCCO kept them on file, along with the correspondence between counselors and petitioners, instructing them how to improve their answers and respond to hearing officers and appeal boards. The beliefs explained in these attached answers range from seemingly orthodox yet verbose statements of belief (seminarians had a penchant for this type of expression) to the musings of those who clearly had no case. Some petitioners needed to account for apparent incon-

8. I am grateful to Dana Logan for suggesting this point. On the relentlessly weird relationships between ritual acts and discursive avowals, see Logan, *Awkward Rituals*.

9. The number of questions varied. In the 1950s, there were seven; by the late 1960s, after the 1967 draft act, there were four.

10. The first edition of the handbook advised, "To check 'no' means automatic elimination from consideration for [exemption]. Therefore, every C.O. whose belief has any basis should check 'yes' if it is possible for him to do so in the light of the broadest possible meaning of Supreme Being. If a C.O. cannot conscientiously check 'yes,' the next best thing to do is to check neither square but write in following the squares, 'It depends on the definition,' or some similar phrase which is satisfactory to him" (Lyle Tatum, ed., *Handbook for Conscientious Objectors* [CCCO, 1952], 88).

11. [Petitioner name redacted], SSS Form 150, Series V, Box 30, Central Committee for Conscientious Objectors Records. Swarthmore College Peace Collection, Swarthmore, PA. Hereafter cited as CCCO Records.

12. The wording varied slightly throughout the years, but from the 1950s through 1967 it was either exactly this sentence or close to it.

sistencies, such as their previous participation in ROTC, earlier registration for combatant service, work related to the military or weaponry (or, in one case, membership in a riflemen's club), or application for a student deferment without mention of religious objection. And by the late 1960s many had to explain why they objected to all wars, not just the one in Vietnam, even if consideration of that particular war had led to their total objection.

Many of the harder cases involved believers with liberal, pluralistic ideas that skirted traditional categories and pushed against the Supreme Being language. To the second question, about the "nature of your belief" and its relation to a Supreme Being, one petitioner responded, "I believe in love, Godliness and humanism within each man and its recognition and expression through his conscience."[13] Petitioners played with the language of the statute, finding a way to make their beliefs strike the right chord, as set by the statutory language. One wrote, "I believe in faith, hope, and love. I affirm these qualities to be my supreme being, as things that I am ultimately committed to without which my whole existence is meaningless."[14] This claimant believed in a Supreme Being, but on his own terms. Whether the secular state would affirm those terms depended on which state agents were evaluating it, which words the petitioner used, how he presented himself before the boards and hearing officer, the contents of his letters of recommendation, and the results of the federal investigation. Some petitioners— and the people writing their letters of recommendation—were better at playing these language games than others, and the differences among them led to confusion and discrepancy. There were hundreds of difficult cases like this. And the one straightforward, simple question—"Do you believe in a Supreme Being?"—turned out not to be so simple.

FOREST BRITT PETER

In response to the Supreme Being question, Peter wrote, "It depends on the definition." In an addendum to his Form 150, he explained the nature of his beliefs: "Since human life is for me a final value, I consider it a violation of moral law to take human life."[15] His reverence for human life was in some

13. [Petitioner name redacted], SSS Form 150, Series V, Box 30, CCCO Records.
14. [Petitioner name redacted], SSS Form 150, Series V, Box 30, CCCO Records.
15. Quoted in *Peter*, 324 F.2d at 175.

sense religious, he argued. It was absolute and paramount, a "final value," and it entailed a "moral law." Expounding upon this belief, Peter referred to the Unitarian minister and civil rights leader John Haynes Holmes's definition of religion as "the consciousness of some power manifest in nature which helps man in the ordering of his life in harmony with its demands" and "the supreme expression of human nature."[16] Peter thus attempted to use the religious bona fides of a minister to bolster his argument that his own beliefs were religious. In other cases, boards, officers, and courts looked approvingly on citations of theologians not just as sources or inspirations for religious beliefs but as general experts on "religious belief" itself. In this case, though, the argument was unpersuasive. During Peter's hearing before the Appeal Board for the Northern District of California, the board approached the Supreme Being issue from a few different angles, and each time Peter's beliefs were found to be not religious. The hearing officer asked Peter if he was "prayerful," reasoning that if he prayed, he must be praying to something, and thus must really believe in some Supreme Being. Peter replied, "No, I don't pray." When he refused to be inducted into the armed forces, Peter was indicted and found guilty by a district court. He appealed the decision and his case moved on to the Ninth Circuit Court.

As Peter and the judges played the language game of religion and sincerity, they exposed a problem: whether it was ultimately the registrant's or the court's description of beliefs that mattered. In starker terms, how significant was one's description of his own beliefs? Did he have the final word? If not, could agents of the secular state interpret, evaluate, and label citizens' beliefs better than they could? In this case, the Ninth Circuit affirmed the lower court's decision, and Peter remained 1-A, available for combatant service. The court based its decision on a careful consideration of the words of the federal statute, especially the term "Supreme Being." Judge Oliver Deveta Hamlin Jr. noted that "nowhere in the record of the proceedings before the administrative bodies did appellant manifest clearly and unequivocally a belief in a Supreme Being to Whom he owed obedience." At trial, Peter had elaborated, "I can define it as a belief in the mystery of the heart of [other living objects], the essence of being alive, and my respecting and loving

16. Frederick Reel had also cited Holmes. *Reel*, 141 F.2d at 846. I do not know if Peter was aware of Reel's case at the time that he filled out the Form 150, though it is possible. Holmes, along with Paul Tillich, appeared regularly on Form 150s, owing in part to their popularity but also, perhaps, because objector advocacy organizations recommended them as potential sources of belief.

this livingness in other objects and human beings." But did he believe in a Supreme Being? "I suppose," Peter responded, "you could call that a belief in the Supreme Being or God. These just do not happen to be the words I use."[17] For the Ninth Circuit, this was not enough. They cited their own decision from a 1952 case in which they had interpreted the statute to define a religious belief as one that was "couched in terms of the relationship of the individual to a Supreme Being, and [that] comport[ed] with the standard or accepted understanding of the meaning of 'Religion' in American society."[18] Peter's terminology was out of step with common usage and thus not in line with the statutory phrasing. Indeed, Hamlin wrote, Peter's "statements were quite consistent with 'a merely personal code.'"[19]

Peter was in many ways a standard-issue conscientious objector case, but it had at least three distinctive features. First, Peter's claim itself was note-worthy. He was one of a small but growing number of petitioners, many of whom had help from organizations such as the CCCO, who carefully parsed the Supreme Being requirement rather than answering the yes-or-no question directly. Secondly, the case raised the issue of whose description of a belief was authoritative. Most subtle but most important was the third issue Peter brought out, which would be pivotal in the Seeger Supreme Court case. The statute did not require, at least directly, a belief in a Supreme Being. The content of the belief, the thing believed in, is not the Supreme Being. The crucial belief is that war is wrong. That belief, to be religious, must be "in relation to" a Supreme Being. So, "Do you believe in a Supreme Being?" was clearly a relevant question, but it was not the question. The court knew that Peter believed war was wrong; they needed to determine whether that belief was in relation to a Supreme Being. The point was not really what he believed but why and how he believed it.

The sources Peter cited for his belief were not inarguably religious, according to the Ninth Circuit. In his original letter, he had cited "Blake (christian mystic), Emerson, Whitman, and more modern poets who have touched on the question." He further clarified, more generally, "I would

17. Peter, 324 F.2d at 176.

18. George v. United States, 196 F.2d 445, 451 (9th Cir. 1952). In the preceding sentence, which they also quoted in Peter, the court explained, "[Congress's language] comports with the spirit in which 'Religion' is understood generally, and the manner in which it has been defined by the courts." Thus, Congress's speech was both an abstraction of the public, "understood generally," and as it was defined by the courts. It was common language and technical legal language at the same time.

19. Peter, 324 F.2d at 177.

say that the source of my conviction concerning the sacredness of human life and the human spirit has been my experience and study in our democratic american culture, with its values derived from the western religious and philosophical tradition."[20] Again, Peter was describing the "source of [his] conviction," not the content of the conviction itself. This distinction was reminiscent of *Evans*, in which the registrant's beliefs were inspired by Gandhi and other apparently "political" leaders, not the Methodist Church of which he was a member. The sources of Peter's belief were not religious, per se, but they led him to a belief that *was* authentically religious. Or so he argued. In the end, however, the court held that "there was ample basis in fact" for the board's decision to deny Peter an exemption.[21]

ARNO SASCHA JAKOBSON

In the fifteen pages appended to his Form 150, Arno Jakobson articulated his beliefs and their sources. He also attached three letters of support. And, for good measure, when his case moved on to the Appeals Board, he offered them a supplementary "43-page discussion of his views."[22] The hearing officer found that Jakobson was "not sincere" in his beliefs, citing the facts that Jakobson originally had reported a back injury rather than filing conscientious objector paperwork and, furthermore, that he had changed his request from 1-A-O (exemption from combatant service) to 1-O (exemption from all military service).[23] The local board, conversely, had not questioned his sincerity, but they had concluded that his beliefs were not religious. After a "generally favorable" FBI investigation, the Department of Justice recommended that Jakobson be classified 1-A, for, though he was an upstanding individual, his beliefs were neither religious nor sincere.

When the case eventually made it to the Second Circuit, Judge Henry Friendly was primarily concerned with interpreting the Supreme Being

20. *Peter*, 324 F.2d at 175. "Christian" and "American" were not capitalized.

21. *Peter*, 324 F.2d at 177. Following *Estep*, courts could overturn a previous ruling only when that ruling was found not to be based in fact. Thus, the FBI investigations' role as a "fact-finding" enterprise was an important component of the process. *Estep*, 327 U.S. 114.

22. *Jakobson*, 325 F.2d at 411.

23. Seeming inconsistencies like this sank many objectors' cases. Draft counselors constantly stressed the importance of consistency and, if possible, establishing a track record of conscientious belief, lest beliefs appear to be, conveniently, newly acquired.

requirement.[24] "To summarize Jakobson's religious views is not altogether easy," Friendly admitted.[25] Via a lengthy elucidation of Fyodor Dostoevsky's *The Brothers Karamazov*, Jakobson had explained that the "central problem of religion" was "an inescapable choice between acceptance or rejection of the order of the universe." He accepted this order, which, he explained, was created by an ultimate cause he called "Godness." Humans could relate to Godness "vertically" or "horizontally." A vertical relationship was not truly possible, since "God is unknowable to man," and thus, attempts to engage God vertically are "egocentric" and inevitably "must lead to error." Jakobson engaged in a horizontal relationship to Godness, "binding himself to the qualities of Godness that exist in every creation in Mankind and throughout the world." Jakobson (like Dostoevsky's Zosima) accepted life and the universe by affirming "the basic blessedness of the fact of being—of goodness and 'yesness,'" and this affirmation precluded the taking of human life.[26] With the beliefs summarized, Friendly could move on to an evaluation of their religiosity. He recognized the court's task as a matter of statutory interpretation: whether Congress had intended to include beliefs like Jakobson's within the purview of the statute.

The language Congress had used to define "religious training and belief" in section 6(j) was, as we have seen, difficult to interpret. Congress drew its definitional language in section 6(j) from Chief Justice Hughes's 1931 dissent in *Macintosh*, which had been quoted approvingly by the Ninth Circuit in *Berman*. Many courts, including the Ninth Circuit in *Peter*, reasoned that Congress had endorsed *Berman*'s narrower understanding.[27] However, Friendly determined that "the statutory definition need not be regarded as precisely bounded by the Berman opinion when the compulsion to read

---

24. It was no coincidence that the Second and Ninth Circuits were in disagreement again, two decades after the *Kauten* and *Berman* decisions. In the 1940s the Second Circuit had issued favorable rulings in *Kauten*, *Reel*, and *Phillips*, taking a broader interpretation of the 1940 draft act. The Ninth Circuit, in *Berman*, had advanced a more limited, stricter understanding and had ruled against Berman. Once again, the Second Circuit took a broader view in *Jakobson* and *Seeger*, and the Ninth Circuit was stricter. In some sense, at the highest levels, conscientious objection law between 1943 and 1964 played out as a fundamental disagreement between the Second and Ninth Circuits, with the Supreme Court choosing sides and Congress occasionally reacting.

25. *Jakobson*, 325 F.2d at 412.

26. *Jakobson*, 325 F.2d at 413. The quotations are from Friendly's summary of Jakobson's beliefs.

27. *Peter*, 324 F.2d at 177.

it broadly is so strong." Though perhaps bending Congress's meaning creatively to his own ends, Friendly resolved the tensions bound up in the phrasing and genealogy of the statute. To make this argument, he referred to the Protestant theologian Paul Tillich (whom Jakobson had not cited) as an authority who "has written of God in terms that would surely embrace Jakobson's beliefs."[28]

Invoking the sincerity test by citing *Ballard*, Friendly argued that it was not the local draft board's job to evaluate theological beliefs. In *Ballard*, Justice Jackson had argued in a dissent that the secular state ought not to weigh in on the theological correctness or the ultimate veracity of an individual's religious belief. And because it was impossible to consider sincerity apart from veracity, Jackson argued, the state should evaluate neither. Friendly did not agree that state agents could not wade into sincerity questions, but he argued that at least certain agents of the state should not make theological pronouncements. Congress, he thought, had not intended for the statute to "require lay draft boards and personnel of the Department of Justice to pass on nice theological distinctions between vertical and horizontal transcendence."[29] It was above their pay grade, so to speak. But Friendly was quite willing to talk about transcendence and draw distinctions, and to that end he found Tillich useful. It might seem odd that Friendly supported his definition of religion—or, technically, his interpretation of Congress's definition—by citing theologians. It was common, though, to understand theologians to be experts on the religious in general, not just their own traditions, and many judges did similarly, especially with Tillich. Through these sources, the court found that Jakobson's beliefs were indeed religious. And, according to Friendly's Tillichian theory of religion, Jakobson's beliefs were religious whether he called them that or not. He held his beliefs "in relation

28. *Jakobson*, 325 F.2d at 415. Friendly also cited Bishop John A. T. Robinson's then recently published *Honest to God* (1963), specifically the chapter excerpted in *Horizon* magazine in September of 1963. Although Jakobson had not cited Tillich, his "vertical and horizonal" framing was remarkably similar to that in Tillich's essay ("Vertical and Horizontal Thinking," *American Scholar* 15, no. 1 [Winter, 1945–1946]: 102–105). Tillich also discussed the "dimension of depth" as "vertical" relations. This dimension had been lost, he argued, despite religious revival in the United States. Paul Tillich, "The Lost Dimension in Religion," *Saturday Evening Post*, June 14, 1958. On this article and its reception, see Finstuen, *Original Sin and Everyday Protestants*, 157–167. Oddly, Judge Friendly did not include these essays among his Tillich citations.

29. *Jakobson*, 325 F.2d at 415.

to a Supreme Being," whether he called it a Supreme Being or God or a god or "Godness" or "yesness" or anything else.

DANIEL ANDREW SEEGER AND THE SUPREME BEING

Neither Peter nor Jakobson could answer the Supreme Being question without some further explanation, but they both assented to some belief in a higher power to which they owed some devotion. Their cases were similar, but the Second and Ninth Circuits came to opposite conclusions. The third case, taken with *Peter* and *Jakobson* in the Supreme Court case *U.S. v. Seeger*, was the most difficult. Dan Seeger did not affirm a belief in a Supreme Being. Beyond the legal questions it raised, Seeger's agnosticism garnered him some level of fame and generated national interest in not only the case but, for some, his very soul. Shortly after the *Schempp* decision had helped make Madalyn Murray O'Hair "the most hated woman in America" and sparked massive letter-writing campaigns to protest the Supreme Court's recent decisions, Americans remained fascinated by unbelievers and fearful of secularization and "secular humanism."[30] The news coverage of Seeger's case brought him letters of support, derision, condescension, and proselytization.[31] Following *Engel* (1962) and *Schempp* (1963), which found public-school prayer and devotional Bible reading, respectively, unconsti-

30. See Benjamin Eric Sasse, "The Anti-Madalyn Majority: The Secular Left, Religious Right, and the Rise of Reagan's America" (Ph.D. diss., Yale University, 2004), 44–203.

31. Seeger's case also galvanized many in the peace movement. In the early 1960s, smaller organizations around the country were becoming affiliated and networked, especially in connection with the American Friends Service Committee, for which Seeger began working in 1962. For instance, a representative of the Peace Center in Coral Gables, Florida, which had recently become a Peace Education Office of the AFSC, wrote to Seeger after his Circuit Court of Appeals case to say, "There were many of us in the Miami area who beamed with pride that your case was brought to the courts. For years, I have heard people say that SOMEONE should be a test case. Finally I saw the good news about you" (Thalia Stern to Daniel Seeger, Jan. 30, 1964, Box 1, Seeger Papers). Daniel A. Seeger Papers, Swarthmore College Peace Collection. Hereafter cited as Seeger Papers.

Seeger collected a number of these letters of support as well as opposition. Among them was a tract published by the Catholic Information Society, titled "It Does Make a Difference! What I Believe," by Father Richard Ginder ("A Friend" to Daniel Seeger, Jan. 31, 1964), and a letter chiding him, "I was 28 once upon a time, today I am past 70. I, too, at 28 knew all the answers" (Thomas P. Byrnes to Daniel Seeger, Feb. 6, 1964). Box 1, Seeger Papers.

tutional violations of the establishment clause, Americans were tuned in to the Supreme Court and religion.[32] Seeger became the face of the next major reassessment of religious belief and public life. This was not an accident. It was a carefully chosen test case, and Seeger himself became deeply involved in the peace movement and work on behalf of conscientious objectors.

When he turned eighteen, Seeger registered for the draft, but he had a student deferment and did not attempt to become a conscientious objector at that time.[33] Four years later, in 1957, he wrote a letter to his local board and asked to be classified 1-O (exempt from service). That letter, which would be quoted six years later in the Court of Appeals decision, stated:

> As a result of the resolution of a number of problems of conscience with which I have been preoccupied for the past months, I am bound to declare myself unwilling to participate in any violent military conflict, or in activities made in preparation for such an undertaking. My decision arises from what I believe to be considerations of validity from the standpoint of the welfare of humanity and preservation of the democratic values which we in the United States are struggling to maintain. I have concluded that war, from the practical standpoint, is futile and self-defeating, and that from the more important moral standpoint, it is unethical.[34]

32. Engel v. Vitale, 370 U.S. 421 (1962); Abington School District v. Schempp, 374 U.S. 202 (1963).

33. Conscientious objector organizations often advised eighteen-year-olds to file for CO status even if they had student deferments, since it later would be good evidence of their sincerity. Many men, like Seeger, first expressed their pacifist views after college, when their deferments had expired.

34. *Seeger*, 326 F.2d at 848. In the decision, Kaufman wrote that this quoted portion was the entirety of the letter, that he had quoted it in full. However, in the original letter, there were two more paragraphs. Seeger continued, "The contention that war is futile needs little explanation, I suspect, since it is quite generally acknowledged. The ethical considerations may not be so obvious, but I have chosen not to undertake to explain them in this preliminary letter as the argument is somewhat lengthy and involved. I should be happy, any time at your convenience, to discuss my position with you and to submit, either in person or in writing, a clarification of my considerations. Please advise me as to your wishes. Thank you for your attention." Daniel A. Seeger to Selective Service System, Local Board No. 66, Flushing, NY, July 12, 1957. Box 1, Seeger Papers. Most other documents from this era are restricted, and identifying information cannot be published. However, Seeger donated his papers, which include trial documents, official forms, private correspondence, and his own FBI file (which he obtained through a Freedom of Information Act request) to the Peace Collection in 2014.

After that letter, Seeger received another one-year student deferment, during which time he took courses at New York's Queens College, including a course on the philosophy of religion.[35] Also in the summer of 1957, Seeger filled out his Form 150. In his response to the Supreme Being question, he affirmed neither belief nor disbelief. Instead, he wrote, "Of course, the existence of God cannot be proven or disproven, and the essence of his nature cannot be determined. I prefer to admit this and leave the question open rather than answer 'yes' or 'no.' However, skepticism or disbelief in the existence of God does not necessarily mean lack of faith in anything whatsoever." He then quoted Plotinus and concluded, "I feel more respect for this nobler spirit of pagan antiquity, i.e., belief in a devotion to goodness and virtue for their own sakes, and religious faith in a purely ethical creed."[36] This phrase, "religious faith in a purely ethical creed," would be pivotal to his case years later. At the time, though, Seeger's local board was not persuaded. They classified him 1-A in August of 1958.

Seeger sought help from the Central Committee for Conscientious Objectors. He explained his beliefs and asked if he would be better off simply changing his answer to "yes" and affirming his belief in a Supreme Being. He did not *deny* the existence of such a being, after all; he just did not surely believe. Agnostic, not atheist. Seeger received a response from George Willoughby, a well-known peace activist and draft counselor and a founding member of the CCCO who helped produce the handbook. Willoughby advised him to be as honest as possible, presciently noting that doing so "will probably prevent you from getting a 1-O classification from the appeal board, [but] it is always possible that a court may reverse the draft board if your case ever comes into court."[37] They decided to play the long game. They would win, eventually; but it was indeed a very long game.

The FBI investigation commenced in the spring of 1959. Agents interviewed nearly thirty of Seeger's friends, relatives, acquaintances, and associates. They talked to his teachers, childhood neighbors, family friends, and his girlfriend (the last of whom identified Seeger as an "agnostic"). All inter-

35. Daniel Seeger, "Flow Chart," Box 1, Seeger Papers. Seeger created this "flow chart" of his life with four parallel columns for "some autobiographical material," "court case," "historical material," and corresponding "legal documents."

36. Daniel Andrew Seeger, SSS Form 150 answers. Box 1, Seeger Papers.

37. George Willoughby to Dan Seeger, Nov. 5, 1959. Box 1, Seeger Papers. On Willoughby and his wife, Lillian, who was also a prominent peace activist, see Gregory Allen Barnes, *A Biography of Lillian and George Willoughby: Twentieth-Century Quaker Peace Activists* (Edwin Mellen Press, 2007).

viewees spoke highly, if vaguely, of Seeger's character.[38] The vagueness was common in these FBI files, and the majority of interviews were unhelpful. If a high school science teacher *did* recall, years later, that a former student had discussed religion and pacifism, then that was quite pertinent information. But if such an authority figure didn't, that did not really affect the case. Most interviews had little effect. A hearing officer reviewed the résumé of the FBI investigation and interviewed Seeger personally. Based on this, he recommended that Seeger be classified 1-O, exempt from military service.

However, the Department of Justice disagreed. Surveying the facts available and considering the hearing officer's report, they found Seeger to be sincere but not religious. He did not believe in a Supreme Being, and he had not joined a religious organization. He listed no one as a spiritual adviser, instead citing texts by Bertrand Russell and Mohandas Gandhi. So, against the hearing officer's recommendation, Seeger remained 1-A. Willoughby advised Seeger to move to the next step—seeking a presidential appeal— though he admitted that they "seldom reverse the state boards. But one never knows."[39] Willoughby then asked Harold Sherk, of the NSBRO, for help with the case, and he sent Sherk a file containing all Seeger's documents to that point.[40] Despite the institutional support and expert advice, the appeal was unsuccessful; the Presidential Appeal Board classified Seeger 1-A in August of 1960.

Early on the morning of his hearing, Seeger walked to the New York subway through a downpour and appeared as scheduled at 7:30. It was October 20, 1960. In his pocket he carried a few copies of the AFSC's pamphlet *Speak Truth to Power* and some Bertrand Russell essays, both of which he had cited in his Form 150 as sources of his beliefs.[41] He had been coached, knew what to expect, and was ready to answer any questions or challenges. When his time for induction came, Seeger refused. The officer asked if he was aware of the penalties, to which Seeger replied, correctly, "Five years in

38. Seeger FBI file. Box 4, Seeger Papers.

39. George Willoughby to Dan Seeger, May 31, 1960. Box 1, Seeger Papers.

40. George Willoughby to J. Harold Sherk, June 13, 1960. Box 1, Seeger Papers.

41. Daniel Seeger, "Experience of a Conscientious Objector at the Induction Station," Feb., 1961. Box 1, Seeger Papers. Seeger wrote this five-page summary of his experience, based on his notes, for the CCCO to keep on file. On October 12 Willoughby had sent Seeger a CCCO memorandum on "Refusal of Induction for Conscience Sake," which guided objectors through the induction refusal process and informed them of the legal ramifications of their actions. Both the letter and a copy of the memo are in Box 1, Seeger Papers.

jail or ten thousand dollars fine or both."[42] No longer was this strictly a matter for draft boards and the Department of Justice; Seeger was now a federal criminal defendant. He had filed his Form 150 over three years earlier, but his case was only beginning.

By that time the CCCO had decided to support Seeger and see his case through. In February of 1961 they declared that they would accept financial responsibility for the case, shortly after Kenneth Greenawalt had agreed to serve as Seeger's attorney.[43] Greenawalt had a successful track record with conscientious objectors and had become a specialist in the area. Over the next two years, courts pored over the files Seeger had amassed, including his Form 150, the FBI report, the Department of Justice's summary, and letters of support, as well as Seeger's own writings, including his rebuttals to government reports. In collaboration with various state agents, friends and family, and draft counselors, Seeger had helped create his own dossier, a documentary record of his sincerely held religious belief. These were the facts of the case, written on paper, accumulated, reproduced, distributed, rehashed. The paperwork compensated for the ineffability and inaccessibility of religious belief. Seeger's sincerity left a trail, vestiges of belief that could be subjected to secularism's calculative reason.

In the meantime, Seeger's life had been changing. He began attending Society of Friends meetings late in 1958, though he had not become a Quaker. In 1962 he took a full-time job at the AFSC, where he would work until the twenty-first century. The case itself had become central to his life, shaping his work and identity. But the legal matter remained the same: whether his objection to war, as expressed in 1957 on the Form 150 and lived out when he refused induction in 1960, was both sincere and religious. And the sticking point remined the same, too. Seeger did not affirm a belief in a Supreme Being, and that seemed to be what the statute required.

Behind the scenes, CCCO leaders debated the merits of Seeger's case. Was this really the high-profile test case they wanted? Shortly before the district court case in 1963, the executive secretary, Arlo Tatum, balked. He spoke to Seeger directly and suggested that they not go through with it. Tatum had an affinity for Seeger and was partial to his case—both men referred to themselves as "religious agnostics"—but he wondered whether the courts might

42. Seeger, "Experience of a Conscientious Objector at the Induction Station."

43. George Willoughby to Kenneth Greenawalt, Feb. 7, 1961. Box 1, Seeger Papers. Greenawalt estimated a fee of $4000: $2500 for a professional fee and $1500 for expenses, which were mostly printing costs.

be more successfully persuaded by someone who was agnostic but more obviously "religious." Seeger relayed their conversation to the draft counselor Albon Man, who had taken a lead role in the case and served as a point person between the CCCO and Greenawalt. "Arlo feels," Seeger wrote, "that at this point an appropriate test case would involve someone who is definitely *religious* but who does not believe in a Supreme Being.... A Buddhist or an atheist who is a bona-fide member of the Unitarian Church or the Religious Society of Friends would, to Arlo's mind, make a better candidate. In such a situation the religiousness would be institutional religiousness and as such would not be likely to be questioned by the Court and the discussion could concentrate on the Supreme Being clause itself."[44] Apparently other interested parties, such as Vail Palmer of the AFSC's Rights of Conscience Fund, agreed with Tatum.[45] Seeger doubted this line of reasoning, since the draft acts of 1940 and 1948 were designed to isolate individual belief from institutional affiliation. Leaning on "institutional religiousness" might actually undercut their case rather than strengthen it. They were trying to test the bounds of sincere belief itself, to open the possibility of conscientious objection to more believers. Seeger concluded, "I am not anxious to undertake litigation unless there is a reasonable chance it might be beneficial to CO's generally."[46] Eventually, the CCCO overcame their doubts and agreed with Seeger; his would be their test case.

Seeger was unsuccessful before the district court in May of 1963 because the court concluded that after leaving Catholicism he had acquired "a religious attitude" but did not have a new *religion*. The more generous Second Circuit opinions in *Kauten, Phillips,* and *Reel* were not persuasive. Greenawalt repeatedly brought them up, arguing that under "the *Kauten* standard" Seeger clearly fit within the purview of the statute.[47] Judge Richard Levet countered that these cases were under the 1940 statute, not the 1948 one, and thus they were tasked with interpreting a different law.[48] At sentencing, Seeger tried once again to define religion: "I think that our age is character-

44. Dan Seeger to Albon Man, Jan. 9, 1963. Box 1, Seeger Papers.

45. Palmer was a new consultant on the case. A month earlier Seeger had sent her copies of his Form 150, the résumé of the FBI inquiry, his own comments on the résumé, the DOJ recommendations, and his comments on those recommendations. Dan Seeger to Vail Palmer, Dec. 10, 1962. Box 1, Seeger Papers.

46. Seeger to Man, Jan. 9, 1963.

47. United States v. Seeger, U.S. District Court, Southern District of NY, 62 Cr. 100.

48. He thus argued by implication that the 1948 clarification had corrected the *Kauten* interpretation, which, of course, is not what Congress had claimed.

ized by abstract hatreds and by the kind of relentless mobilization of the resources of the good earth for terror and destruction and I think it is a matter of religion, how each of us relates to this very serious situation." Religion was a way of believing, a way of responding to the world, an orientation. Judge Levet responded, "I would be the last one in the world to question that right to think as you please, to worship as you please . . . [but] I have a statute to interpret." He also worried about the precedent it might set to find Seeger, who had no religion, to be religious. "I do not believe, therefore," he continued, that for "all your good record, with all your sincerity, with all your idealism, . . . I can conscientiously as a matter of public policy suspend sentence."[49] For the time being it looked as though Tatum had been right; perhaps someone with a clear religious affiliation would have been a better test case. But they would push the case as far as they could. Seeger, Greenawalt, and the draft counselors spent the summer preparing their appeal.[50]

The Second Circuit Court of Appeals heard their arguments on November 15, 1963, and the key question—was Seeger's belief *religious*, as defined by the statute?—was the same as ever, but with a strange twist. Seeger was clearly sincere, everyone agreed, but that didn't mean he was religious, and on that point Judge Irving Kaufman zeroed in on a minute piece of evidence. Form 150 reproduced the words of the statute, "by reason of my religious training and belief," below which conscientious objectors were to sign. When he did his paperwork in 1957, Seeger had crossed out the words "training and" and added quotation marks around the word "religious." Those inserted quotation marks raised a slightly absurd but pertinent question: was "'religious'" the same as "religious"? Did Seeger's supplementary punctuation negate or change or enhance or diminish the word's meaning? We might read Seeger's

49. Stenographer's minutes, Southern District Court Reporters, May 28, 1963. Box 3, Seeger Papers.

50. Perhaps the case also influenced Seeger's conception of his job at the AFSC. In a contentious internal memo only a month before his appeal case, he advocated that the organization be more open to nonbelievers and skeptics. "Labels like 'humanist,' 'atheist,' 'agnostic' and 'skeptic' are convenient labels for the purposes of conversation, but for an organization operating in a Quaker spirit there can be no packaged judgments derived from such labels, for persons are more important than any 'standards.' It seems to me that the AFSC, if it is to truly minister to the sweep and diversity of the human family, must always stand for the priority of persons and personal relationships over any heteronomy, even of the supernatural." Dan Seeger to Catherine Evans, memo, Oct. 16, 1963. Box 3, Seeger Papers.

scare quotes as an instance of irony, distancing one's intention and meaning from one's own words. But the word "religious" was not Seeger's word. It was from the form, which was from the statute. So perhaps we might read Seeger here as pointing out the irony of the whole procedure, not of his own speech act. As an expression of his own sincerely held beliefs, he signed a legal document with someone else's words on them. The added quotation marks, then, might actually have been a signal of his sincerity, a way to show, to quote Britt Peter, that "these are not the words I use."

Kaufman, writing for the court, argued that according to the standard set in *Kauten*, Seeger's "'religious'" belief was indeed religious. He quoted that case's definition of religious belief as arising from "a sense common to men in the most primitive and in the most highly civilized societies."[51] However, Kaufman noted, *contra* Congress's own explanation of their statute, the 1948 addition to the draft act "rejected [*Kauten*] in favor of a narrower standard [in *Berman*]." In his understanding, "Congress expressly approved the *Berman* definition." Thus, unlike Friendly in *Jakobson*, Kaufman thought any interpretation of the statute had to mesh with *Berman*. For this reason, because the *Berman* decision was wrong, the statute itself was misguided. Kaufman's opinion became an apologia for the *Kauten* opinion, which, he argued, was correct and prescient and should not have been supplanted by *Berman* (though, as noted, Congress apparently had not seen a stark contradiction between the two). Religion was essential to humanity and found in all civilizations; thus, the range of what should count as a religious belief was necessarily quite wide.

Whereas the district court had found that Seeger had no religion, the Second Circuit found that neither group affiliation nor belief in a deity was required. Favoring the Second Circuit's opinion was the fact that the Supreme Court had recognized the authentic religiosity of nontheistic beliefs a few years prior in 1961's *Torcaso v. Watkins*. In that case, the Court found unconstitutional a Maryland law requiring public officials to profess a belief in God, because it violated such a believer's free exercise. Torcaso's lawyer was Leo Pfeffer, head of the Commission of Law and Social Action for the American Jewish Congress and a prolific author on religious freedom, civil rights, and related issues. Pfeffer argued that the free exercise clause was "understood by the Fathers of our Constitution to encompass

51. *Seeger*, 326 F.2d at 850, quoting *Kauten*, 133 F.2d at 708.

those without religion," though the Court did not go quite so far.[52] However, in the opinion of a unanimous Court, Justice Hugo Black dropped into a footnote this capacious interpretation of religion: "Among religions in this country which do not teach what would generally be considered a belief in the existence of God are Buddhism, Taoism, Ethical Culture, Secular Humanism and others."[53] Although the *Torcaso* Court had not cited *Kauten*, Kaufman argued that *Kauten* "in a very real sense . . . was the precursor of *Torcaso*." Citing *Torcaso*, then, Kaufman was "compelled to recognized that a requirement of belief in a Supreme Being, no matter how broadly defined, cannot embrace all those faiths which can validly claim to be called 'religious.'"[54] Like Judge Friendly in *Jakobson*, Kaufman felt obliged to interpret broadly.

Using *Kauten* and *Torcaso*, Kaufman situated Seeger's beliefs in two immediate contexts: human hearts and the secularized 1960s. Those two decisions recognized that "today, a pervading commitment to a moral ideal is for many the equivalent of what was historically considered the response to divine commands. . . . [F]or many in today's 'skeptical generation,' just as for Daniel Seeger, the stern and moral voice of conscience occupies that hallowed place in the hearts and mind of men which was traditionally reserved for the commandments of God."[55] The *Kauten* court had anticipated and proactively accommodated secularization and skepticism. By 1964 many journalists, scholars, and clergy were celebrating, chronicling, and warning of secularization, particularly amid the rise of "death of God" theology and the early stages of the "counterculture." If many young people were turning away from traditional religion, did that make them irreligious or incapable of religious belief? For Kaufman, the answer was no. Everyone has a "hallowed place" where deep moral commitments dwell. A commitment was religious (or something like religious) because of its place, not its source

52. Torcaso v. Watkins, oral argument, April 24, 1961 (part II, 4:15), https://www.oyez .org/cases/1960/373.

53. Torcaso v. Watkins, 367 U.S. 488, 495n11 (1961). This definition had plenty of unintended consequences, including efforts by some evangelical Christians to label certain teachings "secular humanism" and thus a religion and thus in violation of the establishment clause when taught in public schools. See Smith v. Board of School Commissioners of Mobile County, 827 F.2d 684 (11th Cir. 1987), and Mozert v. Hawkins, 827 F.2d 1058 (6th Cir. 1987). See Gordon, *The Spirit of the Law*, 156–167.

54. *Seeger*, 326 F.2d at 853, 852.

55. *Seeger*, 326 F.2d at 853.

or inspiration. Seeger believed religiously, even if his belief was *in* a "purely ethical creed" rather than a religion.

U.S. V. SEEGER AND THE REDEFINITION OF RELIGIOUS BELIEF

Seeger, Jakobson, and *Peter,* with their similar facts yet different outcomes, had made a muddle. And once again, the Second and Ninth Circuits had issued divergent interpretations: it was *Kauten* and *Berman,* part two. But this time, instead of a legislative fix, the Supreme Court would sort it out. They heard the *Seeger* case, with *Peter* and *Jakobson* on certiorari, in late 1964 and issued their judgment in 1965. The Court had before it a tangle of issues, but the main thread was the same: What counted as "religious training and belief"?

The Court's answer helped cement a two-pronged sincerity test—"truly held an religious and religious in nature," as one judge later summarized it—and, more fundamentally, it also changed the meaning of "religious in nature."[56] If the Court were to find in Seeger's favor, it would need to find that his belief was "in relation to a Supreme Being" even though he did not affirm belief in a Supreme Being. As Justice Tom Clark noted, the immediate question was "a narrow one: does the term 'Supreme Being,' as used in section 6(j), mean the orthodox God or the broader concept of a power or being, or a faith, 'to which all else is subordinate or upon which all else is ultimately dependent?'"[57] Narrow as that question was, the answer had a broad effect. The Court tried to restrict its decision to interpretation of the statutory language, not to answer bigger questions about the definition of "religious." Nevertheless, judges, lawmakers, and academics referenced the opinion often. Whether they intended to do so or not, the *Seeger* Court offered an expansive, useful definition with a few handy quotable phrases.

Though the legal and definitional questions were not new, historical circumstance framed them in new ways. First, perceived secularization had changed the meaning of religious belief. Increasing religious diversity, indi-

---

56. Martinelli v. Dugger, 817 F.2d 1499 (11th Cir. 1987).

57. *Seeger,* 380 U.S. at 174. The quotation is from *Webster's New International Dictionary,* 2nd ed.

vidualization, and deinstitutionalization weighed heavily on the justices' deliberations. Second, Cold War fears of communism, along with the rise of "Judeo-Christian" or "tri-faith" America, reinforced the importance of religious freedom and the protection of religious belief itself.[58] Third, as *Ballard*'s sincerity test required, the government should consider carefully the fact of a claimant's belief but not its theological veracity. Fourth, decisions of recent decades had yielded contradictory results and a glossary of flexible phrases. These contexts left the Court a shaky footing on which to evaluate the religiosity of these three individuals' beliefs. Perhaps the trickiest task of all was to interpret section 6(j) in a way that took a broad enough view of religion to find in Seeger's favor but did not find the statute unconstitutional.

"We're in an intensely difficult area here," admitted Solicitor General Archibald Cox, with hesitation and strain in his voice, during oral arguments.[59] Cox presented the government's position: there were some beliefs that were obviously just political and some that were obviously religious, but they existed on a continuum, and the government had to demarcate a point of division somewhere along it. Further complicating the issue, religion contained or included certain features, such as humanitarianism or mysticism, but these features alone did not constitute religion. Cox said, "I have no doubt that Peter had, in a sense, [a] poetic, a deep, a mystical feeling, a belief in life, in existence, that he had a feeling that was stirred by living things, by the processes of creation. He apparently had a mystical sense of oneness with those things."[60] That all sounded quite religious to Justice Arthur Goldberg. But Cox responded, "Well, again, Mr. Justice . . . you take some *one* thing that enters into religion and want to *make* that religion."[61] Peter's mystical sense of oneness could enter into religion or could be part of religious belief, but it was not in itself religion.

These difficult questions were not merely academic: they had arisen in

---

58. "Tri-faith" refers to Protestantism, Catholicism, and Judaism. In the mid-twentieth century, many observers saw the tri-faith model replacing the hegemony of Protestant America. See Kevin M. Schultz, *Tri-Faith America: How Catholics and Jews Held Postwar America to Its Protestant Promise* (Oxford University Press, 2011). In this same period, "Judeo-Christianity" arose as an ambiguous term that named an imagined Western tradition that was amenable to democracy and liberalism. See Gaston, *Imagining Judeo-Christian America*.

59. U.S. v. Seeger, oral argument, November 16, 1964, 17:13. https://www.oyez.org/cases/1964/50.

60. U.S. v. Seeger, oral argument, November 16, 1964, 1:14:57.

61. U.S. v. Seeger, oral argument, November 16, 1964, 1:15:38.

the context of secular governance. Far from just abstract questions about the definition of religion, they were, more importantly, questions about how to manage a huge, messy bureaucracy. Judges played their roles, but so did local draft boards. As Judge Kaufman had put it, "[W]e would create an impossible task for draft boards were we to insist upon a distinction between Arno Sascha Jakobson's devotion to a mystical force of 'Godness' and Daniel Andrew Seeger's compulsion to follow the paths of 'goodness.'"[62] What is the difference between Godness and goodness? If there is one, it seemed unfair—and certainly impractical—to ask draft boards around the country to find it. Amid the high-minded discussion and debate, the fine-line-drawing and vexing hypotheticals, it could have been easy to forget that the point was to apply federal law to systems of secular governance.

Of all the practical and theoretical problems at issue, perhaps the most difficult to resolve was what we might call the *Torcaso* problem. If religions did not necessarily involve a god, then how could Congress define "religious training and belief" as that which was "in relation to a Supreme Being"? In conference on November 20, 1964, Chief Justice Earl Warren acknowledged this issue, reasoning that the requirement that conscientious objectors believe "in relation to a Supreme Being" could be discriminatory.[63] If all religious beliefs were to receive equal protection, and if some religious beliefs were nontheistic, then the law discriminated along religious lines when it limited exemptions only to those holding theistic beliefs. For this reason, the Court could find in petitioners' favor by finding the statute itself in violation of the Constitution's free exercise and equal protection clauses. Or, as Justice John Harlan argued, they could find that Congress had favored one religion over another and thus "run afoul of the establishment clause."[64] Simply put, they did not want to do that. Certainly Congress would rewrite such a provision, were it stricken from the law, but the statute in question already had been rewritten as a congressional response to judicial rulings,

62. *Seeger*, 326 F.2d at 853.

63. Dickson, *The Supreme Court in Conference*, 434.

64. Other legal thinkers already had anticipated the difficulties that *Torcaso* might cause for conscientious objection cases. See, e.g., Francis J. Conklin, "Conscientious Objector Provisions: A View in the Light of Torcaso v. Watkins," *Georgetown Law Review* 51 (1963): 252–283; "Comment: Conscientious Objectors: Requirement of a Belief in a Supreme Being Held to Create an Unconstitutional Classification," *Duke Law Journal* 4 (Autumn, 1964): 901–907; and "Comment: Constitutionality of Requiring Belief in a Supreme Being for Draft Exemption as Conscientious Objector," *Columbia Law Review* 64, no. 5 (May, 1964): 938–950.

using judges' phrases. It would be better, the justices thought, to interpret the existing statute creatively.

The fundamental tension remained between the Second Circuit's *Kauten* standard and the Ninth Circuit's more limited definition in *Berman*, the latter of which seemed to have been "expressly approved" by the 1948 statute.[65] Rather than choosing between *Kauten* and *Berman* standards, the Court essentially merged the two by creating two broad categories: the religious and, on the other side, the political, philosophical, sociological, and/or personal. But the religious side would not be defined by a strict reading of the Supreme Being clause. The justices were left to conclude, as Clark said in conference, that "the phrase 'Supreme Being' in the act does not mean a God, but includes all religious belief. I would affirm *Seeger* by construing the act to include this man," adding, "I would follow the procedures established in *Berman*."[66] Thus, the Court relied on *Berman* for its procedural recommendations and reread it as simply establishing a distinction between religious and nonreligious. This distinction, coupled with the broadened interpretation of religious belief, allowed them to affirm the statute's constitutionality while still finding in the favor of all three claimants.

Writing for a unanimous Court, Justice Clark argued that section 6(j) "excludes persons who, disavowing religious belief, decide on the basis of essentially political, sociological or economic considerations that war is wrong and that they will have no part in it."[67] The key to this generous interpretation was that, although the 1940 act used Chief Justice Hughes's words from *Macintosh*—"The essence of religion is belief in relation to God involving duties superior to those arising from any human relation"— Congress had changed "God" to "Supreme Being." Because of this change, Clark argued, "it becomes readily apparent that the Congress deliberately broaden[ed]" the phrase's meaning. Furthermore, because they "did not elaborate on the form or nature of this higher authority which [they] chose to designate as 'Supreme Being,'" they must have been allowing for a wide diversity of beliefs and even, perhaps, changes in what "religion" and "reli-

---

65. The phrase "expressly approved" is from *Seeger*, 326 F.2d at 850. In conference, Justice William O. Douglas said Hand's was "the correct view. As Hand best says it, they are not here discussing philosophical or political ideas—if their conscience is hooked to one or three or no gods, they all fall into the broad conception of religion" (Dickson, *The Supreme Court in Conference*, 435).

66. Dickson, *The Supreme Court in Conference*, 435.

67. *Seeger*, 380 U.S. at 173.

gious belief" would come to mean.[68] *Contra* the Second Circuit's finding and the government's argument, Congress did not endorse the *Berman* definition. The Senate report on the 1948 bill, which cited *Berman* as it clarified "religious training and belief," was meant to reenact "substantially the same provisions as were found" in the 1940 act. If the 1940 act was meant to broaden the definition of religion, the 1948 changes could not substantially narrow that meaning, especially via a simple citation.

Clark considered the statute's meaning in light of increasing religious diversity and reasoned that Congress must have thought similarly, as indicated by the change from "God" to "Supreme Being." Clark remarked on the complexity of the Court's task, made more difficult "by the richness and variety of spiritual life in our country."[69] Clark's opinion showed the dynamic interplay between the political project of pluralism and the demographic fact of diversity. Society, including the law, accommodates and celebrates religious differences even as in so doing it can reinforce them. *Seeger*, in an attempt to harmonize *Berman* and *Kauten*, asserted a clear distinction between religion and not-religion. Religion was one thing, an identifiable category of human life, and religious beliefs existed necessarily in relation to a Supreme Being. However, religious differences complicated the idea that there was indeed a clearly demarcated segment of beliefs called "religion." "Over 250 sects inhabit our land," Clark noted. "Some believe in a purely personal God, some in a supernatural deity; others think of religion as a way of life envisioning, as its ultimate goal, the day when all men can live together in perfect understanding and peace. There are those who think of God as the depth of our being."[70] He mentioned various Christian sects and subsects and splinter groups, including the historic peace churches. And there were Buddhists and Hindus, whose American populations would grow significantly in number after the changes to immigration law enacted that same year. These are all religions, and they all have some conception of a Supreme Being, very broadly interpreted. And, citing *Torcaso*, the Court also acknowledged that some religions were explicitly nontheistic. If religion were to exist as a stable unified category, it would need to accommodate significant differences.

However, the appellants were not religions, but people. They were three idiosyncratic individuals with different beliefs, ways of expressing

68. *Seeger*, 380 U.S. at 175.

69. *Seeger*, 380 U.S. at 174.

70. *Seeger*, 380 U.S. at 174.

those beliefs, and varying degrees of connection to established religions. Religious beliefs often became intelligible through their relation to established churches and doctrines, but what mattered legally was individual conscience. Thus, the fact that the Court had labeled Buddhism, Hinduism, Ethical Culture, and Secular Humanism as religions served only as a guide to which beliefs were indeed religious. In conference, Justice Goldberg remarked, "The only difference between Seeger and Buddhism is that Seeger isn't a Buddhist."[71] Seeger was not a Buddhist, but his beliefs seemed Buddhist, and Buddhism was definitely a religion. This argument made some logical sense, but the Court hesitated to define religious belief only through references to established religions. After all, if the point of the 1948 act had been to encompass more beliefs and believers—who were growing ever more diverse—then individuals' beliefs should be able to be tried without direct reference to established religious traditions. The 1940 draft act had removed the membership requirement. Seeger did not need to be a Buddhist to believe like one. That is, to believe religiously. Nonreligious beliefs were philosophical, sociological, economic, and political; religious beliefs were religious. Thus, for the statutory phrase "religious training and belief" to have meaning, religion needed to stand discrete and coherent with some identifiable qualifying markers.

Clark devised a test: "a sincere and meaningful belief which occupies in the life of its possessor a place parallel to that filled by the God of those admittedly qualifying for the exemption comes within the statutory definition."[72] This parallel-belief test naturalized religion in much the same way as other legal thinkers had theorized it. Religious belief was an inborn and universal,

---

71. Dickson, *The Supreme Court in Conference*, 436.

72. *Seeger*, 380 U.S. at 176. This test had a precursor in the 1957 tax-exemption case *Fellowship of Humanity v. County of Alameda*. Clark did not cite *Alameda*, though it certainly seems that he borrowed some phrases. The *Alameda* court held that "the only inquiry in such a case is the objective one of whether or not the belief occupies the same place in the lives of its holders that the orthodox beliefs occupy in the lives of believing majorities, and whether a given group that claims the exemption conducts itself the way groups conceded to religious conduct themselves." Fellowship of Humanity v. County of Alameda, 153 Cal. App. 2d 673, 692 (Dist. Ct. App. 1957). The judge went on to offer an anthropological/psychological theory of religion: "Religion fills a void that exists in the lives of most men. Regardless of why a particular belief suffices, as long as it serves this purpose, it must be accorded the same status of an orthodox religious belief" (692–693). Justice Black cited this case in *Torcaso*. The key difference was that *Alameda* was about institutions and *Seeger* was about individuals.

though special, part of the human. Thus, it could not be limited to theists. Clark went so far as to argue that Congress had intended such a broad interpretation. The phrase "religious training and belief," combined with the use of "Supreme Being" instead of "God," he argued, were Congress's ways of "embrac[ing] the ever-broadening understanding of the modern religious community." Clark again cited Tillich, as well as David Saville Muzzey, the leader of the Ethical Culture movement (the latter a shrewd citation in light of *Torcaso*'s explicit mention of Ethical Culture). Muzzey had written, "Religion, for all the various definitions that have been given of it, must surely mean the devotion of man to the highest ideal that he can conceive."[73] The Court had solved a delicate problem, but it did so at the expense of a more coherent and usable test. Clark was careful to stipulate that this was strictly a matter of statutory interpretation, not free exercise jurisprudential standard-setting. Nevertheless, many courts would look to *Seeger* as they adjudicated free exercise cases, particularly when judges searched for usefully expansive definitions.

"HIS OWN SCHEME OF THINGS"

The Supreme Court in *Seeger* held that courts, draft boards, and appeals boards had "to decide whether the beliefs professed by a registrant are sincerely held, and whether they are, in his own scheme of things, religious."[74] This was the standard two-pronged sincerity test—but with the added qualification of "in his own scheme of things." This phrase recognized and accommodated the inherent individuality of religious experience. On this point, Clark returned to *Ballard*, this time quoting Justice Douglas: "Religious experiences which are as real as life to some may be incomprehensible to others."[75] Clark did "hasten to emphasize," though, "that while the 'truth'

---

73. *Seeger*, 380 U.S. at 180, 184; quotation from David Saville Muzzey, *Ethics as a Religion* (Frederick Ungar Publishing, 1967 [1951]), 95. Later, Clark again quoted Tillich's *The Shaking of the Foundations* (1948): "And if that word [God] has not much meaning for you, translate it, and speak of the depth of your life, of the source of your being, or your ultimate concern, *of what you take seriously without any reservation*. Perhaps, in order to do so, you must forget everything traditional that you have learned about God" (187; Clark added the emphasis).

74. *Seeger*, 380 U.S. at 185.

75. *Ballard*, 322 U.S. at 86; cited in *Seeger*, 380 U.S. at 184.

of a belief is not open to question, there remains the significant question whether it is 'truly held.' . . . It is, of course, a question of fact—a prime consideration to the validity of every claim for exemption as a conscientious objector."[76] The first step, then, was to demonstrate the facts of belief, with the help of draft counselors, investigators, and others. Once that fact was established, courts and draft boards had to figure out whether the beliefs were religious on a case-by-case basis, with reference to the beliefs of more "orthodox" believers yet still respecting individuality. As the legal scholar Robert Rabin pointed out shortly after the case, *Seeger* set up a distinction "between restrictions on one's *tenets* of belief and restrictions on one's *system* of belief."[77] Religious beliefs as tenets could be considered apart from religions as systems. Though Clark did not offer a new definition of religion, his formulation presented an innovative view of religious belief.

On his draft form, Dan Seeger struck out words and added quotation marks, along with his own explanation of his terminology. When the Supreme Court approved Seeger's belief as religious, it effectively allowed Seeger to redefine the statute's meaning—or, at least, they authorized and affirmed his redefinition. Though it was not meticulously analyzed at the time (or since, for the most part), Seeger's phrase "religious faith in a purely ethical creed" deserves further elucidation. There are two adjective-noun combinations in that phrase: "religious faith" and "ethical creed." "Religious belief," the key term in the draft act, can refer to two different things. Throughout most of American history, and in most conscientious objector cases, it had referred to beliefs in religion, that is, in established doctrines, teachings, or texts. After *Seeger*, "religious" could also indicate a mode of believing, not necessarily the content believed. In other words, religious belief meant to believe *religiously*.

76. *Seeger*, 380 U.S. at 185.
77. Rabin, "When Is a Religious Belief Religious," 241.

6

BELIEVING RELIGIOUSLY

THE *SEEGER* CASE MARKED A PIVOTAL movement in the history of American religion. There is no one story of American religion, no singular grand narrative, but there are major themes. Two of them—individualization and pluralism—worked together to redefine religion as categorically a matter of sincerely held belief. Considering two key 1965 texts, the Supreme Court's *Seeger* opinion and the Second Vatican Council's *Dignitatis humanae*, Winnifred Sullivan has argued that in that year the Court and Council were "in agreement, as revealed in two of their most significant writings on the subject, that religion, insofar as it is the state's business at all, is, in some sense, primarily about individual conscience."[1] The imaginary of sincerely held religious belief, I have been arguing, defines religious belief more by its style than by its content. As religious diversity increased simultaneously with supposed secularization, many in the United States and beyond doubled down on the individual as the seat of religiosity. Of course, this shift was not total, and churches did not go away.[2] But there was a general trend toward individualization of belief and the rise of conscience. Dan Seeger found these

1. Sullivan, "'The Conscience of Contemporary Man,'" 108–109. On the Catholic Church and conscience in this period, see Cajka, *Follow Your Conscience*.

2. Sherbert v. Verner, 374 U.S. 398 (1963), for example, found the claimant religious by identifying her as a belonging to a church. I'm grateful to an anonymous reviewer for pointing this out and asking for clarification on this point. One aspect of the story I have been tracing in this book is the tension between individuality and membership—how, even when sincere belief is imagined as an individual phenomenon, the "religious" is still defined with touchstones in established and recognized religion(s). The parallel-belief test is an example of this. Even though it does not tie individuals to their churches, it reads their religiosity obliquely through others' churches. On the persistence and resurgence of churches and "the Church" in twenty-first-century law, see Sullivan, *Church State Corporation*.

changes liberating. The state afforded him an opportunity to redefine his own religious subjectivity, pushing against the limits of bureaucratic language and prewritten forms. Still, according to the new understanding, his religiosity was legible. He believed religiously.

Other believers, including other conscientious objectors, did not find liberation through individual belief and liberal humanism. It would be too simple, and a little glib, to say that the courts were really rewarding Seeger for his whiteness, maleness, and class, rather than his religious belief. But it is true that the benefits of racial liberalism, including religious freedom, are reaped more fully by people like Seeger than by others, even in an era in which those rights expanded. And, relatedly, it is true that religion, perhaps especially when it is understood more individually than institutionally, is often most legible to agents of the secular state when expressed in familiar idioms and with particular affective comportments.

This chapter extends the previous two chapters' study of conscientious objection both as historically significant to the genealogy of "sincerely held religious belief" and as a case study in secular governance. But it also carries the narrative and analysis beyond conscientious objection, placing *Seeger* (and, later, *Welsh*) in the context of academic and legal discussion of religion and secularism from roughly 1965 to 1972. Using conscientious objector cases as a touchstone, I discuss the utility of citing the Protestant theologian Paul Tillich, particularly his definition of religion as "ultimate concern," for judges, claimants, and scholars. Next, I consider a major intellectual development of this moment: secularization theses, such as Harvey Cox's *The Secular City* (1965), that provided popular explanations for the "death of God" and the secularization of "Western" society. These narratives shared investments in civilizationalist progress and individual conscience. Scholars too, in the then-burgeoning academic study of religion and related disciplines, trafficked in the politics of sincerity, understood as affective. The chapter concludes by taking up the historian of religion Sydney Ahlstrom's suggestion, based on a sort of secularization thesis, that scholars ought to consider "'secular' movements and convictions" within our religious histories of the American people.[3] Rather than debunk the secularization thesis, I am inclined to situate and engage it. To track the rise of believing religiously is to trace the trajectory of a certain sort of secularization.

3. Ahlstrom, *A Religious History of the American People*, xiv.

"ULTIMATE CONCERN" AND THE HANDBOOK

In the developing consensus around "religion," to believe religiously meant to have an "ultimate concern." This phrase, borrowed from Tillich, has served many as a handy definitional tool for broad conceptions of religion. As noted in the previous chapter, Judge Henry Friendly cited Tillich in the *Jakobson* case, even though Arno Jakobson had not mentioned Tillich in his own explanation of his beliefs. Friendly included a lengthy footnote elucidating Tillich's theology, quoting the second volume of his *Systematic Theology* (1957), *Courage to Be* (1952), and *The Shaking of the Foundations* (1948), and he cited Bishop John A. T. Robinson's much-discussed *Honest to God* (1963). Tillich wrote that in "absolute faith" the language of theology and religion is inadequate. There is a "depth" to human experience beyond language and convention, and "the name of this infinite and inexhaustible depth and ground of all being is God. That depth is what the word God means. . . . He who knows about depth knows about God."[4] Quoting this passage from *The Shaking of the Foundations*, Friendly asserted that Jakobson clearly knew about depth. He knew about a Supreme Being.

For Friendly, Tillich's ideas were useful, but so was his status as both a religious authority and an authority on religion. He comparatively analyzed Jakobson's and Tillich's beliefs, finding that in some ways "Jakobson comes closer to a traditional reading of 'Supreme Being.'"[5] Thus, he implied, if Jakobson was not religious, then Tillich certainly could not be either. But Tillich *was* religious and, furthermore, an expert of "high distinction and wide influence." In the oral arguments of *Seeger*, U.S. Solicitor General Archibald Cox affirmed Friendly's assessment and even said that the government "adopt[ed] a more liberal interpretation" of the Supreme Being clause of the conscientious objector statute. They adopted this view, he said, "having in mind not only the diversity of religions in this country, but also the fact that such eminent theologians such as Professor Tillich and Dr. Robinson, the Anglican Bishop of Woolwich . . . construe the idea of the personal god and defined god in such terms as the ultimate ground or root of our being."[6] Justice Clark cited Cox's oral argument and quoted both Tillich and

4. *Jakobson*, 325 F.2d at 416.
5. *Jakobson*, 325 F.2d at 416.
6. *Seeger*, 380 U.S., oral arguments. Nov. 16, 1964. Cox's opening statement, 3:41.

Robinson at some length, as well as the Ecumenical Council at Vatican II and Ethical Culturist David Saville Muzzey.[7] These thinkers each were part of a secularizing trend that worked, in part, through sincerity. David Hollinger has argued, for example, that Robinson "made the generic ideal of honesty, rather than any specifically Christian doctrine, the touchstone for his testimony, and he blurred the line between what most people thought Christianity was and the rest of modern life."[8] In other words, "secular" sincerity substituted, or at least blended with, the role traditionally played by religion. Americans held a wide variety of authentically religious beliefs, Clark wrote, and thus a too-narrow conception of the religious clearly could not account for the nation's pluralism.

Pluralism, Pamela Klassen and Courtney Bender have argued, has created "the paradox that with its expanding reach, invocations to celebrate difference may themselves breed a hegemonic unity."[9] In his concurring opinion in *Seeger*, Justice William Douglas noted that "the words 'a Supreme Being' have no narrow technical meaning in the field of religion," and he went on to cite ideas of God predating "our Judeo-Christian civilization." He discussed various Buddhist and Hindu concepts, quoted from the Rig Veda, and cited *Life* magazine's "The World's Great Religions."[10] For Douglas, almost everyone believed in a Supreme Being, and thus religious diversity reinforced essential human sameness. Tillichian "ultimate concern"— Protestant theology refigured as a secular theory of religion—thus abetted both secularism and pluralism.

After *Seeger*, a Tillich citation could go a long way for a would-be conscientious objector. In the late 1960s, as the United States ramped up the draft and sent hundreds of thousands of troops to Vietnam, thousands more men sought conscientious objector status. The process was no less labyrinthine than in previous eras. Many men continued to seek help from the Central Committee for Conscientious Objectors, both directly and through their handbook, which guided objectors through the process. Draft counselors

7. *Seeger*, 380 U.S. at 180–183.

8. Hollinger, "After Cloven Tongues of Fire," 28.

9. Courtney Bender and Pamela E. Klassen, "Introduction: Habits of Pluralism," in *After Pluralism*, ed. Bender and Klassen, 8.

10. *Seeger*, 380 U.S. at 189. Douglas also quoted from Nancy Wilson Ross's *The World of Zen* (1960) and Edward Conze's *Buddhism: Its Essence and Development* (1959). He referred to Conze as "one eminent student of Buddhism." On the *Life* "The World's Great Religions" issues, see Eden Consenstein, "Religion at Time Inc.: From the Beginning of *Time* to the End of *Life*" (Ph.D. diss., Princeton University, 2021).

who worked for the CCCO and similar organizations also provided counsel, helping objectors keep up with changes in law as well as the latest and most effective strategies. After 1965 the handbook included an excerpt of the passage from Tillich's *Systematic Theology* quoted in *Seeger*. That passage, because it was quoted in the Supreme Court case, became a go-to explanation and authentication for those who believed religiously but not theistically—not in "the God of traditional theism, but the 'God above God.'"[11]

In the CCCO's files, where they kept their correspondence with thousands of objectors and potential objectors, one can see pluralism at work. Often, especially in the clearest and most detailed letters and forms, it is a sort of liberal Protestant or post-Protestant ecumenism.[12] They look like 1960s (or 1990s or sometimes 2010s) religious studies scholarship. One man, who was not particularly religious but had affiliated loosely with an Episcopal church and spent time at the Episcopal Student Center in college, described the nature of his belief: "I believe in love, Godliness and humanism within each man and its recognition and expression through his conscience. I believe this inner spirit or soul to be a part of a universal, intangible and indescribable benevolent force most aptly described and most justly exalted as the love it manifests. As Christ preached and as is indeed the basis for the world's major religions, I believe wholly in the power of love and the doctrine of 'Peace on earth, Good will to men.'" He cited the Upanishads, Buddhist and Confucian texts, "the scriptures of Taoism," and the Hebrew Bible, along with Bertrand Russell, Henry David Thoreau, and Martin Luther King Jr.[13] The petitioner recognized that Christianity remained the standard by which the religious was calculated, aligning his beliefs with those that "Christ preached." However, these beliefs were not sectarian; they were not even essentially Christian. Furthermore, the con-

11. Arlo Tatum, ed., *Handbook for Conscientious Objectors*, 10th ed. (Philadelphia: Central Committee for Conscientious Objectors, 1968), 39.

12. See Hollinger, "After Cloven Tongues of Fire."

13. [Petitioner's name redacted], Form 150. One of this petitioner's coworkers wrote a letter of support to the draft board, assessing, "I consider his beliefs about the pervasiveness of love and the efficacy of pacifism to be unrealistic and romantic, but I feel he adheres to them with a sense of reverence which is religious." [Redacted] to [redacted, Local Draft Board Chairman], April 12, 1968, Series V, Box 30, CCCO Records. This letter is representative of a large number of letters of support, which often made it a point to state their personal disagreements. What is more interesting about this letter, though, is the phrase "sense of reverence which is religious." This letter writer, likely familiar with the *Seeger* decision and the 1967 draft act change, perfectly used the believing-religiously framework.

tent of the belief itself was in a universal human nature. This pluralism is double-layered: the "benevolent force" is universal and accessible to all, *and* all major religions recognize this.

Petitioners cited Tillich, sometimes quoting him directly on their Form 150s, to argue that their views were truly religious. It did not always work. One English professor was in the army but had attended Quaker meetings for some time and wanted to become a conscientious objector. In his 1968 appeal for discharge, wrote a three-page explanation of his "religious training and belief" in which he declined to answer the Supreme Being question, saying rather that "the Divine is discovered by men through the thoughts, emotions, and experiences of his life," and suggested that "Paul Tillich's phrase 'ultimate concern'" captured this better than "conscience." Perhaps the most useful thing about "ultimate concern" was how its seriousness as religion and radical individuality worked together. Ultimate concern was something for individuals, even over and against institutions or official doctrines, even those to which believers belonged.

A Tillich citation was not a fail-safe ticket to exemption from military service, just as the statutory redefinition of the religious was not a totalizing revolution. Local boards might be unsympathetic to petitioners' self-definitions for any number of reasons, even if they did everything "right." One local board, considering the case of a doctoral student who was a Fulbright fellow in Germany, reclassified him as 1-A, stripping him of his student deferment and rejecting his conscience claims.[14] The petitioner wrote a long letter replete with highfalutin language and careful parsing of terms and concepts. One representative passage reads: "The absolute concept is the 'power of being'—or the 'ground of being,' as Tillich sometimes says—because the understanding of which my consciousness consists is of itself the extent of my existence. I cannot exist as consciousness unless I can apprehend an essential order in reality, and this is the reason why I necessarily believe in the Supreme Being."[15] After a series of procedural mishaps, including a missing form, the board illegally denied his request on the stated basis that only members of historic peace churches deserved exemption. When a board was predisposed to disagree with a claimant, it could be nearly impossible to win a case. That is, if one had the resources and knowledge to bring a case in the first place.

---

14. Regarding the student deferment, they reasoned that a Fulbright fellowship was not education but a job. This was not the typical judgment.

15. [Name redacted], Form 150, series II, question 2. Series V, Box 30, CCCO Records.

"THE UNACKNOWLEDGED THEORETICIAN
OF OUR ENTIRE ENTERPRISE"

Conscientious objector cases were not the only secular sites where Til-lich was useful. His work has featured prominently in the field of religious studies, which was beginning to take shape as a secular discipline in the 1960s. Religious studies scholars and U.S. judges were beholden to what John Thatamanil has called a "loose Tillichianism."[16] Jonathan Z. Smith remarked, referring to the academic study of religion writ large, "Tillich remains the unacknowledged theoretician of our entire enterprise."[17] At the 1893 World's Parliament of Religions, Smith notes, the slogan was "To unite all Religion against irreligion."[18] Religion, in the capitalized singular, was a phenomenon, a thing, a substance, that could be found within all world religions. In other words, what all religions had in common was Religion, a bigger category to which no one religion had exclusive access and all had some (but some more than others).[19] Similarly, the *Kauten* standard, by which the courts differentiated religious beliefs from other types of belief, united all Religion over and against irreligion (or nonreligion). It was pre-cisely this standard, the religious/political distinction, that *Seeger* reinforced via a reference to Tillich. Religious studies scholars were doing something similar. Tracing the history of the discipline, Smith argued that "there can be little doubt that, by the 1960s, the formulation 'ultimate concern' was eagerly and strategically deployed as a translation for more traditional theological vocabulary (e.g., God), serving, it was thought, as a more appropriate lan-guage for students of religion, especially in public institutions."[20] It is not

16. Thatamanil, "Comparing Professors Smith and Tillich."

17. Jonathan Z. Smith, "Connection," *Journal of the American Academy of Religion* 58 (1990): 1–15.

18. Smith, "Tillich['s] Remains . . . ," 1143.

19. Winnifred Sullivan's differentiation of "small 'r' religion" from "big 'R' religion" is useful here. The former "is a nearly ubiquitous and perhaps necessary part of human cul-ture," whereas the latter "is a modern invention, an invention designed to separate good religion from bad religion, orthodoxy from heresy—an invention whose legal and political use has arguably reached the end of its useful life" (Sullivan, "The Impossibility of Religious Freedom," *The Immanent Frame*, July 8, 2014). I depart from Sullivan insofar as I do not think that small "r" religion exists, but I argue that in the 1960s and 1970s, if not before, the imagination of small "r" religion was integral to the manufacture of big "R" religion.

20. Smith, "Tillich['s] Remains . . . ," 1147.

a coincidence, then, that conscientious objectors and draft counselors also used the phrase to make their legal arguments. Tillichian language was flexible and, ultimately, quite useful.

Ultimate concerns were not always liberal, post-Protestant, and pluralist. Writing in the late 1980s, James McBride showed how the language of "ultimate concern" has served a wide variety of parties, including conservative Christians who wish to remove the religion of "secular humanism" (citing *Torcaso*) from public schools because it violates the establishment clause. In one such case, the social scientist James Davidson Hunter testified as an expert witness and directly cited Tillich to argue that secular humanism was indeed a religion.[21] McBride argued that a more careful reading of Tillich might actually provide a workable standard, since for Tillich "the affective attitude of 'ultimate concern' itself must be grounded in the transcendent reality of the 'substance' which 'grasps' the believer."[22] So perhaps the sincere believer was not so in control; to have a real ultimate concern means to be "grasped" by the agency of another "substance." McBride continued, "Tillich's definition of 'ultimate concern' should be recognized not only as a useful elaboration of the *Ballard* standard of 'sincerity' but also as a judicial guideline by which religion and nonreligion may be objectively judged."[23] McBride thus brings the conversation back to the sincerity test. If courts search for sincerity, it must be as objective a fact-finding mission as possible, and the requisite "substance" to which Tillich points could serve as just such an objective marker of authenticity.

Religious studies scholars in the late twentieth century, especially in the heyday of "lived religion" studies in the 1990s, turned their attention to the vernacular practices of "everyday" people rather than the "official" religion of church doctrine and professional theology.[24] Many (but not all) of the lived religion scholars gave short shrift to the production of religious experience and the relevance of the construction of the category religion. Instead, like the local draft boards, they homed in on a local example and found within it (emblems of) a universal category. The draft boards, hearing officers, and courts were even less conscientious and self-reflexive in their

21. McBride, "Paul Tillich and the Supreme Court," 248. *Smith*, 827 F.2d 684.

22. McBride, "Paul Tillich and the Supreme Court," 272.

23. McBride, "Paul Tillich and the Supreme Court," 272.

24. Orsi, *Madonna of 115ᵗʰ Street*, inspired a generation, or rather multiple generations, of scholarship on lived religion, although he used the phrase "popular religion." See especially the preface to the 2nd ed. (Yale University Press, 2002). See also Hall, ed., *Lived Religion in America*; and Tweed, ed., *Retelling U.S. Religious History*.

evaluations of petitioners' religiosity and sincerity, lacking much interest in "those processes that *produce* a felt difference between, for example, the sacred and the profane."[25] My point here is not simply to critique lived religion for being insufficiently genealogical or attuned to the production of experience. Rather, I am arguing that such scholarship has often trafficked in a politics of sincerity and authenticity, understood as affective, that was central to both legal and scholarly accounts of religion in the 1960s and early 1970s. The religious/political distinction (as in the *Kauten* standard) was in large part affective, and the inarticulate or unarticulated feltness of "religion" became one of its identifying markers.

Many scholars, including J. Z. Smith in the above-quoted piece on Tillich, have repeated the received myth that Justice Clark's opinion and the Supreme Court's ruling in *Abington v. Schempp* (1963) inaugurated, even legalized, the secular academic study of religion.[26] The commonplace truism about religious studies—teaching *about* religion, not teaching religion—finds justification in Clark's *Schempp* opinion, where he made a similar distinction. The argument is that *Schempp* made religious studies possible as a secular pursuit in public universities. As Sarah Imhoff has definitively shown, this "creation story" folds under historical scrutiny, though it persists as a mythic origin.[27] The *Schempp* opinion is nevertheless illuminating. For Clark, there was a set of content that could be labeled religion, and this could be approached with or without critical distance, secularly or religiously. In this way, Clark's distinction between teaching religion and teaching *about* religion resonates with his *Seeger* opinion that distinguished between believing *in* religion and believing *religiously*.

Clark's opinion in *Seeger*, even as it followed the *Kauten* standard in dif-

---

25. O'Neill, "Beyond Broken," 1102. This follows O'Neill's critique of lived religion, which missed the spatial turn in the humanities "by assuming a local instead of exploring its production; by juxtaposing this presumed local against an equally amorphous global; by wrestling over questions of center and periphery (a distinctly horizontal debate) rather than engaging issues of scale (with its more vertical concerns); and by seeking religious significance in diaspora rather than assessing how religion contributes to the very construction of a diaspora" (1100).

26. *Schempp*, 374 U.S. 203.

27. Imhoff, "The Creation Story." Imhoff argues that, contrary to the popular story, departments of religious studies and the academic study of religion did not "take off" because of *Schempp*. These changes were already under way, and besides, *Schempp* dealt with compulsory public kindergarten-through-high-school education, not colleges and universities.

ferentiating religion from nonreligion, poked a few holes in the wall between religion and culture by locating both within the person. But this also reflected a Tillichian view. Tillich wrote, "There is not a wall between the religious and the non-religious. The holy embraces itself and the secular. Being religious is being ultimately concerned, whether this concern express itself in secular or (in the narrower sense) religious forms."[28] If true religious belief is interior, it might even be physical, embodied. Sullivan has described what she calls the New Establishment in American religion law, within which every individual is essentially religious or spiritual, and this part of the person's self requires "spiritual care."[29] Individuals now have levels of "spiritual fitness" that can be measured. The faculty of spirituality has a place in each brain. John Modern has shown, with regard to the role of spirituality in faculty psychology, how this embodiment works toward disenchantment: for William Ellery Channing, for instance, "rational knowledge of the mental faculties—conscience, memory, and perception in particular—even more so than revelation, secured the ground of theological inquiry as well as pastoral care."[30] Psychologists of religion, from foundational scholars such as William James to twentieth- and twenty-first-century scientists and social scientists, have attempted to isolate and study that kernel of human experience called religious.[31] On Ann Taves's account, "James theoretically constituted 'religious experience' as an object of study, defining it as a generic 'something' that informed 'religion-in-general' apart from any tradition in

28. Paul Tillich, *The Protestant Era*, abridged ed. (University of Chicago Press, 1957), xi.

29. Winnifred Fallers Sullivan, "Religion Naturalized: The New Establishment," in *After Pluralism*, ed. Bender and Klassen, 82–97; Sullivan, *A Ministry of Presence*.

30. Modern, *Secularism in Antebellum America*, 144–145.

31. It is worth noting here that in *Ballard*, the case that initiated the sincerity test, Justice Robert Jackson discussed William James to explain the role of religion and religious experience in the lives of individuals. *Ballard*, 322 U.S. at 93.

Years later the Ninth Circuit also cited James, in Navajo Nation v. U.S. Forest Service, 479 F.3d 1024. In deciding whether the desecration of sacred land was a violation of religious free exercise, they wrote, "Religious belief concerns the human spirit and religious faith, not physical harm and scientific fact. Religious exercise sometimes involves physical things, but the physical or scientific character of these things is secondary to their spiritual and religious meaning. The centerpiece of religious belief and exercise is the 'subjective' and the 'spiritual.' As William James wrote, religion may be defined as 'the feelings, acts, and experiences of individual men [and women] in their solitude, so far as they apprehend themselves to stand in relation to whatever they may consider the divine'" (1039). For more on this case, see Howe, *Landscapes of the Secular*.

particular."[32] The administration, investigation, and litigation involved in conscientious objection might be understood as practical implications of such a view of religion.[33]

Beyond secular courts and scholars, religious groups were also rethinking religion and the human. Most notably, the Second Vatican Council endorsed religious freedom in 1965 with *Dignitatis humanae*. Like the United Nations' 1948 Universal Declaration of Human Rights, *Dignitatis humanae* recognized religious freedom as a fundamental human right.[34] The council declared "that the human person has a right to religious freedom" and, further, "that the right to religious freedom has its foundation in the very dignity of the human person as this dignity is known through the revealed word of God and by reason itself." The council naturalized and secularized religion at the same time they explained it theologically and supernaturally. Religious freedom was secular because it was universal, putatively available

---

32. Taves, *Fits, Trances, and Visions*, 351.

33. *Seeger* and *Welsh* and to a lesser extent *Gillette* have been cited widely, not only in free exercise cases but in legal studies and political philosophy as well. For example, Bruce Ledewitz has argued that these cases provide a model for treating "nonreligious conscience . . . as basically identical to religious conscience." Writing in 2014 and concerned with "the growing divide in America between believers and nonbelievers," Ledewitz hoped that "the recognition that those who practice traditional religions share similar beliefs with many of those who do not, will lead to reconciliation and a reduction in the enmity that currently characterizes American life" ("The Vietnam Draft Cases," 4 and 5). Ledewitz was responding especially to Brian Leiter, *Why Tolerate Religion?* (Princeton University Press, 2012).

The moral philosopher Melissa Moschella has found the *Seeger* decision a helpful reference point from and with which to "speak of religion as a basic human good, one among many intrinsically choiceworthy goods that perfect us as human beings—goods like health, knowledge, and friendship" ("Beyond Equal Liberty," 126). Religion here means "the good of knowing the truth with regard to ultimate questions of existence and meaning, and of being in harmony with the transcendent source of existence and meaning (usually referred to as God)" (124). Moschella intentionally removed *Seeger* from its statutory context (and even its First Amendment context, such as it is) to propose instead "broad principles for determining *what justice requires* from a moral perspective, with regard to respect and accommodation of belief and practice on the part of the state" (140).

34. Article 18 of the Universal Declaration of Human Rights states, "Everyone has the right to freedom of thought, conscience and religion; this right includes freedom to change his religion or belief, and freedom, either alone or in community with others and in public or private, to manifest his religion or belief in teaching, practice, worship and observance." See also Kessler, "The Invention of a Human Right"; Samuel Moyn, *The Last Utopia: Human Rights in History* (Harvard University Press, 2010); and Samuel Moyn, *Christian Human Rights* (University of Pennsylvania Press, 2015).

to all individuals rather than those of a particular race or creed or affiliation ("within due limits"), and it was to be ensured by secular governments. But it also imagined, in the figure of the sincere believer, a normative human who was naturally religious.

SECULARIZATION AND AUTHENTICITY

In the same year that the Supreme Court handed down the *Seeger* decision, the theologian Harvey Cox published his influential secularization narrative, *The Secular City*. Theologians, sociologists, historians, and cultural critics debated and discussed the fate of religion in the twentieth century, and many agreed that it was withering. Soon belief in gods, particularly the personal god of Christianity, would be a relic of the past in the modern secular West. The next year, *Time*'s cover story, "Is God Dead?," presented the secularization thesis to a general reading public. In 1967 Peter Berger's *The Sacred Canopy* offered a widely influential sociological explanation for the decline in traditional religious belief and affiliation. In recent decades scholars have critiqued, amended, and largely discarded the standard secularization thesis, which charted and predicted the decline of belief in a deity, participation in religious groups, and the retreat of religion from the public square. Nevertheless, the older theories are worth revisiting as both primary and secondary sources. They illuminate the intellectual and cultural history of an era, but they also shape the contours of conversations scholars still have.

Although *The Secular City* does not take up the question of authenticity and sincerity directly, the book can help explain connections between individual subjectivity and the religious. Cox argued that secularization, which was all but inevitable, was linked with urbanization. As "man" transitioned away from local ways of being, old, dogmatic religions naturally would fall away, their theologies inadequate for the modern city and era. Modern man was transitory, unmoored from static communities and local relations.[35] Anonymity and transience—defining qualities of the world of masquerade into which Melville poured the *Fidèle*'s "strange particles"—worried nineteenth-century Americans and justified investigation and surveillance. But for Cox, secularization via urbanization was "a liberating process. It

35. See also Davis, *Periodization and Sovereignty*.

dislodges ancient oppressions and overturns stultifying conventions."[36] Moralists such as Anthony Comstock warned that the anonymity of urban life created opportunities for immoral men to shape-shift, trying on one persona after another. The public face, the mask, was not a true expression of the private self, and this disconnect threatened the moral order. Cox argued instead that the secular city allowed the individual to be more authentic, to be true to himself rather than constrained by superstitious traditions and "tribal" affiliations.

Even though Cox celebrated city life and urbanization, he did not delight in or attempt to hasten religion's demise. But he did not lament it, either. Instead, the decline of religion was simply a fact of modernization, and churches, along with the rest of society, had to adapt. "The forces of secularization have no serious interest in persecuting religion," he wrote in the book's opening pages. "Secularization simply bypasses and undercuts religion and goes on to other things. It has relativized religious world views and thus rendered them innocuous. Religion has been privatized."[37] In Cox's Protestant-secular story, religion finds its proper place in the private realm, and the public realm does not so much expunge it as ignore it and let it drift away into its designated spot. Thus, it is also a modernization narrative. Just as society progresses from the forest to the village to the technopolis, individuals progress from tribal to liberal and national to truly individual. The individual becomes a self. "Tribal man," conversely, "is hardly a personal 'self' in our modern sense of the word. He does not so much live in a tribe; the tribe lives in him."[38] The modern secular man is, then, a sincere man, or at least one with the capacity for sincerity. He can express himself as an individual.

In the late 1960s and early 1970s, some literary and art critics reconsidered sincerity and its role in modern society. The most popular and influential of these works was Lionel Trilling's *Sincerity and Authenticity*, first delivered as the Charles Eliot lectures at Harvard University in 1970. As a

36. Cox, *The Secular City*, 75.

37. Cox, *The Secular City*, 2.

38. Cox, *The Secular City*, 9. The discourse of "tribe" and "tribalism" was common among public commentators in the 2010s. Tribalism, as an accusation, refers to supposedly innate tendencies in humans to make in-groups and out-groups, and it also implies a failure to transcend these tendencies as liberal democracy requires. For more on this usage of the term, and its connection to secularism and liberal subjectivity, see Charles McCrary, "The Trump Era's Tribalism Discourse: Reflections on a 'Weird Euphemism,'" *Revealer*, May, 2020.

Jewish critic who never quite considered himself an insider in the worlds he studied, Trilling offered an observation of "the moral life" as a partial outsider, at a moment when that life was "in the process of revising itself."[39] The revision Trilling noticed was the rise of authenticity and the decline of sincerity, the former ideal supplanting the latter. Trilling defined sincerity as "a congruence of avowal and actual feeling." The truth of this congruence is difficult to determine, not least because it implies a stability to one's belief—as if this belief were an object, an unchanging doctrine written on the heart and mind. And yet, Trilling argued, "certain men and classes of men conceived that the making of this effort was of supreme importance in the moral life, and the value they attached to the enterprise of sincerity became a salient, perhaps a definitive, characteristic of Western culture for some four hundred years."[40] But then, decline. The ethic of sincerity was on the wane. This was especially the case in the worlds of high art and literature, where "sincere" was almost an insult, akin to calling an artwork treacly, sappy, or cloying.

On Trilling's account, authenticity had become the new dominant ethic. The difference between the two terms is that sincerity was about expressing oneself to and for others, whereas authenticity is turned ever inward. By 1970, owing especially to the influence of psychoanalysis and existentialism, "highbrow" literature and art had capitulated to an ethic of authenticity. Because society itself was rife with inauthenticity and façade, it became good taste, even ethical, to strive for an individual authenticity, to be true to oneself.[41] This model of subjectivity did not do away with, but rather

39. On Trilling's "always qualified Jewish identity," see Thomas Bender, "Lionel Trilling and American Culture," *American Quarterly* 42, no. 2 (June, 1990): 324–347, at 333.

40. Trilling, *Sincerity and Authenticity*, 1, 2, 6.

41. The philosopher Charles Taylor carried on these themes two decades later, in *Sources of the Self* and more directly in the lectures published as *The Ethics of Authenticity* (Harvard University Press, 1991). Taylor's project, which he continued with *A Secular Age*, was to uncover and provide some history of the contours of "modern identity," which designates "the ensemble of (largely unarticulated) understandings of what it is to be a human agent: the senses of inwardness, freedom, individuality, and being embedded in nature which are at home in the modern West" (*Sources of the Self*, ix).

Trilling noted that earlier thinkers such as Rousseau believed that misrepresentation was inherently detrimental to the public good. Rousseau's disapproval of theater, then, "was based on no puritanical dislike of pleasure, only on his perception of the extent to which the theatrical art falsifies the self and thus contributes to the weakening of society" (*Sincerity and Authenticity*, 65). Focusing on sincerity and the secular, Andrea Most has shown how twentieth-century secular Jews participated in theater and popular culture that celebrated

internalized, the public/private dichotomy. Just as Cox theorized that "tribal man" was not a modern self, Trilling argued, "we cannot say of the patriarch Abraham that he was a sincere man. That statement must seem only comical. The sincerity of Achilles or Beowulf cannot be discussed: they neither have nor lack sincerity."[42] Even if sincerity was fading away as an ideal, many people still found it necessary—before a draft board if not before an art critic—to perform authenticity and consistency of conviction and belief in recognizably sincere ways.

Sincerity and Authenticity is a secularization narrative. Sincerity, by codifying the liberal individual and naturalizing the public/private dichotomy, appears to attend to secularization. However, Trilling argued, albeit somewhat obliquely, that the rise of authenticity and the concomitant decline of sincerity was secularizing. Though he was impressed by Michel Foucault's work on madness and civilization, Trilling decried the fashionable idea that "madness is liberation and authenticity." Society feels constraining, and it certainly takes disciplinary measures, he admitted, but "it might seem that no expression of disaffection from the social existence was ever so desperate as this eagerness to say that authenticity of personal being is achieved through an ultimate isolateness and through the power that this is presumed to bring."[43] Authenticity, as self-obsessed rather than for others, would not lead to freedom. Instead, the ideal of authenticity facilely fashioned people into gods, in society but not of it. He concluded, "The falsities of an alienated social reality are rejected in favour of an upward psychopathic mobility to the point of divinity, each one of us a Christ." And he added, wryly, "but with none of the inconveniences of undertaking to intercede, of being a sacrifice, of reasoning with rabbis, of making sermons, of having disciplines, of going to weddings and to funerals, of beginning something and at a cer-

---

the public performance and the public self as more important, and in some ways more real, than the "private" self. "Theatrical liberalism privileged this external and public version of a self, the acting self. Americans have long wrestled with questions about where the 'truth' of a self lies, and although action in the world has often been seen as a sign of good internal character, for most Protestants, internal, private faith is the driving force that animates action (rather than the other way around); faith, and the kinds of character traits that allow for and support Christian faith, determine one's chances of salvation and move one to act morally in the world" (Andrea Most, "The Birth of Theatrical Liberalism," in After Pluralism, ed. Bender and Klassen, 144).

42. Trilling, Sincerity and Authenticity, 2.

43. Trilling, Sincerity and Authenticity, 171.

tain point remarking that it is finished."[44] These new Christs, their religions fully deinstitutionalized, inhabited a secular world of blissfully individualized spirituality.[45] On Trilling's account, then, the virtue of authenticity is secular because the religious is inherently social, and sincerity requires sociality.

Cox's secularization narrative jibed with Trilling's, though Cox placed a greater emphasis on the functionalism of the modern secular. "In the functional era," he wrote, citing C. A. van Peursen, "things become things to do."[46] From here, he contrasted this secularity with Paul Tillich's, arguing that Tillich was not a wholly secular thinker because he remained interested in "ultimate" questions rather than functionality. "Tillich spoke to those who still feel the need to ask 'religious' questions even when they are asked in nontraditional ways," Cox wrote. "These are questions he believed to be inherent in the very structure of human existence."[47] This reading of Tillich illuminates the courts' understanding of religion during this same period.

---

44. Trilling, *Sincerity and Authenticity*, 171–172.

45. This critique of reminiscent of Robert Bellah's critique of "Sheilaism," which he figured as a form of spirituality impoverished by its lack of depth and tradition. Bellah, Madsen, Sullivan, Swidler, and Tipton, *Habits of the Heart*. For more on Bellah in the historical context of midcentury pluralism, see Stahl, "A Jewish America and a Protestant Civil Religion." Stahl contrasts Will Herberg's "American Way of Life" with Bellah's "civil religion." Stahl argues that Herberg's "civic religion was simultaneously too Jewish and too neo-Orthodox—too tied to particular forms of immigration and too vexed by the future of religion qua religion" (447). Bellah's work, conversely, was well received in part because it was so thoroughly Protestant. On Herberg's use of "religion" and authenticity, see K. Healan Gaston, "The Cold War Romance of Religious Authenticity: Will Herberg, William F. Buckley Jr., and the Rise of the New Right," *Journal of American History* 99, no. 4 (Mar., 2013): 1133–1158. She argues that "Herberg used the new concept of a Judeo-Christian tradition to incorporate religious Jews in the social mainstream and to marginalize secular-minded Americans, regardless of their religious or ethnic ancestry. An adequate understanding of Herberg's role in American history requires attention to the deeply antisecularist strain in his work" (1134).

In his 1970 work, *Beyond Belief: Essays on Religion in a Post-Traditional World* (Harper and Row), Bellah defined his topic in simultaneously autobiographical and Tillichian terms: "The religious need, the need for wholeness, which has been strong in me from adolescence, was partly filled in these years [during graduate school] through my encounter with the theology of Paul Tillich. Here was the Protestantism of my childhood transmuted through the deepest encounter with the twentieth century" (xiv–xv).

46. Cox, *The Secular City*, 56.

47. Cox, *The Secular City*, 69.

The parallel-belief test, for instance, conceives of religion as an essential component of the human, recognizable for what it does, the function it serves. Religion "occupies a place." But it is not inert; it also "compels."

The politics of defining of religion is a politics with real stakes beyond the stuff of academic debate. But it is also the stuff of academic debate. These two realms, the legal and lived on one hand and the academic on the other, are intertwined in numerous ways. Claimants quoted certain scholars; judges cited other scholars; yet other scholars cited judges. They made the history of American religion and secularism together. In the 1960s, and in many ways since, scholars of religion have found Tillich, *Seeger*, and *Seeger's* citation of Tillich as useful justifications for their own self-consciously secular enterprises. The secularization story that Cox and others advanced was mostly wrong. But that does not mean that it did not do work. And it does not mean that "secularization" is an altogether useless framework. As Peter Coviello has written, "'secularism' names the ideology that, in an occluded way, *operates* the secularization thesis."[48] When judges cited imagined secularization as a rationale for reinterpreting "religious belief," they manifested secularization in the form of secular governance. In that sense, at least, secularization did happen.

THE DEATH OF THE SUPREME BEING (CLAUSE)

As troop deployments to Vietnam increased, thousands more conscripted men filed for exemptions. Facing a backlog in reviewable cases, the government stopped conducting investigations into each claim. In the end, definitional difficulties could be resolved, statutes could be interpreted, legal tests could be forced to harmonize, and investigators could discover what someone truly believed. What the state could not overcome, though, was an administrative morass. The hearings took up massive amounts of time. Hearing officers, judges, FBI agents, and appeal boards were swamped. Cases took up to eighteen months from the submission of Form 150 to final decision, and those whose cases moved into and through the federal court system took much longer. Sometimes secularism is about paperwork. And there was too much of it (paperwork, not secularism). When Congress passed a new draft act in 1967, they eliminated the special appeals process.

48. Coviello, *Make Yourselves Gods*, 43.

In that same act, in the wake of *Seeger*, they also eliminated the Supreme Being requirement but kept the negative definition that contrasted "religious" belief with "essentially political, sociological, or philosophical views, or a merely personal ethical code."[49] With the investigatory mechanisms diminished, even more interpretive onus fell on the courts.

The 1967 act would shine a brighter light on the petitioner's style and appearance, some critics warned, because it shifted the "major evidentiary emphasis" from the FBI report to the petitioner's own self-presentation before the local draft board.[50] Boards would judge his affect of sincerity, in lieu of the notionally more objective dossier, the "fair résumé" that resulted from the FBI's fact-finding. Petitioners would be subject to the personal judgments and whims of the local boards without as much recourse through the appeal process. There was a simple practical problem: if local boards relied on demeanor to determine sincerity, then they relied on data that were inaccessible to appeal boards and judges. With the Department of Justice's report, problematic as it could be, at least all parties making judgments had access to the same facts. This practical problem exposed deeper conceptual issues in addition to the practical ones. A believer's conscience and innermost beliefs are, in some sense, never totally accessible. But these beliefs are precisely what state agents must identify in order to approve a conscientious objection claim—and to protect one's free exercise of religion. The legal scholar Ralph Reisner, writing in 1968, argued that the law erred too far on the side of ease and efficiency and that the FBI investigations should have continued. His argument demonstrates the dual nature of the secular state's regulation of religious believers. On one hand, the investigations epitomized the inquisitional nature of secular governance and the probing search for sincere beliefs. People normally do not take great comfort from the knowledge that they are under federal investigation. On the other hand, the investigations at times provided believers their best defenses. Without these investigations and their authoritative air of objectivity and thoroughness, petitioners were left alone, exposed before the state, to give an account of themselves.

Even after 1967 the Supreme Being language was still relevant to anyone who had filed before the 1967 act. Although Seeger had opened a space for vaguely Tillichian, white, (post-)Protestant expressions to be read as reli-

---

49. 50 U.S.C. App. § 456(j) (1964), as amended by P.L. 90–40, § 1(7), 81 Stat. 104 (1967). On this change, see Reisner, "The Conscientious Objector Exemption," 668–689.

50. Reisner, "The Conscientious Objector Exemption," 714.

gious, many believers still could not quite fit. One such claimant wrote to the CCCO's executive secretary, Arlo Tatum, after his local draft board was dissatisfied with his answer to the Supreme Being question. One of his letter writers had described him as a "religious young man, in the Jewish faith," although he did not believe in a god. Apparently seeing this as a contradiction, the local board had denied his claim. The claimant clarified to Tatum that he *could* be a "religious young man" if that could mean a "conscientious, moral young man who cherishes human life and many traditional Judaeo-Christian values; is of Jewish parentage and upbringing; is loyal to what is his; esteems the therapeutic effect, on both individual and society, of heartfelt ritual properly carried out; and tends to study classical Hebrew texts, finding many of them to be full of power."[51] Here he writes in a particularly Jewish way while translating that experience into the secular language of "Judaeo-Christian" and an almost anthropological account of the benefits of religious ritual. Stretching the term "religious young man," he offered different terms—"Judaeo-Christian," "conscientious," "moral," appreciating the "therapeutic effect" of ritual—that might accord well with secularized, liberal, pluralist understandings of religion as well as his own Judaism.

But would the hearing officer, appeal board, and courts understand that? He believed that he should pass *Seeger*'s parallel-belief test, but he also recognized that it could be an uphill battle to prove it, especially if certain secular state agents were unsympathetic. "Will the slippery G-men," he asked, "through either ignorance or design, grant my I-O status without at the same time making it any easier, in the future, for like-minded skeptics to be granted theirs?"[52] In this way, *Seeger* added more language and possible citations (most notably that of Tillich) from which objectors might draw, and the case perpetuated the interpretive dance the involved numerous state and nonstate actors. Despite the rhetoric of Judeo-Christianity, the changes generally fit liberal Christians or post-Christians better than Jews or, in many cases, Black Protestants or Catholics. While the 1967 act might have undone the immediate effect of the Supreme Court's creative interpretation of the phrase "Supreme Being"—it didn't really matter what "Supreme Being" meant if it was no longer in the statute—the *Seeger* decision's effects were far-reaching and its premises prescient. Courts used the parallel-belief test, as it came to be called, to define religion in dozens of free exercise cases in

51. [Redacted] to Arlo Tatum, Dec. 11, 1967. Series V, Box 28, CCCO Records.
52. [Redacted] to Arlo Tatum, Dec. 11, 1967. Series V, Box 28, CCCO Records.

the following decades.[53] Against the backdrop of the war in Vietnam, a few high-profile cases made their way through the courts after 1967, and courts again had to determine what it meant to believe religiously. Among the most influential of these cases was *Welsh v. United States* in 1970.[54]

RELIGION AND POLITICS

Elliott Ashton Welsh II's Selective Service System Form 150, submitted on April 24, 1964, was filled out but marked up. It now read, "by reason of ~~my religious training and~~ belief." And, crucially, Welsh marked "no" in response to the question "Do you believe in a Supreme Being?" On the face of it, it would seem as though Welsh clearly failed to meet the standards for conscientious objection. After *Seeger*, though, Welsh had a case. Even so, it would be difficult for him to argue that he was religious or believed in a Supreme Being, given his doctoring of the form and his explicitly negative answer. How do you prove that you believe religiously, and "in relation to a Supreme Being," when you cross out the word "religious" and do not believe in a Supreme Being? Welsh tried a couple of arguments. The first was that the Supreme Being clause itself was "an unconstitutional distinction between theistic and nontheistic religious beliefs."[55] Thus, the decision based on it was invalid. To support this argument, Welsh cited Judge Irving Kaufman's Second Circuit opinion in *Seeger*, although this was precisely the argument that the Supreme Court Justices had tried to stave off in their decision. The Ninth Circuit Court rejected this piece of Welsh's argument. Leaving the constitutionality argument aside, Welsh contended that he passed the parallel-belief test. Again, the court found otherwise, holding that Welsh's direct rejection of the term "religion" forestalled his ability to lay claim to that term in a different context.

After *Seeger*, the meaning of the Supreme Being clause was given "such a broad reading that, in effect, it added nothing to the 'religious training and

---

53. One of the earliest uses of this phrase is in "Comment: Conscientious Objectors— The New Parallel Belief Test—United States v. Seeger, 33 U.S.L. Week 4247 (U.S. March 8, 1965)," *Catholic University Law Review* 14, no. 2 (1965): 238–246.

54. Welsh v. United States, 398 U.S. 333 (1970).

55. Welsh v. United States, 404 F.2d 1078, 1081 (9th Cir. 1969).

belief' clause."[56] Or so Judge Frederick George Hamley argued in his dissent, which took issue with the majority opinion on multiple counts. Either Welsh's beliefs should count under the *Seeger* definition, he reasoned, or the statute was so limited that it was indeed unconstitutional. It was difficult to make both arguments at the same time, but both worked within the flexible logic of the parallel-belief test. The next year, during oral arguments before the Supreme Court, Chief Justice Warren Burger put the question to Welsh's lawyer, J. B. Tietz, a well-known expert on conscientious objection law. "Well," Burger asked, "are you arguing now that his—the case is based on religious belief and conviction *or* that it is not and it doesn't make any difference?" Citing Hamley's dissenting opinion Tietz responded, "I say both of them."[57] Welsh's argument was essentially this: my beliefs should be covered by the statute, but if they aren't, then the statute must be unconstitutional, because it favors some religions over others.[58]

Welsh believed that humans possess "some sort of ethical apparatus, a conscience, if you will."[59] His beliefs were not only religious according to the parallel-belief test; they rested on the same conceptual framework as that test. He theorized religious belief as not only individual and internal but natural. If everyone has such an ethical apparatus, and that apparatus is itself religious, then all humans must be religious or at least have the capacity for religion. Welsh believed religiously because his belief, although it was not religious in content per se, stemmed from the indelibly religious part of him, his conscience.

But *did* Welsh believe in conscience? He called it a "conscience, if you will." It was a curious addition—*if you will*. A few years later the legal scholar Laurence Tribe argued, regarding the rights of the environment, that we are "capable of perceiving intrinsic significance—sanctity, if you will—in the very principles, however variable, according to which we orchestrate our

56. *Welsh*, 404 F.2d at 1087.

57. *Welsh*, 398 U.S., oral argument, Jan. 20, 1970. The quoted exchange begins at about the 11:30 minute mark.

58. The federal government also agreed with the Ninth Circuit's argument that Welsh's case must rest on a "judicially cognizable administrative error," i.e., a factual mistake. The hearing officer or a DOJ agent or someone along the way must have erred in their fact-finding mission into Welsh's religious beliefs, and no such error had been found. So a key component of this case was about procedure as well as definitional interpretation. It is worth noting that Hamley disagreed with this piece of the majority opinion too.

59. *Welsh*, 404 F.2d at 1090.

relationships with one another and with the physical world of which we are a part."[60] As Nicolas Howe argued, Tribe's "if you will" might be read as a "tolerant affirmation of ethical pluralism" or a "diffident or even distrustful nod to that language."[61] For Tribe, as for Welsh, there is a real. What we call it—that's a different issue. Welsh was, of course, not the first claimant to express sincere belief through ironic distance. Recall Dan Seeger's inserted scare quotes or Britt Peter's remarks: "I suppose you could call that a belief in the Supreme Being or God. These just do not happen to be the words I use."[62]

The "you" in Welsh's "if you will" was not a generic term. It was a hearing officer. When the hearing officer asked Welsh if he was religious, he replied "no," but only because, as he explained in another letter, he assumed that the officer "was using the word 'religious' in the conventional sense, and, in order to be perfectly honest [I] did not characterize my belief as 'religious.'" But in fact, Welsh argued, the origins as well as the contents of his belief were essentially religious, because all religion, even in its "primitive" forms, was about concern for others. "Perhaps I erred in taking such pains to point out that I not believe in the 'standard notion' of God," he reflected. "I think my beliefs could be called religious, in the sense I have just explained. I do not *call* myself religious, simply because most people then assume that I believe in God, in the conventional sense."[63] Welsh subjected his own self-description to the calculative reason of the state and found himself outside the bounds of the religious—that is, until he retranslated in a different context.

In a secular age, popular understandings of religion were changing, and courts worked to keep up with these modern changes. They cited demographic diversity, considered Buddhism, and looked to liberal theologians. Even so, disconnections between legal definitions, academic and theological stances, and "conventional" or "standard" meanings could lead to miscommunication. The *Seeger* decision intended to reflect something like a "modern" understanding, but not all relevant parties had modernized their worldviews. Indeed, most people had not; this modern definition was not yet conventional. When talking to the hearing officer, Welsh answered in

60. Laurence H. Tribe, "Ways Not to Think about Plastic Trees: New Foundations for Environmental Law," *Yale Law Journal* 83, no. 7 (1974): 1315–1348, at 1339.

61. Howe, *Landscapes of the Secular*, 119.

62. *Peter*, 324 F.2d at 176.

63. *Welsh*, 404 F.2d at 1091.

keeping with what he assumed the officer would understand the religious to be, which was different from Welsh's own anthropological understanding of religious, and neither was exactly the same as the Supreme Court's explication in *Seeger*. What "religious" means, Welsh recognized, depends on who's asking.

The Supreme Court used the parallel-belief test to overturn the Ninth Circuit's ruling. Welsh's sincerely held belief did indeed occupy "in the life of its possessor a place parallel" to that in a more traditional religious believer. The government had argued that Welsh was different from Seeger (and Jakobson and Peter) in two key ways. First, "Welsh was far more insistent and explicit than Seeger in denying that his views were religious." Second, Welsh, unlike Seeger, had "essentially political, sociological, or philosophical views," since he mentioned world politics, "the military complex," and "our responsibility as a nation."[64] To the first argument, Justice Hugo Black, writing for the majority, granted Welsh's point that he used the word "religious" in a way he thought the hearing officer would understand it, not how he might mean it or how the courts might interpret it.[65] Further, Black stipulated that "the Court's statement in *Seeger* that a registrant's characterization of his own belief as 'religious' should carry great weight, does not imply that his declaration that his views are nonreligious should be treated similarly."[66] Claiming to be nonreligious did not mean that one was in fact nonreligious. To the government's second argument, that Welsh's beliefs were "essentially political, sociological, or philosophical," Black maintained that political beliefs did not disqualify a petitioner so long as these beliefs existed alongside religious beliefs. Religious belief happens in context and must be applied to real-world situations. The fact that Welsh mentioned specific historical circumstances in addition to general abstract principles did not tarnish the religiosity of his sincere beliefs.

Black made one more key distinction: the beliefs themselves were not protected but the *roots* of what was protected. Regarding section 6(j), he

---

64. *Welsh*, 398 U.S. at 341, 342.

65. Black, who died the year after *Welsh*, was one of the most influential figures in the history of religion law, particularly in establishment cases. Black's own religious background, practice, and thought have thus been the subject of scholarly interest. See Bertucio, "The Political Theology of Justice Hugo Black." Bertucio argues, "Black's religion took on a certain civic instrumentalism. Once sufficiently atomized, religion could serve as a bulwark to unified civic life, rather than a potential rival with the liberal state for an individual's loyalty, as might be the case in more 'thick' or hierarchically structured tradition" (96).

66. *Welsh*, 398 U.S. at 341.

clarified, "That section exempts from military service all those whose consciences, spurred by deeply held moral, ethical, or religious beliefs, would give them no rest or peace if they allowed themselves to become a part of an instrument of war."[67] It was a subtle clarification, but these linguistic quibbles were nothing if not subtle. This sentence, the last in Black's opinion, has gone mostly unremarked upon, but it is worth some brief consideration. Notice the order of operations in Black's formulation. First, an individual has beliefs, which can be moral, ethical, or religious, but must necessarily be "deeply held." Then, those beliefs "spur" one's conscience. The conscience then requires one to perform or not perform certain actions. In this imaginary, religion is a prime mover, elided with morality and ethics, that qualifies a certain type of deeply held belief. Subsequent positions stem from these roots. In this sense religious beliefs are starkly different from political, economic, or sociological beliefs, which are the result of consideration of external circumstances. Religious (and/or moral and/or ethical) belief comes first. It is not a conclusion. And yet, that was just the way Seeger, Jakobson, Peter, and Welsh talked about their beliefs. They read things, thought carefully, and provided citations. But their beliefs became something spiritual and thus nonpolitical but also nonintellectual. Deeply held, deeply felt. These beliefs were inside, in their souls, their consciences. Welsh had political beliefs. He railed against the "military complex" and believed that the Vietnam War was unjust. But alongside or underneath the politics, he also had religious beliefs, regardless of whether he or the hearing officer or the Ninth Circuit called them that.

Capacious as *Welsh* was, there were still believers who didn't meet the standard. The next year, the Court drew some limits. In *Gillette v. United States*, the last of the major conscientious objector cases, two claimants, a Catholic and a humanist, claimed their religious objections not to all war or war in general but specifically to the war in Vietnam. Louis Negre cited Catholic teachings against unjust wars. But because the Church did not officially oppose the war, the Court found that Negre's selective application of its religious principles to particular political stances was an essentially political move, not a religious one.[68] Thurgood Marshall found that Negre and Gil-

---

67. *Welsh*, 398 U.S. at 344.

68. This problem arose with some regularity among Catholics. Catholic organizations, including universities, employed draft counselors to try to help Catholics make their arguments in the proper frames and language. Other groups, like the CCCO, did their best but sometimes had to throw up their hands. In one letter, the CCCO's executive secretary, Arlo

lette wanted "greater 'entanglement'" by judicial expansion of the exemption to cover objectors to particular wars. Necessarily, the constitutional value at issue is 'neutrality.'"[69] Marshall, the only Black justice and whose background was in civil rights, recognized that approving such "political" objections would deepen the inequalities further, granting exemptions to those who could make the most persuasive political arguments. However, this decision also helped shut out "political" actors, especially Black civil rights activists, as it reinforced the idea that religion was truly a matter of intrinsic individual ultimate concern. The *Kauten* standard persisted: a religious belief is essentially not political, which is to say, not really arising from the real world. This was a stubborn secular imaginary. The gradual processes by which it arose, became common sense, and was implemented could be aptly named secularization: an account of how the secular is instituted through techniques and repertoires of secularism.[70]

ON WIDENING THE SCOPE

On December 16, 1971, having completed his magnum opus, *A Religious History of the American People*, Sydney Ahlstrom penned a preface in

---

Tatum, wrote to a lawyer about a claimant, "[He] has perplexed me somewhat, for I have been unable to get him to express his conscientious objection in terms of personal belief. He insists upon quoting Roman Catholic authorities, and takes a stand as a Catholic as if he were going to be taken into court to determine whether he was a good Catholic or not." However, even though he cited Catholic doctrine about just wars, he retained his right as an individual believer to decide when and to which wars the doctrines applied. His lawyer worried, "Thus he brings himself into the area of a personal moral code." The young man's claim was ultimately unsuccessful. He was sentenced to two years in prison, but then the judge suspended the sentence and gave him five years' probation, "on condition that for 3 of those years he do work of national importance, as directed by the Probation Office."

The first quotation is from Arlo Tatum to Caleb Foote, Mar. 31, 1965. Foote was a professor at Penn Law School and a lawyer who worked with the CCCO. The second is from [the petitioner's lawyer] to Arlo Tatum, Feb. 24, 1965; and the third is from [the petitioner's lawyer] to Carol Krauthamer, Apr. 9, 1968. Series V, Box 25, CCCO Records.

Catholic organizations, such as the Catholic Peace Fellowship and on-campus groups at Catholic colleges, offered their own draft counseling services. See Cajka, *Follow Your Conscience*.

69. Gillette v. United States, 401 U.S. 437, 450 (1971).

70. The language of "repertoire" is borrowed from Berger, *Law's Religion*, 196–197.

which he thought once again about American religion writ large. Ahlstrom devoted that preface to a series of reconsiderations and recommendations for future scholars who might build on his work.[71] He had just completed a grand narrative (not *the* grand narrative) of American religion, and he wondered how other scholars might use it to tell new stories. Among his historiographical suggestions was this one: "The concept of religion must be extended to include 'secular' movements and convictions, some of which opposed or sought to supplant the churches. Agnosticism does not preclude religiosity and moral seriousness. In 1970 the courts were taking this step by broadening the acceptable grounds for conscientious objection to war, and religious historians must similarly widen their scope."[72] Underwriting Ahlstrom's suggestion was the assumption that a more expansive definition in the *Seeger-Welsh* moment was, in a word, correct. The courts recognized a truth about what religion really is. For Ahlstrom—as for John A T. Robinson, Harvey Cox, and Paul Tillich, as well as for the courts in *Kauten*, *Seeger*, and *Welsh*—belief in a deity was not an essential feature of religion. The imperative to widen religion's scope was not about a proper interpretation of the 1948 draft act, and not (directly) about good governance; rather, it was a call to capture religion's essence more truly. Ahlstrom advised that historians write a history of Americans believing religiously.

In the remainder of this chapter, I think through Ahlstrom's suggestion historically and historiographically. I argue that the intellectual and cultural environment that occasioned Ahlstrom's call—the same one that made Seeger's and Welsh's beliefs legible as *religious*—depended on a fundamentally disciplinary, often racializing, conception of religion and the secular. The Supreme Court opinions and oral arguments, *The Secular City* and the debates surrounding it, and the Tillichian texts produced by the early generations of religious studies scholars demonstrate how the putative universality of religion was shaped by an unmarked politics of whiteness. It was a liberal project that produced difference as it regulated subjectivities.

71. I understand myself to be very much a part of this public. I read Ahlstrom's book in a course on the historiography of American religions, which was a required course for my degree in American religious history. So, when I take up Ahlstrom's suggestions, I do so in good faith as someone he was addressing. And I consider this book to be part of an ongoing effort by a big-tent "field" to understand the "religious history of the American people."

72. Ahlstrom, *A Religious History of the American People*, xiv.

These actors conceptualized religion as inherent to the human, and yet they limited the benefits of religious freedom only to certain subjects (even as that range of subjects was expanding).

Secularization narratives propped up the civilizationalist project of liberalism. The religious, as a category, depends on the universalization of particulars. The question, then, is about which particulars are universalized and how that process happens. Tracy Fessenden has asked, "How have specific forms of Protestant belief and practice come enduringly to be subsumed under the heading of 'Christian'—to the exclusion of non-Protestant and differently Protestant ways of being Christian—and how, in many cases, does the 'Christian' come to stand in for the 'religious' to the exclusion on non-Christian ways of being religious?"[73] In this way, state practices construct and reinforce the epistemic frame, and the secular state becomes a de facto defender and promoter of Protestantism. In this view, secularization advanced by *Seeger*, the 1967 draft act, and *Welsh* is, in a sense, Protestantization. These processes produce and protect liberal subjects, which are gendered and racialized, just as the governing rationalities of liberalism are inexorably bound up with genealogies of gender and race. To put a finer point on it, this is how Seeger's and Welsh's whiteness and maleness helped them translate their beliefs into recognizably religious registers.

One remarkable feature of the *Seeger* case is how the courts not only accepted the petitioners' self-descriptions but actually helped them craft their secular translations, most blatantly when Judge Friendly interpreted Jakobson's beliefs as Tillichian. For his own part, Jakobson included a detailed discussion of Dostoevsky and philosophical ruminations on the "central problem of religion." He found a sympathetic audience before the courts—much more so than at his local draft board or the appeal board— because his manner of explanation was compelling. Conscientious objectors who had letter writers who knew what language to use (e.g., successful letters did not use the word "philosophical," since that was expressly counterposed to "religious" in the 1948 draft act) faced much better odds. Some claimants found it more difficult to translate their beliefs into the religious, especially when they were read as political actors. Differentiation of the religious from the political—putting religion in its place—is secularization.

73. Fessenden, *Culture and Redemption*, 4.

"ALMOST ENTIRELY IN THE CASES OF WHITE MEN"

In the early 1970s the Southern Conference Educational Fund (SCEF) produced a fact sheet entitled "Black Draft Resisters: Does Anybody Care?" They
celebrated Elliott Welsh's recent victory at the Supreme Court but noted that
so far "the breakthroughs that have been made in establishing rights under
the draft law have occurred almost entirely in the cases of white men." Often
because they had some affiliation with civil rights organizations, or even
simply had expressed support for civil rights, Black objectors had had their
appeals denied at a higher rate and had faced more difficulty in the courts.
Since 1965, the fact sheet stated, the Supreme Court had decided twenty-
eight draft-resister cases, finding in favor of the resisters all but four times.
Of those four, two were Black. Only one of the twenty-four young men who
won a case that year was Black. "This gap between the expanding rights of
white men under the draft and those of blacks simply cannot be explained
away," they wrote. "It is racism in a most poisonous form—a form that leads
to prison or often to death on the battlefield. White America must look at
the facts about this gap. The white peace movement must look at it."[74] Conscientious objector advocates from the peace movement—groups like the
CCCO, the AFSC, and the ACLU's National Committee on Conscientious
Objectors—helped objectors framed their objections in ways that would be
legible as religious and sincere. As the SCEF's fact sheet pointed out, though,
these organizations worked primarily with white men, and their success rate
was much higher.

Michael Simmons, a Black man from Philadelphia, organized dem-
onstrations against the draft and was arrested and charged. Shortly afterward, having had his conscientious objector application denied, he refused
induction anyway, was indicted, and served two and a half years in prison.
He had been active in the Student Nonviolent Coordinating Committee
(SNCC) and other civil rights organizations, associations that marked him
as political rather than religious. Years later, Simmons recounted his negative experiences with the peace movement. "Back in those days, I went to
CCCO, and talked to a guy, one of the founders of CCCO. I told them that I
was a conscientious objector, and they told me that I wasn't. They refused to
help me, the Friends Peace Committee, the whole Quaker community, there

74. Southern Conference Educational Fund, "Black Draft Resistors: Does Anybody
Care?" Series V, Box 29, CCCO Records.

was no white group that helped me. In fact it was the civil rights movement that became a support mechanism for me." Though the civil rights movement offered support, these leaders lacked expertise in conscientious objector law, and associations with them hurt Simmons's case. And again, the CCCO and AFSC were of no help. "Back in those days," Simmons recalled, "they were very hostile toward African-Americans, and really poor people in general. . . . I mean, they saw conscientious objection as this precious little group of narrow, upper-middle-class strata, and then they saw people like me as riff-raff, who would dilute conscientious objection."[75] Simmons understood clearly, and personally, how upper-middle-class white Protestantism is taken as synonymous with "religion" itself.[76] Through conscientious objector law, the scope of the religious grew wider, but that growth primarily meant more white people on the side of the religious, and mostly white people like Seeger and Welsh.

Rarely were race and class discussed explicitly in the conscientious objection court cases. Almost all of the high-profile or influential cases dealt with claimants who were white. This was for a variety of reasons, including the lack of institutional support that all but ensured that Black claimants in particular would not make it that far. There were a few exceptions. In 1969 Londell Brown, a Black conscientious objector from Arkansas who was stationed in western Louisiana, had his case heard by the Fifth Circuit Court, although in the end it was unsuccessful. The local draft board had rejected his claim, and the Selective Service had upheld it, because he was not a "member of a religious organization or Sect."[77] But neither was Seeger. Brown argued that if he did not pass *Seeger*'s parallel-belief test, then not

75. Central Committee for Conscientious Objectors, "A Black Man Fights the Draft: Interview with Michael Simmons," 2003. This interview was made available by the Civil Rights Movement Veterans as part of the Civil Rights Movement Archive; https://www.crmvet.org/comm/draft.htm.

See also James A. Daly and Lee Bergman, *Black Prisoner of War: A Conscientious Objector's Vietnam Memoir* (University Press of Kansas, 2000 [1975]). Daly's text focuses primarily on his time as a prisoner of war in Vietnam, but he also includes the story of his unsuccessful attempts to become a conscientious objector.

76. On the whiteness of U.S. secularism, see Fessenden, *Culture and Redemption*; Kahn and Lloyd, eds., *Race and Secularism*, esp. Lloyd's introduction; and Fessenden, "Forum: American Religion and 'Whiteness,'" *Religion and American Culture* 19, no. 1 (Winter, 2009): 11–19.

77. This phrase is from Adjutant General H. F. Wise's statement denying Brown's appeal. Quoted in Brown v. Reaves, 294 F. Supp. 858, 860 (W.D. La. 1966).

only would the government have misapplied the case law, but they "would also have violated the Due Process Clause of the Fifth Amendment, as well as the Free Exercise and Establishments Clauses of the First Amendment in that it would have rewarded church membership while discriminating against non-church membership."[78] This is an important and prescient argument for a few reasons, not least that it applied the *Seeger* ruling to First Amendment law, even though *Seeger* was technically only a matter of statutory interpretation. Brown appealed to the Fifth Circuit, where he lost again. In his brief on appeal, he cited the "systematic exclusion of negroes [*sic*] from his local board and the Selective Service System of Louisiana."[79] Unfortunately, this was the first time he had brought this up, and his case counsel withdrew the point during oral arguments. But here we can see, just for a moment, and too late, an attempt to bring a critique of the racist structure of the Selective Service bureaucracy together with a critique of the limits of "religious sincerity."

Local draft boards, appeal boards, FBI agents, Department of Justice officials, hearing officers, and federal judges—the array of state agents who would evaluate petitioners' religiosity and sincerity—were predominantly white men. In many cases, they apparently were more sympathetic to claimants who were also white men. Such claimants performed their sincerity and religiosity, which was judged by the boards in person and secondhand by the investigators, in recognizable affective and rhetorical styles. These styles were a matter of education and class status as well, which in some cases caused rifts at the local levels. Race, class, and gender inflect the secular, though in ways obscured by design.[80] Ultimate concern was imagined as religious experience and, more basically, an essential part of what it meant to be human. Joshua Dubler and Vincent Lloyd call this "Tillich's normative anthropology," in which "every life is built on such epistemic bedrock—or, at the very least, every life *ought* to be."[81] Ultimate concern presumably leveled the playing field by individualizing religious belief, but the religious remained ensconced in a putatively universal yet implicitly gendered and racialized normative conception of the individual human.

78. *Brown*, 294 F. Supp. 862.

79. Londell Brown and Warren E. Gillam, Jr., Appellants, v. Stanley R. Resor, As Secretary of the Army, Appellee, 407 F.2d 281 (5th Cir. 1969).

80. See Kahn and Lloyd, eds., *Race and Secularism in America*; and Cady and Fessenden, eds., *Religion, the Secular, and the Politics of Sexual Difference*.

81. Dubler and Lloyd, *Break Every Yoke*, 168.

A SECULARIZATION NARRATIVE

———————

At the same time, and swimming in the same intellectual and social circles, the new discipline of religious studies advanced the cause of religious pluralism. Using theoretical models from Tillich and others, including Mircea Eliade and the History of Religions school, they posited religion as a universal aspect of humanity and hoped that recognition of this fact could overcome religious differences.[82] As Lucia Hulsether has shown, this project distracted from the ongoing realities of racialization and colonialism, sometimes intentionally. Divinity schools and secular religious studies programs sought interfaith engagement, building bridges across religious divides, thus papering over racial difference and eschewing racial justice.[83] This echoed the "Judeo-Christian" and "tri-faith" movements of a generation or two prior, as well as, for that matter, the white peace movement.[84] The category of religion was a useful apparatus for construing the human.[85] The ideal of pluralism, as it promoted religious freedom and produced religious difference, was part of this ongoing project. Hulsether advises that "to fathom the history of multicultural discourse in and beyond higher education, we must combine critiques of the Protestant secular with critiques of liberal multiculturalism."[86] How might we take up this advice alongside Ahlstrom's recommendation that historians of religion "widen the scope" of their objects of study?

Here is what I propose. One way we can combine the two lines of critique Hulsether mentions while widening the scope of our objects of study is by narrating new histories of individuals and institutions that show the racializing power of liberal projects such as religious freedom. This neces-

82. Masuzawa, *The Invention of World Religions*; and Long, *Significations*.

83. Hulsether, "The Grammar of Racism."

84. On the whiteness of Judeo-Christian interfaith tolerance, see Wenger, *Religious Freedom*, and Gaston, *Imagining Judeo-Christian America*. For a more in-depth explanation of how this rhetoric was enacted in particular forms of racial and secular governance in a specific site, namely New York City public schools, see Leslie Ribovich, *Without a Prayer: Race and the Transformation of Religion in American Public Education* (forthcoming).

85. Wynter, "Unsettling the Coloniality," 260. On connections between Wynter's work and critical secularism studies, see Robinson, "Racialization and Modern Religion." See also Alexander G. Weheliye, "After Man," *American Literary History* 20, nos. 1–2 (Spring–Summer, 2008): 321–333.

86. Hulsether, "The Grammar of Racism," 31.

sitates a critique of "religion" *and* "freedom." Both religion and freedom are often imagined to be universal or timeless, but as ideologies and institutions, they are not. In recent decades, postcolonial scholars have demonstrated that freedom is not a universal human longing; rather, what is often called simply "freedom" is a particular formation of liberal humanism.[87] As Lisa Lowe has argued, "The uses of universalizing concepts of reason, civilization, and freedom effect colonial divisions of humanity, affirming liberty for modern man while subordinating the variously colonized and dispossessed peoples whose material labor and resources were the condition of possibility for that liberty."[88] Like reason, civilization, and freedom, religion is a universalizing concept. Indeed, drawing from Alexander Weheliye's work on racialization, Tisa Wenger has shown that religion, as deployed in "religious freedom talk," is part of a civilizationalist assemblage that serves racial empire.[89] This is perhaps more obvious or more blatant in straightforwardly colonial or imperial projects, as in the U.S. occupation of the Philippines or Haiti, or the governance of Native Americans, or constitution writing in post-2003 Iraq.[90] But religious freedom, because it is liberal freedom, always disciplines.[91]

87. See Patterson, *Freedom in the Making of Western Culture.* For a particularly insightful critique of the Hegelian freedom-slavery dialectic and suggestion of alternative models, see Neil Roberts, *Freedom as Marronage* (University of Chicago Press, 2015).

88. Lisa Lowe, *The Intimacies of Four Continents* (Duke University Press, 2015), 6.

89. Wenger, *Religious Freedom*; and Weheliye, *Habeas Viscus.* The theoretical language of assemblages was popularized by Deleuze and Guattari, *A Thousand Plateaus.*

90. Wenger, *Religious Freedom*; and Su, *Exporting Freedom.*

91. Cécile Laborde offers a valuable critique of the argument I'm insinuating here. She argues, "Critics sometimes write as though state definition and regulation of religion is per se troubling or embarrassing for liberals. But it is not. The fact that regulation of religion is 'normative' in a Foucauldian sense—it shapes the ways that people experience the world— does not entail that it is impermissible in a liberal normative sense" ("Rescuing Liberalism," 65). Some scholars, in a less critical vein, have argued that the problem with the regulation of religion is that it is done *unequally,* as in, not recognizing all the "religions" equally (see, e.g., Gin Lum and Harvey, "Introduction," in *The Oxford Handbook of Religion and Race in American History*). Such regulation is troubling, as I argue at length in the next chapter, because "religion" is constructed in racializing terms and thus abets state violence; religion itself, like sincerity, can and does serve as a technology of racial governance.

It is important also to recognize that liberalism, even U.S. constitutional liberalism, is not necessarily or entirely reliant on a radically individual subject. Freedom of assembly is, after all, one of the First Amendment's freedoms, alongside that of religion. So, while collective action might and perhaps should overthrow liberalism, radical critiques of individualism can still be fundamentally liberal.

What comes after the critique of secularism, perhaps unexpectedly, might be a reformed secularization narrative.[92] Secularization did happen, in the sense that the religious and the secular were defined against each other, with religion becoming increasingly individualized and thus putatively depoliticized. This framework, in which the religious is essentially nonpolitical and noninstitutional, dominated the following decades of American public life and shaped the context of religious freedom in the late twentieth and twenty-first centuries. I see the *Kauten* standard, persistent in *Seeger* and backed by Tillichian citation, still regnant if embattled in the study of religion and certainly in popular and legal discourse. The proliferation of "religion and x" frameworks—including "religion and politics," as in the name of the well-funded center where I wrote most of this book—attest to the ways that attempting to situate religion within broader contexts often can leave "religion" relatively untroubled. These "religion and *x*" formulations, common in articulations of religious studies scholars' research interests, can be illuminating when the conjunction destabilizes both categories and explores their dynamic interrelations. Often they do the opposite. Finally, against assertions that genealogical critique lacks story or characters, I think that this critique of secularism, perhaps rendered as a secularization narrative, can feature a wide variety of agents, in keeping with Ahlstrom's suggestions, from the conventionally religious to the officially secular.[93] And, in telling these stories, as Sylvester Johnson suggests, we "must begin to appreciate religion as, at times, a racialized formation, one located squarely at the center of biopolitics."[94] The next chapter attempts such an appreciation.

92. See "What Comes After the Critique of Secularism? A Roundtable," *Journal of the American Academy of Religion* 88, no. 1 (Mar., 2020).

93. Stephen Prothero, "Liberalism vs. Pluralism as Models of Interpretation," *Proceedings: Fourth Biennial Conference on Religion and American Culture* (2015): 71–74.

94. Johnson, *African American Religions*, 400.

7

TROUBLING SECULARISM

FRANK AFRICA SINCERELY BELIEVED that he should eat a diet only of uncooked vegetables and fruits. "To eat anything else," he said, "would be a direct violation of my Religion and I will not violate my Religion for anyone."[1] In the short time that Africa was an inmate at Holmesburg Prison in Philadelphia, his belief was accommodated and he received the special diet. After his sentencing, he was transferred to the state prison at Graterford, Pennsylvania.[2] There prison officials denied his request. So Africa requested either to go back to Holmesburg and remain there for the duration of his seven-year sentence or, if he had to stay at Graterford, that they accommodate his diet and thus ensure his free exercise of religion. The district court heard Africa's case and decided that he should serve his time at Graterford and was not entitled to religious accommodations. A few months later the Third Circuit Court of Appeals affirmed the decision, agreeing that Africa's religion was not really a religion. He believed sincerely, but his beliefs were not sincerely held *religious* beliefs.

Federal courts found, in Africa's belief, the limits of sincerity. Or, more accurately, they established those limits. After *Seeger* and *Welsh*, it seemed like almost any belief could be considered religious. Throughout the 1970s legal scholars carefully parsed case law, the phrase "ultimate concern," and the relationship between the free exercise and establishment clauses. Surely, they reasoned, *some* beliefs were not religious, but how can we know which ones? They worked to develop standards, all of which trafficked in the discourse and politics of sincerity.

1. Africa v. Commonwealth of Pennsylvania, 662 F.2d 1025 (3d Cir. 1981). The quotation is from a statement Africa submitted to the court.

2. On religion at Graterford, though in a later period, see Joshua Dubler, *Down in the Chapel: Religious Life in an American Prison* (Farrar, Straus, and Giroux, 2013).

Africa was not the only claimant to lose a free exercise case in these years, but his case was particularly illustrative and influential. Africa's religion—or not-religion, the courts decided—was MOVE. MOVE was a group of mostly Black people in Philadelphia who followed the teachings of John Africa. The district court in Frank Africa's case categorized MOVE not as a religion but, rather, "merely a quasi-back-to-nature social movement of limited proportion and with an admittedly revolutionary design."[3] Judge Arlin Adams, writing for the Third Circuit, did not endorse this characterization, but for his own reasons he did not find MOVE to be a religion either. Legally, the *Africa* case was straightforward. If Frank Africa's beliefs were religious, then state officials at Graterford would be violating his free exercise if they denied him his special diet. If the beliefs were something else, anything other than essentially religious, then the prison had no such obligation. But the case was not simple. A close look at the case in its context shows how racialized secular governance intersects with secular imaginaries.

Frank Africa ended up in an odd position: all the relevant authorities thought he was sincere, but none of them thought he was religious, and yet one thing he sincerely believed was that *his beliefs were religious*. Religiosity was a matter of fact, and if Africa were in fact not religious, then his sincere belief otherwise did not matter. Africa and MOVE seemed to check all the right boxes, and yet the courts, police, and even their advocates could not think of them as religious, of MOVE as a religion. Judge Adams, even after finding Africa not-religious according to a number of guidelines, admitted that the outcome was "troubling." There was something unsettling about the whole thing.

In this chapter I analyze the *Africa* case in the context of the post-*Seeger* sincerity test and late-1970s legal scholarship on religious freedom. I argue that Frank Africa's religion did not fall within a secular frame. His self was not buffered. MOVE was not liberal. In claiming the label of religion—which MOVE people did long before they sought First Amendment protections; this was not a matter of adopting "religious freedom talk" in order to get rights and privileges—he was making a case against a liberal, secular society, not an appeal to be included in or protected by it. That is how Frank Africa came to define the limits of sincerity: he was not religious because he was not secular.

---

3. Africa v. Commonwealth of Pennsylvania, 520 F.Supp. 967, 970 (E.D.Pa. 1981).

MOVE PEOPLE

———————

In the late 1960s a Black man from West Philadelphia named Vincent Leaphart became John Africa.[4] He began gathering followers and preaching a radical message of liberation. His teachings, collected in a text called *The Guidelines of John Africa*, explained how "the System" had corrupted the world and held it captive. Political corruption, environmental degradation, the systematic oppression of people and animals—these were the result of the System, more of a force than a built institution. people struggled against the System and sought to live in accordance with the "Law of Mama," or of Life itself. Many of the MOVE people lived in a house together, with dozens of dogs, no electricity, and, for the children, little or no clothing. And they often ate raw food, although they sometimes made allowances because the adults had become accustomed to the food of the System. (The children thus were especially important; they were uncorrupted by the ideas and habits of the System.) Most members changed their last name to Africa to indicate a break from their previous histories and their integration into a new community. As Richard Evans has summarized, "The uniquely human experience of living in alienation from Life is what John Africa meant by the System."[5] When Frank Africa requested his diet of uncooked fruits and vegetables, he was trying to live the Teachings of John Africa, to stay connected to Life while literally imprisoned by the System.

The lives of MOVE people from the mid-1970s to 1985 were marked

4. There is a small but growing body of scholarly historical work on MOVE, much of which focuses, from various disciplinary perspectives, on the bombing of May 13, 1985. Tajah Ebram's "'Can't Jail the Revolution'" is a valuable recent exception. She focuses on the 1970s and Philadelphia's "carceral landscape." The first academic historical monograph on MOVE is Evans, *MOVE*. Much of my knowledge about MOVE's early years is from Evans's book, as well as MOVE's own publications and website (onamove.com) and some brief archival research I did in 2016 in the Philadelphia Special Investigation Commission (MOVE) Papers at Temple University (henceforth cited as MOVE Commission Papers). I am extremely grateful to Richard for his conversation and for sharing his drafts with me before his book's publication.

I use the term "MOVE people" throughout, because it encompasses members and nonmembers. Also, this is what MOVE people tended to call themselves. See Evans, *MOVE*, xvii.

5. Evans, *MOVE*, 38.

by violent encounters with police and tense relations with city officials. The group's history, as it is often told, is structured around these conflicts. Because of coverage in the local and sometimes national media, these conflicts were the primary or only exposure most people had to MOVE. Violent flash points—the 1976 death of an infant named Life Africa during a scuffle with police officers; the "guns on the porch" standoff of 1977; a starvation blockade the city imposed on the MOVE house; the death of Officer James Ramp in 1978, for which nine MOVE people were imprisoned; most famously, the 1985 bombing that killed John and Frank Africa and nine others, including five children, and burned down dozens of houses— became what Susan Harding has called "representational events." Such an event is "a complex, multilayered, polyvocal, open-ended discursive process in which participants (including self-appointed 'observers') created and contested representations of themselves, each other, and the event."[6] In more ways than one, MOVE was formed through these representational events. They shaped the group's practices and ideology, and they changed or intensified police strategies for interacting with the group. Frank Rizzo, the former police commissioner who became Philadelphia's mayor in 1972, used racist tough-on-crime rhetoric and tactics to win the support of white working-class Philadelphians. Targeting MOVE was a key prong of his governing and political strategy.[7]

In the group's early years, city officials watched MOVE carefully— documents later revealed small-scale surveillance operations as early as 1974—but rarely engaged in open conflict with the members.[8] For its part, MOVE looked more like a small religious group oriented around social justice and community service than a potentially violent revolutionary movement. Its tone and tactics changed in 1976, when police officers responded to a disturbing-the-peace call at the house where MOVE people lived. This led to a physical altercation in which a police officer knocked the infant Life Africa from his mother Janine Africa's arms to the ground, where he was crushed. The police not only denied responsibility for the death; initially, they denied that Life had ever existed. As Evans has shown, this event

6. Harding, "Representing Fundamentalism," 380.

7. See Lombardo, *Blue-Collar Conservatism*, 204–213.

8. Civil Disobedience Police Unit Surveillance File on MOVE, Apr. 22, 1974, Box 51, MOVE Commission Papers. Ebram also mentions this briefly ("'Can't Jail the Revolution,'" 337).

proved pivotal, as "MOVE abandoned their commitment to nonviolent resistance and embraced a doctrine of armed self-defense."[9] MOVE made
the change quite public by brandishing guns on the porch of their home in
Powelton Village. In response, city officials demanded that they leave their
home. They initially agreed to comply and find a new residence outside
of the city. But by the time the evacuation date arrived, they had changed
their minds. They were not going anywhere. City officials set up a starvation
blockade around the house.[10]

In the early months of the blockade, a cadre of community leaders and
other sympathetic Philadelphians offered their support to MOVE in the
form of food, water, and medicine passed over and through fences, as well
as public statements of solidarity. For example, the Reverend Paul Washington, a Black Episcopal priest, who already had a friendly relationship
with MOVE, used his religious bona fides and stature in the civil rights
movement to advocate on MOVE's behalf as he denounced the blockade.
(Washington later served on the MOVE Commission, which investigated
and reckoned with the 1985 bombing.) He served as a sort of secular transla-
tor. Fluent in the rhetoric of rights and freedom and well respected by the
city and the broader community, he used his position and skills to advocate
for MOVE and their rights. However, sympathetic though he was, Washington did not acknowledge that MOVE was a religion. Even though he
regarded them as a misunderstood and oppressed group, he nevertheless
perpetuated what MOVE people would call a misunderstanding. They were
not just political activists calling attention to the horrors of capitalist exploitation and governmental suppression; they were a religious group remaking
the world. Even their supporters, much less the press and the courts, seemed
not to grasp the nature of their project.

MOVE had support from some familiar translators: the American
Friends Service Committee. The AFSC had decades of experience helping
individuals explain to government officials why their beliefs were religious.
They knew how to speak the state's language and use it to protect one's rights
and had helped conscientious objectors win their cases. Dan Seeger himself

---

9. Evans, *MOVE*, 90.

10. Temple University's Digital Collections have made accessible online some photographs of the blockade. See, e.g., Don Camp, "MOVE Headquarters Blockade," *Philadelphia
Evening Bulletin*, May 21, 1977. In the George D. McDowell *Philadelphia Evening Bulletin*
Photographs collection. https://digital.library.temple.edu/digital/collection/p15037coll3/id
/63682.

worked for the AFSC in these years. Who would be better at helping people explain to state agents why their beliefs should be recognized as religious? As a Philadelphia institution with decades of legal expertise and community activism, they were perfectly positioned to make the case that MOVE was a religion, to make the Teachings of John Africa legible within the System's secular frame. But, like Washington, the AFSC treated MOVE not as religious group but as a minority group whose human rights were endangered by repressive police operations. It was in the context of their Philadelphia Police Abuse Project, which brought together the ACLU, interfaith groups, and other advocacy organization, that the AFSC supported MOVE. As Timothy Lombardo has explained, the police abuse of Delbert Orr Africa after a raid on MOVE headquarters in 1978, caught on tape, confirmed in the minds of many "allegations they had long waged against the police department and Frank Rizzo. It also made MOVE seem like a sympathetic victim of longstanding patterns of police misconduct."[11] Likewise, when Washington led a march on City Hall on MOVE's behalf, he did so in his capacity as the leader of the Citywide Black Coalition for Human Rights. In short, sympathetic community leaders consistently emphasized MOVE people's human rights, not their religious freedom.[12]

By the time Frank Africa's case made it to the Third Circuit in 1981, it was difficult for him to mount a free exercise defense. Public opinion had largely turned against MOVE. Some journalists were sympathetic and fair observers, but, again, even sympathizers rarely discussed MOVE as a religion, even though that is how MOVE people had long described themselves.[13] But their defenders generally trafficked in human rights talk, not religious freedom talk. There is a strange tension in these arguments, since at this time religious freedom was often conceptualized as a human right, and sincere religious belief was a capacity of the normative human subject. Perhaps if MOVE had been more widely considered a religious group, the press would not have worked to turn public sympathies against MOVE

11. Lombardo, *Blue-Collar Conservatism*, 205.

12. Evans, chap. 4, "Pastoral Power," in *MOVE*.

13. Linn Washington was the most prominent of these journalists. He began covering MOVE in 1975, and his work is among the best and most reliable of that period. He later went on to a legal career and then a professorship of journalism at Temple University. He wrote a longer piece on MOVE in 1989 in which he argued for their human rights. See Linn Washington, "MOVE: A Double Standard of Justice?" *Yale Journal of Law and Liberation* 1 (1989): 67–82.

and "dehumanize . . . its members."[14] (It is important to note here, though, that the status of "human," much less the liberal project of human rights, does not forestall anti-Blackness; in fact, anti-Black racism works through humanization just as much as through dehumanization.[15]) Some scholars of religion have since recognized MOVE's religiosity, applying their own labels to it. Juan Floyd-Thomas argued that they were "Black humanists," representing "a radical alternative to both traditional Judeo-Christian theology and American civil religion that offers new ways of analyzing black religiosity and its relation to radical politics."[16] Joshua Dubler and Vincent Lloyd have used the term "abolition religion" to refer to MOVE's "combative religious mood," a mood "nurtured in collective struggle within and against an oppressive system it vows to destroy."[17]

These scholars' descriptions of MOVE prompt an important question: If MOVE's religion was an alternative to both Judeo-Christian theology and American civil religion and, what's more, enmeshed with (radical) politics, then would the post-*Seeger* law recognize their beliefs as sincere and religious? Or, more bluntly, could that kind of religion be recognized as religion? As it happened, Africa's case came at just the wrong time for another reason, too. In the late 1970s and early 1980s many jurists and legal academics, reflecting on what they saw as the excesses and implications of cases like *Seeger* and *Welsh*, had been debating the limits of religious freedom and the sincerity test, thinking about how to curb its creeping expansion.

"GROUPS AS YET UNIMAGINED"

While MOVE people insisted that they had a religion, advocates marched for their human rights, and the City of Philadelphia put up a blockade, academics and judges kept outlining the religious and finding its others. But they weren't the only ones. Debates about good and bad religion and their place in public life captured public attention and filled newspaper and magazine pages. Many Americans were obsessed with "cults," especially after the

14. Sanders and Jeffries, "Framing MOVE," 572.

15. See Jackson, *Becoming Human.*

16. J. M. Floyd-Thomas, "The Burning of Rebellious Thoughts: MOVE as Revolutionary Black Humanism," *Black Scholar* 32, no. 1 (Spring, 2002): 11–21, at 12.

17. Dubler and Lloyd, *Break Every Yoke*, 160.

deaths of over nine hundred people at Jonestown, Guyana. "Fundamental-ism," another of good religion's others, was supposedly on the rise, from the religious right in the United States to the Ayatollah Khomeini's "unthink-able" ascent in Iran.[18] These tropes were close at hand as interested par-ties debated the scope of the religious clauses and the nature of religious freedom.

In the years since *Seeger* and *Welsh* had used the sincerity test to stretch the religious as far as it could go, perhaps to the point of ripping, many legal scholars had tried to ease the tension and mend the tears. Religion, they cautioned, needed some definitional edges lest it be overextended beyond a reasonable frame. These concerns were not brand new. Immediately follow-ing *Seeger*, some worried about the implications of such an expansive under-standing. One legal scholar wrote in 1966, "When this forbearance toward religious objection is combined with the new permissiveness in defining religion, other kinds of possibilities come into view. Dissidents of all kinds—nudists, LSD users, racists, utopians, and groups as yet unimagined—can be expected to present claims for religious freedom."[19] By the late 1970s those yet-unimagined groups had been realized. In this context, in the sober morning light, a growing number of legal thinkers saw a need for new, clear definitions of religion. One such thinker—whose thoughts led to rulings with consequences—was Judge Arlin Adams, who wrote the Third Circuit opinion ruling against Frank Africa.

Adams intervened in a number of ongoing debates with his 1979 opinion in *Malnak v. Yogi*, from which he would draw directly in *Africa*. The main issue, if it could be boiled down to one question, was this: How broad should the "religious" be? Or, framed differently: If *Seeger* and *Welsh* went too far, how far should we go? One proposed answer—really, a dodge and a new question more than an answer—was that "religion" had two meanings: one for the establishment clause and one for the free exercise. The excesses of

18. Charles Kurzman, *The Unthinkable Revolution in Iran* (Harvard University Press, 2004). On fundamentalism as a cross-cultural category of analysis, see David Harrington Watt, *Antifundamentalism in Modern America* (Cornell University Press, 2017). Watt cri-tiques the Fundamentalism Project. See R. Scott Appleby and Martin E. Marty's five-volume edited work, published by the University of Chicago Press between 1991 and 1995, the result of a grant-funded project begun in 1987. For an overview, see Marty, "Too Bad We're So Relevant: The Fundamentalism Project Projected," *Bulletin of the American Academy of Arts and Sciences* 49, no. 6 (Mar., 1996): 22–38.

19. Marc Galanter, "Religious Freedoms in the United States: A Turning Point?" *Wis-consin Law Review* 1966 (1966): 217–296, at 270.

the Tillichian moment largely served free exercise jurisprudence. Applying those same standards to the establishment clause could create impossible situations, where any foundational "ultimate concern" could not be
funded by the government. Avoiding these implications, another solution
was to assert that the law could instead recognize that the "religion" whose
free exercise was protected was not exactly the same "religion" that could
not be established. In his influential 1978 work, *American Constitutional
Law*, Laurence Tribe argued for such a dual model—"expansive for the
free exercise clause, less so for the establishment clause."[20] Although Tribe's
position remained a minority view (and he later revised it), it did spark
further debates about a constitutional definition of religion. Most people
recognized the need for some limits, so how would courts figure out where
to set them?

John Sexton's 1978 note in the *Harvard Law Review*, "Toward a Constitutional Definition of Religion," was among the clearest and most influential
arguments on the side of a broad definition of religion. Fifteen years after
Judge Irving Kaufman situated Dan Seeger's beliefs in a historical moment
at the intersection of secularization and pluralism, Sexton perceived some of
the same trends. In one sense, pluralism was age-old and foundational: "the
essence of America is its diversity and radical pluralism."[21] But, he continued, "there are far more blossoms in the theological garden than there were
at the time of the adoption of the Constitution." And yet, at the same time,
Sexton mentioned the death of God.[22] There were more religions, and more
religion, but less "traditional" religion. God had died or was dying, and yet
religion was everywhere. In a simultaneously pluralizing and secularizing
nation, what should count as "religion" for constitutional purposes? "Against
a background of such heterogeneity, it becomes increasingly difficult to dis-
regard the claim of a group that it is a 'new religion,'" Sexton admitted.[23]

Sexton concluded that a functional definition was necessary. The question was not so much what religion *is* but what religion *does*. The category
of religion, then, could "be limited only by a broader inquiry which seeks
to identify those functions worthy of preferred status in the constitutional
scheme. This is precisely the kind of inquiry at the root of the ultimate concern test espoused by Tillich and relied upon by the Court in *Seeger* and

20. Tribe, *American Constitutional Law*, 827.
21. Sexton, "Note: Toward a Constitutional Definition of Religion," 1069.
22. Sexton, "Note: Toward a Constitutional Definition of Religion," 1060, 1068.
23. Sexton, "Note: Toward a Constitutional Definition of Religion," 1071.

Welsh."[24] The phrase "worthy of preferred status" is a striking example of secularism's calculative reason, jarring alongside the flowery language earlier in the piece. It seems to sound a dissonance against the Tillichian idea of each person's inherent religiosity. But the point was not simply that every human had an ultimate concern or was naturally religious, but rather that these deeply held concerns were religious *only* when they were deepest and most basic. "Tillich's thesis," Sexton summarized, "is that the concerns of any individual can be ranked, and that if we probe deeply enough, we will discover the underlying concern which gives meaning and orientation to a person's whole life."[25] Calculation, investigation, pulling back masks: everyone may be religious, but only some religious people are worth protecting—and only some beliefs are worth "preferring."[26]

Adams followed these discussions with concern and fascination. In 1979's *Malnak v. Yogi* he seized the opportunity to stake out his position in the conversation. His contribution was more than academic; it set precedent. Adams was a proponent of religious freedom, but he also worried that its dramatic expansion in the previous few decades needed to be curtailed. As Sarah Barringer Gordon has written, Adams's opinion was "a bold attempt to rein in a galloping scholarly and judicial debate about the meaning of the Constitution's religion clauses."[27] This opinion was, in effect, Adams's solution to the problem of the ever-expanding and unwieldy scope of the religious. The test he devised in *Malnak*, his way of limiting sincerely held religious beliefs in a post-*Seeger* world, was the very one he would use two years later to deny religious freedom to Frank Africa.

SPIRITUAL COUNTERFEITS

Alan and Edwina Malnak, along with two other sets of parents, alleged that New Jersey public schools had violated the establishment clause by teaching the Science of Creative Intelligence/Transcendental Meditation (SCI/TM). In so doing, a government institution was endorsing and promoting a

---

24. Sexton, "Note: Toward a Constitutional Definition of Religion," 1075.

25. Sexton, "Note: Toward a Constitutional Definition of Religion," 1067.

26. Evaluations of preference and importance were key factors in the doctrine of "strict scrutiny." *Sherbert*, 374 U.S. 398.

27. Gordon, "Malnak v. Yogi," 11.

religious belief—and a "false religion" at that, Edwina said.[28] They brought suit against Maharishi Mahesh Yogi, the Indian guru who popularized TM, as well as the New Jersey Board of Education, the local board of education, and the United States Department of Health, Education and Welfare. In the years leading up to the case, TM leaders had been re-presenting their practices and beliefs as less spiritual and more scientific. As part of that effort, they had established a nonprofit corporation called the World Plan Executive Council (WPEC).[29] Through this organizational structure and the introduction of SCI, which emphasized the scientific legitimacy and secular benefits of TM practices, the World Plan had won numerous grants and developed a curriculum for teaching SCI/TM in institutions including prisons and schools. New Jersey schools offered this program as an elective class.

The Malnaks enlisted the help of a Californian anticult group called the Spiritual Counterfeits Project (SCP). The SCP was founded in the early 1970s by members of the Jesus People movement, a charismatic group that incorporated the style and rhetoric of the "counterculture" into its evangelical spirituality.[30] The SCP's founders had come to the Jesus People after experiences in what they understood as "cults," particularly TM. The SCP published periodicals that warned evangelical readers about the dangers of New Age groups, Scientologists, and others.[31] When they got the call from the Malnaks, three members of the SCP, one of whom had attended law school, moved into the Malnaks' house and began plotting their legal strategy.[32] Anticult leaders—including deprogrammers, whose job was to reverse the effects of brainwashing—alleged that cults stripped individuals

28. The "false religion" quotation is from an interview the Malnaks conducted with Sarah Barringer Gordon. Cited in Gordon, "Malnak v. Yogi," 14.

29. The WPEC had branches in multiple countries, and they incorporated in the U.S. in 1975. Eugene L. Meyer, "TM Takes on Corporate Look in U.S.," *Washington Post*, Sept. 22, 1975. The WPEC–United States was also a named defendant in the *Malnak* case, and its president gave a key deposition.

30. See Eskridge, *God's Forever Family*.

31. Eskridge, *God's Forever Family*, 207, 262–263; and Tim Stafford, "The Kingdom of the Cult Watchers," *Christianity Today*, Oct. 7, 1991, 18–22. As of 2018, the *SCP Journal* and *SCP Newsletter* are still in publication. See scp-inc.org/ckbody.php. The SCP was an offshoot of the Christian World Liberation Fellowship.

32. In the Malnaks' words, in an interview with Sarah Barringer Gordon in 2009, "Three guys came and lived in our house for *months*" (Gordon, "Malnak v. Yogi," 14).

of their agency, their ability to choose and explain their religious beliefs.[33] In other words, cults foreclosed the possibility of sincere religious belief. You cannot be sincere if you are not in control of your own faculties and not fully aware of the meaning of your own religious practices. Even if students did not know the true meaning of the mantras—indeed, even if the World Plan claimed that the mantras were "meaningless," as they did—the Malnaks believed that TM was nevertheless a spiritually real practice with real (harmful) effects, regardless of its discursive window dressing.

In her discussion of *Malnak*, the religious studies scholar Candy Brown endorses the SCP's arguments. She writes, "The tendency of courts to identify religion by belief statements makes it easier for practices to pass as nonreligious if promoters subtract religious-sounding language."[34] Religious(-sounding) language, Brown and the SCP argue, could be a cloak for anything, and so too could secular(-sounding) language disguise religion. Rather than exposing a fake religion masquerading as real, the SCP in this case held up to the light the fake science of SCI/TM and demonstrated that it was, in fact, real (bad) religion—a counterfeit science *and* a counterfeit religion.

Normally, religious freedom cases work the other way: someone claims to be religious and the government or its representatives argue otherwise. Frank Africa insisted that MOVE was a religion and thus his diet was an expression of sincere religious belief; prison officials said it was not. In *Malnak*, though, appellees found religious belief in a program whose designers contended that it was actually secular. The basic facts of the case were not in dispute. In the opinion of the District Court of New Jersey, the judge spent

---

33. See James Bennett, "Pseudo Religion and Real Religion: The Modern Anticult Movement and Religious Freedom in America," in *The Lively Experiment: The Story of Religious Toleration in America, from Roger Williams to the Present*, ed. Chris Beneke and Christopher Grenda (Rowman and Littlefield, 2015).

34. Brown, *Debating Yoga and Mindfulness*, 40. Brown seems to endorse the position that words and practices have real, essential meanings regardless of the practitioner's interpretation. She cites Mircea Eliade's description of Hindu mantras as a "vehicle of salvation" that "*are* (or at least, if correctly recited, *can become*) the 'objects' they represent." Eliade, *Yoga, Immortality, and Freedom*, 2nd ed. (Princeton University Press, 2009 [1958]), 215; quoted in Brown, *Debating Yoga and Mindfulness*, 44. She continues, "By this metaphysical logic, whether or not a practitioner understands the mantra, recitation is spiritually transformative. . . . This leads to the question: Even if mantras, the meaning of which is not understood, can be experienced as invoking the Divine, is this necessarily so" (44)?

dozens of pages going over the content of the main pieces of evidence World Plan had submitted: a textbook written by the Maharishi and a description of the *pūjā* ceremony, in which practitioners chanted mantras. The defense also supplied affidavits from two teachers who taught the course in New Jersey schools, a linguist, eleven students who took the course, and two religious studies professors who argued that the *pūjā* was not religious.[35] The question was not about the facts, about what actually happened in the classroom. The question was about interpretation: Was TM really religious or not? The defendants insisted that the practices were scientific, while the Malnaks and SCP maintained that they were stealthily yet essentially religious. The district court decided that TM was religious and that the program thus unconstitutionally breached the wall between church and state.

When *Malnak* was appealed to the Third Circuit, Adams seized his chance to intervene in the debates about the religion clauses. It was a "great opportunity," he later recalled, "to untangle some of the web surrounding church and state, [and to resolve] confusion about what is covered by the religion clauses."[36] He had two main bones to pick. First, he disagreed with the idea advanced by Tribe and others that "religion" took different meanings in free exercise and establishment contexts. He thought it was necessary to have a definition of religion that fit both clauses. Second, Adams believed that the emphasis on individual belief and sincerity, bolstered by the "ultimate concern" language, had led the law too far afield of what religion was really about. Ultimate concerns were not necessarily religious just because they were "ultimate." To be religious, they had to be part of a structure, a larger system of thinking and living religiously. The Third Circuit affirmed the previous ruling, and the Malnaks won their case. But the outcome is not why this case became influential. It was Adams's long concurring opinion, in which he attempted a sweeping solution to the definitional problem, that would live on.

35. The professors, according to the court, were not very helpful, since they simply explained that in India "many secular activities begin with a puja ceremony or ceremony of gratitude," without providing analysis of the difference between the religious and the secular or a textual analysis of the particular *pūjā* performed in New Jersey. "While the court, of course, accepts these generalizations," Judge Meanor wrote, "they shed little or no light on the religiosity or lack thereof of the puja conducted in the presence of New Jersey high school students because there is no indication that the puja performed for the high school students was similar to 'secular pujas' performed in India" (Malnak v. Yogi, 440 F.Supp. 1284 [D.N.J. 1977], at 1310).

36. Quoted in Gordon, "Malnak v. Yogi," 17.

INDICATING RELIGION

Adams's definition was not, strictly speaking, a definition. Instead, he outlined three "indicia," features that religions had and not-religions lacked. With these criteria—which pointed to religion but did not constitute it— Adams attempted to sidestep the stilted, stifling constraints of definition. Stopping short of saying definitively what a religion *is*, Adams identified *markers* or *signs* of religion. He believed that it was ultimately up to the secular state, not the individual believer, to declare whether a belief was religious. But it behooved the state to be flexible, to have some capacity to accommodate the idiosyncrasies and intricacies of sincere beliefs. Despite the implication in *Welsh* that all deeply felt sincere beliefs were basically religious, Adams agreed with other legal thinkers who found it necessary to distinguish religious from nonreligious sincere beliefs.[37] Individuality mattered, though, and beliefs were held by sincere people, not churches or corporations. Thus, the indicia afforded Adams a way to find religion without putting it in too small a box. These indicia became the three-part test that Frank Africa failed, according to Adams himself, two years later.

Adams began his *Malnak* concurrence by discussing the previous few decades of judicial definitions of religion, from the "traditional" deity-belief version to the "new constitutional definition" that included secular humanists and others. Adams understood the historical context for the "modern definition of religion," which was "not confined to the relationship of man with his Creator, either as a matter of law or as a matter of theology." He continued, "Even theologians of traditionally recognized faiths have moved away from a strictly Theistic approach in explaining their own religions."[38] Here he cited familiar texts, including Paul Tillich's *The Shaking of the Foundations* and Harvey Cox's *The Secular City*.[39] If he were to propose new definitional standards, Adams realized, they would have to be in line with the "modern" view of religion.

With the stage set, Adams laid out his three indicia: (1) "ultimate" ideas,

---

37. As Terry Slye argued, this might be because Adams understood *Yoder* (1972) as limiting the reach of *Welsh*, forestalling the possibility of "merely personal moral codes" being understood as religious. Slye, "Rendering unto Caesar," 238. I discuss this further below.

38. *Malnak*, 592 F.2d at 207.

39. In addition to these two, Adams also mentioned Thomas J. J. Altizer, *The Gospel of Christian Atheism* (1966); Robert L. Richard, *Secularization Theology* (1967); and Gustavo Gutiérrez, *A Theology of Liberation* (1973).

(2) comprehensiveness, and (3) formal signs and structures. The first was a nod to Tillich's phrase "ultimate concern." In this way, Adams's *Malnak* opinion did not do away with individual sincere belief as a criterion. If anything, he solidified and centralized it. He wrote, "The 'ultimate' nature of the ideas presented is the most important and convincing evidence that they should be treated as religious."[40] The second indicium, comprehensiveness, was a sort of check on ultimateness. "A science course," for example, "may touch on many ultimate concerns, but it is unlikely to proffer a systematic series of answers to them that might begin to resemble a religion."[41] The comprehensiveness test, as it were, was a direct response to arguments like Sexton's, that "any concern deemed ultimate" should be protected for free exercise purposes, "regardless of how 'secular' that concern might seem to be."[42] Ultimate ideas, Adams argued, were not enough; they had to be part of a larger system. And the third indicium would help differentiate totally secular systems from authentically religious ones: there should be "formal, external, or surface signs that may be analogized to accepted religions." He elaborated, "Such signs might include formal services, ceremonial functions, the existence of clergy, structure and organization, efforts at propagation, observation of holidays and other similar manifestations associated with the traditional religions."[43] Not all of these formal structures were always present in a religion, Adams noted, but sincere religious beliefs generally had some external manifestation, such as, say, chanting a mantra.

The three indicia were perhaps the best—and, so far, the last—attempt at something like an across-the-board constitutional definition of religion offered by a federal judge. According to Sarah Barringer Gordon, "No definition has been as long-lived or widely used," though she notes that "the law has swirled away from such foundational questions."[44] Fittingly, in a case where the winning party was supported by anticult activists devoted to exposing "spiritual counterfeits," the indicia are a sort of fakecraft. By describing the markers of religious belief, Adams gave judges a way to identify real religion but also to find the fakes. The indicia were tools to craft the sincere believer as a secular subject; they refined this ongoing project. The indicia added up to something *like* a definition, but not truly a definition.

40. *Malnak*, 592 F.2d at 208.

41. *Malnak*, 592 F.2d at 209.

42. Sexton, "Note: Toward a Constitutional Definition of Religion," 1075.

43. *Malnak*, 592 F.2d at 209.

44. Gordon, "Malnak v. Yogi," 27.

Ultimate ideas, comprehensiveness, and outward signs *indicated* a religion. They were the smoke of religion's fire. True religion was still an individual's belief, held deeply inside, and courts could look only for its signs, its smoke.

FRANK AFRICA'S (NOT-)RELIGION

In some ways, it is surprising that Frank Africa's case would be the one to curtail the Tillichian moment. Even according to Adams's indicia, which were designed to clip the overgrowth of the religious, Africa could have won his case. In fact, MOVE's own intellectual genealogy, by which members understood themselves to be part of a religious group, shared some tangled roots with the courts' definitions of religion. Historicizing the earliest teachings of John Africa, Richard Evans writes:

> Across the country, in organizations ranging from the YMCA to the Student Nonviolent Coordinating Committee, from the Students for a Democratic Society to the Black Panthers, the generation that came of age in the 1960s developed a religious and political radicalism upon the language of Christian Existentialists such at Kierkegaard, Tillich, and Bonhoeffer. To them, the key to escaping alienation was to live lives of "authenticity." Certainly John Africa was not reading in Christian Existentialism, but he was undoubtedly engaging with these ideas in other forms. Christian existentialism was in the zeitgeist of late 1960s.[45]

Modern religion, authenticity, Tillich—it was all there. But there was also a "political" orientation, and a radical one at that. The *Kauten* standard, a religious/political binary, still set the terms. And courts and other state actors applied it to more stringently to radical politics, particularly Black radical politics. Nonetheless, the translations should have been easy. The AFSC should have been able to explain to city officials and federal judges that Africa was really religious, that he had an "ultimate concern." Instead, Africa and his fellow MOVE people were largely on their own. Ramona Johnson, a MOVE supporter (later Ramona Africa, she would be the sole adult survivor of the 1985 bombing and served as the de facto leader and spokesperson for MOVE for decades), had some legal training, and she offered legal counsel.

45. Evans, *MOVE*, 41.

An analysis of Africa's self-explanations and Adams's opinion reveals a contest between the religious and the secular, with Africa's antisecular religion pitted against Adams's proreligious secularism.

Africa submitted materials to the Court of the Eastern District of Pennsylvania, including a statement of his beliefs and an explanation of his diet. Judge John Hannum wrote that the decision came down to three issues: (1) Is MOVE a religion? (2) If so, does the First Amendment require active accommodation (it was one thing to exempt a believer from a potentially discriminatory law, but it was something more to accommodate them, to go out of their way to make sure religious needs were met)? And (3) Did the exigencies of prison life and the goals of the carceral state outweigh "any infringement upon the plaintiff's purported first amendment protections"?[46] To answer the first question, Hannum used Adams's *Malnak* indicia. For Hannum, none of the three indicated that MOVE was really a religion. It was by these criteria that he dismissed MOVE as "merely a quasi-back-to-nature social movement of limited proportion and with an admittedly revolutionary design."[47] Even though MOVE people "may respect and respond to religious concepts," MOVE itself was not a religion, because it lacked ultimate ideas, a comprehensive system, and, apparently, a formal structure with guiding texts, holidays, and other markers of religion.[48]

The Third Circuit affirmed the district court's decision. Adams wrote the opinion of the court, and he used his own indicia to test the religiosity of MOVE and Frank Africa. The first indicium of a real religion was the presence and centrality of "ultimate" ideas, dealing with questions and concerns like "life and death, right and wrong, and good and evil." Adams found that MOVE had no such ideas. "MOVE does not appear to take a position with respect to matters of personal morality, human morality, or the meaning and purpose of life," he wrote.[49] On its face, this is obviously not true. In the brief submitted to the court, Frank Africa wrote that "our religion is simply *the* way of life, as our religion in fact *is* life."[50] His wristband at Holmesburg Prison had listed his religion as "Life."[51] How could MOVE not have a position on "the meaning and purpose of life"? Adams admitted that it

---

46. *Africa*, 520 F.Supp at 969.
47. *Africa*, 520 F.Supp at 970.
48. *Africa*, 520 F.Supp at 970.
49. *Africa*, 662 F.2d at 1033.
50. *Africa*, 662 F.2d at 1027.
51. Evans, *MOVE*, 158.

was a difficult question, but ultimately he determined that Africa's "mindset seems to be far more the product of a secular philosophy than of a religious orientation."[52] This parsing—at once exacting and impressionistic—recalls the distinction at the crux of *Seeger* and *Welsh*. The hazy category "religious" is defined against the even hazier not-religious, which goes by such names as "political," "philosophical," "secular," and "terrorist." The first indicium was meant to give specificity to religion, using the Tillichian "ultimate" to refine rather than expand. Africa's ideas, by Adams's calculations, were not religious because they lacked systematicity and thoroughgoing rigor. In a strange and telling turn of phrase, Adams wrote that MOVE had a "preoccupation with living in accord with the dictates of nature" but other than that did not have "what might be classified as a fundamental concern."[53] Even though Adams claimed that Africa's sincerity was not in question, a preoccupation cannot be sincere in the same way a deeply held belief is. Adams downgraded this seemingly fundamental belief to a "preoccupation." A preoccupation is a quirk, pathology, obsession, fetish, a hang-up.[54] Not a sincere belief. Not a religion.

The second indicium was "comprehensiveness."[55] Acknowledging that again "our conclusion in this regard is not unassailable," the court concluded that Africa's beliefs were not-religious because a religion "must consist of something more than a number of isolated, unconnected ideas."[56] Africa had lots of ideas, but they were not quite "ultimate," and the connections between them were not clear enough to Adams and the other circuit judges. Really, the problem was that Africa's beliefs were *too* comprehensive. He wrote in his brief, "We are practicing our religious beliefs all the time: when I run, when I put information out like I am doing now, when I eat, when I breathe. All of these things are in accordance to our religious belief."[57] There was no buffer between religion and the rest of life. Secularism indexes

---

52. *Africa*, 662 F.2d at 1033–1034.

53. *Africa*, 662 F.2d at 1031.

54. On fetishes as not-religion, see Matory, *The Fetish Revisited*, and chap. 2 of Johnson, *African American Religions*.

55. Later cases that cite the "comprehensive test" include United States v. Meyers, 906 F.Supp. 1494 (D.Wyo. 1995); Alvarado v. City of San Jose, 94 F.3d 1223 (9th Cir. 1996); Carpenter v. Wilkinson, 946 F. Supp. 522 (N.D. Ohio 1996); Altman v. Bedford Cent. School District, 45 F.Supp.2d 368 (S.D.N.Y. 1999); and Strayhorn v. Ethical Society of Austin, 110 S.W.3d 458 (Tex. App. 2003).

56. *Africa*, 662 F.2d at 1035.

57. *Africa*, 662 F.2d at 1027.

differences between the religious and the secular, and it was precisely this division that MOVE rejected. "There is no comparison between the absolute necessity of our belief and this system's interpretation of religion," Africa wrote.[58] The system was secular; MOVE was not. And they were not aspiring to secularity and falling short. They were intentionally antisecular. This antisecularity is what made them illegible as religious.

Third and finally, real religions had "structural characteristics." The court found that MOVE lacked an organizational structure, rituals, services, and sacred texts (*The Guidelines of John Africa* might have counted, but Africa did not submit a copy as evidence at trial, since MOVE did not share the *Guidelines* with outsiders). They did not celebrate holidays or perform religious rituals, per se, and they did not have a hierarchy. John Africa had given Frank the title "Naturalist Minister," but apparently it carried with it no special duties, responsibilities, or privileges. Adams disagreed with Hannum's characterization of MOVE as "merely a quasi-back-to-nature social movement," but he agreed that they were not a religion. MOVE's philosophy, Adams wrote, was something "more akin to Thoreau's rejection of 'the contemporary secular values accepted by the majority.'"[59] The reference to Thoreau called back to the Supreme Court's 1972 decision in *Wisconsin v. Yoder*, in which Chief Justice Burger had written, "If the Amish asserted their claims because of their subjective evaluation and rejection of the contemporary secular values accepted by the majority, much as Thoreau rejected the social values of his time and isolated himself at Walden Pond, their claims would not rest on a religious basis. Thoreau's choice was philosophical and personal, rather than religious, and such belief does not rise to the demands of the Religion Clauses."[60] Burger invoked Thoreau to explain why the Amish *were* religious: their rejection of the world was not like *Walden*. Adams used the comparison to the opposite purpose. For him, MOVE's rejection of "contemporary secular values" was reminiscent of Thoreau's. When Frank Africa critiqued and rejected "secular values," then, he did so kind of like Thoreau did, which is to say, not religiously.

Adams's citation of *Yoder* is worth lingering on. In that case, the Supreme Court found in favor of Old Order Amish believers who sought exemption from a state law requiring all children to attend school through age sixteen. They "sincerely believed that high school attendance was contrary to the

58. *Africa*, 662 F.2d at 1027.
59. *Africa*, 662 F.2d at 1035.
60. Wisconsin v. Yoder, 406 U.S. 205, 216 (1972).

Amish religion and way of life."[61] The case is noteworthy because the Court applied "strict scrutiny" and found that, although the state of Wisconsin had a "compelling government interest" in ensuring that its citizens are educated, their right to free exercise outweighed that interest. Adams invoked *Yoder* for another reason, though. He read *Yoder* against *Welsh*, since in *Yoder* the Court evaluated the claimants' religiosity by looking to church doctrine, teachings, and tradition, rather than solely to individual sincere belief. And, further, they argued that Thoreau's beliefs were *merely* ethical and *thus* not religious, thereby undoing *Welsh*'s contention that ethical or moral codes were tantamount to religion. In this way, the legal scholar Terry Slye argued, Adams "must have been saying that *Yoder* to that extent *sub silentio* overruled *Seeger* and *Welsh*."[62] Adams seemed to agree with this assessment. In his 1990 book on religious liberty, he cited *Yoder* as evidence that the Supreme Court had "retreated from *Seeger*."[63] But it was not just the Supreme Court who had retreated. In *Africa*, Adams used *Yoder*, via his own opinion in *Malnak*, to find that Frank Africa's beliefs were ethical or political but not religious. The supposed excesses of *Seeger* and *Welsh*, namely the inclusion of "merely personal moral codes" under the big tent of the religious, had been undone—at least in some cases.

SINCERELY HELD RELIGIOUS BELIEF, CIRCA 1981

As it happened, *Africa* was not the first important free exercise case of 1981. That year the Supreme Court decided in *Thomas v. Review Board* that an individual's sincerely held beliefs were religious, even if they were out of step with the official doctrine of his church.[64] Eddie Thomas, a Jehovah's Witness, asked to be laid off from his job fabricating sheet steel because the product was being used for military tanks. Even though his church did not explicitly discourage working in weapons production—and even though his friend, coworker, and coreligionist told him working on weapons was "not 'unscriptural'"—Thomas concluded that his religious beliefs forbade such work. After he was laid off, he was denied unemployment benefits. The

---

61. *Yoder*, 406 U.S. at 216..
62. Slye, "Rendering unto Caesar," 238.
63. Adams and Emmerich, *A Nation Dedicated to Religious Liberty*, 90.
64. Thomas, 450 U.S. 701, 707 (1981).

Indiana Supreme Court upheld this decision, in part because Thomas had made a "personal philosophical choice, rather than a religious choice."[65] The U.S. Supreme Court found that the Indiana court had erred in this judgment, and that they were also wrong to weigh the seemingly more orthodox opinion of Thomas's friend and in their reliance "on the facts that petitioner was 'struggling' with his beliefs and that he was not able to 'articulate' his beliefs precisely."[66] Some commentators, including Arlin Adams, had thought the Court in *Seeger* and *Welsh* had individualized religion too much. But in *Thomas*, the Court doubled down on individual sincerity as the defining feature of religious belief.

That summer, Adams served as a visiting judge for the Ninth Circuit case *Callahan v. Woods*. The case was argued in June, following the Supreme Court's *Thomas* decision in April. In *Callahan* a man had refused to obtain a Social Security number for his daughter because he believed, based on his interpretation of the Bible, that these numbers are the "'mark of the beast,' the sign of the Antichrist who threatens to control the world."[67] The district court had ruled that, although Callahan drew his beliefs from a "traditional religious text," he did so "to justify and support a secular, philosophical objection."[68] Writing for the circuit court, Adams contended instead that "there can be little doubt that Callahan's interpretation of social security numbers as tools of the Antichrist is religious in nature."[69] The only real issue, then, was the same one as in *Thomas*: Callahan's belief was not clearly based in official church teaching.[70]

Given the *Thomas* decision, it was easy to find in Callahan's favor. The court found his beliefs both sincere and religious. How Adams presented the decision, though, was telling. "Although traditional religious beliefs are entitled to no greater protection than many nontraditional dogmas,"

65. Thomas v. Review Board of Indiana Employment Sec. Div., 391 N.E.2d 1127 (1979). On this point, the court cited *Yoder*.

66. *Thomas*, 450 U.S. at 707–708.

67. Callahan v. Woods, 658 F.2d 679 (9th Cir. 1981).

68. Callahan v. Woods, 479 F.Supp. 621, 625 (N.D.Cal.1979).

69. *Callahan*, 658 F.2d at 685.

70. Callahan was a member of the West Santa Rosa Baptist Church. The court noted that he had not been particularly religious until he began to read the Bible while incarcerated in 1973. While teachings about the mark of the beast and Social Security numbers were not official doctrine at Callahan's church, his beliefs were not uncommon at the time. See Paul S. Boyer, *When Time Shall Be No More: Prophecy Belief in Modern American Culture* (Harvard University Press, 2009 [1992]), 427.

he wrote, "their status as religious beliefs is often *more readily ascertained.*
Indeed, such doctrines are the standard by which other beliefs are measured
for inclusion in the First Amendment guarantee."[71] On this point, he cited
his own *Malnak* concurrence. And he elaborated,

> Callahan is a member of the Baptist church; his ascription of diabolical
> status to social security numbers is derived from the New Testament's
> *Book of Revelation*, a text which his church, and indeed most churches,
> consider holy. Callahan's interpretation of the scriptures may differ from
> the meaning members of his church generally find in that text, but such
> disagreement cannot itself invalidate his free exercise right.[72]

This passage hints at what Winnifred Sullivan has called "the peculiar legal
phenomenology of religion produced by American-style disestablishment."[73]
Jurists continue to use the figure of the church—"his church" and "most
churches"—as a way to conceptualize the realm of the religious. Callahan's
apparently idiosyncratic views were validated, in part, by his own churchli-
ness. Frank Africa's "church" and "scripture," MOVE and the *Guidelines*,
according to Adams's own indicia, were not a church and scripture. And
thus, Africa's beliefs were not religious—or at least not so "readily ascertained" as such. Even in the year that the Supreme Court upheld individual
sincerity as the defining market of religiosity, over and against group membership or church doctrine, "traditional" beliefs, or those most easily analogized to them, held sway.

"IRRATIONAL RADICALS OR CONFUSED TERRORISTS"

The *Africa* case was surely not the first time Arlin Adams had heard of
MOVE. A lifelong Philadelphian and consumer of the city's news media
throughout the 1970s, he very likely had read about the "guns on the porch"
standoff, the death of Officer Ramp, and the nine MOVE people imprisoned for it. At the same time as Frank Africa's trial, incarcerated MOVE
women were conducting a hunger strike, and the local news media followed

71. *Callahan*, 658 F.2d at 685. Emphasis added.
72. *Callahan*, 658 F.2d at 685.
73. Sullivan, *Church State Corporation*, 11.

it closely. Without speculating too much about Adams's biases or assumptions, we can at least say that before the case he already had access to frameworks for thinking about MOVE.

By the late 1970s police and city officials had begun describing MOVE as a "terrorist" organization. According to Robin Wagner-Pacifici, who has studied the public rhetoric around MOVE, especially the 1985 bombing and its aftermath, "the label *terrorist* was congealing around" the group by the early 1980s.[74] MOVE contested this label by reiterating that they had a religion. In 1978 they sent a letter to George Fencl, the head of the police department's Civil Affairs Unit (formerly known as the Civil Disobedience Unit), in which they explained that they were "not a bunch of frustrated, middle-class college students, irrational radicals or confused terrorists." On the contrary, they were a "deeply religious organization totally committed to the principle of our belief as taught to us by our founder, John Africa."[75] Drawing from the work of Hortense Spillers, Aisha Beliso-De Jesús has argued that "religious irrationality within American blackness is also central to the imputing of white rationality."[76] In the case of MOVE, ideas about Black religious irrationality—the "frenzy" of the "Negro church," the "superstitious" practices of conjure and hoodoo, and the like—combined with discourses on terrorism and civilization to mark MOVE people as outside the bounds of "religion," which is to say white, rational, *sincere* religion.[77] MOVE directly contested charges of irrationality and terrorism by explaining that their beliefs were, instead, religious.

MOVE's claim to be religious was not only or primarily about receiving First Amendment protections; it was an argument about civilization.[78]

74. Robin Wagner-Pacifici, *Discourse and Destruction: The City of Philadelphia Versus MOVE* (University of Chicago Press, 1994), 36.

75. MOVE to Commissioner O'Neill, May 20, 1978, Box 8, Folder 1, MOVE Commission Records.

76. Beliso-De Jesús, "Confounded Identities," 323.

77. On these tropes of Black religiosity, see Evans, *The Burden of Black Religion*, and Josef Sorett, "Secular Compared to What? Toward a History of the Trope of Black Sacred/Secular Fluidity," in *Race and Secularism in America*, ed. Jonathon S. Kahn and Vincent W. Lloyd (Columbia University Press, 2016). On "superstition" as a racialized third category in the United States between religious and secular, see McCrary, "Superstitious Subjects." In that piece, I make a version of this argument at greater length, with reference to the *Africa* case.

78. Some scholars have shown how individuals and communities strategically argue that they have a religion in order to receive the protections of religious freedom. See, e.g., Wenger, *We Have a Religion*. Many of the earlier examples in this book, such as the fortune-

Explaining MOVE's teachings, Ramona Africa wrote, "Man's system is built on all of these things—crime, disease, pollution, exploitation, enslavement, brutality and torture, etc. As long as this system exists, all of these problems will continue to exist because they ARE the system."[79] Depictions of MOVE in the Philadelphia media, however, often emphasized their "uncivilized" practices, including their health code violations and potential endangerment of children. For their part, MOVE people considered civilization to be synonymous with the System and were thus perfectly happy to be considered uncivilized. This clash animated media coverage as well. Neighbors' accounts of the MOVE house, amplified in the weeks leading to the 1985 bombing, often relied on comparisons between MOVE life and "normal" domestic family structures. Media campaigns against MOVE leaned heavily on sentimental discourses. Many stories, in describing the scene before the bombing, noted that the previous day was Mother's Day. MOVE people had spent much of the day yelling obscenities through a bullhorn at police. In the investigations after the bombing, city officials often emphasized the reports that Frank had beaten his mother, Louise James Africa (who was also John Africa's sister), and they questioned her about it in public hearings.[80] Domesticity—the racialized imaginary of "normal" or "healthy" family structures—was central to the city's campaign against MOVE. But MOVE people were not failed liberal subjects; rather, they openly confronted domesticating ideologies of civilization and the legitimacy of state authority.[81]

In MOVE's analysis and experience, the System was debilitating. It kills by poisoning gradually. Jasbir Puar has theorized debility as the "slow wearing down of populations instead of the event of becoming disabled."[82] In Frank Africa's testimony, he made a similar argument: that the System's

---

tellers and the conscientious objectors, fall in or near this category. But MOVE people insisted on their religious sincerity before they attempted any First Amendment arguments or talked about religious freedom.

79. Ramona Africa, "Long Live John Africa!" in *This Country Must Change: Essays on the Necessity of Revolution in the USA*, ed. Craig Rosenbraugh (Arissa Media Group, 2009), 141.

80. Some of Louise's testimony before the MOVE Commission can be seen in Jason Osder's 2013 documentary film *Let the Fire Burn*.

81. See also Spencer Dew, "The State 'Don't Own a Goddamn Thing': Illiberal Religification of the Legal System," *Political Theology Network*, Nov. 24, 2020. https://politicaltheology .com/the-state-dont-own-a-goddamn-thing-illiberal-religification-of-the-legal-system/.

82. Puar, *The Right to Maim*, xiv.

food was poisoning him, debilitating him. From that, he sought exemption. But his unwillingness to submit to the System, to contextualize his religion within a secular frame, meant that he remained subjected to its most debilitating institution. After Frank was released from prison, the state's subjugation and repression of MOVE transitioned from institutional debilitation into enactments of necropolitical power to take life.[83]

"SUCH A CONSEQUENCE, HOWEVER TROUBLING"

When Arlin Adams decided against Frank Africa, he struck a note of almost sad resignation. The prison officials had no constitutional obligation to provide Africa with the food he needed to stop his debilitation. "Such a consequence," Adams wrote, "however troubling, follows directly from our declaration that MOVE is not a religion."[84] It was as if he wanted to find in Africa's favor but was prevented from doing so by the objective standard he had established. In Winnifred Sullivan's words, the court "put up a mirror to Africa in which only white religion could be seen."[85] The three indicia framed that mirror. In this way, the *Africa* case illustrates Vincent Lloyd's argument that "whiteness is secular, and the secular is white. The unmarked racial category and the unmarked religious category jointly mark their others."[86] The secular frame that determined what counted as *religious*, as well as the (bio)political projects of enforcing those boundaries, were instantiations of whiteness.[87] Sullivan explains that *Africa*, along with *Seeger* and *Welsh*, has been "simply accepted . . . as one of the limit cases defining religion for legal purposes. Yet it is arguable," she continues, "that its real significance is in its capacity to illustrate the illegibility and threat to law posed by African-American religious collectivity."[88] She connects this point directly to state repression and governance of Black religious life, particularly in form of FBI investigations and surveillance. It is instructive

83. Mbembe, "Necropolitics," 17. On MOVE and mundane biopolitical violence, see Ebram, "'Can't Jail the Revolution,'" especially on zoning laws and gentrification.

84. *Africa*, 662 F.2d at 1036–1037.

85. Sullivan, *Church State Corporation*, 151.

86. Lloyd, "Introduction," in *Race and Secularism in America*, ed. Kahn and Lloyd, 5.

87. On the biopolitics of secularism, see Coviello, *Make Yourselves Gods*.

88. Sullivan, *Church State Corporation*, 151.

to note, then, that Seeger and Welsh were also the objects of FBI investigations, which yielded favorable results. Surveillance can produce "terrorists"
and "sincere believers." Thinking again with Beliso-De Jesús and Spillers, we
can see how the legibility of Seeger's and Welsh's religiosity—"the imputing
of white rationality"—relied on the foil of the irrational radical, the confused
terrorist, the unbuffered Black religious self.

In the lectures published as *"Society Must Be Defended"*, Michel Foucault
said, "What in fact is racism? It is primarily a way of introducing a break
into the domain of life that is under power's control: the break between what
must live and what must die."[89] This break sometimes cuts along the axis
of sincere religionist and confused terrorist. Puar demonstrated how ideas
about the failed sexuality of the terrorist other were necessary to construct
the homonationalist subject. As the biopolitical state gradually extended
the "right to live" to white gay men, they emphasized the repressive (and
repressed) sexuality of the terrorist, who must die. In this way, a mainstream
version of the struggle for gay rights became attendant upon a violently
nationalist agenda.[90] In the City of Philadelphia's repression of MOVE,
accusations of deviance from normative family structure and proper citizenship marked them as racial others unfit for incorporation into society.
Some communities, such as nineteenth-century Mormons, as Peter Coviello has shown, became white liberal subjects by changing their queer family structures and embracing settler colonialism.[91] And in so doing, they
remade themselves, albeit incompletely and gradually, into the character of
the sincere believer, followers of a quintessential American religion.

That sort of secularizing shift was impossible for MOVE, owing to structures of anti-Blackness and their own inability—and, of course, absolute
unwillingness—to lay claim to whiteness. And thus, they had no foothold
on the path toward claiming the mantle of religion in a way that would be
recognizable to and legitimated by the secular state. That total rejection,
that principled stance, looks a lot like religion. And it was certainly sincere.
But it was not secular and thus was not religion. The uneasiness of that

---

89. Foucault, *"Society Must Be Defended"*, 254. See also Ruth Wilson Gilmore: "Racism, specifically, is the state-sanctioned or extralegal production and exploitation of group-
differentiated vulnerability to premature death" (*The Golden Gulag: Prison, Surplus, Crisis,
and Opposition in Globalizing California* [University of California Press, 2007], 28).

90. Puar, *Terrorist Assemblages*. See also Reddy, *Freedom with Violence*.

91. Coviello, *Make Yourselves Gods*.

logic, the way it lays bare the anti-Blackness and particularity of the sincerity test and religious freedom in general—that, or something like it, I think, is what troubled Arlin Adams. He was troubled by the instability of the secular frame and the racialized modernity of the religious.[92] And, probably most troubling of all was the fact that Frank Africa recognized all of this and actively rejected secularity.

"THIS IS AMERICA"

Frank Africa died early in the day on May 13, 1985, before police dropped a bomb from a helicopter, before they shot at children fleeing, before the neighborhood burned. That morning, a smaller bomb ripped apart his body, alongside John Africa's. Before they started shooting, police announced through a bullhorn, "Attention, MOVE. This is America." The message was clear: you are not part of the nation. Outside the national community, outside of the System, willingly and intentionally undomesticated, MOVE was refigured as the terrorist other, marked for death, on one side of a clash of civilizations.

Thirty-one years later, on May 13, 2016, the Philadelphia hardcore punk band Soul Glo released an untitled album, the lyrical content of which deals with race, violence, and policing, from the perspective of their Black lyricist and vocalist, Pierce Jordan. The first lyrics on the album are "I want to be a terrorist / I want to terrorize this world of men / Which vilifies my self-defense from constant acts of violence from police, military, and government."[93] MOVE claimed that they did *not* want to be terrorists, but the sentiment is the same. It was the choice MOVE people made after the death of Life Africa. If "terrorism" is what it means to oppose a racist state, then the emphasis in MOVE's letter shifts to the adjectives: "We are not

92. Hesse, "Racialized Modernity."

93. Soul Glo, "1," *Untitled LP* (2016). Soul Glo have not publicly mentioned the significance of that date, so far as I can find. I asked them if the May 13 date was chosen because of the bombing, and they replied, "We dont really remember to be honest. but it does feel cosmic the way the dates lineup at the very least." SOUL GLO (@soulglophl) to Charles McCrary (@charlesmccrary), Twitter direct message, Dec. 19, 2019.

irrational radicals or *confused* terrorists." The letter to George Fencl, like the
Soul Glo song, was an argument for the *rationality* of opposition.[94]

Years after the case, *Africa* haunted Arlin Adams's imagination of religious freedom. In his 1990 book, *A Nation Dedicated to Religious Liberty*,
he told a short celebratory history of American religious freedom from
Roger Williams through the present, with meditations on the "animating
principles" of constitutional religious freedom. The end point was *Africa*.
There, Adams made a defense, albeit not a very strident one, of his decision. He wrote, "It may be that MOVE was central to Africa's life, but the
centrality of an idea or belief system does not necessarily transform it into
a religion."[95] This word, "transform," can be read alongside a similar sentence from Adams's *Africa* opinion. There he admitted that "the notion that
all of life's activities can be cloaked with religious significance is, of course,
neither unique to MOVE nor foreign to more established religions."[96] Just
as the team in *Malnak* argued, exposing spiritual counterfeits, there is a gap
between words and real states. A "cloak" could not "transform." The law
builds a secular framework that did not apply to MOVE. Africa did not
have a religion that could be applied to, overlaid on, linked with supposedly
secular life, thus sacralizing it. There were no cloaks. Thus, Adams's problem
was not that Africa's religion was a duplicitous masquerade, but that it wore
no mask at all.

The sincere believer, I have argued throughout this book, is a secular subject. Their religious belief belongs in its own compartment, on one side of a

---

94. In the song's next line, they further indict the System for mistaking victims as
dangerous, for taking colonized and racialized subjects as inherently violent: "Do I seem
dangerous in a weaponized world, on seized land no less? Do I seem dangerous with pro-
jectiles ripping through my flesh?" The lyric recalls Sara Ahmed's Marxian analysis of how
"the movement between signs allows others to be attributed with emotional value, as 'being
fearsome'" (*The Cultural Politics of Emotion*, 67).

The reference to seized land, situating state violence in the context of settler colonial
pasts and presents, highlights the shortcomings of the sincerity test and free exercise as
well. Native American claimants in the twentieth century were generally unsuccessful in
translating their sacred-land use into the language of religious freedom and belief. See,
e.g., Lloyd, *Arguing for This Land*, and Howe, *Landscapes of the Secular*. Howe writes about
the San Francisco Peaks, sacred land where colonizers built a ski resort and pumped fake
snow, as a "story about translation and mistranslation," of "interpretive frameworks" and
their failures (85).

95. Adams and Emmerich, *A Nation Dedicated to Religious Liberty*, 92.

96. *Africa*, 662 F.2d at 1035.

public/private divide. It was this frame that Frank Africa rejected. But Africa was not the first incarcerated Black claimant to be called political instead of religious because his beliefs were *too* comprehensive. In previous decades, members of the Nation of Islam, as Sarah Barringer Gordon has shown, "brought something new to the world of law": "They argued that theirs was a religious movement, even though prison officials, politicians, and others claimed that the Nation was political."[97] For example, a New York prison official alleged, "They attempt to express everything on a religious basis. But it is our opinion that they are not religiously sincere—that they have ulterior motives."[98] This suspicion of "ulterior motives" recalls again the political/religious distinction from *Kauten*, which structured conscientious objection law. And it highlights the oddly ineffectual nature of law's religion, that it invites suspicion and condemnation when it seems to be responding to real-world situations. Instead, it must be an ahistorical, timeless sort of belief. But at the same time, religion remains a marker of identity, a way of calculating and sorting people.[99]

As much as scholars can and should talk about the "liberal regime of religious freedom" or the "modern ideology of religious freedom," it is, like both religion and freedom, an always-changing institution with no real essence. Black and indigenous people lose religious freedom cases more often than white people because the United States is a racialized state that affords rights disproportionately and excludes certain subjects from the governance of their own country. More specifically, secular governance enforces secular ideology, and the Protestant secular is enmeshed in whiteness. Resisting whiteness and coloniality often is resistance of secularity. And religious freedom is awarded to secular subjects who translate their religiosity into secular registers through sincere affects. At the beginning of this chapter I

97. Gordon, *The Spirit of the Law*, 113.

98. "Prisoner Group Held Anti-White," *New York Times*, Oct. 31, 1959, 48. Quoted in Gordon, *The Spirit of the Law*, 113.

99. Jolyon Thomas has argued that "'What are you?' is the implicit question in religious freedom talk" (*Faking Liberties*, 267). Connecting this to other texts cited in this chapter, I again cite Beliso-De Jesús reading Spillers: "Identity should not be understood as a quest for self, but instead is a racialized and sexualized national ordering technology—a practice of racialized state governance" ("Confounded Identities," 323); and Puar, whose rereading of terrorist bodies is "a queer praxis of assemblage [that] allows for a scrambling of sides that is illegible to state practices of surveillance, control, banishment, and extermination" (*Terrorist Assemblages*, 221). Religious freedom talk beyond identity is hard to imagine; abolition (religion) probably means abolishing both.

wrote that secular agents "find" people outside the secular frame because they put them there. And that is true. Secularism as an institution must be maintained, sometimes with violence, and modern liberal subjects assure themselves of their own modernity and liberalism by pointing out, or pointing at, who isn't. But what Frank Africa and MOVE demonstrate, with their "abolition religion," is that some people do not want to be secular.

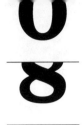

SINCERITY NOW

IN 2016 MISSISSIPPI LAWMAKERS PASSED a bill, HB (House Bill) 1523, that would protect believers who hold three specific "sincerely held religious beliefs": that "(a) Marriage is or should be recognized as the union of one man and one woman; (b) Sexual relations are properly reserved to such a marriage; and (c) Male (man) or female (woman) refer to an individual's immutable biological sex as objectively determined by anatomy and genetics at time of birth."[1] The bill was passed by the legislature but enjoined at the last minute by the Federal District Court for the Southern District of Mississippi, which found that the law violated the Fourteenth Amendment's Equal Protection Clause. The next year the Fifth Circuit lifted the injunction, and then the Supreme Court declined to hear the case. So in 2018 HB 1523 became a law officially called the Protecting Freedom of Conscience from Government Discrimination Act. The law is significant (and, according to some critics, unconstitutional) because, unlike most similar laws, it specifies *which* sincerely held religious beliefs are being protected.[2] But in design and purpose, if not totally in execution, it was perfectly generic. In fact, it was one of dozens of such laws and bills, at state and local levels, in the 2010s.

In that decade, religious freedom and sincere belief were everywhere. Conservative Christian investments in the politics of religious freedom, which began with the antisecularist movements in the 1960s, accelerated with the rise of the Religious Right in the 1980s, and came to fruition in the

---

1. Miss. Code. Ann. § 11–62–3 (2016).

2. See Mark Strasser, "Neutrality, Accommodation, and Conscience Clause Legislation," *Alabama Civil Rights and Civil Liberties Law Review* 8, no. 2 (2017): 197–238; and Lindsay Krout Roberts, "Protecting Sincerely Held Religious Beliefs: Lessons from Mississippi's HB 1523," *Mississippi College Law Review* 36, no. 3 (2018): 379–396.

2010s with a more fully realized conservative Christian legal movement and further expansions of free exercise. During these years religious freedom became not just a legal issue or a political ideology supported by a relatively stable bipartisan consensus, but a frequent culture-war flash point. In 2014 I set up a Google alert for a few variations of the phrase "sincerely held religious belief." Every afternoon since then I have received an email with links to stories about local and national controversies: school board debates, calls to arms from embattled evangelicals, high-minded liberal theorizing, employment discrimination filings, vitriolic op-eds, fact sheets on mandatory vaccinations, viral videos, and many thousands of words about real and hypothetical wedding cakes.

Sincerely held religious belief permeated these public debates about religious freedom and (anti)discrimination. Religious freedom has been imagined by many policymakers and theorists alike as a universal secular good, an "indispensable condition for peace in our time."[3] As such it has been entrenched in global politics and U.S. culture wars—particularly as the latter steadily creeps into the former. Religious freedom in the United States has always been limited and never protected everyone who might lay claim to it, as many Native Americans, incarcerated persons, and others could readily attest. But when the courts found against sincere believers, Congress stepped in multiple times to make laws that would protect or "restore" religious freedom.[4] Religious freedom was not a zero-sum game. By the 2010s, though, religious freedom and sincere belief seemed to conflict with other freedoms.

This chapter analyzes the "new politics of religious freedom" and the place of "sincerely held religious belief" in this landscape. Departing from previous chapters' extended analyses of court cases, it situates religious free-

---

3. Sullivan, Hurd, Mahmood, and Danchin, eds., *Politics of Religious Freedom*, 1.

4. For example, the American Indian Religious Freedom Act (1978) attempted to help Native Americans win more cases, since their beliefs and practices often did not translate easily into the secular frame of the religious. In 1993, in response to *Employment Division v. Smith* (1990), Congress passed the Religious Freedom Restoration Act (1993), which I discuss later in the chapter. A few years later the International Religious Freedom Act (1998) made religious freedom an explicit foreign-policy goal and set up multiple offices, one in the State Department and one independent, to promote and protect religious freedom abroad. The most recent federal law on domestic religious freedom is the Religious Land Use and Institutionalized Persons Act (2000), which attempted to remedy the fact that RFRA had not been effective in protecting the freedoms of indigenous people making land-use claims or of incarcerated people.

dom controversies as artifacts of the cultural politics of the early twenty-first century. Sincerely held religious belief is both more and less than a legal issue. Less because sincerity, despite jurists' and scholars' persistent convention of citing and discussing *Ballard*, has become a weak legal test. It is usually easy to pass—though not everyone does—and courts tend to give claimants the benefit of the doubt regarding their individual sincerity. This book, though, is not just a history of the sincerity test, and I am not arguing that is so central to the actual practice of religion law in the United States.[5] But in the twenty-first century, sincerely held religious belief, coincident and enmeshed with expansively conceived rights of conscience, is far more than a specific legal test. In ways different from and more significant than in earlier periods, religious freedom is a feature of U.S. culture and culture wars. For example, a county clerk in Kentucky named Kim Davis, to whom I will make frequent reference in this chapter, became a sort of celebrity for her refusal to issue a marriage license to a same-sex couple and for her well-publicized yet long-shot religious freedom claim.[6] Attention to sincerely held religious belief in this moment, both in and beyond the courts, situated at the end of a long history of secular governance, allows for new critical perspectives and cultural histories of the present.

RFRA: A BRIEF HISTORY

Before we proceed, a short history of the Religious Freedom Restoration Act (RFRA) is in order, since that 1993 law set the terms for much of the ensuing legal, political, and cultural debate about religious freedom and sincerity. RFRA was Congress's response to the U.S. Supreme Court's decision in *Employment Division of Oregon v. Smith* (1990), often known as the "peyote

---

5. I am grateful to Sarah Barringer Gordon and John Inazu for stressing this point. They each (mis)understood my argument this way, so it is important to me to clarify the scope of my claim. I am not saying that the sincerity test, as a formal legal test, is centrally important to the actual business of free exercise jurisprudence in the twenty-first century.

6. For an overview of the legal issues in Davis's case, see Ruth Colker, "Religious Accommodations for County Clerks?" *Ohio State Law Journal Furthermore* 76 (2015): 87–101; and Jeffrey B. Hammond, "Kim Davis and the Quest for a Judicial Accommodation," *Faulkner Law Review* 7, no. 1 (Fall, 2015): 105–128.

case."[7] Two men were denied unemployment benefits because they were fired with cause after failing a drug test when it disclosed their peyote use. They had ingested the peyote as part of a ceremony of the Native American Church. Thus, they claimed, the government violated their free exercise of religion when it denied them their benefit, unduly discriminating against them. But the Court, in an opinion written by Justice Antonin Scalia, held that individuals' religious beliefs did not exempt them from "generally applicable" laws. The believers' peyote use was indeed religious, and an expression of sincerely held belief, but that did not mean that they could violate laws that applied to everyone.

One of the central points of contention in the case was the "compelling interest" test. The Court needed to balance two good things: the government's interest in enforcing generally applicable laws and its interest in protecting individuals' free exercise of their religion. Which interest wins out in a given case? Scalia explained the decision, in part, by citing religious diversity: "Precisely because 'we are a cosmopolitan nation made up of people of almost every conceivable religious preference,' and precisely because we value and protect that religious divergence, we cannot afford the luxury of deeming *presumptively invalid*, as applied to the religious objector, every regulation of conduct that does not protect an interest of the highest order."[8] In other words, there are lots of religions now, with lots of different beliefs, and the free exercise clause does not demand that we accommodate every last one of them.[9]

The twenty-first-century landscape of free exercise law and discourses of religion take place in what Winnifred Sullivan memorably called "the world that *Smith* made." In response to the Court's decision, a broad irenic coalition formed: "Baptists, evangelicals, Jews, Seventh-day Adventists, Presbyterians, Unitarians, Pentecostals, Quakers, and more. All agreed that *religion* itself—religion-in-general—was under threat as a result of the *Smith*

7. Employment Division, Department of Human Resources of Oregon v. Smith, 494 U.S. 872 (1990).

8. *Smith*, 494 U.S. at 888; quoting Braunfield v. Brown 366 U.S. 599, 606 (1961).

9. Earlier in the opinion, Scalia quotes *Reynolds v. U.S.*: "Can a man excuse his practices to the contrary because of his religious belief? To permit this would be to make the professed doctrines of religious belief superior to the law of the land, and in effect to permit every citizen to become a law unto himself" (*Smith*, 494 U.S. at 879, quoting *Reynolds*, 98 U.S. at 167).

decision."[10] Sullivan related this change to mid-twentieth-century religious studies. Two different assumptions about religion, both of which found voice in religious studies scholarship throughout the second half of the twentieth century, began to work together. First, religion was everywhere, and religious belief became less about content and more about intensity or style of belief, what I called in this book "believing religiously." Second, there was a rise in pluralism and, after 1965, a proliferation of religious diversity (alongside perceived secularization). More religion, more religions. These developments track with the rise of the sincerity test and the history of conscientious objection, which influenced free exercise law. If there is a near-endless set of religions and the capacity within each person to be religious, then individual sincere belief becomes the defining criterion of religion—it becomes religion itself. A variety of religious organizations teamed up to lobby in support of RFRA. It passed the Senate almost unanimously. Sullivan argued in 2012, "It is plausible, I think, to see *Smith* as a turning point in the consolidation of a broad religious alliance that is at work today, one which collectively opposes secularism while each member aggressively seeks to shore up its own ecclesiological position."[11] I am not sure that such a coalition is at work as I write this in the early 2020s—although the conservative evangelical and Catholic legal organizations have maintained, on some issues, a tentative alliance—but nevertheless there was an effort by many different parties to protect religion-in-general and to uphold religious freedom as an ideal. Many people thought—and still think, though probably less commonly now—that protecting one religious person's freedom would help protect everyone's.

RFRA requires that the government "shall not substantially burden a person's exercise of religion even if the burden results from a rule of general applicability," unless two conditions are met: the law furthers a "compelling governmental interest," and it is "the least restrictive means" of furthering said interest. Each of these terms, especially "substantially burden," is vague and has been the subject of debate and conflicting interpretations. In 1997 the Supreme Court found that RFRA applies only to the federal government, not to the states. In the following years, many states passed their own state-level versions, most of which borrowed the federal statute's exact language.[12]

---

10. Sullivan, "The World That *Smith* Made."

11. Sullivan, "The World That *Smith* Made."

12. The case limiting the reach of RFRA to federal laws was City of Boerne v. Flores, 521 U.S. 507 (1997).

RFRA became freshly relevant in 2014 and 2015 for two reasons. First, it was used in the *Hobby Lobby* case, which dealt with a federal law. Second, as same-sex marriage was being legalized across the country, in 2014 and 2015 over a dozen states quickly proposed their own RFRAs or updated their existing ones. These issues also brought "sincerely held religious belief" newly to the fore of public deliberation and local legislation.[13]

The most controversial of these new RFRAs was Indiana's.[14] It became a culture-war flash point, with opinion pieces and cable-news debates, boycotts and threats of boycotts, and, among other things, grassroots fundraising campaigns for a pizza parlor whose owners claimed they would not serve pizza at a same-sex wedding.[15] Despite Governor Mike Pence's many public assurances that it was the same as the federal RFRA, Indiana's law was different in two key ways. First, its definition of "persons" included not only individuals and religious organizations but also "a partnership, a limited liability company, a corporation, a company, a firm, a society, a joint-stock company, an unincorporated association," or any other entity that might exercise beliefs held by people who "have control and substantial ownership of the entity, regardless of whether the entity is organized and operated for profit or nonprofit purposes."[16] But it was not only governmental actions that could not infringe on the religious beliefs of these "persons." The second noteworthy feature of the Indiana RFRA was that, unlike other religious freedom legislation, which protects people from government's infringements, this law allowed any person to "assert the violation or administrative proceeding, regardless of whether the state or any other governmental entity is a party to the proceeding." Many people were alarmed by the implications, fearing that a person, quite broadly defined, could bring suit against almost

13. See Koppelman, *Gay Rights vs. Religious Liberty?*, esp. 21–42, for an overview of this history. Some politicians and legal scholars recognized the potential conflicts between antidiscrimination law and RFRA early on. For example, California Governor Pete Wilson vetoed a state RFRA in 1998 for just this reason. See Robert M. O'Neil, "Religious Freedom and Nondiscrimination: State RFRA Laws Versus Civil Rights," *University of California Davis Law Review* 32, no. 3 (1999): 875–910.

14. Arizona passed a similar law first, but Governor Jan Brewer vetoed it.

15. Daniela Galazara, "Supporters Raise Over $500K for Indiana Pizza Parlor that Discriminated against Gays," *Eater*, Apr. 3, 2015. The pizza parlor, Memories Pizza, received thousands of negative Yelp reviews and had to close temporarily. Through a viral GoFundMe campaign, they raised $846,000. Memories Pizza closed in 2018. Erin DeJesus, "Indiana Pizzeria at Center of Marriage Equality Controversy Has Closed," *Eater*, Apr. 25, 2018.

16. Senate Enrolled Act No. 101, Indiana Senate (2015).

anyone who violated their capaciously defined religious beliefs. Amid public scrutiny and nationwide backlash, including threats from multinational corporations and the National Collegiate Athletics Association (which is headquartered in Indianapolis) that they would take their business elsewhere, the legislature quickly amended the law to include a provision that religious freedom did not give a person the right to impinge upon someone else's civil rights.

The new politics of religious freedom are bigger than RFRA, but they are shaped by the federal and state-level versions. These laws make possible the protection of "sincerely held religious beliefs" against the advance of LGBTQ rights. RFRA and other developments in *Smith*'s world construe religion-in-general in order to instantiate religious people as such, as individual sincere believers. In unresolved and perhaps counterintuitive ways, conservative Christian claimants reassert their secularity, as sincere believing subjects, *and* their nonsecularity, as deeply religious people persecuted and unduly regulated by overreaching political secularism. These beliefs are correlated strongly with whiteness.

THE NEW POLITICS OF RELIGIOUS FREEDOM

In the summer of 2015—the summer of the Indiana RFRA controversy and *Obergefell v. Hodges*, which legalized same-sex marriage throughout the United States—a county clerk named Kim Davis refused to issue a marriage license to a same-sex couple and was subsequently jailed. Championed by the conservative media figure and former Arkansas governor Mike Huckabee and backed by the Christian legal organization Liberty Counsel, Davis became a celebrity. She was celebrated but also mocked and derided. And along the way, in a bizarre bit of public relations, she met Pope Francis I.[17] Davis's case mattered not because it had especial legal importance

17. The full story of this encounter has not been reported, so far as I can tell. Davis claims that Archbishop Carlo Maria Viganò himself called her to set up the meeting (*Under God's Authority*, 118–122). The pope later claimed that his meeting with Davis was not an endorsement of her views and that he had not known about her story prior to their meeting (Ed Payne and Daniel Burke, "Pope's Meeting with Kim Davis Not an Endorsement, Vatican Says," *CNN*, Oct. 2, 2015). See also Cindy Wooden, "Vigano, Vatican Spokesmen Dispute Facts of Pope Meeting Kim Davis," *National Catholic Reporter*, Sept. 3, 2018.

but because Davis became a figurehead in the pitched skirmishes between religious freedom and LGBTQ rights. She was a prominent representative of conservative white American Christianity, even though the particularities of her apostolic belief and practice were atypical.[18] Further, her case shows how these conflicts were structured by the politics of gender, race, and class in the early days of what has come to be called "the Trump era." I will return to Davis's case throughout this chapter.

Davis sought an exemption from some of her duties because to fulfill them would, she maintained, make her complicit in what she believed to be sinful. In the same way, Hobby Lobby objected to helping its employees access healthcare because the company believed certain forms of birth control were abortion. Whether the content of these beliefs is true is not relevant—*contra* many commentators who pointed out Hobby Lobby's apparent misunderstandings of biology and reproduction—since these cases are still subject to the sincerity test. There is something about religious belief that removes it from the realm of facticity. That aspect of the cases is not new; it is the foundational assumption of the sincerity test. These cases and others from the era did have some new features, though. The following sections sketch out three of the most salient aspects of the new politics of religious freedom: complicity-based claims, religious-liberty legal specialists, and local political activism.

Complicity-Based Claims

Davis, Hobby Lobby, and many others made what Douglas NeJaime and Reva Siegel have called "complicity-based conscience claims." They did not seek exemption or accommodation for their own actions; rather, they wished not to be forced to be complicit in other people's actions. Such claims, NeJaime and Siegel write, "differ in *form* and in *social logic* from the claims featured

---

18. Her church is different from that of most of the key players on the Christian Right. She uses words like "anointed," and she does not wear makeup or style her hair. Also, she is not ensconced in the world of conservative media and Fox News (in her memoir, she notes that she did not know what prominent Fox anchor Megyn Kelly looked like until they met in person). Her exact beliefs and conceptions of sin, sanctification, and redemption were not analyzed by most media outlets. Nor was her religious difference mentioned, even by journalists specializing in religion, who frequently lump all evangelicals together, failing to make distinctions among Pentecostal, holiness, Mennonite, and other traditions.

in the free exercise cases RFRA invokes."[19] None of the three cases cited in RFRA—*Sherbert*, *Yoder*, and *Smith*—was about complicity. They were about whether the state could compel an individual to action or whether one's sincere religious beliefs could lead to adverse legal consequences. Closely related to the issue of complicity is "third-party harm." The cases cited in RFRA were essentially two-party issues, conflicts between an individual and the state. The law says you must do something that violates your conscience, or you sincerely believe you must do something that is against the law. Either way, no one else is directly involved, usually.

But many of the cases brought in the 2010s and early 2020s directly involve third parties who could incur harm.[20] Justice Ruth Bader Ginsburg addressed these implications in her *Hobby Lobby* dissent. She wrote, "No tradition, and no prior decision under RFRA, allows a religion-based exemption when the accommodation would be harmful to others—here, the very persons the contraceptive coverage requirement was designed to protect."[21] A counterexample came before the court the next year, in *Holt v. Hobbs*. That case was decided unanimously in favor of an incarcerated Muslim who wanted to grow a half-inch beard as an expression of his sincerely held religious belief. Ginsburg penned a very short concurrence to highlight the difference. "Unlike the exemption this Court approved in [*Hobby Lobby*]," she wrote, "accommodating petitioner's religious belief in this case would not detrimentally affect others who do not share petitioner's belief."[22] A short beard doesn't harm anyone; denial of healthcare does. Whether and how these harms should be weighed against the harm of

19. NeJaime and Siegel, "Conscience Wars," 2519.

20. While I was finishing this book, the Supreme Court granted a Pentecostal church's members' application for injunctive relief from California's ban on indoor religious services, which was part of the state's public safety efforts to curb the spread on COVID-19. (South Bay United Pentecostal Church v. Newsom, 592 U.S. ___ [2021]). Justice Neil Gorsuch wrote that the state had "single[d] out religion for worse treatment than many secular activities." In her dissent, though, Justice Elena Kagan argued that the state's policies satisfied the "neutrality rule by regulating worship services the same as other activities 'where large groups of people [come together] in close proximity for extended periods of time." There is much that could and will be said about this case, but for now I want to note its relevance to this discussion of third-party harms. Believers and churches were granted the right to worship freely, but their actions will undoubtedly harm others—in significant numbers, and sometimes fatally.

21. *Hobby Lobby*, 573 U.S. at 27.

22. Holt v. Hobbes, 574 U.S. 352 (2015)

impinging upon sincerely held religious belief complicates the two-way strict scrutiny of substantial burdens and compelling interests.[23]

The Christian Legal Movement

"The aftermath of *Smith*," Winnifred Sullivan noted, "saw the development of a vigorous and well-funded specialized bar promoting the rights of religion." Some of these specialists were ostensibly nonsectarian, like the Becket Fund for Religious Liberty. But many others are explicitly Christian, working on behalf of mostly white evangelicals and some Catholics. The "Christian legal movement" includes groups such as the Alliance Defending Freedom (ADF) and Liberty Counsel, the latter of which represented Davis. The political scientist Daniel Bennett has studied these "Christian conservative legal organizations" (CCLOs) and what he calls the "CCLO industry," which is lucrative, powerful, and growing.[24] CCLOs often focus on religious freedom, but, especially through complicity-based claims, they conceptualize it as a far-reaching right, even if exercising that right directly harms others.[25] In the 2010s these groups became influential in the courts, particularly after Trump appointed many sympathetic federal judges, as well as in Republican Party politics.

The Christian Right has styled themselves champions of "religious liberty," which groups like ADF and Liberty Counsel frequently assert is under attack and must be protected. This is a twist on a persecution myth that casts Christians as under attack by the forces of "secularism" both in the United States and globally.[26] Defenses, sometimes earnest and sometimes in

23. See also Amy J. Sepinwall, "Conscience and Complicity: Assessing Pleas for Religious Exemptions in *Hobby Lobby*'s Wake," *University of Chicago Law Review* 82, no. 4 (Fall, 2015): 1897–1980.

24. Bennett, *Defending Faith*; and Hollis-Brusky and Wilson, *Separate but Faithful*. See also Kelsey Dallas, "Serving God by Suing Others: Inside the Christian Legal Movement," *Deseret News*, Aug. 2, 2017. Though the United States is distinctive in its approach to religious freedom, specialized Christian legal organizations exist in other countries as well. See, e.g., Méadhbh McIvor, *Representing God: Christian Legal Activism in Contemporary England* (Princeton University Press, 2020).

25. Their "arguments for religious liberty," Bennett writes, "bleed into most aspects of CCLO advocacy, providing a useful and principles frame for the CLM [Christian legal movement] as it moves to rein in the expansion of legal rights for certain segments of the population" (*Defending Faith*, 7).

26. See, e.g., Jason Bruner, *Imagining Persecution: Why American Christians Believe There Is a Global War against Their Faith* (Rutgers University Press, 2021).

bad faith (but who can tell which, in every case?), against imagined animus have formed a key part of this strategy. The journalist Sarah Posner has called this the "'anti-Catholic' playbook," propagated by millions of dollars in dark money and lobbying, which advises that allegations of bigotry be countered with the same.[27] In 2019 Missouri Senator Josh Hawley questioned Michael Borgen, who was nominated by Trump to serve on the U.S. District Court for the Western District of Michigan. Borgen was a conservative, but Hawley went after him, in apparent bad faith, because he had "equated" a Catholic family with the Ku Klux Klan. While representing the City of East Lansing, Borgen had written that it was difficult to distinguish legally between allowing a Catholic family to discriminate against same-sex couples and, for instance, allowing KKK members to discriminate based on their sincerely held religious beliefs.[28] Clearly, Borgen had not "equated" the parties; he had just said that if "sincerely held religious belief" allows someone to flout antidiscrimination law, it is hard to draw a line. So why did Hawley decide to paint Borgen as anti-Catholic? As Posner pointed out, Borgen's error, for Hawley, was not so much the content of his argument as the fact that he had opposed the ADF, who represented the Catholic family.[29]

Davis was represented, pro bono, by Liberty Counsel. They courted media attention and sought to make Davis famous. Her memoir was written with Mat Staver, an attorney and former pastor who cofounded Liberty Counsel, as well as with John Aman, who also works for Liberty Counsel.[30] The memoir was published by their in-house publishing imprint, New Revolution Publishers, and was sold exclusively through the Liberty Counsel website.[31] In the memoir Davis offers a personal account, in plainspoken and sincere style, of the Christian legal movement's ideology. She is a kind

27. Sarah Posner, "The 'Anti-Catholic' Playbook," *Nation*, Sept. 5, 2018.

28. Brief in Support of a Motion—Document 14, docket number 1:17-cv-00487. Country Mill Farms and Stephen Tennes v. City of East Lansing.

29. Sarah Posner, "Inside the Christian Legal Army Weakening the Church-State Divide," *Talking Points Memo*, Oct. 4, 2019.

30. Staver cofounded Liberty Counsel with Anita Staver, who is also an attorney. On Staver and the early history of Liberty Counsel, see chap. 3 in Hans J. Hacker, *The Culture of Conservative Christian Litigation* (Rowman and Littlefield, 2005).

31. See https://www.lc.org/nrp. According to the website, "New Revolution Publishers publishes educational resources regarding worldview, Judeo-Christian thought and values, cultural issues and engagement, and Israel."

person with no personal animus toward gay people, but she was the victim of persecution. The villains in her story are "the ACLU and its clients," who in her case "had what, to some, looked like a big win—and a lucrative payday—just ahead."[32] Rather than defenders of civil rights, in Davis's narrative they are villainous bullies.

The Christian legal movement is a public relations movement as well as a legal one.[33] It is not just about winning cases but shifting conversations and swaying public opinion, such that "religious liberty" has become a central concern for many Republican and/or white Christian nationalist voters, and politicians court these votes by "standing up for" religious liberty and defending them against the secularists.[34] CCLOs like are the new secular translators—hewing to strategic rhetorical guidelines—working against the ACLU. In 2012 someone leaked internal ADF documents, including "Branding and Identity Standards." The document advises employees on how to use language to reflect ideology properly. For example, "USE: cross-dressing, sexually confused; DON'T USE: transgender"; "USE: abortion-inducing drug, morning-after abortion pill; DON'T USE: emergency contraception, birth control, morning-after pill"; "USE: 'hate' crimes, so-called 'hate' crimes; DON'T USE: hate crimes."[35] The ironic quotation marks—"hate" crimes, not hate crimes—are part of Davis's repertoire too. She refers only to "same-sex 'marriage.'" Sincere beliefs, while individual and personal, must be translated into politically effective language; in quintessentially early twenty-first-century style, this can be called a "branding strategy."

32. Davis, *Under God's Authority*, 17.

33. Amanda Hollis-Brusky and Joshua Wilson explain how the Christian legal movement cultivates various sorts of capital—human, social, intellectual—in order to create networks and promote their ideas, sometimes through "infiltration" of mainstream institutions but more often through creating "parallel alternatives" and "supplemental alternatives." They write, "The ultimate goal of engaging in support structure building is not only to win in court, but also to build a movement capable of affecting the legal, political, and broader culture. Success is, therefore, not all or nothing" (*Separate but Faithful*, 204). Bennett, *Defending Faith*, analyzes press releases from CCLOs, showing how they frame their activities and ideas. The ADF's Kristen Waggoner explained to Bennett that it is imperative that CCLOs—and related interest groups—focus on winning arguments in the cultural realm as well as in the legal and political realms. 'You can win in the courtroom and lose in the culture,' Waggoner told me, 'and we have to win in both of them'" (132).

34. See Whitehead and Perry, *Taking America Back for God*, 133–138.

35. Alliance Defending Freedom, "2012 Branding and Identity Standards," 26–32, https://assets.documentcloud.org/documents/6444427/ADF-Lexicon.pdf.

Local Laws

Beyond the state-level RFRAs, smaller governing entities have worked religious freedom into legislation. In some cases, legislators have introduced these bills in response to—or even as addenda to—antidiscrimination protections. For example, in 2019 legislators in Daviess County, Kentucky proposed a "fairness ordinance" that would add "gender identification and sexual orientation" to existing antidiscrimination laws. The ordinance would also include an opt-out clause, ensuring that people did not have to comply if their noncompliance was motivated by "sincerely held religious belief." Still, local religious groups opposed the legislation, citing a national attack on religious freedom. According to a business owner and former county commissioner, a then-recent 2019 debate among Democratic presidential candidates showed "where some of this stuff is headed": "When it comes to our religious freedoms, Christians and other people who are opposed to these types of lifestyles which we don't approve of . . . we are concerned that our rights will also be in jeopardy."[36] This is a zero-sum freedom, where advances for some entail infringements on others' rights. If "complicity" with other's "lifestyles which we don't approve of"—by, say, signing a marriage license or sharing a bathroom with someone—tramples on religious freedom, then it is a fragile thing indeed, and one might be right to think it's under threat.[37] This is the framework many CCLOs use, and it has become axiomatic for Christian Right politics. Local jurisdictions around the country, including school boards, have passed similar ordinances. Proscriptions of discrimination against people because of their queer identification were understood not just to necessitate preemptive religious exemptions but to be an attack on sincere believers.

These laws are often model legislation. In 2018 Frederick Clarkson, a journalist and research analyst, discovered a "playbook" from "Project Blitz," designed by a coalition of Christian Right activists.[38] It had been distributed to over 750 lawmakers throughout the United States.[39] In addition to bills

36. Jacob Mulliken, "Views Voiced on Fairness Ordinance," *Paducah Sun*, Oct. 19, 2019.

37. On trans rights and religious freedom, see Alexis M. Florczak, "Make America Discriminate Again: Why Hobby Lobby's Expansion of RFRA Is Bad Medicine for Transgender Healthcare," *Health Matrix* 28 (2018): 431–468.

38. Frederick Clarkson, "'Project Blitz' Seeks to Do for Christian Nationalism What ALEC Does for Big Business," *Religion Dispatches*, Apr. 27, 2018.

39. Hayes, "Bracing for the Blitz." This piece was published in *Church and State*, the magazine of American United for the Separation of Church and State.

protecting "sincerely held religious belief," the model bills included "In God We Trust" legislation, specifically designed to troll opponents into taking "unpopular stands on seemingly symbolic issues."[40] Based on the players involved, it seems clear that Project Blitz is an effort to use religious freedom and the language of sincerely held religious belief to advance their brand of Christian nationalism. Critics such as Katherine Stewart have alleged that the architects of these bills, including Mississippi's HB 1523, with which this chapter opened, are themselves insincere—that the point isn't really religious freedom, but some admixture of bigotry and greed. Bills like HB 1523 would protect religious activists from the "governmental threat of losing their tax exemption."[41] (These critiques often can slide into a classed distinction between knaves and fools, imagining believers like Kim Davis as duped by knavish theocrats like Mat Staver.) Americans United for the Separation of Church and State (AU), in an official statement, characterized Project Blitz as "part of a national trend to redefine religious liberty as a sword used to harm others instead of a shield that protects people."[42]

SWORDS AND SHIELDS

Throughout U.S. history, most claimants in high-profile free exercise cases have been religious minorities—Mormon polygamists, Jehovah's Witnesses, members of the Native American Church, Santería practitioners, MOVE people. In many cases these claimants were minoritized in other ways that intersected with their religious identities. I would argue that religious freedom, as a liberal institution, serves to grant freedoms selectively, protecting certain dissenters while upholding normative subjectivities. From this critical perspective, "religious" has no proper or true referent, and thus religious freedom is the stuff of power and politics, and its affordances will always be partial not because not "all religions" have yet to be recognized but because the process of recognizing people on the basis of their religiosity is always a technique of governance under racial liberalism. On many liberal accounts, though, the denial of the status of "religious" to minority groups is an effect

40. Stewart, *The Power Worshippers*, 159.

41. Katherine Stewart, "Why Mississippi's New Anti-LGBT Law Is the Most Dangerous One to Be Passed Yet," *Nation*, Apr. 6, 2016.

42. Hayes, "Bracing for the Blitz."

of misrecognition, in which people who are really religious are mistakenly denied that status. For instance, Khyati Joshi has argued that "many religious issues come to be incorrectly labeled as racial."[43] In the same way, Kathryn Gin Lum and Paul Harvey write, the project of religious freedom and equality remains "incomplete," because "when challenged, the power of the state does not recognize all 'religion' equally."[44] As time goes on, this "standard story" goes, there are setbacks here and there, but for the most part religious freedom laws ensure more freedom of expression for minorities and makes the right to free exercise accessible to more and more of them.[45] This story charts a trajectory of uplift, of minoritized identity groups fighting for and earning rights that were rightfully theirs all along.

This story seemed to have been knocked off its narrative arc. By the 2010s many liberals had noticed something of a reversal. High-profile religious freedom issues often centered white Christians, not minoritized groups. What's more, these claimants and the organizations backing them sought to use their freedoms to do harm to more vulnerable people. Religious freedom had a new meaning.[46] And so, many liberals began turning against religious freedom—or religious liberty, the term conservatives increasingly preferred.[47] People for the American Way (PFAW), for example, argued in a 2015 report that "'religious liberty' has become an ideological rallying cry for

43. Khyati Y. Joshi, "South Asian Religions in Contemporary America," in *The Oxford Handbook of Religion and Race in American History*, ed. Gin Lum and Harvey, 470.

44. Gin Lum and Harvey, "Introduction," in *The Oxford Handbook of Religion and Race in American History*, ed. Gin Lum and Harvey, 14. For a more thorough version of this critique, see my review of this book in *Religion* 50, no. 1 (Jan., 2020): 182–185.

45. The term "standard story" is borrowed from Steven D. Smith, *The Rise and Decline of Religious Freedom* (Harvard University Press, 2015), although my usage is a little different from Smith's.

46. See, e.g., Marsha B. Freeman, "Holier than You and Me: 'Religious Liberty' Is the New Bully Pulpit and Its New Meaning Is Endangering Our Way of Life," *Arkansas Law Review* 69, no. 4 (2017): 881–910. Andrew Koppelman, in a narration of the "reversal" (across two chapters, titled respectively "Liberals Used to Love Religious Freedom" and "But Now They Denounce It as a Mere Excuse for Bigotry"), cites the "surge in news stories mentioning religion, homosexuality, and bigotry together" and, specifically, two stories: Indiana's RFRA law and the story of the Kentucky county clerk Kim Davis (*Gay Rights vs. Religious Liberty?*, 30).

47. Stephanie Russell-Kraft has argued that "by reclaiming *liberty*, members of the religious right are reclaiming a world in which Christianity provided the moral structure for the founding of the nation." Also, Russell-Kraft writes, citing conversations with legal scholars, "*liberty* is the language of exemption, of freedom from government intervention."

a collection of culture warriors—and the linchpin of their legal and political strategies." On their account, there used to be a consensus that religious freedom was a good thing. However, "that consensus has been shattered because social conservatives are trying to turn laws meant to shield individuals' religious exercise into swords that individuals and corporations can use against antidiscrimination laws and other measures opposed by conservative religious groups."[48] I argue that, while certain aspects of the "new politics of religious freedom" are actually new, as discussed above, religious freedom has sometimes been used as a shield but has always been a sword.[49] And neither use, sword or shield, is the "correct" one; people advocate for the politics they want, and they use the tools available.

For liberal proponents of the reversal thesis, the new anti-antidiscrimination politics are seen as a perversion of religious freedom, rather than an example of its inherent coerciveness. The journalist Katherine Stewart writes, following her discussion of the coordinated attempt by right-wing organizations to draft and pass religious freedom bills, that "at this point, it would be apparent to any listener that the agenda" of that project "had nothing to do with religious freedom in the *proper sense of the term.*" She continues, "By 'religious freedom,' participants simply meant privilege for those with the right religion."[50] Religious freedom becomes "religious freedom." Stewart's ironic quotations marks—which call to mind Davis's use of "same-sex 'marriage'"—imply that there is a true referent for

---

Thus, "liberty" signals a defense against imposition, rather than positive freedom to practice per se. See Russell-Kraft, "'Freedom' vs. 'Liberty': Why Religious Conservatives Have Begun to Favor One Over the Other," *Religion Dispatches*, Oct. 12, 2016.

48. People for the American Way Foundation, "Religious Liberty: Sword or Shield?" report, Feb. 2015. http://www.pfaw.org/report/religious-liberty-shield-or-sword/. On PFAW and its founder Norman Lear's liberal vision of religion in public, see L. Benjamin Rolsky, *The Rise and Fall of the Religious Left: Politics, Television, and Popular Culture in the 1970s and Beyond* (Columbia University Press, 2019).

See also the Public Religion Research Institute's 2021 survey on "perceptions of the meaning of religious liberty." PRRI, "Is Religious Liberty a Shield or a Sword?" Feb. 10, 2021, https://www.prri.org/research/is-religious-liberty-a-shield-or-a-sword/.

49. Critical studies of religious freedom among scholars owe less to this recent history and more to postcolonial theory (and the postcolonial roots of secularism studies) and critiques of liberalism, which have more purchase among scholars than among, say, U.S. policy makers. However, studies of the swordliness of religious freedom might be especially resonant in this new era. See, e.g., Curtis, *The Production of American Religious Freedom*; Wenger, *Religious Freedom*; and Hurd, *Beyond Religious Freedom*.

50. Stewart, *The Power Worshippers*, 168; emphasis added.

religious freedom and a "proper" use of it. Stewart and her fellow critics traffic in a familiar politics of sincerity. By insinuating that discriminatory applications of religious freedom are not real religious freedom, they insinuate that religion is not really, sincerely, the motivating factor. Sometimes this is quite explicit, as in the finding by the U.S. Commission on Civil Rights that such bills and lawsuits "represent an orchestrated, nationwide effort by extremists to promote bigotry, cloaked in the mantle of 'religious freedom'" and "are pretextual attempts to justify naked animus against lesbian, gay, bisexual, and transgender people."[51] It's not religion underneath. This supposed perversion of religious freedom, according to critics like Stewart, is a new development, orchestrated by savvy operatives with a sinister agenda. Many of the claimants, though, the people whom bills like HB 1523 or the Daviess County ordinance are putatively designed to protect, would say that their need for protection is new, that Christianity is under unprecedented attack, and that they simply are protecting *themselves* from "naked animus" against Christians, "cloaked" as reproductive and LGBTQ rights.[52]

THE EMPIRE OF RELIGIOUS FREEDOM

During the 2016 presidential campaign, and then in the Trump administration, religious liberty was a foundational plank of the Republican Party's platform, evident in the track records of judicial nominees as well as public rhetoric. In this section I want to critique the reversal thesis through a brief departure from domestic religious freedom, showing how these politics, including the discourse of sincerity, has also permeated U.S. promotion of international religious freedom. In that arena, the Trump administration (2017–2021) accelerated a two-decade push, beginning with the 1998

51. U.S. Commission on Civil Rights, "Peaceful Coexistence: Reconciling Nondiscrimination Principles with Civil Liberties" (Sept., 2016); quoted in Koppelman, *Gay Rights vs. Religious Liberty?*, 112.

52. In her memoir, Kim Davis frequently asserts that the couples who sought marriage licenses from her did so not simply out of a genuine desire to get married (or "married") but to stick it to her personally, to punish her for stance (*Under God's Authority*). *Masterpiece Cakeshop* turned on this sort of "revelation," in which members of the Colorado Civil Rights Commission seemed to have personal animus toward the baker Jack Phillips.

International Religious Freedom Act, to protect the human right to religious freedom throughout the world. In 2018 Sam Brownback, the former governor of Kansas, was appointed Ambassador-at-Large for International Religious Freedom. That same year, Secretary of State Mike Pompeo hosted the first Ministerial to Advance Religious Freedom, which convened religious and political leaders to discuss religious freedom and persecution globally. At the second iteration of that ministerial, in 2019, Brownback said, "Let this be the time the worlds' [sic] faiths came together to stand for each others' [sic] ability to exist peacefully, without fear. Let's bring our faiths alive, and respect—even love one another no matter what we believe or don't believe. We are all part of a common humanity."[53] There is no room in this worldview for illiberal religion, because authentic religiosity necessitates tolerance.

As the administration globalized domestic culture-war issues, it reproduced the discourse of sincerity when championing international religious freedom. In September of 2019 President Trump convened an event at the United Nations dedicated to religious freedom. In his speech Trump described widespread religious persecution around the world and stressed the moral and political imperatives to protect religious freedom. Addressing the assembly, he said:

> As we speak, Jews, Christians, Muslims, Buddhists, Hindus, Sikhs, Yazidis, and many other people of faith are being jailed, sanctioned, tortured, and even murdered, often at the hands of their own government, simply for expressing their deeply held religious beliefs. So hard to believe. Today, with one clear voice, the United States of America calls upon the nations

53. Samuel D. Brownback, "Opening Keynote Remarks at the 2019 Ministerial to Advance Religious Freedom," July 16, 2019. August 22, 2019 was the first International Day Commemorating the Victims of Acts of Violence Based on Religion or Belief. In the press statement announcing the commemoration, Secretary Pompeo said: "This day serves as a reminder of the need to promote and protect the unalienable right of religious freedom, and the consequences when countries fail to do so. . . . No one should face persecution on account of their faith, for changing beliefs, or switching their membership in a belief community. All governments have a duty to protect people from harm regardless of their beliefs, and to hold perpetrators of persecution accountable." Michael R. Pompeo, Press Statement, Aug. 22, 2019. On the phrase "religion or belief," see Sherwood, "On the Freedom of the Concepts of Religion and Belief," in *Politics of Religious Freedom*, ed. Sullivan, Hurd, Mahmood, and Danchin.

of the world to end religious persecution. To stop the crimes against people of faith, release prisoners of conscience, repeal laws restricting freedom of religion and belief, protect the vulnerable, the defenseless, and the oppressed, America stands with believers in every country who ask only for the freedom to live according to the faith that is within their own hearts.[54]

The language of sincerity permeates this passage: "people of faith," "deeply held religious beliefs," "the faith that is within their own hearts." Religion, in domestic as well as foreign policy, is a generalized category paradoxically naming group identities (which are severable from other identities, like ethnicity) *and*, essentially, a way of believing for individuals.[55] The secular subject has a "faith" and keeps it in their "own heart."

As scholars such as Anna Su and Elizabeth Shakman Hurd have shown, religious freedom is attendant on U.S. empire. Hurd writes, "Guarantees for religious freedom are a modern technique of governance, authorizing particular forms of politics and regulating the spaces in which people live out their religion in specific ways."[56] This insight explains how, for instance, the Department of Justice formed a "Religious Liberty Task Force" while also surveilling and suppressing Muslims and "Black Identity Extremists."[57] The relationship between these projects should be explained and analyzed.[58] When liberal critics of the new politics of religious freedom assert that a "license to discriminate" is not true religious freedom, and that discriminatory beliefs are simply a mask for bigotry, they maintain the same assemblage in which Trump, Pompeo, and Brownback locate religion: civilizationalist liberalism. Both sides understand (good) religious belief as inherently liberal, pro-freedom, and sincere.

54. Donald Trump, "Remarks by President Trump at the United Nations Event of Religious Freedom," Sept. 23, 2019. https://www.whitehouse.gov/briefings-statements/remarks-president-trump-united-nations-event-religious-freedom-new-york-ny/.

55. On religion as both individual and communal and the problems this contradiction creates for constitutional law, see Benjamin Schonthal, "Why Religion Is Different: Five Contradictions of Religion in Law," *Immanent Frame*, July 25, 2019.

56. Hurd, *Beyond Religious Freedom*, 38.

57. Jeff Sessions, "Attorney General Sessions Delivers Remarks at the Department of Justice's Religious Liberty Summit," July 30, 2018.

58. Here I am taking a cue from Sylvester Johnson: "The relationship between freedom and its others has to be *explained* instead of being dismissed as hypocrisy or contradiction" (*African American Religions*, 5).

THE "SEXUAL PROTOCOLS OF SECULARISM"

The pitched battle between Christian conservatives fighting for religious liberty on one side and advocates for LGBTQ rights on the other is a clash not between religion and secularism, but between two types of secularism.[59] The debate is not about whether we should have secularism, but about what type of secular governance the various parties want.[60] One way to conceptualize the conflict, and the stakes of secularism, is as being between religious freedom and "sexual freedom." The legal scholar Frank Ravitch has used the catchall term "sexual freedom" (though admitting it is "not an ideal term") to refer to "both LGBT and reproductive freedom[, which] concern one's ability to be oneself, to be free, and to control one's destiny."[61] Sexual freedom, then, looks a lot like secular subjectivity. As Talal Asad argues, "The human being is a sovereign, self-owning agent—essentially suspicious of others—and not merely a subject conscious of his or her own identity. It is on this basis that the secularist principle of the right to freedom of belief and expression was crafted."[62] There are always limits, of course. As Janet Jakobsen and Ann Pellegrini have explained, "promises of 'freedom' and 'privacy'—promises supposedly made to every American by virtue of begin a citizen—are actually held out as rewards, not rights, and only to those who belong to the right kind of family."[63] Sexual freedom and religious freedom, then, are different species of the same genus, an always selective secular liberalism.

59. Jacobsen, Fernando, and Jakobsen, "Gender, Sex, and Religious Freedom," 97. The quotation ("sexual protocols of secularism") is from Fernando.

Self-identified secularist organizations, some of which are atheist or freethinker societies and some of which are church-state separation advocates, often perpetuate this distinction. On groups such as AU, the Freedom from Religion Foundation, the Secular Coalition, and American Atheists, the overlaps among them, and the coalitions they form, see Blankholm, "The Political Advantages of a Polysemous Secular."

60. I think that most scholars of secularism would agree on this. For a different perspective, from a scholar who conceptualizes secularism less critically, as a desirable liberal value of church-state separation, rightfully and admirably geared toward policing bad religions, see the work of Jacques Berlinerblau.

61. Frank S. Ravitch, *Freedom's Edge: Religious Freedom, Sexual Freedom, and the Future of America* (Jacobsen, Fernando, and Jakobsen, "Gender, Sex, and Religious Freedom," 97. The quotation ("sexual protocols of secularism") is from Fernando.

62. Asad, *Formations of the Secular*, 135.

63. Jakobsen and Pellegrini, *Love the Sin*, 9.

The regulation of sex and gender in the United States has often been understood as essentially religious. But secularism is regulatory too, and sex is one of its primary targets for regulation. "In fact," Janet Jakobsen writes, "sexual regulation is such a passion in U.S. politics because sexual regulation is constitutive of (secular) American freedom. . . . Freedom in this sense—and this market-based sense of freedom becomes dominant in modernity—is not the repression of activity, but it is the regulated enactment of activity along particular lines."[64] Thus, following Mayanthi Fernando, we should understand secularism "not so much as a site of emptiness or a kind of space-clearing neutrality but rather as a formation that has a series of norms and protocols about sex and gender."[65] Secularism encourages people to express their sex, like their religion, in public, so long as those sexual and/or religious expressions are properly (self-)regulated. For certain post-9/11 feminists and xenophobes, the promotion of sexual and gender freedom combines with racist condemnations of the repressive Islamic other, resulting in what Sara Farris calls "femonationalism."[66] Concern for women's rights, however sincere, can thus underwrite imperial ambitions and nativist politics.

The conflict between religious freedom and sexual freedom is enabled by a generally unquestioned assumption that "conservative Christians" hold their views about sex both sincerely and religiously. Winnifred Sullivan has noted, for instance, how for all members of the Supreme Court in *Hobby Lobby* "opposition to legal contraception and abortion was assumed to be religiously motivated. No evidence was required."[67] This easy assumption is due, at least in part, to the elision of conservative Christianity with religion itself—which also elides the differences among conservative Christians, as I will discuss later with reference to Davis.[68] And in turn, the "sexual," which is to say LGBTQ rights and even identities and practices, has been cast as irreligious or secular. This is what Jasbir Puar meant when she described "queer secularity" as "demand[ing] a particular transgression of norms, religious norms that are understood to otherwise bind that subject

64. Jakobsen, "Sex + Freedom = Regulation," 286.

65. Jacobsen, Fernando, and Jakobsen, "Gender, Sex, and Religious Freedom," 93.

66. Farris, *In the Name of Women's Rights*. See also Lila Abu-Lughod, *Do Muslim Women Need Saving?* (Harvard University Press, 2013).

67. Sullivan, *Church State Corporation*, 97.

68. Jakobsen and Pellegrini, *Love the Sin*; and Fessenden, *Culture and Redemption*.

to an especially egregious interdictory religious frame. The queer agential subject can only ever be fathomed outside the norming constrictions of religion, conflating agency and resistance."[69] Indeed, as Christian groups claim the broad mantle of religious freedom in a post-*Smith* world, religion itself is locked in an existential contest over the future of a zero-sum freedom. Or, as Mike Huckabee put it in his foreword to Kim Davis's memoir, "same-sex 'marriage' directly assaults religious liberty."[70] Through this contrast between LGBTQ rights and religious freedom, Huckabee, Liberty Counsel, and others become secular regulators who produce "good religion." Of course, this is only one side in an argument about good religion. Their opponents often charge them with having bad religion. They are fakes, their "religion" merely a mask for discrimination and bigotry. This contest is not simply two-sided. Instead, it indicates a complex civilizationalist assemblage.[71]

The secular queer subject, presenting as a liberal deserving of marriage rights, constructs their homonationalist bona fides by contrasting themselves with the deviant terrorist—as Puar writes, "constitutive of and constituted by the queer autonomous liberal subject against and through the reification of the very pathological irrational sexualities that are endemic to discourses of terrorist culpability."[72] The "other side" knows this move too. In defense of Davis's good religion, Huckabee argues that Davis's sincere beliefs cast her outside the bounds of liberal society (unfairly and perversely, we are led to presume) even as the Muslim terrorist's bad religion is protected. "Why," Huckabee asks, "could we not be at least as accommodating of Kim's religious convictions as we are for Muslim terrorists held at Gitmo, the Guantanamo Bay Naval Base? I have visited Gitmo and observed how the U.S. government provides these men, who want to destroy America, with prayer rugs, halal meals, even painted stripes on the floor pointing toward Mecca. But for Kim and her conscience, there was no accommodation."[73] In Huckabee's telling, the terrorist other has had their religion accommodated, perhaps unduly or overgenerously, but the same government that would grant those accommodations actively persecutes Davis. Again, it

69. Puar, *Terrorist Assemblages*, 13.
70. Davis, *Under God's Authority*, xii.
71. Wenger, *Religious Freedom*.
72. Puar, *Terrorist Assemblages*, 15.
73. Davis, *Under God's Authority*, xiii.

works in all directions, as secular liberals have compared the Christian Right to the illiberal Islamic other.[74] For instance, Bill Maher said on his television show *Real Time* in 2015, "If you say, as Kim Davis and her ilk and [Texas Senator] Ted Cruz and these people say, that, 'actually, I can ignore the rule of man because the rulebook of God said,' then you are Iran. Then you are Saudi Arabia. Then you are Shari'a law."[75] For Huckabee, Davis's good religion is cast into stark relief with bad ("terrorist") religion. The U.S. government grants religious freedom to detained men "who want to destroy America," but they fail to protect Davis. Huckabee hints at the question: Is Kim Davis really (like) a terrorist? For his audience, the answer is an obvious no. For Maher, though, it's yes.

The politics of good and bad religion, of sincerity and insincerity, are wrapped up in a sexual politics. As Puar argued, the homonationalist subject demonstrates their own good sexuality by juxtaposing it with aberrant terrorist sexualities. In the early 2000s the queer secular defined itself against the repressive religious, which could be expressed as the deviant yet repressive Muslim or the authoritarian and puritanical Christian. Davis's complicity-based claim was an exercise in (religious) freedom that attempted to deny (sexual) freedom to others. In this way, like the terrorist's failed sexuality, Davis's failed religion is contrasted with that of the homonationalist subject, the white Christian Kentucky couple who just want to get married.

In unsympathetic media outlets, critics scrutinized Davis's own deviant sexuality. In her memoir, though, Davis describes her own sexual and marital history as evidence that God uses unlikely people to accomplish his aims: "In a divine irony—if not comedy—He was about to take someone married four times, twice to the same husband, and give me an international platform to defend marriage."[76] She was not, she admitted, a perfect vessel for the message of the sanctity of marriage. Her critics agreed, but for them the irony was not so divine. Her divorces, they argued, showed her hypocrisy, her attempt to regulate others' sexual freedom while she misused her own. In so doing, they constructed good sexuality—sexual pleasure and monogamous marriage—over and against Davis's dual excesses: sexual repression

---

74. On the Islamic other as the perennial foil against which liberalism is constructed, see Massad, *Islam in Liberalism*.

75. Trudy Ring, "WATCH: Bill Maher to Kim Davis: 'You Are Sharia Law,'" *Advocate*, Sept. 12, 2015.

76. Davis, *Under God's Authority*, 30.

and sexual infidelity. In her work on sex, gender, and secularism, Joan Scott argued that "the normative constraints [of sexual freedom] are obscured by defining them in opposition to some excess. . . . The excesses go both ways: sexual overindulgence on the one side, and sexual repression on the other."[77] Davis's excesses went both ways, and thus she becomes doubly unsecular. She is zealously religious, to the point of irrationality and incivility. *And* her past indicates failure to comply with the civilizing norms of monogamous domesticity that she now prevents others from achieving. She is, above all, undisciplined.

The twenty-first-century secular subject is sexually free, but Davis is not. Some of Davis's harshest critics mocked her appearance. Unlike many of the most visible U.S. white evangelical women, such as megachurch pastors and pastors' wives, Davis did not perform her gender as conventional white femininity.[78] As a member of an apostolic holiness church, she dressed modestly, without makeup, and wore her hair long and unstyled.[79] Derisive comments and jokes about Davis's appearance underscored her deviance, her failure to conform to patriarchal norms while she was still authoritarian enough to repress others. In her analysis of anti-Davis memes, Sarah Walker argues, "Memes that emphasize Davis's sexual (un)desirability or promiscuity or mock her religious convictions restrict public displays of unpopular belief."[80] The goal of these critiques, in other words, is secular regulation, barring bad belief from the public sphere.[81] If a reversal has taken place, it is

77. Scott, *Sex and Secularism*, 163.

78. On self-presentation, femininity, and white evangelical celebrity, see Kate Bowler, *The Preacher's Wife: The Precarious Power of Evangelical Women Celebrities* (Princeton University Press, 2019).

79. Davis has not addressed these choices often or at much length in her public speech and writings. Her memoir does contain a short passage about refusing hair and makeup styling when she appeared on Megyn Kelly's Fox News television show. Davis, *Under God's Authority*, 115–116.

80. Sarah Walker, "Kim Davis vs. the Gay(ze): A Problematic Response to Religious Freedom Advocates," in *The Rhetoric of Religious Freedom in the United States*, ed. Eric C. Miller (Lexington Books, 2018), 133.

81. Nevertheless, the fact of Davis's religiosity—that her beliefs were indeed *religious*—went unquestioned. "Liberal" claimants have fared less well, although there have been some recent exceptions, such as the case of Scott Warren, an activist who provided water to migrants on the southern border. A jury found that his actions were an exercise of his sincere religious beliefs. See Ryan Devereaux, "Humanitarian Volunteer Scott Warren Reflects

that Davis's sexuality is now less normative, less tolerated, than that of the couples whose marriage rights she denied.[82]

Why is religious freedom seemingly all about sex now? Despite the rise of sincerity and individual belief, the content of the belief still matters, and in the twenty-first-century United States religion has been "reduced to a matter of individual sincere and usually devout belief—about sex and reproduction."[83] Many Americans—on the right and the left, "religious" and "secular"—have conceded that this is what religion is really about.[84] Comparisons to racial discrimination help illustrate this point. Many critics have argued that anti-LGBTQ bigotry is like racism or is as bad as racism, but what about cases in which sincerely held religious beliefs are actually

---

on the Borderlands and Two Years of Government Persecution," *Intercept*, Dec. 23, 2019. See also Elizabeth Reiner Platt, Katherine Franke, Kira Shepherd, and Lilia Hadjiivanova, "Whose Faith Matters? The Fight for Religious Liberty Beyond the Christian Right" (Nov., 2019). This report, from the Columbia Law School's Law, Rights, and Religion Project, is available on their website, https://lawrightsreligion.law.columbia.edu.

It remains to be seen whether more claimants like Warren will be successful, or if these defenses will remain primarily tools of the Christian Right. Drawing from anecdotal evidence, which I will sneak into a footnote, I will say that I am doubtful. At a dinner in the fall of 2019, a prominent religious-freedom specialist who has successfully represented high-profile claimants discussed Scott Warren and similar claimants as liberals "trying to *use*" religious freedom toward their own political ends. She strongly insinuated that their true aims were not really religious, and yet that night she gave an entire talk (and indeed wrote an entire book) that never questioned the sincerity or religiosity of conservative evangelicals.

82. Tolerance implies a power differential, the normative and powerful tolerate certain others, but in so doing reinforce their status as others. Wendy Brown reminds, "Despite its role in identity production, regulation and governance, tolerance represents itself as a benign and power-free discourse" ("Civilizational Delusions"). See also Brown, *Regulating Aversion*.

83. Sullivan, *Church State Corporation*, 170.

84. This is one reason that the exposés about Project Blitz and critical analysis of ADF and Liberty Counsel are interesting. Although I disagree with the normative assumptions about religion and religious freedom of critics such as Katherine Stewart, they make interesting and valuable points when they allege that religious freedom is *really* about tax exemptions or hurting queer people. In so doing, they question the easy assumption that such views are necessarily religious. Ultimately, though, this is not really the concern of courts, since they consider the religious sincerity of the claimants, not the people representing them or writing the bills (or appointing and approving judges, or sitting on the bench).

racist?[85] The owner of a wedding venue in Mississippi cited HB 1523 in her refusal to host "mixed-race" weddings. When asked why she was denying service to an interracial couple, she cited her Christian beliefs.[86] Unlike the many churches and venues who refuse to host same-sex weddings, this venue owner received widespread condemnation. She changed her stance a few days later, saying that she had recently learned, contrary to what she had been taught, that "biracial relationships were NEVER mentioned in The Bible!"[87] She did not apparently change her view on same-sex weddings. But by enumerating the content of sincerely held beliefs—not the theological content, per se, but the application of that content—HB 1523 implies that religion is about sex in a way that, presumably, it is not about race. And the courts would probably agree. This is rarely explained, defended, or contested; it has become common sense.

SUBSTANTIAL BURDENS

"Sincere" has become another word for devout or serious or deep. It's an intensifier. And it is how courts (and others, including some scholars) recognize real religiosity. In this way, sincerity has become connected, awkwardly, to another key term: *substantially*. RFRA requires that governmental action "shall not substantially burden a person's exercise of religion." What work

85. On comparisons of anti-LGBTQ discrimination to racial discrimination, see Shannon Gilreath and Arley Ward, "Same-Sex Marriage, Religious Accommodation, and the Race Analogy," *Vermont Law Review* 41, no. 2 (Winter, 2016): 237–278. They recognize the compatibility and even mutual reinforcement of racist beliefs and religious beliefs, and they argue that "both the source of the opposition to black and gay rights and the structure of the principle arguments have been virtually identical" (278). Legally, then, "the repression of same-sex marriage *is the same as* the repression of interracial marriage" (278). Most legal scholars and commentators do not recognize this point, failing to understand the historical compatibility of religion and racism or, put slightly differently, to acknowledge that racist religions are "authentic" religions too. Andrew Koppelman provides an overview of these debates in *Gay Rights vs. Religious Liberty?*, 108–127.

86. The exact quotation, heard on video, was "because of our Christian race, I mean our Christian belief." Ashton Pittman, "No 'Mixed' or 'Gay' Couples, Mississippi Wedding Venue Owner Says on Video," *Deep South Voice*, Sept. 1, 2019.

87. Allyson Chiu, "A Mississippi Wedding Venue Rejected an Interracial Couple, citing 'Christian Belief.' Facing a Backlash, the Owner Apologized," *Washington Post*, Sept. 3, 2019.

does the intensifier do? When does a negligible or minor burden become a substantial one? The 2014 *Hobby Lobby* case exacerbated the confusion over an already unclear standard. Justice Samuel Alito, in the opinion of the court, cited the financial penalties Hobby Lobby would incur should they fail to comply with the law—"as much as $1.3 million per day or about $475 million per year." Alito surmised, "If these consequences do not amount to a substantial burden, it is hard to see what would." But these consequences were a financial burden, not a religious one.

This confusion led to what Anna Su called "the main worrisome development in *Hobby Lobby*"—"that the Supreme Court made short shrift of the substantial burden prong of the RFRA test."[88] Substantial burdens, like sincere beliefs, are supposed to be matters of fact.[89] And the matter is, specifically, about the degree to which a governmental action impacts one's belief, not about how much money it might cost to follow one's belief. As Abner Greene argues, "It cannot be legally substantial just because the penalty for disobeying is high."[90] A substantial burden on religious exercise means the government is substantially burdening someone's exercise of religion; in *Hobby Lobby*, it's substantially burdening their bottom line. In Alito's misreading of RFRA, we can see a blurring of sincerely and substantially, such that both are intensifiers that change the kind of belief or burden by changing its degree. Following *Seeger* and *Welsh*, a belief becomes religious when it is believed sincerely and deeply. A burden becomes substantial when it deeply affects the believer. On Nathan Chapman's analysis, Alito's opinion "appears to conflate the requirement that a claimant be sincere with the requirement that the claimant show that the government has 'substantially burdened' the claimant's religious exercise."[91] Alito is not alone in this misunderstanding, and his opinion has allowed others to perpetuate his misreading of RFRA.

Kim Davis's substantial burden was on her potentially complicit conscience, but she also spoke of the financial burden she and others could incur. The lawsuit against her, she wrote, "sent a potent message to every

88. Su, "Judging Religious Sincerity," 42. See also Su, "Varieties of Burden in Religious Accommodations."

89. See Kara Loewentheil and Elizabeth Reiner Platt, "In Defense of the Sincerity Test," in *Religious Exemptions*, ed. Kevin Vallier and Michael E. Weber (Oxford University Press, 2018).

90. Greene, "Religious Freedom and (Other) Civil Liberties," 181.

91. Chapman, "Adjudicating Religious Sincerity," 1185.

county clerk across Kentucky: If you obey your conscience, the ACLU will paint a bull's-eye on your back, too. You could lose your job and face financial ruin."[92] Many of Davis's critics indeed argued that she was simply refusing to "do her job" and thus should lose it.[93] The nature of Davis's job was different from that of many other claimants: she was, herself, an agent of the secular state. She was its public face, interacting with members of her community who needed licenses and forms. She did paperwork. She was, in this way, less like a conscientious objector and more like an FBI agent or Anthony Comstock.[94] Kathryn Lofton asked, "Is it possible that conscience is something only a nongovernmental employee has the right to possess?"[95] This question has no easy answer, but another way of posing it is to ask how it is that an agent of the secular state could be antisecular. And what happens when the state's compelling interest (in ensuring marriage equality, for instance) must be accomplished through the violation of a state employee's rights of conscience? This will likely be a pertinent and even central question for free exercise in the coming years and decades.

In closing, I want to revisit how Davis felt religious. A sincerely held religious belief is, in so many words, an *important* belief, deeply felt. Through attention to affect, the gendered and racialized nature of religion again comes into view. Ann Pellegrini suggests, "We could say that being sincere not only encodes whiteness but also aligns it with Christianity, allowing some subjects to position themselves as above secular law. In a country as deeply religious as the United States, the performance of citizenship is bound up in being and feeling religious in the right way: sincerely."[96] There is a reason Davis's memoir is titled *Under God's Authority*. Hers is a freedom with an oxymoronic edge.[97] When she told David Ermold and David Moore that issuing them a marriage license "would violate a central teach-

---

92. Davis, *Under God's Authority*, 18.

93. See Lofton, *Consuming Religion*, 198. On religious freedom and workplace accommodations, see Weiner, "The Corporately Produced Conscience."

94. Thanks to an anonymous reviewer for drawing out these specific comparisons.

95. Lofton, *Consuming Religion*, 218.

96. Pellegrini, "Sincerely Held," 81.

97. Wendy Brown, "Religious Freedom's Oxymoronic Edge," in *Politics of Religious Freedom*, ed. Sullivan, Hurd, Mahmood, and Danchin. "If liberalism configures freedom as unhindered choice, it does not appear this way within most religions, including Islam, Christianity, and Judaism, where not only messianism but many everyday practices connect freedom with divine truth and authority" (327).

ing of Scripture and of Jesus Himself regarding marriage," Ermold asked, "Under whose authority?" "Under God's authority," Davis answered.[98] She freely exercised her religion by denying their constitutional right to marry. But, by her own description, she did so not of her own volition as a self-motivated agent, but because God instructed her so and she could do no other.[99] Davis's god, like Frank Africa's, does not fit in a secular frame. She sees through the fake worldly authority of the Supreme Court. "Unelected lawyers in robes," she calls them. But there was also something wrong with her performance of citizenship. Her sincere belief, though clearly white and Christian, was affectively amiss. When Davis was released from prison, she cried and praised God, triumphantly raising her arms, flanked by Mike Huckabee, Mat Staver, and her husband, Joe Davis—whose straw hat and denim overalls underscored the class identity that structured the mockery of Davis and her bad religious affect.[100] Individual claimants of all religions can win religious freedom, "but," to quote Pellegrini again, "the successful claimant will already have internalized the pastorate and the affective codes

98. Davis, *Under God's Authority*, 67–68. Earlier in the exchange, Moore asks Davis if she would also refuse to issue a license to an interracial couple. "'A man and a woman? No,' I responded, leaving the two men momentarily speechless" (67). I wonder about this exchange, what the men's speechlessness is supposed to signify, why the passage is included in the memoir. The implication, I think, is that the men had wrongly expected Davis to be bigoted with regard to race in addition to sex, and Davis (along with her coauthors) wants the reader to know that she is not racist and has an ideologically coherent and sex-based definition of marriage. But I also wonder, what if she had said yes? Would it make her case any different?

99. This is a theme throughout *Under God's Authority*. In Davis's telling, God told her to run for county clerk, an office her mother held for thirty-seven years before her retirement. She recounts full arguments with God about this decision (23–30). She told God that she did not want to run and would not do so freely, "so you have to make this happen" (24). She exercised her religion freely, then, by submitting. On agency and submission among conservative white evangelical women, see also R. Marie Griffith, *God's Daughters: Evangelical Women and the Power of Submission* (University of California Press, 1997).

100. A photograph of this scene, taken by a CNN photographer, can be found in a *Daily Mail* article entitled "The Tangled Marriages of Kentucky's Anti–Gay Marriage Martyr: Court Clerk Kim Davis Conceived Twins in Adulterous Affair with Lover She Branded Violent," which includes a detailed account of Davis's family history and includes photos of her children. Louise Boyle, "The Tangled Marriages," *Daily Mail*, Sept. 9, 2015.

that certify compliance with a law beyond the law."[101] In the coming decades, only politics will yield answers as to which believers will be read as sincere enough and religious enough to live beyond secular law.[102]

101. Pellegrini, "Sincerely Held," 82.

102. In October of 2020 the Supreme Court declined to hear Davis's suit against the men whom she had denied a license. But, even though he agreed that the court should not hear the case, Justice Clarence Thomas, joined by Justice Samuel Alito, issued a statement about it. Thomas criticized the Court's *Obergefell* decision, which legalized same-sex marriage, alleging that the Court had "bypassed" the "democratic process" of allowing states to work out marriage law for themselves through legislation. Then he added, "Worse still, though it briefly acknowledged that those with sincerely held religious objections to same-sex marriage are often 'decent and honorable,' the Court went on to suggest that those beliefs espoused a bigoted worldview." Turning then to Davis, Thomas predicted that "Davis may have been one of the first victims of this Court's cavalier treatment of religion in its *Obergefell* decision, but she will not be the last. Due to *Obergefell*, those with sincerely held religious beliefs concerning marriage will find it increasingly difficult to participate in society without running afoul of *Obergefell* and its effect on other antidiscrimination laws." Davis v. Ermold, 592 U.S. ___ (2020). By calling Davis a "victim" and choosing her case as the one to make a statement about *Obergefell*, Thomas (who, it is worth mentioning, is not a white evangelical but a Black Catholic) continued the Christian legal movement and right-wing media's efforts to make Davis a symbolic martyr for religious liberty, under attack by secularists. This statement seems to imply that Thomas and Alito, at least, will look favorably upon sincere believers whose very ability "to participate in society" is supposedly threatened by the freedoms and civil rights of others.

EPILOGUE

On Being Sincere

I WROTE THIS BOOK DURING a golden age of scams. Most of these words were written between 2018 and 2020, a time when urgent crises and pervasive dangers coincided with all manner of fakery. Phrases like "alternative facts" and "fake news" entered the lexicon. Conspiratorial thinking circulated everywhere, from niche online circles to the White House.[1] In 2016, the year that Donald Trump was elected president of the United States, the *Oxford English Dictionary*'s word of the year was "post-truth."[2] A few years earlier, as I was forming the initial ideas for this book, I began noticing

1. See, e.g., Nancy L. Rosenblum and Russell Muirhead, *A Lot of People are Saying: The New Conspiracism and the Assault on Democracy* (Princeton University Press, 2019). On Trump's rhetoric and his complex relationship with conspiracy and truth and sincerity, see Jennifer Mercieca, *Demagogue for President: The Rhetorical Genius of Donald Trump* (Texas A&M University Press, 2020).

2. Oxford Languages, "Word of the Year 2016," https://languages.oup.com/word-of-the -year/2016/. They define it as an adjective meaning "relating to or denoting circumstances in which objective facts are less influential in shaping public opinion than appeals to emotion and personal belief." See also Michael Dango, "How Contempt Became a Genre," *New Inquiry*, Sept. 11, 2018.

For what it's worth, it seems clear to me that Trump is emblematic of a "post-truth" age not in the sense that he lies or obscures the truth, although he does those things, but rather in that he is indifferent to truth. The technical term for this is "bullshit." See Harry Frankfurt, "On Bullshit," *Raritan Quarterly Review* 6, no. 2 (Fall, 1986): 81–100. See also Philip Kitcher, "Dangerous Bullshit," *Los Angeles Review of Books*, Feb. 12, 2018. https:// lareviewofbooks.org/article/dangerous-bullshit/.

Trump's most loyal followers love him not because what he says is factual, but because it makes them feel good. See Schaefer, "Whiteness and Civilization." Schaefer argues that

another phrase—"sincerely held religious belief"—popping up everywhere. How was it that the demise of truth coincided with the rise of sincere belief? These might seem like incompatible trends. But, especially when modifying religious belief, "sincerely held" has come to mean not just truthful but deeply felt and personal. This distinction indexes a form of secularization. Religious belief becomes a different type of belief, not exactly in the realm of veracity, not subject to public scrutiny or deliberation. We do not consider whether religious beliefs are true; we just consider whether the believers are truthful. In this way, "sincerely held religious belief" and "post-truth politics" work together. Both are marked by inability or unwillingness to deliberate in public about the content of ideas.

On January 6, 2021, rioters stormed the U.S. Capitol in an attempt to stop the certification of Joe Biden's election to the presidency. They were motivated by conspiracies and lies, a sea of misinformation. False stories about voter fraud and election interference (as well as deeper conspiracies about secret sex-trafficking rings and cannibalism) flowed through various social media. They were also propagated by established right-wing media outlets. Elected officials, including the outgoing president, spread the conspiracies as well, suggesting that the election had been "stolen." Even while insurrectionists were inside the Capitol building, some of them trying to find members of Congress so they could execute them, Trump released a video in which he said "it was a landslide election" in his favor and that "this was a fraudulent election."[3] Commentators took to calling it the Big Lie. But a lot of people believed it—sincerely, even religiously. Many of the rioters were white Christians, although the religious makeup of the mob was far from monolithic.[4] Some of them, including a conspiracy-believing "shaman" figure, prayed to Jesus in evangelical style in the Senate chamber.[5] A few days later, I received some physical mail from Liberty Counsel, the Christian legal organization that represented Kim Davis. Their leader

---

Trump's supporters feel their shame repudiated through Trump's rhetoric. In 2005 Stephen Colbert coined the term "truthiness" to refer to a similar dynamic, citing George W. Bush's defense of a judicial appointment by saying, "I know her heart."

3. Donald J. Trump, @realDonaldTrump, tweet, Jan. 6, 2021.

4. See Peter Manseau, "Some Capitol Rioters Believed They Answered God's Call, Not Just Trump's," *Washington Post*, Feb. 11, 2021.

5. That shaman, Jacob Angeli (legal name Jacob Chansley), was arrested for his role in the insurrection. In prison, he successfully sought a dietary accommodation, citing his sincerely held religious belief that he should eat only USDA-certified organic food. As a

and founder, Mat Staver, wrote: "Election integrity is crucially important because it affects ALL our rights. If an election can be stolen, our rights can be stolen." There was a return envelope with an enclosure reading, in bright red, "URGENT REPLY FROM: Charles McCrary." And below it, my reply, a prewritten note: "Mat, I understand the solemn importance of this season in which Christians in America are coming under attack as never before. That's why I'm partnering with you." They promised that all donations would be doubled.

In the weeks following the events at the Capitol, many scholars in and adjacent to religious studies wrote op-eds and hosted webinars about that day, what led to it, and how to make sense of it. Jacques Berlinerblau excoriated religious studies scholars, and scholars of secularism in particular, for failing to predict the day's events. They had celebrated religion too much, failing to study bad religions and thus being insufficiently attentive to white Christian nationalism.[6] In addition to overlooking so much scholarship on just the topics it claimed scholars haven't studied, Berlinerblau's essay misrepresented (or misunderstood) the point of the critique of secularism. By secularism, which he takes to be a good thing, Berlinerblau means liberal church-state separation and the governance, through violence and the threat thereof, of bad believers.[7] Because religion scholars celebrate religion and denigrate secularism, he argued, they side with those who misuse free exercise to illiberal and dangerous ends. Rather than pick apart the essay, I want to make use of its misunderstandings. Berlinerblau claims that we need something he calls "secular analysis." This type of scholarship is "relentlessly critical, self-critical, rude, and suspicious of all orthodoxies."[8] There is a name for this: debunking. It is the style of the secular modern. If you study secularism, then this style, this sort of character, is "part of your data set."[9] But I do want to take up one aspect of Berlinerblau's call for "secular

---

shamanic practitioner, he eats only "traditional food that has been made by God." United States v. Chansley, Case No. 21-er-2 (RCL), Doc. 8, Feb. 3, 2021.

6. Jacques Berlinerblau, "Bad Religion in the Ivory Tower," *Chronicle of Higher Education*, Jan. 21, 2021.

7. On the violence implicit in Berlinerblau's essay, see Caleb Smith, "Bad Religion, or Bad Faith?" *Chronicle of Higher Education*, Jan. 25, 2021.

8. Berlinerblau, "Bad Religion in the Ivory Tower."

9. Berlinerblau writes that if you study secularism, "religious believers gone wild are part of your data set" ("Bad Religion in the Ivory Tower"). I would like to suggest that if you

analysis," because, while rudeness is not a scholarly virtue, I do agree that being self-critical is. For me, being self-critical means to interrogate one's own investments in the object of one's critique, namely, secularism.

GETTING LAW AND RELIGION

Over the past decade, the study of religion and law, especially First Amendment cases, has become popular in American religious studies. *Hobby Lobby* was a sort of tipping point, it seemed, after which almost everyone was familiar with the basic history of free exercise, from *Cantwell* to *Seeger* to *Smith* to RFRA to *Hobby Lobby*. In fact, these cases might be, at least in some circles of American religious studies, the set of texts we hold most in common. They are the topics that show up on every syllabus, the phrases we all know. We keep Supreme Court cases in a parallel place to where an earlier generation kept, say, the writings of Jonathan Edwards. As Winnifred Sullivan put it, "US religious studies has got law!"[10]

The reason I got law is that religious freedom hinges on contests over the word and concept "religion," and so I could do religious studies while sidestepping questions about why I defined my "data set" as "religious." Plus, the law has clear stakes. It has winners and losers.[11] Amid consternation and hesitation about the category "religion"—ethical objections to perpetuating our field's colonialist legacies, hand-wringing about reifying a "folk taxon," and other fallouts from the acknowledgment that the thing we were studying does not really exist—I took comfort in studying the *discourse* of religion. Loath to call something religious, to use that as an analytical term, I discovered that I could simply study how other people use that term. This

---

study secularism, your data set more properly includes the politics of defining some believers as "wild," the colonialist histories of such designations, and the forces that construct and enforce such boundaries between good beliefs and bad, wild ones.

10. Sullivan, "Afterword," in *Religion, Law, USA*, ed. Dubler and Weiner, 283.

11. On winners and losers, see Lincoln, "Theses on Method." He writes, "The same destabilizing and irreverent questions one might ask of any speech act ought be posed of religious discourse . . . [These include] 'Who wins what, and how much? Who, conversely, loses?'" (226).

position is premised on a neat split between scholars and their object of study, their "data."[12] *They* use that term; *I* study them using it.[13]

But I realized, embarrassingly late, that this is the same secularist move that the sincerity test makes. This move, separating veracity from sincerity—or, in Bruce Lincoln's terms, "truths" from "truth-claims"—reifies the same division it aims to deconstruct.[14] The line between scholars and their data draws the line between the secular and the religious.[15] Some scholars draw this line too eagerly and thus mistake most or all normativity for (crypto-)theology. And, with theology being an off-limits "religious" discourse, there is little to no space left for critique, especially critique of or engagement with religious discourses or actors. This often leads to a weak sort of antipolitics, a general allergy to "normativity."[16]

In this book I have tried to undertake a postsecular project that critiques and historicizes its own presumptions and modalities of thought in an aspirational, incomplete endeavor to undo them.[17] By postsecular, I mean

12. Russell McCutcheon has used the word "data" to describe the people religious studies scholars study, a usage that Robert Orsi described as "chilling." Russell T. McCutcheon, *The Discipline of Religion: Structure, Meaning, Rhetoric* (Routledge, 2003); and Robert A. Orsi, "Fair Game," *Bulletin of the Council of Societies for the Study of Religion* 33, no. 3 (Sept., 2004). See also McCutcheon, "'It's a Lie. There's No Truth in It! It's a Sin!' On the Limits of the Humanistic Study of Religion and the Costs of Saving Others from Themselves," *Journal of the American Academy of Religion* 74, no. 3 (Sept., 2006): 720–750.

13. On uses of "folk" in classifying religions, see Levene, "Marx's Eleventh Thesis," and Drake, "Folk Religion and the Medical Engineering of Rural Black Laborers."

14. Lincoln, "Theses on Method," 227. For a similar critique of Lincoln's theses, see Tim Fitzgerald, "Bruce Lincoln's 'Theses on Method': Antitheses," *Method and Theory in the Study of Religion* 18, no. 4 (2006): 392–423.

15. In his critique of Lincoln, Russell McCutcheon, and other scholars, Tyler Roberts shows how this type of "critical" approach is secularist, in that it imagines and creates "clear, impermeable boundaries between religion or theology and the study of religion" (*Encountering Religion*, 62).

16. The term "crypto-theology" is from Donald Wiebe, "Disciplinary Axioms, Boundary Conditions and the Academic Study of Religion: Comments on Pals and Dawson," *Religion* 20 (1990): 17–29. See also William E. Arnal, Willi Braun, and Russell T. McCutcheon, eds., *Failure and Nerve in the Academic Study of Religion* (Routledge, 2014).

17. As much as the previous section critiques others' scholarship, it is more a self-critique. After all, those very scholarly positions are why I took to studying religious freedom in the first place, and that work was a major part of the foundation of my training.

While I am writing a sincere and self-critical footnote, I also want to note that for a long time I thought that the study of religion and law—and other instances of discourse *about*

what Peter Coviello and Jared Hickman have described as "quite literally postsecular in the sense that it dares to suggest that we might do our thinking about modernity—including our thinking about what in fact instigates modernity—under a sign other than 'the secular.'"[18] This is hard to do. Phillip Maciak sums up the predicament: the secular "is both the subject of argument and the ground upon which that argument is fought." Scholars critique secularism in order to think under other signs, but we also "identify the ways the secularization thesis might still structure even the premises of its own critiques."[19] Being self-critical is just one step toward unmaking and remaking worlds. But it is a crucial one. The critique of secularism, for me at least, demands that we not only dig up and critique secularism's epistemological and historical roots or simply identify its disciplinary functions, but interrogate why they feel good and understand what violence they do.

---

religion—was the only defensible way to study "religion." I still think that is a good way to study religion, especially in the context of secularism studies (which is basically what I am doing in this book), but it is important to note that this is not in fact the only way to study religion. It is true that plenty of religious studies scholarship, especially in the 1980s and 1990s, relied on dubious assumptions about religion's specialness, as something ineffable and distinct from culture or politics. But it actually is very possible to study religion, and to call something religion, *without* making such assumptions.

And, further, the archive of religious studies, the history of our own discipline, contains frameworks and tools and vocabulary that many scholars have discarded prematurely and unwisely, wrongly assuming that categories such as "ritual" and "sacred text" somehow scare up old Eliadean ghosts or lack a critical edge. They don't. I am grateful to Dana Logan, whose work, along with Katie Lofton's, helped me understanding this point. See Lofton, *Consuming Religion*; Logan, "The Lean Closet"; and especially Logan, *Awkward Rituals*.

18. Coviello and Hickman, "Introduction: After the Postsecular," 649.

19. Maciak, *The Disappearing Christ*, 12. John Modern argued that "the problem with the field of American religious history is that it has largely failed to question religion and its attendant categories in a sustained manner, so much so that a particular kind of human is assumed to be at the center of any narrative about religion, a secular subject who must take a stand vis-à-vis religion, who chooses, with the capacity of free will, to believe in their belief, unbelief, or even their indifference" (John Lardas Modern, "My Evangelical Conviction," *Religion* 42, no. 3 (July, 2012): 439–457, at 444. This secular subject is the sincere believer, but they are also, often, the scholar.

WHAT NOW

What comes after the critique of secularism?[20] At this point, putting secularism through its paces can be a tired exercise. We know the critiques, and we repeat them, as I have done in this book. But there are ways to push forward, to develop new and different kinds of critique or rediscover old ones. What comes after the critique of secularism, for me, is more critique of secularism. These critiques should be specific, attentive always to iterations of secular governance rather than an imagined monolithic ideology. The fact that secularism is regulatory is a starting point, not a conclusion. We should study better how various agents, perhaps in unexpected archives and settings, perform these acts of regulation, as well as their lived effects.

What I am after is a style of postsecular critique that refuses the stance of the debunker.[21] Discussing scholarship and postsecular style in literary studies, Kate Stanley noted how some scholars have resisted that stance by "thinking, feeling, and writing *with* the intensity of their subjects, by flagging the hegemonic and exclusionary secular presumptions inherent to their own critical authority, and by showing how other postsecularists might labor to do the same."[22] My aim in this book is slightly different, in terms of topic and style, but I consider it part of this same project. For me, endeavoring to undertake postsecular scholarship in this book has meant critiquing "sincerely held religious belief" while wrestling with my own desire to take religion "seriously" and to be sincere.

Sincerity could bring us together. It is, or could be, a democratic and communal way of thinking, feeling, and writing with others. Sincerity is a public ethic; the point is to be true to others.[23] In public societies, we all play

---

20. Udi Greenberg and Daniel Steinmetz-Jenkins, "Introduction to Roundtable: What Comes After the Critique of Secularism?" *Journal of the American Academy of Religion* 88, no. 1 (Mar., 2020): 1–14.

21. Jason Ānanda Josephson Storm, *Metamodernism: The Future of Theory* (University of Chicago Press, 2021), offers one version of this style, beyond religious studies and broadly applicable to the human sciences, that moves beyond deconstruction and discourse analysis without discounting the foundational work those modes of analysis do.

22. Kate Stanley, "Postsecular Style," *American Literary History*, advance article (Feb., 2021), 2. The piece is a review essay of Coviello, *Make Yourselves Gods*; Maciak, *The Disappearing Christ*; and Reckson, *Realist Ecstasy*.

23. For a defense of sincerity's place in liberalism, see Micah Schwartzman, "The Sincerity of Public Reason," *Journal of Political Philosophy* 19, no. 4 (2011): 375–398. I am critical of

roles. To be sincere does not mean to be without style or affectation, as if that were possible, but to craft a persona that matches one's private self. Underneath, behind, within the words of this book are the socialities that made it—my publics, my networks, my friends, and the institutions at which I've spent my entire adult life. The forms in which I've written this book reflect an authorial persona made up of other persons. I address certain audiences because I am bound up with them, attached to them.[24]

In U.S. culture, politics, and law today, sincerity—and especially sincerely held religious belief—does not usually work like that. It is not only the separation of truth from truthfulness but the related redefinition of "sincerely" as an affective style rather than a marker of good faith and clear intention. Religious beliefs are lived experiences. But this issue extends beyond religion. It is increasingly common in U.S. public discourse to invoke "lived experience" to defend one's own position. It is true that our own experiences of the world shape the way we see it, and that there is no objective "view from nowhere." But it is one thing for lived experience to be the standpoint from which one makes an argument and another for it to stand in for an argument. Kwame Anthony Appiah has argued, "What makes the invocation of lived experience such a powerful move—the fact that it's essentially private, removed from inspection—is exactly what makes it such a perilous one."[25] It

---

liberal projects, but nevertheless I agree with many of Schwartzman's points here, including the conclusion that "sincerity is not an independent requirement that needs to be added to the ideal of public reason as an *ad hoc* measure designed to meet certain objections. It is an integral part of any adequate theory of political discourse" (398). I do not think this should imply that we should give everyone a pass if they seem sincere; on the contrary, we ought to be more vigilant about exposing bad faith.

24. Bruno Latour wrote, "Emancipation does not mean 'freed from bonds,' but *well-attached*" (*Reassembling the Social*, 218). Rita Felski quotes this line and adds, "What is needed, in short, is a politics of relation rather than negation, of mediation rather than co-option, of alliance and assembly rather than alienated critique" (*The Limits of Critique*, 147).

This book is not the place, and I am not the scholar, to wade into debates about postcritique. But I do want to say that I agree with Felski, in the quote above, about what is needed. There is a version of postcritical scholarship, though, that to me looks akin to certain sorts of religious studies scholarship that focuses on objects and subjects to which scholars are attached, and with whom they have affinities, without sufficiently critiquing those attachments and affinities. Critique can and should be careful, full of care. Scholarship that is not critical (and self-critical) is likely not very careful.

25. Kwame Anthony Appiah, "Why Are Politicians Suddenly Talking about Their 'Lived Experience?,'" *Guardian*, Nov. 14, 2020.

is rude to question lived experiences and difficult to argue with them, even as they serve as motivations or justifications for actions that affect others. This problem is compounded when religion is involved, since few people are both willing and equipped to have a theological conversation, in a public setting, about specific beliefs. The assumed specialness of religion widens the intelligibility gap.[26] This situation, in which everyone claims to respect everyone else's beliefs but cannot really discuss them, is not conducive to democracy, not least because it too often lets the powerful off the hook.

What are the alternatives? How might we undertake a postsecular critique of sincerity and religious freedom? Some scholars have turned toward political theology, combining that approach with the critical study of law. Winnifred Sullivan describes the

26. This is one reason that I am skeptical of another brand of postsecular studies, one that also stands in contrast to debunking. Some scholars have embraced a style of radical enchantment or reenchantment, or what Emily Ogden calls "the enlightened-enchantment approach" (*Credulity*, 11). Often, this looks like a reversal of disenchantment, in which the scholar finds that magic and spirituality are perhaps real and liberating and certainly delightful. But, as Tracy Fessenden has explained, this does not really upend or critique secularist presumptions. She cautions, "It's one thing to admit to the inadequacy of our descriptive vocabularies, another to let an intelligibility gap stand in for an encounter with sacred depths" ("The Problem of the Postsecular," 161). Related trends in religious studies to "take seriously" the agency of spirits, while in some cases quite exciting and potentially revolutionary, often strike me as fashionable and constrained by unacknowledged rules about which type of reenchantment is permissible.

Nevertheless, this question animates some of the most lively and vital conversations in religious studies and the anthropology of religion and secularism today. How do scholars working in the context of universities—the "citadel of secular modernity," as Susan Harding has put it—work through and beyond the constraints of secularity? Courtney Bender has described how scholars maintain boundaries, unspoken until they're not, around what is reasonable and believable for scholars. So, even among sympathetic, careful scholars of religion and the secular, talk of ghosts, for instance, is supposed to be talk of "ghosts" or (others') *belief in* ghosts: "literary ghosts, metaphorical ghosts, secular hauntings" (Courtney Bender, "Modernity's Resonances—An Introduction," *Immanent Frame*, Feb. 22, 2019). Critiquing modernity and secularism goes only so far when the critic herself is constrained by those very objects of critique. See Mayanthi L. Fernando, "Supernatureculture," *Immanent Frame*, Dec. 11, 2017; and Mayanthi L. Fernando and Susan J. Harding, "Practices of Relation: Fernando and Harding," *Immanent Frame*, Apr. 27, 2020. Perhaps my choices in this book have been designed to sidestep deep investigation of (religious) experiences, in nervous anticipation of my descriptive vocabularies' inadequacies. But such avoidance offers only fleeting relief, for the epistemological thicket of postsecular scholarship is no less tangled.

current tautological legal practice in the United States and in many other countries, that is, that a sincere (i.e., nonfraudulent) representation that one's refusal to obey the law is founded in religious belief sufficiently proves the presence of religion and triggers the relevant protective law, without further proof. Litigants today, at least white christian litigants refusing to conform to the law, are not usually asked to offer any evidence that anyone else has such a belief or that their belief is attached to a community, found in a text, or otherwise formalized or institutionalized. The religiousness or not of their belief is not measured according to any specific conception of or history of religion. It is enough that they believe it to be so.[27]

One way out of this problem, then, Sullivan argues, is to engage with people, to have actual theological discussions. To scrutinize claims and weigh their effects. Scholars of religion have these tools, if not often this disposition. Such conversations would require us to think, feel, and write with our subjects, to use sincerity to bridge, not exacerbate, the gaps between us.

The courts imagine religion not only as a matter of individual belief but also as an aspect of identity, which then conflicts with other identities, including those protected by civil rights laws.[28] Elizabeth Markovits argues that it would be better to do away with this stifling obsession with inner states and consistency and sincerity. "Instead of trying to strip people to some authentic being," she writes, "we should move in the other direction, where we can acknowledge the performative aspect of all public interaction."[29] As I have shown throughout this book, the imagination of sincere belief and the character of the sincere believer is conceptually incoherent and, when enforced, frequently involves investigation, surveillance, and intrusion. Sincerely held religious belief, beyond the sincerity test itself, exposes the "rotten core at the heart of religious freedom."[30] The rot is not the impossibility of religious freedom, per se, or the way that it will never apply equally to all religions or believers. It is religious freedom's imbrication with the liberal

27. Sullivan, *Church State Corporation*, 167.

28. On religion as both individual and communal, and the problems this contradiction creates for constitutional law, see Benjamin Schonthal, "Why Religion Is Different: Five Contradictions of Religion in Law," *Immanent Frame*, July 25, 2019.

29. Markovits, *The Politics of Sincerity*, 183.

30. Winnifred Fallers Sullivan, "The Impossibility of Religious Freedom," *Immanent Frame*, July 8, 2014.

subject, a "practice of racialized state governance" figured as a person.[31] I return to Aisha Beliso-De Jesús, who argues that "identity should not be understood as a quest for self, but instead is a racialized and sexualized national ordering technology—a practice of racialized state governance."[32] Is sincerity after identity possible? The modern politics of sincerely held religious belief, denying freedom to some in order to shore up others' power, suggests not. But while this politics is one logical outcome of a particular history of American religion, secularism, and belief, it is not the only one.

31. See also Sylvester Johnson, "Person," in *Religion, Law, USA*, ed. Dubler and Weiner.

32. Beliso-De Jesús, "Confounded Identities," 323. Here she is drawing from the work of Hortense Spillers.

ACKNOWLEDGMENTS

MY BEST HOPE FOR THIS BOOK is that it is a good one to discuss with colleagues and friends. I hope it can serve as a starting point for useful, enriching, and fun conversations; it is the product of such conversations. I am grateful to everyone who talked with me along the way.

My first real foray into secularism studies was in the summer of 2013, when Martin Kavka graciously led a small independent study group for no reason other than his kindness. We worked through every page (even the infamous 207) of books thick as the Tallahassee humidity. It was a turning point in my thinking and influenced all my scholarship since. The second origin story of this book begins when Mike Graziano asked me, "You study religion and law, right?"—to which I responded, "No, why?" He asked me to co-teach a class on religion and law, which we did in the fall of 2014. I had been planning a dissertation on nineteenth-century hucksters and charlatans while also reading for my comprehensive exams that December. Somewhere between that reading and research and figuring out, with Mike, how to teach a survey of religion and law that might explain *Hobby Lobby*, the ideas in this book started taking shape.

I was incredibly fortunate to go to graduate school at Florida State University. By sheer luck, I enjoyed just about every minute of it, and I made lifelong friends. This is an uncommon experience, and I will always cherish it. Many of those friends read drafts of this book at various stages. Our constant conversations—in seminars and colloquia in person and virtual, over beers, via text, across my rambling emails and their smart replies, in settings formal and very informal—have been invaluable. Thanks especially to Cara Burnidge, Tim Burnside, Emily Clark, Mike Graziano, Haley Iliff, Andy McKee, Adam Park, and Jeff Wheatley.

John Corrigan was and continues to be a helpful and supportive advisor who pushes in the right directions and asks the right questions. I received thoughtful feedback from Jamil Drake, Andrew Epstein, Sarah Barringer Gordon, Mike McVicar, and Amanda Porterfield. I am especially grateful to Sally, who has always been so kind and generous with her time, without expecting (or, so far I can tell, receiving) anything in return. My research assistants, Nicole MacMillan and Nicholas Meier, who worked with me through FSU's Undergraduate Research Opportunity Program, were very helpful at the early stages of the project.

The vast majority of this book was written while I was a postdoctoral fellow at the John C. Danforth Center on Religion and Politics at Washington University in St. Louis. It was a wonderful place to work, and I remember my St. Louis years fondly. Thanks to Tazeen Ali, Fannie Bialek, Marie Griffith, John Inazu, Sandy Jones, Debra Kennard, Laurie Maffly-Kipp, Lerone Martin, Sheri Peña, Leigh Schmidt, and Mark Valeri. I learned from all of you. And special thanks to my fellow postdocs Aaron Griffith, Dana Lloyd, and Cyrus O'Brien. I also learned from my students, especially those in my spring of 2019 course "American Religion and the Politics of Sincerity." I know you didn't like The Confidence-Man, but thanks for talking about it with me while I wrote chapter 1. My St. Louis years were further enriched by friendships with Elena Kravchenko, Rachel Lindsey, and Adam Park. Thanks also to the Cultures of American Religion group at St. Louis University, led by Kate Moran, who formed a welcoming intellectual community and read the first version of a drafty chapter 8. The final stages of writing were completed in Phoenix, where my collaborators on the Beyond Secularization project at Arizona State University have been ideal conversation partners. I am again fortunate to have smart and generous fellow postdocs in Heather Mellquist Lehto and Schuyler Marquez. They, along with Gaymon Bennett, Jen Clifton, Taylor Genovese, and Annie Hammang, helped me sort out some crucial sections of the introduction. I am also grateful to Evan Berry, John Carlson, Tracy Fessenden, Ali Hussain, and Karen Taliaferro for convening to read a freshly written epilogue and offer incisive feedback.

Swapping drafts is always a double pleasure, getting to learn from friends' writing as well as their comments on mine. In addition to those already mentioned, Finbarr Curtis, Sarah Dees, Jamil Drake, Richard Evans, Sonia Hazard, Bradley Kime, Dana Logan, Shari Rabin, and Jolyon Thomas—thanks for letting me learn from you. Leslie Ribovich deserves special mention. For years, we've exchanged drafts regularly, and this book is much better (and completed much sooner) because of her comments and conversation.

I presented pieces of this work for audiences at Florida State, Northwestern University, the Newberry Library (thanks especially to Pete Cajka for the response), the Danforth Center, and St. Louis University, as well as a number of conferences. I'm grateful to panel respondents—Finbarr Curtis, Sarah Dees, Emily Johnson, John Modern, and Bethany Moreton—for their comments and questions. Tracy Fessenden read the whole manuscript (or the six chapters that were done) and flew to St. Louis to discuss it with me. Her feedback was invaluable and perfectly timed. An earlier version of chapter 3 was published in *Religion & American Culture* 28, no. 2 (Summer, 2018). My thanks to the editors and reviewers there, who made the article and thus the chapter much better.

I am grateful to archivists at the Library of Congress Manuscript Division, Temple University Special Collections Research Center, and the National Archives at Riverside. And a special thanks to Wendy Chmielewski, Mary Beth Sigado, and Anne Yoder at the Swarthmore College Peace Collection, an idyllic place to spend a couple of weeks in October. Thanks also to Maria Santelli at the Center on Conscience and War for allowing me to access restricted materials housed at Swarthmore.

Katie Lofton, John Modern, and Kyle Wagner have been ideal editors. They believed in the project from the start, and they encouraged me to lean into what made it interesting and original. They found excellent readers too, who understood what I was trying to do and helped me do it better. Thanks to all of them. I have been fortunate to work with a talented and meticulous team at the University of Chicago Press. To Dylan Montanari, Barbara Norton, Caterina MacLean, Jenny Volvovski, and everyone else, thank you.

Last, I want to thank my family. My parents, Colleen and Jay McCrary, never told me what to do or questioned my career choices, although skepticism would have been, and still is, warranted. My grandparents, Bonnie and Jack McCrary, always showed interest and offered support. My in-laws, Kelly and Neal Haaland, welcomed me into their family and make me feel at home. And finally, Haley Haaland McCrary. From Grand Forks to Tallahassee to St. Louis to Phoenix to anywhere, always with you. My best friend, strongest support, constant companion. For everything, Haley, "thank you" isn't enough.

BIBLIOGRAPHY

Adams, Arlin M. and Charles J. Emmerich. *A Nation Dedicated to Religious Liberty: The Constitutional Heritage of the Religion Clauses*. University of Pennsylvania Press, 1990.

Adams, Ben, and Cynthia Barmore. "Questioning Sincerity: The Role of the Courts after Hobby Lobby." *Stanford Law Review Online* 67 (Nov. 7, 2014): 59–66.

Adcock, C. S. *The Limits of Tolerance: Indian Secularism and the Politics of Religious Freedom*. Oxford University Press, 2013.

Agrama, Hussein Ali. "Notes on the Idea of Theorizing Secularism." *Political Theology Network*, June 10, 2013. https://politicaltheology.com/notes-on-the-idea-of-theorizing-secularism-hussein-ali-agrama/.

———. *Questioning Secularism: Islam, Sovereignty, and the Rule of Law in Modern Egypt*. University of Chicago Press, 2012.

Ahlstrom, Sydney E. *A Religious History of the American People*. Yale University Press, 1972.

Ahmed, Sara. *The Cultural Politics of Emotion*, 2nd ed. Edinburgh University Press, 2014 [2004].

Albanese, Catherine L. *A Republic of Mind and Spirit: A Cultural History of American Metaphysical Religion*. Yale University Press, 2007.

Anidjar, Gil. *Blood: A Critique of Christianity*. Columbia University Press, 2014.

Ansorge, Josef Teboho. *Identify and Sort: How Digital Power Changed World Politics*. Oxford University Press, 2016.

Asad, Talal. *Formations of the Secular: Christianity, Islam, Modernity*. Stanford University Press, 2003.

———. *Genealogies of Religion: Discipline and Reasons of Power in Christianity and Islam*. Johns Hopkins University Press, 1993.

———. *Secular Translations: Nation-State, Modern Self, and Calculative Reason*. Columbia University Press, 2018.

Beier, A. L. *Masterless Men: The Vagrancy Problem in England, 1560–1640*. Methuen, 1985.

Beisel, Nicola. *Imperiled Innocents: Anthony Comstock and Family Reproduction in Victorian America*. Princeton University Press, 1997.

Beliso-De Jesús, Aisha M. "Confounded Identities: A Meditation on Race, Feminism, and Religious Studies in Times of White Supremacy." *Journal of the American Academy of Religion* 86, no. 2 (June, 2018): 307–340.

Bell, Catherine M. "Belief: A Classificatory Lacuna and Disciplinary 'Problem.'" In *Introducing Religion: Essays in Honor of Jonathan Z. Smith*, ed. Willi Braun and Russell T. McCutcheon. Equinox, 2008.

Bender, Courtney and Pamela E. Klassen, eds. *After Pluralism: Reimagining Religious Engagement.* Columbia University Press, 2010.

Bellah, Robert N., Richard Madsen, William M. Sullivan, Ann Swidler, and Steven M. Tipton. *Habits of the Heart: Individualism and Commitment in American Life.* University of California Press, 1985.

Bennett, Daniel. *Defending Faith: The Politics of the Christian Conservative Legal Movement.* University Press of Kansas, 2017.

Berger, Benjamin L. "Belonging to Law: Religious Difference, Secularism, and the Conditions of Civic Inclusion." *Social & Legal Studies* 24, no. 1 (Mar., 2015): 47–64.

———. *Law's Religion: Religious Difference and the Claims of Constitutionalism.* University of Toronto Press, 2015.

Berger, Peter L. *The Sacred Canopy.* Doubleday, 1967.

Bergmann, Johannes Dietrich. "The Original Confidence Man." *American Quarterly* 21, no. 3 (Autumn, 1969): 560–577.

Bertucio, Brett. "The Political Theology of Justice Hugo Black." *Journal of Law and Religion* 35, no. 1 (2020): 79–101.

Blackwood, Sarah. *The Portrait's Subject: Inventing Inner Life in the Nineteenth-Century United States.* University of North Carolina Press, 2019.

Blankholm, Joseph. "The Political Advantages of a Polysemous Secular." *Journal for the Scientific Study of Religion* 53, no. 4 (Dec., 2014): 775–790.

Blumenthal, Susanna L. *Law and the Modern Mind: Consciousness and Responsibility in American Legal Culture.* Harvard University Press, 2016.

Boaz, Danielle. "Fraud, Vagrancy, and the 'Pretended' Exercise of Supernatural Powers in England, South Africa, and Jamaica," *Law and History* 5, no. 1 (2018): 54–84.

———. "Obeah, Vagrancy, and the Boundaries of Religious Freedom: Analyzing the Proscription of 'Pretending to Possess Supernatural Powers' in the Anglophone Caribbean." *Journal of Law and Religion* 32, no. 3 (2017): 423–448.

Braucher, Jean, and Barak Orbach. "Scamming: The Misunderstood Confidence Man." *Yale Journal of Law and the Humanities* 27, no. 2 (Summer, 2015): 249–290.

Braude, Ann. *Radical Spirits: Spiritualism and Women's Rights in Nineteenth-Century America*, 2nd ed. Indiana University Press, 2001 [1989].

Brown, Candy Gunther. *Debating Yoga and Mindfulness in Public Schools: Reforming Secular Education or Reestablishing Religion?* University of North Carolina Press, 2019.

Brown, Wendy. "Civilizational Delusions: Secularism, Tolerance, Equality." *Theory and Event* 15, no. 2 (2012). http://muse.jhu.edu/journals/theory_and_event/v015/15.2.brown.html.

———. *Regulating Aversion: Tolerance in the Age of Identity and Empire.* Princeton University Press, 2006.

Butler, Judith. *Bodies that Matter: On the Discursive Limits of "Sex"*. Routledge, 1993.

Cady, Linell E., and Tracy Fessenden, eds. *Religion, the Secular, and the Politics of Sexual Difference*. Columbia University Press, 2013.

Cajka, Peter. *Follow Your Conscience: The Catholic Church and the Spirit of the Sixties*. University of Chicago Press, 2021.

Calhoun, Craig, Mark Juergensmeyer, and Jonathan VanAntwerpen, eds. *Rethinking Secularism*. Oxford University Press, 2011.

Cameron, Euan. *Enchanted Europe: Superstition, Reason, and Religion, 1250–1750*. Oxford University Press, 2010.

Carter, J. Kameron. *Race: A Theological Account*. Oxford University, 2008.

Casanova, José. "The Secular and Secularisms." *Social Research* 76, no. 4 (Winter, 2009): 1049–1066.

Chakrabarty, Dipesh. *Provincializing Europe: Postcolonial Thought and Historical Difference*. Princeton University Press, 2008 [2000].

Chapman, Nathan S. "Adjudicating Religious Sincerity." *Washington Law Review* 92 (2017): 1185–1254.

Cheney-Lippold, John. *We Are Data: Algorithms and the Makings of Our Digital Selves*. New York University Press, 2017.

Chidester, David. *Authentic Fakes: Religion and American Popular Culture*. University of California Press, 2005.

———. *Empire of Religion: Imperialism and Comparative Religion*. University of Chicago Press, 2014.

Chireau, Yvonne P. *Black Magic: Religion and the African American Conjuring Tradition*. University of California Press, 2003.

Cohen, Lara Langer. *The Fabrication of American Literature: Fraudulence and Antebellum Print Culture*. University of Pennsylvania Press, 2011.

Cole, Rachel. "At the Limits of Identity: Realism and American Personhood in Melville's *The Confidence-Man*." *NOVEL: A Forum on Fiction* 39, no. 3 (2006): 384–401.

Comstock, Anthony. *Frauds Exposed; Or, How the People are Deceived and Robbed, and Youth Corrupted*. New York: J. Howard Brown, 1880.

———. *Traps for the Young*, 2nd ed. Funk and Wagnalls, 1884 [1883].

Comstock, Anthony, O. B. Frothingham, and J. M. Buckley. "The Suppression of Vice." *The North American Review* 135, no. 312 (Nov., 1882): 484–501.

Cook, James W. *The Arts of Deception: Playing with Fraud in the Age of Barnum*. Harvard University Press, 2001.

Corcos, Christine A. "The Scrying Game: The First Amendment, State Regulation of the Crafty Sciences, and the Rise of Spiritualism, 1848–1944." *Whittier Law Review* 38, no. 1 (2017): 59–160.

———. "Seeing It Coming Since 1945: State Bans and Regulations of 'Crafty Sciences' Speech and Activity." *Thomas Jefferson Law Review* 37, no. 1 (Fall, 2014): 39–114.

Corrigan, John. *Religious Intolerance, America, and the World: A History of Remembering and Forgetting*. University of Chicago Press, 2020.

Coviello, Peter. *Make Yourselves Gods: Mormons and the Unfinished Business of American Secularism*. University of Chicago Press, 2019.

Coviello, Peter, and Jared Hickman. "Introduction: After the Postsecular." *American Literature* 86, no. 4 (Dec., 2014): 645–654.

Cox, Harvey. *The Secular City: Secularization and Urbanization in Theological Perspective.* Macmillan, 1965.

Crawley, Ashon T. *Blackpentecostal Breath: The Aesthetics of Possibility.* Fordham University Press, 2016.

Curtis, Finbarr. *The Production of American Religious Freedom.* New York University Press, 2016.

Cusack, Carole M. *Invented Religions: Imagination, Fiction and Faith.* Ashgate, 2013.

Davis, Kathleen. *Periodization and Sovereignty: How Ideas of Feudalism and Secularization Govern the Politics of Time.* University of Pennsylvania Press, 2008.

Davis, Kim. With Mat Staver and John Aman. *Under God's Authority: The Kim Davis Story.* New Revolutions Publishers, 2018.

Deleuze, Gilles, and Félix Guattari. *A Thousand Plateaus: Capitalism and Schizophrenia.* Trans. Brian Massumi. University of Minnesota Press, 1987.

Delgado, Jessica L. *Laywomen and the Making of Colonial Catholicism in New Spain, 1630–1790.* Cambridge University Press, 2018.

Dennis, Donna. *Licentious Gotham: Erotic Publishing and Its Prosecution in Nineteenth-Century New York.* Harvard University Press, 2009.

De Roover, Jakob. "Secular Law and the Realm of False Religion." In Taussig-Rubbo, Yelle, and Sullivan, eds., *After Secular Law,* 43–61.

Dew, Spencer. *The Aliites: Race and Law in the Religions of Noble Drew Ali.* University of Chicago Press, 2019.

Dickson, Del., ed. *The Supreme Court in Conference (1940–1985): The Private Discussions behind Nearly 300 Supreme Court Decisions.* Oxford University Press, 2001.

Drake, Jamil W. "Folk Religion and the Medical Engineering of Rural Black Laborers." *Journal of the American Academy of Religion* 88, no. 2 (June, 2020): 329–353.

Dressler, Markus, and Arvind Mandair, eds. *Secularism and Religion-Making.* Oxford University Press, 2011.

Dubber, Markus Dirk. *The Police Power: Patriarchy and the Foundations of American Government.* Columbia University Press, 2005.

Dubler, Joshua, and Vincent W. Lloyd. *Break Every Yoke: Religion, Justice, and the Abolition of Prisons.* Oxford University Press, 2019.

Dubler, Joshua, and Isaac Weiner, eds. *Religion, Law, USA.* New York University Press, 2019.

Durkheim, Émile. *The Elementary Forms of Religious Life.* Trans. Carol Cosman. Oxford University Press, 2001 [1912].

Dyson, Erika White. "Spiritualism and Crime: Negotiating Prophecy and Police Power at the Turn of the Twentieth Century." Ph.D. diss., Columbia University, 2010.

Ebram, Tajah. "'Can't Jail the Revolution': Policing, Protest, and the MOVE Organization in Philadelphia's Carceral Landscape." *Pennsylvania Magazine of History and Biography* 143, no. 3 (Oct., 2019): 333–362.

Eskridge, Larry. *God's Forever Family: The Jesus People Movement in America.* Oxford University Press, 2016.

Eskridge, William Jr. "Noah's Curse: How Religion Often Conflates Status, Belief, and Conduct to Resist Antidiscrimination Norms." *Georgia Law Review* 45, no. 3 (Spring, 2011): 657–720.

Evans, Curtis. *The Burden of Black Religion.* Oxford University Press, 2008.

Evans, Richard Kent. *MOVE: An American Religion.* Oxford University Press, 2020.

Fabian, Ann. *Card Sharps and Bucket Shops: Gambling in Nineteenth-Century America.* Cornell University Press, 1990.

Farris, Sara R. *In the Name of Women's Rights: The Rise of Femonationalism.* Duke University Press, 2017.

Felski, Rita. *The Limits of Critique.* University of Chicago Press, 2015.

Fenton, Elizabeth. *Religious Liberties: Anti-Catholicism and Liberal Democracy in Nineteenth-Century U.S. Literature and Culture.* Oxford University Press, 2011.

Fernando, Mayanthi L. *The Republic Unsettled: Muslim French and the Contradictions of Secularism.* Duke University Press, 2014.

Fessenden, Tracy. *Culture and Redemption: Religion, the Secular, and American Literature.* Princeton University Press, 2007.

Finstuen, Andrew. *Original Sin and Everyday Protestants: The Theology of Reinhold Niebuhr, Billy Graham, and Paul Tillich in an Age of Anxiety.* University of North Carolina Press, 2009.

Flynn, George Q. *The Draft, 1940–1973.* University Press of Kansas, 1993.

Foucault, Michel. *"Society Must Be Defended": Lectures at the Collège de France, 1975–1976.* Ed. Mauro Bertani and Alessandro Fontana. Trans. David Macey. Picador, 2003.

Franchot, Jenny. *Roads to Rome: The Antebellum Protestant Encounter with Catholicism.* University of California Press, 1994.

Fromont, Cécile. "Paper, Ink, Vodun, and the Inquisition: Tracing Power, Slavery, and Witchcraft in the Early Modern Portuguese Atlantic." *Journal of the American Academy of Religion* 88, no. 2 (June, 2020): 460–504.

Fronc, Jennifer. *New York Undercover: Private Surveillance in the Progressive Era.* (University of Chicago Press, 2009.

Gaston, K. Healan. *Imagining Judeo-Christian America: Religion, Secularism, and the Redefinition of Democracy.* University of Chicago Press, 2019.

Gin Lum, Kathryn and Paul Harvey, eds. *The Oxford Handbook of Religion and Race in American History.* Oxford University Press, 2018.

Glen, John M. "Secular Conscientious Objection in the United States: The Selective Service Act of 1940." *Peace & Change* 9, no. 1 (Spring, 1983): 55–71.

Goffman, Erving. "On Cooling the Mark Out: Some Aspects of Adaptation to Failure." *Psychiatry* 15, no. 4 (Nov., 1952): 451–463.

———. *The Presentation of Self in Everyday Life.* Doubleday, 1959.

Goluboff, Risa. *Vagrant Nation: Police Power, Constitutional Change, and the Making of the 1960s.* Oxford University Press, 2016.

Gordon, Avery. *Ghostly Matters: Haunting and the Sociological Imagination.* University of Minnesota Press, 2008 [1997].

Gordon, Sarah Barringer. "Malnak v. Yogi: The New Age and the New Law." In *Law and Religion: Cases in Context*, ed. Leslie C. Griffin. Aspen Publishers, 2010.

————. *The Spirit of the Law: Religious Voices and the Constitution in Modern America.* Harvard University Press, 2010.

Gray-Hildenbrand, Jenna. "Negotiating Authority: The Criminalization of Religious Practice in the United States." Ph.D. diss., University of California, Santa Barbara, 2012.

Greenberg, Udi. "Is Religious Freedom Protestant? On the History of a Critical Idea." *Journal of the American Academy of Religion* 88, no. 1 (Mar., 2020): 74–91.

Greene, Abner. "Religious Freedom and (Other) Civil Liberties: Is There a Middle Ground?" *Harvard Law and Policy Review* 9 (2015): 161–193.

Greiman, Jennifer. *Democracy's Spectacle: Sovereignty and Public Life in Antebellum American Writing.* Fordham University Press, 2010.

Hall, David D., ed. *Lived Religion in America: Toward a History of Practice.* Princeton University Press, 1997.

Halttunen, Karen. *Confidence Men and Painted Women: A Study of Middle-Class Culture in America, 1830–1870.* Yale University Press, 1982.

Hammerschlag, Sarah. "Believing in the USA: Derrida, Melville and the Great American Charlatan." *Political Theology* 21, nos. 1–2 (2020): 56–70.

Harding, Susan J. "Representing Fundamentalism: The Problem of the Repugnant Cultural Other." *Social Research* 58, no. 2 (Summer, 1991): 373–393.

Harris, Cheryl I. "Whiteness as Property," *Harvard Law Review* 106, no. 8 (June, 1993): 1707–1791.

Harris, LaShawn. *Sex Workers, Psychics, and Numbers Runners: Black Women in New York City's Underground Economy.* University of Illinois Press, 2018.

Hayes, Liz. "Bracing for the Blitz: The Religious Right Has a New Game Plan to Make America More to Its Liking—And If It's Not Already in Your State, It Will Be Soon." *Church and State* 71, no. 10 (Nov., 2018). https://www.au.org/church-state/november -2018-church-state/cover-story/bracing-for-the-blitz-the-religious-right-has-a.

Heisler, Francis. "The Law versus the Conscientious Objector." *University of Chicago Law Review* 20, no. 3 (Spring, 1953): 441–460.

Hesse, Barnor. "Racialized Modernity: An Analytics of White Mythologies." *Ethnic and Racial Studies* 30, no. 4 (July, 2007): 643–663.

Hollinger, David A. "After Cloven Tongues of Fire: Ecumenical Protestantism and the Modern American Encounter with Diversity." *Journal of American History* 98, no. 1 (June, 2011): 21–48.

Hollis-Brusky, Amanda, and Joshua C. Wilson. *Separate but Faithful: The Christian Right's Radical Struggle to Transform Law and Legal Culture.* Oxford University Press, 2020.

Howe, Nicolas. *Landscapes of the Secular: Law, Religion, and American Sacred Space.* University of Chicago Press, 2016.

Hull, Matthew S. *Government of Paper: The Materiality of Bureaucracy in Urban Pakistan.* University of California Press, 2012.

Hulsether, Lucia. "The Grammar of Racism: Religious Pluralism and the Birth of the Interdisciplines." *Journal of the American Academy of Religion* 86, no. 1 (Mar., 2018): 1–41.

Hurd, Elizabeth Shakman. *Beyond Religious Freedom: The New Global Politics of Religion.* Princeton University Press, 2015.

Imhoff, Sarah. "The Creation Story, or How We Learned to Stop Worrying and Love Schempp." *Journal of the American Academy of Religion* 84, no. 2 (June, 2016): 466–497.

Jackson, John L. *Real Black: Adventures in Racial Sincerity.* University of Chicago Press, 2005.

Jackson, Zakiyyah Iman. *Becoming Human: Matter and Meaning in an Antiblack World.* Duke University Press, 2020.

Jacobsen, Christine M., Mayanthi Fernando, and Janet Jakobsen. "Gender, Sex, and Religious Freedom in the Context of Secular Law." *Feminist Review* 113 (2016): 93–102.

Jakobsen, Janet R. "Sex + Freedom = Regulation: Why?" *Social Text* 23, nos. 3–4 (Fall–Winter, 2005): 285–308.

Jakobsen, Janet R., and Ann Pellegrini. *Love the Sin: Sexual Regulation and the Limits of Religious Tolerance.* Beacon Press, 2003.

Jakobsen, Janet R., and Ann Pellegrini, eds. *Secularisms.* Duke University Press, 2008.

Johnson, Brandon Lavell. "Spirits on the Stage: Public Mediums, Spiritualist Theater, and American Culture, 1848–1893." Ph.D. diss., University of Chicago, 2007.

Johnson, Paul C. "Fakecraft." *Journal for the Study of Religion* 31, no. 2 (2018): 105–137.

Johnson, Sylvester A. *African American Religions, 1500–2000: Colonialism, Democracy, Freedom.* Cambridge University Press, 2015.

Johnson, Sylvester A., and Steven Weitzman, eds. *The FBI and Religion: Faith and National Security Before and After 9/11.* University of California Press, 2017.

Jones, Nicole Brown. "Did Fortune Tellers See This Coming? Spiritual Counseling, Professional Speech, and the First Amendment." *Mississippi Law Journal* 83 (2014): 639–670.

Josephson-Storm, Jason Ānanda. *The Myth of Disenchantment: Magic, Modernity, and the Birth of the Human Sciences.* University of Chicago Press, 2017.

———. "The Superstition, Secularism, and Religion Trinary: Or Re-Theorizing Secularism." *Method and Theory in the Study of Religion* 30, no. 1 (Jan., 2018): 1–20.

Kahn, Jonathon S. and Vincent W. Lloyd, eds. *Race and Secularism in America.* Columbia University Press, 2016.

Keane, Webb. *Christian Moderns: Freedom and Fetish in the Mission Encounter.* University of California Press, 2007.

———. "Sincerity, 'Modernity,' and the Protestants." *Cultural Anthropology* 17, no. 1 (Feb., 2002): 65–92.

Keitt, Andrew W. *Inventing the Sacred: Imposture, Inquisition, and the Boundaries of the Supernatural in Golden Age Spain.* Brill, 2005.

Kemper, Steven E. "*The Confidence-Man*: A Knavishly-Packed Deck." *Studies in American Fiction* 8, no. 1 (Spring, 1980): 23–35.

Kessler, Jeremy K. "The Invention of a Human Right: Conscientious Objection at the United Nations, 1947–2011." *Columbia Human Rights Law Review* 44, no. 3 (Fall, 2013): 753–791.

Khabeer, Su'ad Abdul. *Muslim Cool: Race, Religion, and Hip Hop in the United States*. New York University Press, 2016.

Koppelman, Andrew. *Gay Rights vs. Religious Liberty? The Unnecessary Conflict*. University of Chicago Press, 2020.

Kornweibel, Theodore Jr. *"Investigate Everything": Federal Efforts to Compel Black Loyalty during World War I*. Indiana University Press, 2002.

Kosek, Joseph Kip. *Acts of Conscience: Christian Nonviolence and Modern American Democracy*. Columbia University Press, 2009.

Laborde, Cécile. *Liberalism's Religion*. Harvard University Press, 2017.

———. "Rescuing Liberalism from Critical Religion." *Journal of the American Academy of Religion* 88, no. 1 (Mar., 2020): 58–73.

Latour, Bruno. "Has Critique Run Out of Steam?" *Critical Inquiry* 30 (Winter, 2004): 225–248.

———. *The Making of Law: An Ethnography of the Conseil d'Etat*. Polity, 2010.

———. *Reassembling the Social: An Introduction to Actor-Network Theory*. Oxford University Press, 2005.

Laycock, Joseph P. *Speak of the Devil: How the Satanic Temple Is Changing the Way We Talk about Religion*. Oxford University Press, 2020.

Ledewitz, Bruce. "The Vietnam Draft Cases and the Pro-Religion Equality Project." *University of Baltimore Law Review* 43, no. 1 (Spring, 2014): 1–84.

Lee, Blewett. "The Conjurer." *Virginia Law Review* 7, no. 5 (Feb., 1921): 370–377.

———. "The Fortune-Teller." *Virginia Law Review* 9, no. 4 (Feb., 1923): 249–266.

———. "The Fortune-Teller Again." *Virginia Law Review* 16, no. 1 (Nov., 1929): 54–56.

———. "Psychic Phenomena and the Law." *Harvard Law Review* 34, no. 6 (Apr., 1921): 625–638.

———. "Spiritualism and Crime." *Columbia Law Review* 22, no. 5 (May, 1922): 439–449.

Lee, E. G. *The Mormons, Or, Knavery Exposed; Giving an Account of the Discovery of the Golden Plates*. Philadelphia: George Webber, 1841.

Levene, Nancy. "Marx's Eleventh Thesis and the Politics of the Study of Religion: Lessons from *The Sacred Is the Profane*." *Journal of Religion* 98, no. 2 (Apr., 2018): 224–246.

Lincoln, Bruce. "Theses on Method." *Method and Theory in the Study of Religion* 8 (1996): 225–227.

Lindsey, Rachel McBride. *A Communion of Shadows: Religion and Photography in Nineteenth-Century America*. University of North Carolina Press, 2017.

Lloyd, Dana. *Arguing for This Land: Rethinking Indigenous Sacred Sites*. University Press of Kansas, forthcoming.

Lofton, Kathryn. *Consuming Religion*. University of Chicago Press, 2017.

Logan, Dana W. *Awkward Ritual: Sensations of Governance in Protestant America*. Forthcoming.

———. "The Lean Closet: Asceticism in Postindustrial Consumer Culture." *Journal of the American Academy of Religion* 85, no. 3 (Mar., 2017): 600–628.

Lombardo, Timothy J. *Blue-Collar Conservatism: Frank Rizzo's Philadelphia and Populist Politics*. University of Pennsylvania Press, 2018.

Long, Charles H. *Significations: Signs, Symbols, and Images in the Interpretation of Religion*. Fortress, 1986.

Lopez, Donald S., Jr. "Belief." In *Critical Terms for Religious Studies*, ed. Mark C. Taylor. University of Chicago Press, 1998.

Lyon, David, ed. *Surveillance as Social Sorting: Privacy, Risk, and Digital Discrimination*. Routledge, 2003.

Maciak, Phillip. *The Disappearing Christ: Secularism in the Silent Era*. Columbia University Press, 2019.

Mahmood, Saba. *Religious Difference in a Secular Age: A Minority Report*. Princeton University Press, 2016.

Markovits, Elizabeth. *The Politics of Sincerity: Plato, Frank Speech, and Democratic Judgment*. Penn State University Press, 2008.

Martínez, María Elena. *Genealogical Fictions: Limpieza de Sangre, Religion, and Gender in Colonial Mexico*. Stanford University Press, 2008.

Massad, Joseph A. *Islam in Liberalism*. University of Chicago Press, 2015.

Masuzawa, Tomoko. *The Invention of World Religions; Or, How European Universalism was Preserved in the Language of Pluralism*. University of Chicago Press, 2005.

Matory, J. Lorand. *The Fetish Revisited: Marx, Freud, and the Gods Black People Make*. Duke University Press, 2018.

Maurer, David W. *The Big Con: The Story of the Confidence Man*. Anchor Books, 1999 [1940].

Mbembe, Achille. "Necropolitics." Trans. Libby Meintjes. *Public Culture* 15, no. 1 (2003): 11–40.

McBride, James M. "Paul Tillich and the Supreme Court: Tillich's 'Ultimate Concern' as a Standard in Judicial Interpretation." *Journal of Church and State* 30, no. 2 (Spring, 1988): 245–272.

McCrary, Charles. "Superstitious Subjects: US Religion, Race, and Freedom." *Method & Theory in the Study of Religion* 30, no. 1 (Jan., 2018): 56–70.

McCrary, Charles, and Jeffrey Wheatley. "The Protestant Secular in the Study of American Religion: Reappraisal and Suggestions." *Religion* 47, no. 2 (Apr., 2017): 256–276.

McGarry, Molly. *Ghosts of Futures Past: Spiritualism and the Cultural Politics of Nineteenth-Century America*. University of California Press, 2008.

McGreevy, John T. *Catholicism and American Freedom: A History*. W.W. Norton, 2003.

McNally, Michael D. *Defend the Sacred: Native American Religious Freedom beyond the First Amendment*. Princeton University Press, 2020.

Melville, Herman. *The Confidence-Man; His Masquerade*. Ed. Hershel Parker and Mark Niemeyer. 2nd Norton critical ed. W. W. Norton, 2006 [1857].

———. *Moby-Dick; Or, the Whale*. Ed. Hershel Parker and Harrison Hayford. 2nd Norton critical ed. W. W. Norton, 2002 [1851].

Mihm, Stephen. *A Nation of Counterfeiters: Capitalists, Con Men, and the Making of the United States*. Harvard University Press, 2007.

Mills, Charles W. *The Racial Contract*. Cornell University Press, 1997.

Modern, John Lardas. *Secularism in Antebellum America*. University of Chicago Press, 2011.

Moschella, Melissa. "Beyond Equal Liberty: Religion as a Distinct Human Good and the Implication for Religious Freedom." *Journal of Law and Religion* 32, no. 1 (2017): 123–146.

Mullen, Lincoln. *The Chance of Salvation: A History of Conversion in America*. Harvard University Press, 2017.

Murphy, Sharon Ann. *Other People's Money: How Banking Worked in the Early American Republic*. Johns Hopkins University Press, 2017.

NeJaime, Douglas, and Reva B. Siegel. "Conscience Wars: Complicity-Based Conscience Claims in Religion and Politics." *Yale Law Journal* 124 (2015): 2516–2591.

Ngai, Sianne. *Ugly Feelings*. Harvard University Press, 2005.

Noble, Mark. "Reading Melville Reading Character." *J19* 4, no. 2 (Fall, 2016): 237–247.

Novak, William J. *The People's Welfare: Law and Regulation in Nineteenth-Century America*. University of North Carolina Press, 1996.

O'Brien, Geoffrey. "A Nation of Grifters, Fixers, and Marks: David Maurer's *The Big Con*." *Social Research* 85, no. 4 (Winter, 2018): 727–738.

Ogden, Emily. *Credulity: A Cultural History of US Mesmerism*. University of Chicago Press, 2018.

O'Neill, Kevin Lewis. "Beyond Broken: Affective Spaces and Study of American Religion." *Journal of the American Academy of Religion* 81, no. 4 (Dec. 2013): 1093–1116.

Orsi, Robert A. *History and Presence*. Harvard University Press, 2016.

———. *The Madonna of 115th Street: Faith and Community in Italian Harlem, 1880–1950*. Yale University Press, 1985.

Pascoe, Peggy. *What Comes Naturally: Miscegenation Law and the Making of Race in America*. Oxford University Press, 2009.

Pateman, Carole. *The Sexual Contract*. Polity Press, 1988.

Patrick, Jeremy. *Faith or Fraud: Fortune-Telling, Spirituality, and the Law*. UBC Press, 2020.

Patterson, Orlando. *Freedom in the Making of Western Culture*. Vol. 1 of *Freedom*. Basic Books, 1991.

Pellegrini, Ann. "Religion, Secularism, and a Democratic Politics of 'As If.'" *Social Research* 76, no. 4 (Winter, 2009): 1345–1350.

———. "Sincerely Held; or, The Pastorate 2.0." *Social Text* 34, no. 4 (Dec., 2016): 71–85.

Peters, Shawn Francis. *Judging Jehovah's Witnesses: Religious Persecution and the Dawn of the Rights Revolution*. University Press of Kansas, 2000.

Petro, Anthony M. "Ray Navarro's Jesus Camp, AIDS Activist Video, and the 'New Anti-Catholicism.'" *Journal of the American Academy of Religion* 85, no. 4 (Dec., 2017): 920–956.

Pietruska, Jamie L. *Looking Forward: Prediction and Uncertainty in Modern America*. University of Chicago Press, 2017.

Pinheiro, John C. *Missionaries of Republicanism: A Religious History of the Mexican-American War*. Oxford University Press, 2014.

Piper, Alana. "Women's Work: The Professionalisation and Policing of Fortune-Telling in Australia." *Labour History* 108 (May, 2015): 37–52.

Pritchard, Elizabeth A. "Seriously, What Does 'Taking Religion Seriously' Mean?" *Journal of the American Academy of Religion* 78, no. 4 (Dec., 2010): 1087–1111.

Puar, Jasbir K. *The Right to Maim: Debility, Capacity, Disability.* Duke University Press, 2017.

———. *Terrorist Assemblages: Homonationalism in Queer Times.* Duke University Press, 2007.

Rabin, Robert L. "When is a Religious Belief Religious: *United States v. Seeger* and the Scope of Free Exercise." *Cornell Law Review* 51, no. 2 (Winter, 1966): 231–249.

Rana, Aziz. *The Two Faces of American Freedom.* Harvard University Press, 2010.

Rana, Junaid. *Terrifying Muslims: Race and Labor in the South Asian Diaspora.* Duke University Press, 2011.

Reckson, Lindsay V. *Realist Ecstasy: Religion, Race, and Performance in American Literature.* New York University Press, 2020.

Reddy, Chandan. *Freedom With Violence: Race, Sexuality, and the US State.* Duke University Press, 2011.

Reisner, Ralph. "The Conscientious Objector Exemption: Administrative Procedures and Judicial Review." *University of Chicago Law Review* 35, no. 4 (1968): 686–720.

Ribton-Turner, C. J. *A History of Vagrants and Vagrancy, and Beggars and Begging.* London: Chapman and Hall, 1887.

Roberts, Tyler. *Encountering Religion: Responsibility and Criticism after Secularism.* Columbia University Press, 2013.

Robinson, Benjamin G. "Racialization and Modern Religion: Sylvia Wynter, Black Feminist Theory, and Critical Genealogies of Religion." *Critical Research on Religion* 7, no. 3 (Dec., 2019): 257–274.

Rusert, Britt. *Fugitive Science: Empiricism and Freedom in Early African American Culture.* New York University Press, 2017.

Rutenberg, Amy J. *Rough Draft: Cold War Military Manpower Policy and the Origins of Vietnam-Era Draft Resistance.* Digital ed. Cornell University Press, 2019.

Ryan, Susan M. "Misgivings: Melville, Race, and the Ambiguities of Benevolence." *American Literary History* 12, no. 4 (Winter, 2000): 685–712.

Salazar, James B. *Bodies of Reform: The Rhetoric of Character in Gilded Age America.* New York University Press, 2010.

Sanders, Kimberly, and Judson L. Jeffries. "Framing MOVE: A Press' Complicity in the Murder of Women and Children in the City of (Un) Brotherly Love." *Journal of African American Studies* 17, no. 4 (Dec., 2013): 566–586.

Schaefer, Donovan O. "Whiteness and Civilization: Shame, Race, and the Rhetoric of Donald Trump." *Communication and Critical/Cultural Studies* 17, no. 1 (2017): 1–18.

Schuller, Kyla. *The Biopolitics of Feeling: Race, Sex, and Science in the Nineteenth Century.* Duke University Press, 2017.

Schwartzman, Micah, Chad Flanders, and Zoë Robinson, eds. *The Rise of Corporate Religious Liberty.* Oxford University Press, 2016.

Scott, Joan Wallach. *Sex and Secularism*. Princeton University Press, 2018.

Sehat, David. *The Myth of American Religious Freedom*. Oxford University Press, 2011.

Seligman, Adam B., Robert P. Weller, Michael J. Puett, and Bennett Simon. *Ritual and Its Consequences: An Essay on the Limits of Sincerity*. Oxford University Press, 2008.

Sexton, John. "Note: Toward a Constitutional Definition of Religion." *Harvard Law Review* 91, no. 5 (Mar., 1978): 1056–1089.

Siedentop, Larry. *Inventing the Individual: The Origins of Western Liberalism*. The Belknap Press of Harvard University Press, 2014.

Slack, Paul. *Poverty and Policy in Tudor and Stuart England*. Longman, 1988.

Slye, Terry L. "Rendering unto Caesar: Defining 'Religion' for Purposes of Administering Religion-Based Tax Exemptions." *Harvard Journal of Law and Public Policy* 6, no. 2 (1983): 219–294.

Smith, Jonathan Z. "Tillich['s] Remains. . . ." *Journal of the American Academy of Religion* 78, no. 4 (Dec., 2010): 1139–1170.

Smith, Oscar T., and Derrick A. Bell. "The Conscientious-Objector Program—A Search for Sincerity." *University of Pittsburgh Law Review* 19, no. 4 (Summer, 1958): 695–726.

Smith, Steven D. *The Disenchantment of Secular Discourse*. Oxford University Press, 2010.

Snorton, C. Riley. *Black on Both Sides: A Racial History of Trans Identity*. University of Minnesota Press, 2017.

Stahl, Ronit Y. "A Jewish America and a Protestant Civil Religion: Will Herberg, Robert Bellah, and Religious Identity in Mid-Twentieth-Century Liberal America." *Religions* 6, no. 2 (2015): 434–450.

Stewart, Katherine. *The Power Worshippers: Inside the Dangerous Rise of Religious Nationalism*. Bloomsbury, 2019.

Stone-Gordon, Tammy. "'Fifty-Cent Sybils': Occult Workers and the Symbolic Marketplace in the Urban U.S.,1850–1930." Ph.D. diss., Michigan State University, 1998.

Styers, Randall. *Making Magic: Religion, Magic, and Science in the Modern World*. Oxford University Press, 2004.

Su, Anna. *Exporting Freedom: Religious Liberty and American Power*. Harvard University Press, 2016.

———. "Judging Religious Sincerity." *Oxford Journal of Law and Religion* 5 (2016): 28–48.

———. "Varieties of Burden in Religious Accommodations." *Journal of Law and Religion* 34, no. 1 (2019): 42–63.

Sullivan, Winnifred Fallers. *Church State Corporation: Construing Religion in US Law*. University of Chicago Press, 2020.

———. "'The Conscience of Contemporary Man': Reflections on *U.S. v. Seeger* and *Dignitatis Humanae*." *U.S. Catholic Historian* 24, no. 1 (Winter, 2006): 107–123.

———. *The Impossibility of Religious Freedom*. Princeton University Press, 2005.

———. *A Ministry of Presence: Chaplaincy, Spiritual Care, and the Law*. University of Chicago Press, 2014.

———. "The World That *Smith* Made." *Immanent Frame*, Mar. 7, 2012.

Sullivan, Winnifred Fallers, Elizabeth Shakman Hurd, Saba Mahmood, and Peter M. Danchin, eds. *Politics of Religious of Freedom*. University of Chicago Press, 2015.

Taussig-Rubbo, Mateo, Robert A. Yelle, and Winnifred Fallers Sullivan, eds. *After Secular Law*. Stanford University Press, 2011.

Taves, Ann. *Fits, Trances, and Visions: Experiencing Religion and Explaining Experience from Wesley to James*. Princeton University Press, 1999.

Taylor, Charles. "The Polysemy of the Secular." *Social Research* 76, no. 4 (Winter, 2009): 1143–1166.

———. *A Secular Age*. Belknap Press of Harvard University Press, 2007.

———. *Sources of the Self: The Making of Modern Identity*. Harvard University Press, 1989.

Taylor, Mark C. "Discrediting God." *Journal of the American Academy of Religion* 62, no. 2 (Summer, 1994): 603–623.

Taylor, Steven J. *Acts of Conscience: World War II, Mental Institutions, and Religious Objectors*. Syracuse University Press, 2009.

Thatamanil, John J. "Comparing Professors Smith and Tillich: A Response to Jonathan Z. Smith's 'Tillich('s) Remains.'" *Journal of the American Academy of Religion* 78, no. 4 (Dec., 2010): 1171–1181.

Thomas, Jolyon Baraka. *Faking Liberties: Religious Freedom in American-Occupied Japan*. University of Chicago Press, 2019.

Threlkeld, Megan. "'The War Power Is Not a Blank Check': The Supreme Court and Conscientious Objection, 1917–1973." *Journal of Policy History* 31, no. 3 (2019): 303–325.

Tolentino, Jia. *Trick Mirror: Essays on Self Delusion*. Random House, 2019.

Tortorici, Zeb. *Sins against Nature: Sex and Archives in Colonial New Spain*. Duke University Press, 2018.

Tribe, Laurence. *American Constitutional Law*. Foundation Press, 1978.

Trilling, Lionel. *Sincerity and Authenticity*. Harvard University Press, 1972.

Tweed, Thomas A., ed. *Retelling U.S. Religious History*. University of California Press, 1997.

Viswanathan, Gauri. *Outside the Fold: Conversion, Modernity, and Belief*. Princeton University Press, 1998.

Walker, David. "The Humbug in American Religion: Ritual Theories of Nineteenth-Century Spiritualism." *Religion and American Culture* 23, no. 1 (Winter 2013): 30–74.

Warner, Michael. *Publics and Counterpublics*. Zone Books, 2002.

———. "Was Antebellum America Secular?" *Immanent Frame*, Oct. 2, 2012.

Warner, Michael, Jonathan VanAntwerpen, and Craig Calhoun, eds. *Varieties of Secularism in a Secular Age*. Harvard University Press, 2010.

Weber, Max. *The Protestant Ethic and the "Spirit" of Capitalism*. Translated and edited by Peter Baehr and Gordon C. Wells. Penguin, 2002 [1905].

———. "Science as a Vocation." In *Essays in Sociology*, ed. H. H. Gerth and C. Wright Mills. Oxford University Press, 1946 [1919].

Weheliye, Alexander G. *Habeas Viscus: Racializing Assemblages, Biopolitics, and Black Feminist Theories of the Human*. Duke University Press, 2014.

Weiner, Isaac. "The Corporately Produced Conscience: Emergency Contraception and the Politics of Workplace Accommodations." *Journal of the American Academy of Religion* 85, no. 1 (Mar., 2017): 31–63.

Weisenfeld, Judith. *New World A-Coming: Black Religion and Racial Identity during the Great Migration*. New York University Press, 2016.

Wenger, Tisa. *Religious Freedom: The Contested History of an American Ideal*. University of North Carolina Press, 2017.

———. *We Have a Religion: The 1920s Pueblo Indian Dance Controversy and American Religious Freedom*. University of North Carolina Press, 2009.

Werbel, Amy. *Lust on Trial: Censorship and the Rise of American Obscenity in the Age of Anthony Comstock*. Columbia University Press, 2018.

Wernimont, Jacqueline. *Numbered Lives: Life and Death in Quantum Media*. MIT Press, 2019.

Whitehead, Andrew L., and Samuel L. Perry. *Taking Back America for God: Christian Nationalism in the United States*. Oxford University Press, 2020.

Wilcox, Melissa M. *Queer Nuns: Religion, Activism, and Serious Parody*. New York University Press, 2018.

Wilson, Charles H., Jr. "The Selective Service System: An Administrative Obstacle Course." *University of Chicago Law Review* 54, no. 5 (Dec., 1966): 2123–2179.

Wynter, Sylvia. "Unsettling the Coloniality of Being/Power/Truth/Freedom: Towards the Human, After Man, Its Overrepresentation—An Argument." *CR: The New Centennial Review* 3, no. 3 (Fall, 2003): 257–337.

Yacovazzi, Cassandra L. *Escaped Nuns: True Womanhood and the Campaign against Convents in Antebellum America*. Oxford University Press, 2018.

Yelle, Robert A. *The Language of Disenchantment: Protestant Literalism and Colonial Discourse in British India*. Oxford University Press, 2012.

INDEX